W9-ANC-864

Peace and Persistence

Peace and Persistence

Tracing the Brethren in Christ Peace

Witness through Three Generations

M. J. HEISEY

THE KENT STATE UNIVERSITY PRESS · KENT AND LONDON

© 2003 by The Kent State University Press, Kent, Ohio 44242

All rights reserved.

Library of Congress Catalog Card Number 2002006020

ISBN 0-87338-756-2

Manufactured in the United States of America

07 06 05 04 03   5 4 3 2 1

Library of Congress Cataloging-in-Publication Data

Heisey, M. J. (Mary Jane), 1955–

Peace and persistence : tracing the Brethren in Christ peace witness

through three generations / M. J. Heisey

p.   cm.

Includes bibliographical references and index.

ISBN 0-87338-756-2 (hardcover : alk. paper)

1. Brethren in Christ Church—History—20th century.

2. Peace—Religious aspects—Brethren in Christ Church—History—20th century.

3. War—Religious aspects—Brethren in Christ Church—History—20th century.

4. Brethren in Christ Church—Doctrines. I. Title.

BX9675 .H45 2003

289.9—dc21

2002006020

British Library Cataloging-in-Publication data are available.

To

Philip C. Harnden,

Velma Climenhaga Heisey,

J. Wilmer Heisey,

and all others who carry the peace witness

now and in the future.

Every war already carries within it the war which will answer it. . . .

Pacifism simply is not a matter of calm looking on; it is work, hard work.

—Käthe Kollwitz, February 21, 1944

Contents

❦

Preface   xi

Acknowledgments   xv

Abbreviations   xvii

Introduction: A "Plain Church" in American Society   1

1. Nonresistance in World War I   25

2. Nonresistant Thought and Practice in the 1940s and 1950s   49

3. Nonresistance and Home Front Life   76

4. Nonresistant Mobilization   97

5. Conscientious Objection, Civilian Public Service, and
   Community Life   112

6. The Private Life of Nonresistance   135

7. Legacy and Conclusion   160

Appendixes

1. Questionnaire on Brethren in Christ Nonresistance   169

2. Conscripted Men Related to the Brethren in Christ Community
   in World War I   171

3. Brethren in Christ Men in Canadian Alternative Service Work   177

4. Brethren in Christ Men in U.S. Civilian Public Service   179

5. Civilian Public Service and Mennonite Central Committee–
   Related Participants   184

6. Brethren in Christ Service Workers in Mennonite Central
   Committee and Related Programs, 1944–1955   186

7. Brethren in Christ Men in U.S. I-W Service   190

Notes   192

Bibliography   257

Index   274

Preface

❧

Why study the Brethren in Christ, one small community among so many better-known groupings in American society? Why focus on their particular expression of pacifism, which they called *nonresistance?* Doing so provides us a number of opportunities to understand the kind of community life required if such an alternative ethos is to persist alongside mainstream culture. For example, we can search out the diverse and changing nature of nonresistant beliefs and experiences; these nuances remain unexplored in more general studies and in research on larger groups. We can also consider the interaction between nonresistance and other aspects of community life. Furthermore, our exploration of this minority belief in American society can address the relationship of small community life to public life in local, national, and international settings.

I began my study of nonresistance by searching for as many expressions of the concept as I could find in the Brethren in Christ (BIC). Official church doctrine and legislation, the statements of BIC leaders, and the writings of drafted young men expressed the community's nonresistance most visibly in war years. But the Brethren in Christ claimed nonresistance not only as a precept for draft-age men but as a guide for all BIC people in their tasks of being neighbors, choosing occupations, and raising children. Therefore, it was important to hear from neighbors, workers, and children. In addition to uncovering these individual voices, it was also important to examine the community's corporate stand on nonresistance, because until 1958 the belief was officially required for membership.

Because community conflict over belief is just as important as consensus, we must consider conflict in order to understand both nonresistance and community life more generally. "A sense of identity," historian Natalie Zemon Davis writes, "is nourished not by simple boosterism but by important shared quarrels."[1] So I sought out those who embraced nonresistance and those who rejected it. Both reveal something about the nature of nonresistance among the

Brethren in Christ, just as the aspects of group life that fade yield as much insight into a nature of the community as those that persist.

Finally, I turned to the BIC doctrine that nurtured nonresistance—nonconformity, or separation from the world. I wondered if examining the practice, rather than the doctrine, of nonconformity might alter the perception of nonresistance as aloof and isolated. How successful were the nonresistant Brethren in Christ in their exclusiveness? How did their sense of being different affect their ability to contribute in their local neighborhoods and in the larger national arena? Might the concept of nonconformity overestimate the power of people to separate themselves from their neighbors? Again, Davis cogently points to the problem of group boundaries: "Persons belong in fact to multiple groups and rarely have single identities."[2] In work, school, and civic settings, the nonresistant Brethren in Christ assumed identities that they shared with many other people in their society. At different times and in different contexts, they thought of themselves as farmers or professionals; as Mennonites, plain people, holiness advocates, or fundamentalists; as easterners or westerners, Canadians or Americans; as Prohibitionists; as Allied sympathizers, German culture bearers, or as emissaries of Western civilization. Alongside such identifications with larger groupings, they also lived daily life as a defined community. But so did many other Americans in the first half of the twentieth century. Might many Anabaptist groups appear more separate as we look back at them than they appeared to their contemporaries, prior to the homogenizing process of total wars and the rise of mass media? Did the Brethren in Christ's nonresistance and nonconformity simply reflect a sectarian approach? Or did their peace position always require contributions to public life in their neighborhoods and in national communities?

The Brethren in Christ provide grist for Davis's contention that identities are created from multiple strands. Throughout their history, the Brethren in Christ have rarely described themselves in Anabaptist terminology. Furthermore, the Brethren in Christ have consistently distinguished themselves from Mennonites, even while borrowing from and working with them. From their beginnings, however, the Brethren in Christ have chosen beliefs and practices that placed them in the Anabaptist family. In addition, during World War II, the Brethren in Christ began formally affiliating themselves with Mennonites, the largest Anabaptist grouping. As they joined Mennonite coalition organizations, however, they insisted that the larger group acknowledge their separate identity. Many of the strands of BIC identity are similar to those of other small denominations in the Mennonite mosaic. Therefore, in this study I include the Brethren in Christ in that Mennonite mosaic, while delineating their particular historical experience.

Major works on the Brethren in Christ in religion and history—most often synthetic denominational or leadership studies—have primarily identified historical and theological roots, differentiated the BIC community from other related groups, and offered explanations for shifts in theology, church polity, and religious practice. A small group of scholars in the fields of history and religion (and all of those who have been closely connected to the BIC denomination) have produced a historical overview as well as evaluations of religious change in the group. Their work provides a base from which to explore the many other aspects of community life connected to the daily practice of nonresistance. The establishment in 1978 of an interdisciplinary, academic, and lay journal, *Brethren in Christ History and Life,* provided important new sources on the community, especially in the areas of autobiography, biography, family histories, theology, institutional studies, and issues of current identity.

The pursuit of my interest in the internal tensions, the larger society, and the persistence of nonresistant practice required a variety of sources. This study, like existing historiography on the Brethren in Christ, draws on the following: official doctrinal statements; minutes of various levels of the church polity; the *Evangelical Visitor,* the primary denominational periodical; and oral interviews. In the *Visitor* and in other underutilized denominational and church school periodicals, this study found a rich variety of authors, including women, young people, poets, and obituary writers. Minutes of the BIC General Conference, of state and provincial councils, and of district councils made regional variations and women's roles more apparent. Records of four denominational boards and committees provided additional denominational sources. Two compilations of conscientious objector experiences in Civilian Public Service described individual experiences. One Brethren in Christ and two Mennonite archives produced personal papers, diaries, institutional collections, and audiotapes and transcripts of oral interviews.[3] Contributed diaries, letters, and record books added sources scarce in archival holdings. Finally, my research produced a number of new sources: forty-two oral interviews and 151 responses to a questionnaire on nonresistance distributed to members of the BIC community.[4] Although a number of respondents to the questionnaire provided only the most basic personal information, many more included extended descriptions of experiences as well as reflections on their significance. In addition, several respondents commented on my academic endeavor. The comments of these living sources on my academic research reminded me that the best historical dialogue involves people both inside and outside the discipline.

Interviews provided glimpses into aspects of the BIC community ordinarily unavailable to the historian. The willingness of the individuals being interviewed to reflect on difficult or unhappy experiences surprised me, but so did their forgetfulness. Because records from the first half of the twentieth century were far richer than I expected, oral interviews provided not only new information but also a measure of how little of the past we retain. Accuracy was only one problem; passion and complexity too often had disappeared as years passed. Interviews sometimes contradicted letters and diaries from the period. Taken together, these contemporary and retrospective accounts reveal the contrast between the confusion of day-to-day living and the coherence we later impose on it. In response to this contrast, I attempted to pair, whenever possible, contemporary and retrospective accounts. Most importantly, I tried to use a variety of sources, all with their respective problems, in the hope that they would check and qualify each other.

In addition to joining conversations in the academic community, this study also reflects my personal interest in the BIC community (in which I was raised), my continuing participation in the Historic Peace Church family, and my experience as a woman wending her way through all three communities.

Acknowledgments

⁓

Many people have provided substantial support for my research and writing; all of them have enriched my life. The variety of contributions, if detailed, would produce a lengthy acknowledgment section. Therefore, except for a few major categories, I will simply list names, with gratitude: Patti Bohrer, William Boyer, Geoffrey W. Clarke, Elia Filippi, Bill and Dorcas Climenhaga Fischer, Steven Foulke, Mary E. Heisey, Paul Heisey and Melinda Smale, Wilmer and Velma Climenhaga Heisey, Samuel L. Herr, Lela Swalm Hostetler, Karen Johnson-Weiner, Mary Olive Lady, Mark W. Olson, Elisabeth Lasch-Quinn's dissertation seminar, John Linscheid, Paul Lockhardt, Paul Longacre, Richard Mundy, Patricia Niles, Heather L. Ross, Theron Schlabach, Ruth Schrock, Dorothy Sherk and household, Kevin D. Smith, the staff of Frederick W. Crumb Memorial Library at Potsdam College, the staff of Owen D. Young Library at St. Lawrence University, Beth Sutter, Clayton and Elsie Eash Sutter, Ruth Sutter, Marilyn Helmuth Voran, Bonnee Lauridsen Voss, Heidi Wingert, and Joan Byer Wolgemuth.

The richness of historical sources in the study reflects the skills and enthusiasm of three archivists—E. Morris Sider and Dorcas Steckbeck of the Archives of the Brethren in Christ Church and Messiah College, Grantham, Pennsylvania, and Dennis Stoesz of the Archives of the Mennonite Church, Goshen, Indiana.

I am grateful for the generous financial support I received from the Syracuse University Graduate School Research-Creative Project Grant, Syracuse University Roscoe Martin Award, Syracuse University History Department, Syracuse University Dobie-Kampel Scholarship, Mennonite Central Committee Canada, the Board for Ministry and Missions Canadian Conference of the Brethren in Christ Church, Mennonite Historical Society Publication Grant, and the Potsdam College Office of Research and Sponsored Programs Faculty Travel Award.

Extensive comments and criticisms by the following readers sharpened my thinking, went unheeded at certain points, and made my research part of a conversation, which was my ultimate goal: John S. Burdick, Perry Bush, Philip C. Harnden, Nancy R. Heisey, Ronald Helfrich, Otey M. Scruggs, William Stinchcombe, Margaret S. Thompson, and an anonymous reader from The Kent State University Press.

I am particularly grateful for the sustained encouragement and critiques of three scholars whom I admire a great deal: Paul S. Boyer, Elisabeth Lasch-Quinn, and E. Morris Sider.

It was an honor and a pleasure to work with Joanna Hildebrand Craig, John T. Hubbell, and Perry Sundberg of The Kent State University Press.

Much of this study is possible because Brethren in Christ people and people with Brethren in Christ backgrounds generously shared their memories and reflections on questionnaires, in letters or telephone calls, and in interviews.

Abbreviations

∽

AFSC	American Friends Service Committee
AMC	Archives of the Mennonite Church, Goshen, Indiana 46526
ASW	Alternative Service Work
BIC	Brethren in Christ
BICA	The Archives of the Brethren in Christ Church and Messiah College, Grantham, Pennsylvania 17027
BICHL	*Brethren in Christ History and Life*
BYPW	Board for Young People's Work
CO	conscientious objector
CPS	Civilian Public Service
CESR	Committee on Economic and Social Relations, Mennonite General Conference Committee Collection
DC	district council
DCPS	*Directory of Civilian Public Service* (with year)
GC	General Conference
GEB	General Executive Board
ICPC	Inter-College Peace Conference
ICPF	Inter-Collegiate Peace Fellowship
IRC	Industrial Relations Board
I-W	conscientious objector performing civilian work; selective service system classification, 1952–1974
JC	Joint Council, used with state or province abbreviation
MC	Messiah College
MCC	Mennonite Central Committee
MGCC	Mennonite General Conference Committee
MLA	Mennonite Library and Archives, North Newton, Kansas 67117
MSMS	*My Story, My Song*
PRS	Peace, Relief, and Service Committee

QPASC45   Pennsylvania state council questionnaire sent to cps participants in 1945

sc   State Council, used with state abbreviation

WAL   Women's Activities Letter

A "Plain Church" in American Society

⌘

"Bigness ruins everything," said a late-twentieth-century Amish carpenter, expressing in three words a sentiment quite outside the bounds of mainstream American culture.[1] That sentiment and others like it have been shared by many communities throughout American history, especially communities that link their religious lives to countercultural practices. Members of one such community, the Brethren in Christ (BIC), found themselves in the first half of the twentieth century at odds with mainstream America. They were also at odds with each other on a host of social and economic issues—from hair and clothing styles to life insurance and military service.[2] Because of their resistance to mainstream culture, such communities are often misunderstood or considered marginal by the larger society or in their own self-perceptions.

This study seeks to look beyond generalized images of such communities to the complexities of their members' actual lives. These complexities reveal the fact that the Brethren in Christ, despite their uncommon sentiments, faced dilemmas common to other Americans. "Clustered . . . in their 'tribes' and denominations and movements," writes American historian Martin E. Marty, "those who looked for identity, meaning, and belonging in life . . . faced the issue as old as the United States itself: How could they ensure a healthy *communitas communitatum,* a larger community made up of healthily interactive subcommunities? To what extent should they devote themselves to their particular often sectarian belief systems, and how and when should they converge on the claims of the commonweal?"[3]

The Brethren in Christ offer an important case study, because the BIC community participated in many aspects of the larger society while carefully separating itself in other areas. This book considers both the small BIC community and its relationship to larger communities, using the elaboration of a particular expression of pacifism—nonresistance—practiced by the BIC community in war years from 1914 to 1958. Nonresistance—and the larger doctrine of non-conformity—connected the small community to a variety of neighbors even as these understandings symbolized separate worlds.

Nonconformity was a means of visibly marking a new community, set in place by Christ and distinct from the rest of sinful society. Nonconformity manifested itself in patterns of language, personal appearance, consumption, and entertainment. Nonconformist people ideally lived simply and humbly, and they were focused on spiritual matters. The Brethren in Christ, along with a number of other such groups, often used the word "plain" when describing themselves and their practices. They also refused to conform to mainstream assumptions about the use of force, employing the doctrine of nonresistance. The Brethren in Christ defined *nonresistance* as the rejection of force as a way to promote ideas, settle conflicts, or defend themselves. During the three great wars of the century—World War I, World War II, and the early Cold War—the BIC community formalized nonresistance by officially prohibiting participation in the armed forces, in legal prosecutions, and in parts of political and economic life. For example, the Brethren in Christ eschewed jury duty, police work, and labor strikes, because each involved or was instrumental in the use of force.[4]

Those guiding beliefs of difference and separation shaped BIC thinking and practice. But the actual world in which they lived often complicated matters. Although the Brethren in Christ often applied nonresistance and nonconformity in the form of prohibitions, both doctrines also made positive appeals. A 1931 children's catechism, for example, described nonresistance as "love in action"; a 1945 volume for youth defined it as a "powerful alternative" to violence; a 1939 doctrinal statement on nonconformity argued that "being different" should not lead to "reclusiveness, isolation nor insulation" but rather should be accompanied by "an open and approachable spirit toward humanity."[5] Nonresistance and nonconformity, then, required active regulation of a variety of neighborly relationships, even in sectarian formulations. Furthermore, nonresistant Brethren in Christ cooperated with many other religious pacifists and even rubbed shoulders with secular peace advocates. Along with this largest grouping, itself a strand in the story of American reform, the tiny BIC community continually elaborated, debated, and redefined the meanings and goals of its peace witness.[6]

During the world wars, the BIC community increasingly expressed nonresistance in religiously motivated service to humanity. A gradual shift in terminology from *nonresistance* to *peace witness* or *peace testimony* during World War II symbolized the new emphasis. This study, however, demonstrates that daily life always required an active "peace witness," and I therefore use that term to express the ongoing attempts to practice peace at home, in the church, and in the world. At the same time, the term *nonresistance* accurately portrays the particular historical context of small, local communities and the pre–World War II emphasis on prohibitions. Also, the emergence of a self-conscious service ethic during the world wars enlarged the BIC world and increased the national and international social concern of the peace witness. These new settings and concerns helped to create new tensions in the small community. In the 1950s the community's corporate peace stand weakened, as did its appreciation of being a unique, small community.[7]

This study examines nonresistance as defined and practiced by many members of the BIC community in daily life. That community included not only official church members but also children and youth who had not yet joined the church, as well as church attenders and kin networks.[8] Wartime mobilization and Cold War militarism between 1914 and 1958 required explicit nonresistant stands and therefore provided extensive documentation. The study ends in 1958, because in that year the Brethren in Christ discontinued disciplining members who chose to enter military service. The picture of nonresistance that emerges from this study challenges historical analyses that stress the separatist nature of the nonresistant doctrine. In the first half of the twentieth century, the Brethren in Christ practiced, altered, and passed on their generations-old nonresistant position. They did not do so, however, as an isolated community. Because their community was integrated economically and technologically into American society, the Brethren in Christ found it impossible to keep the world out. Furthermore, the religious belief in the necessity of separation from society often served less as a wall against the outer world than as a means to determine what the community would and would not borrow from neighbors. Nonresistance, in particular, pulled this nonconformist community into society. Although nonresistance called members away from the larger society's use of lethal force, it also bid them foster peaceful interactions in local settings. Even more broadly, nonresistant people sometimes described their ideas of peaceful living as a model for national and international problems. In other words, nonconformist people were not as separate as either people in the larger society or they themselves thought.

This study also shows that disunity was an integral part of BIC community life. Disagreements were common and sometimes contentious. During World War II, the definition of nonresistance itself divided the community, causing some members to question the validity of a belief that did not appear to work at home. Differing roles for women and for men, a variety of family patterns, and geographical dispersion contributed to diverse nonresistant positions or the with-ering of the belief among some Brethren in Christ. Although the Brethren in Christ understood nonresistance to be a corporate stand, they also insisted that only individual religious conviction legitimated the belief. Nonresistance, then, was less a unified stance than a constellation of sometimes contending ideas.

Nonresistance in this study appears less coherent than it does in others based more on doctrinal formulations or on the accounts of conscientious objectors. But a consideration of the experiences of a wider range of community members shows that this persistent brand of pacifism survived its interactions with the larger society in spite of its internal tensions. The study of ordinary people in daily routines enlarges our understanding of how values persist. Perhaps they persist most often with compromise, confusion, inconsistency, and even failure at the center. To explore this fully requires giving serious attention to the power of daily life to muddle ideas. This complex picture of nonresistance, however, does not dismiss the ideas of nonconformity, which fostered distinct communi-ties over centuries and in many ways limited their social vision.

The question of persistence is a central one in every peace study. Many indi-viduals and groups have called for peace, but pacifist stands are tenuous. The Brethren in Christ, in contrast, advocated a peace witness in the 1780s and con-tinued to do so at the end of the twentieth century. That unusual persistence is a focus of this study. During the twentieth century, the corporate BIC peace witness weakened. That too is a focus of this study. In fact, it was not because of doctrinal statements or because the path of peace was obvious to people that the peace witness persisted most strongly. Instead, the peace witness proved most durable among BIC people when they remembered and valued the stories of previous generations.

In the first half of the twentieth century, few in mainstream America noticed the tiny community of Brethren in Christ. But in many ways their struggles were similar to those of other Americans. The Brethren in Christ sometimes sacrificed their best traits in search of validation in America's mass society. They embraced, for example, the larger society's often-noted amnesia.[9] Because many forgot the accomplishments of their own nonresistant practice, they deprived themselves of a resource for maintaining their identity as a small group. At the same time, however, they took seriously the important questions being asked in America about the aspirations of individuals versus the claims of the common-weal. As many other Americans, they insisted that despite the costs, peaceful living and neighborly concern should be at the center of life. Parts of their world-view blinded them to that commonality, but nonresistance aligned them with many other attempts to realize America not as empire but as "insistence on community."[10]

Brethren in Christ History

The Brethren in Christ represent one small Protestant denomination among the many communities that give shape to religious life in North America.[11] If asked, members would most likely identify themselves as Evangelicals or as Anabaptists.[12] In the year 2000 some twenty-four thousand official members lived in the United States and Canada and another sixty thousand worldwide. But in 1914, when the church was about 125 years old, it had only an estimated four thousand official members, scattered across North America. Between 1914 and 1958, the period of this study, church membership grew to approximately eight thousand.[13]

The largest concentrations of Brethren in Christ were in Lancaster and Franklin Counties, Pennsylvania; on the Niagara Peninsula in Ontario; and in an area of Kansas around Abilene. Neighbors would have noticed their prosperous farms. BIC farmers had joined most other North Americans in accepting the technologies that accompanied industrialization and thus integrated them economically. For their children and youth, they had accepted the value of education beyond the primary years. Much of their religious expression looked like that of other American Protestants: an annual General Conference, which legislated policy for the church; revival meetings; international missionaries; Sunday schools; and a church periodical.[14]

At the same time, the Brethren in Christ still defined themselves as plain people and would have appeared so to others. The ideals of plainness were dynamic and often divisive. In the first half the twentieth century the Brethren in Christ debated which symbols should be retained and which discarded. Nevertheless, church buildings, doctrines, polity, rituals, dress, hairstyles, and group discipline continued to embody plainness. Nonconformity and nonresistance remained central in doctrinal statements. Church gatherings were in simple buildings without steeples or pulpits. The denomination was divided into districts of one or more congregations, each led by an elected bishop and by elected ministers and deacons. These were not paid leaders; they were expected to provide their own livelihoods. Worship services included a cappella singing, individual testimony about religious experiences, and preaching, often by more than one minister. The church year also included other services: baptism of adult believers in rivers and ponds; a harvest service of thanksgiving in Pennsylvania districts; and biannual "love feasts," which included the service of Communion. Aided by the new ease of travel in the opening years under study, love feasts and harvest services sometimes attracted hundreds of people. Old religious expressions, such as footwashing, which accompanied the service of communion, the holy kiss, and a subsequent fellowship meal, stressed old values of servant-hood and love between community members. Furthermore, strong kinship networks gave the scattered group a personal, local flavor, reflected in the church magazine, the *Evangelical Visitor*. Its pages included obituaries, reports of visitation between community members, notifications of employment possibilities, and individual letters, along with the religious counsel that would be expected. Its flavor melded denominational goals with the interest an extended family shows for its members. Often, in fact, the Brethren in Christ simply called the magazine the *Visitor*.[15]

Dress was the most visible expression of plainness to outsiders. Traditionally, the group had not explicitly defined "plain" dress. In the years between the world wars, however, the BIC church legislated specific dress codes. Adult male members were not to wear ties. Women were to wear long hair up under a "prayer covering." Dresses were to include a cape, an additional vest over the bodice. Both men and women were to avoid additional ornamentation.[16] Photographs from the period, however, show substantial variation. Nevertheless, the Brethren in Christ continued to understand the church as a community with a corporate definition of obedient practice and with the authority to discipline errant members by "disfellowshiping" them. Administered by district leaders, disfellowshiping practices varied from a statement that a member "was not in good standing" to exclusion from church rituals, to an occasional excommunication. The goal was public confession by the person who had strayed, followed by reunion with the community.[17] In this period, abandoning plain dress or joining the military were grounds for disfellowshiping.

A brief history of the group before 1914 will help to provide a context for the substantial change and the persistent traditions in this nonconformist community.

The Brethren in Christ, first called River Brethren, appeared in the 1770s and 1780s as a new gathering of believers on the east bank of the Susquehanna River in Lancaster County, Pennsylvania. Sources, though scanty, suggest that many of the earliest River Brethren were Mennonites drawn into eighteenth-century American pietistic revivalism, which had filtered into Pennsylvania German communities after the 1750s. Reflecting this religious ferment, the River Brethren stressed a personal, emotional conversion experience after a period of inner struggle. They grafted this religious fervor to their Anabaptist roots, which they shared with their Mennonite, Amish, and German Baptist Brethren neighbors.[18]

The sixteenth-century Radical Reformation, or Anabaptism, had shaped all of these groups. Originally, Anabaptism represented diverse and uncoordinated expressions of religious, social, and political protest. Anabaptists met immediate repression in European states from political leaders and also from Roman Catholic and Protestant church officials. Survivors quickly evolved into self-conscious and scattered congregations, often in remote farming areas. Emigration patterns reflected European upheavals and ever more deeply tied Anabaptists to German ethnicity. By the eighteenth century, Mennonites—the largest group of Anabaptist descendents—lived in communities as far west as colonial North America and as far east as Ukraine. Though modified by time and place, decentralized and schismatic Anabaptist communities continued to challenge certain verities of Christendom and of successive political systems. Nonresistant pacifism, of which the earliest written statement is found in the 1527 Schleitheim Confession, and separation of church and state represent the most distinctive Anabaptist beliefs and the centrality of ethical practice among a constellation of ideals. The example and teachings of Jesus, as recorded in the Gospels, were to be followed literally. Church was a fellowship, chosen by members, who were baptized as adults. Those members saw themselves as part of Christ's new kingdom, separate from the state and the larger society. Community unity and purity were to be maintained by mutual aid and by discipline.[19]

BIC historians often represent the experience of the Brethren in Christ and their River Brethren ancestors as an ongoing attempt to balance the fervor of an individual religious experience of salvation, central to evangelical revivalism, with the corporate, lifelong practice required in Anabaptist conceptions of salvation and the church.[20] Despite their distinctive elements, the Brethren in Christ resembled other communities in many ways. For example, all Anabaptists shared with other Protestant groups certain religious beliefs about God, salvation, and the Bible. These commonalities fostered interaction with other Protestants. Similarly, American Anabaptists were firmly lodged in a German language subculture, which connected them to neighbors who were not Anabaptists. Even within the Anabaptist grouping, the new River Brethren could not claim uniqueness. The fires of pietistic renewal had also influenced and changed other Anabaptists. In fact, most River Brethren ideas, church structures, and daily practices had precedents among Mennonites and German Baptist Brethren.[21] Despite these commonalities, the River Brethren put their world together in a particular way; perhaps more importantly, the River Brethren continued to perceive themselves as unique. In addition, unlike their Anabaptist cousins, whose origins were in Europe, the River Brethren emerged in colonial America at about the same time as did a new nation, the United States. And unlike most other religious groups that emerged in North America, the River Brethren embraced and persisted in practicing nonresistance.

Early River Brethren beliefs and practices can only be glimpsed in fragmentary evidence. Members' homes or barns served as church gathering places. All decisions, such as marrying, changing location, and making purchases, were to be made in consultation with the church community. Ideally, marriage partners were to come from within the group. To maintain the community, members who had sinned would accept discipline. Members were not to swear oaths, "bear the sword for revenge or defence," or hold public office. They were urged, however, to obey authorities "in all that is right and good, paying them tax and toll and protection-money[,] . . . else it would be more difficult to live in this world." That complex Anabaptist division of authority between the church and the state bedeviled nonresistant practice and also, undoubtedly, helped the belief to survive.[22]

By the middle of the nineteenth century, a number of disputes within the River Brethren community had led to schisms. During the American Civil War, according to later church accounts, the largest group that had emerged from the schisms registered with the federal government as a nonresistant church. That group gave its name as "the Brethren in Christ." One smaller group continued to refer to itself as the Old Order River Brethren.[23]

Farming as well as religious faith shaped the Brethren in Christ. Until the middle of the twentieth century, farming was the BIC community's primary occupation. By revering community cooperation and—in the Jeffersonian tradition—celebrating rural life, farming reinforced the community's religious beliefs of separation and mutual aid. At the same time, farming served as a powerful force for change, scattering the believers in their search for land and making them part of the continental migration.[24]

Beginning in the last quarter of the nineteenth century, the Brethren in Christ began a slow process of accepting many of the changes that accompanied industrialization. Most of them encountered this change on the farm, as mechanization and electrification spread to rural America. A few highly visible individuals, however, encountered these changes in urban settings, where they had moved as missionaries. Cautious centralization added an annual General Conference to the district setup. The church established an academy, the Messiah Bible School and Missionary Training School, in Harrisburg, Pennsylvania. As waves of non-English-speaking people arrived in North America, the Brethren in Christ slowly shifted from German to English. A number of BIC women, despite their covered heads and their lack of formal political power in the church, resembled women in the larger society in their pursuit of education, their activism in promoting missions and benevolent institutions, and their penchant for voicing opinions in the church magazine.[25]

In these same years, the Brethren in Christ, like many other Protestant groups, were drawn into the revivalism promoted by American holiness traditions. The holiness message promised Christian perfection through an instantaneous personal experience of sanctification. This promise of perfection had obvious appeal for a community that stressed individual religious experience and expected consistent practice in daily life. Holiness advocates sometimes claimed nonconformist symbols as outward expressions of inner perfection. Holiness revivalism, however, challenged Anabaptist traditions of corporate religious authority. And the holiness idea of instantaneous perfection ran contrary to the Anabaptist idea that perfection requires lifelong practice. Furthermore, holiness revivalism reinforced BIC ties with conservative Protestants, many of whom opposed pacifism.[26]

Major change thus occurred in the Brethren in Christ over time. The need to negotiate constant change did not lessen between 1914 and 1958. Institutionalization and bureaucratization of the denomination intensified. The number of home and international missions and denominational schools grew. Two of the schools began offering college programs. More community members received higher levels of education, and more left farms, usually to run small businesses or to enter professions.[27] Nevertheless, until the 1950s—and in some arenas well beyond those years—the Brethren in Christ maintained or strengthened Anabaptist elements of their identity and changed in ways similar to other "progressive" Anabaptists.[28]

Within this dance of continuity and change lies the story of evolving BIC nonresistance. Records from the American War of Independence and Civil War, though rare, reveal nonresistant beliefs, complicated attempts to live them out, and apostasy.[29] From the 1870s to the outbreak of World War I, nonresistant expression appears as only a minor theme in writings and explicit teachings. Clearly, many Brethren in Christ took nonresistance for granted, but the threat of military conscription always roused the old doctrine. As we shall see, the institution of universal male conscription in both the United States and Canada in 1917 dramatically affected the Brethren in Christ. This first total war also required nonresistant responses to home-front mobilization. World War I brought the Brethren in Christ into an informal working relationship with what would come to be called the "Historic Peace Churches"—the Religious Society of Friends (or Quakers); the Mennonites, who increasingly represented smaller Anabaptist groups; and the Church of the Brethren, one of several groups descended from the German Baptist Brethren. In ways that foreshadowed the next world war, the Brethren in Christ joined in pacifist humanitarian relief efforts as a positive corollary to their opposition to war.[30]

After the war, nonresistant expression again took a backseat to more pressing, yet related, issues of nonconformist dress and holiness teachings—all components of being a "peculiar people." But the problems of the World War I experience informed BIC leaders in the interwar years.[31] By the time war broke out in Europe in 1939, both the Canadian and American branches of the BIC church had begun more extensive cooperation with the Historic Peace Church coalition. That coalition was quickly engulfed by the massive requirements of funding and administering Civilian Public Service (CPS), the alternative-service program for conscientious objectors in the United States during World War II. In 1940, the Brethren in Christ became official members of Mennonite Central Committee (MCC), a service agency of churches in the Mennonite mosaic. In this setting and in Civilian Public Service, the Brethren in Christ were identified as "Mennonite." Although the requirements were different, Canadian Brethren in Christ made similar alliances, which also yielded cooperation across the border.

Simultaneously, successive pieces of General Conference legislation in the 1940s imposed discipline on official members who defied the corporate stand against military participation. Perhaps half of BIC men in the United States served in the military, some of them defining their noncombatant military service as conscientious objection. Because the official church members disagreed on definitions of conscientious objection and disciplinary measures, internal conflict became a key part of BIC nonresistance in World War II. If conflict was part of the experience, so too was a strong emphasis on peace teachings and on the institutionalization of voluntary humanitarian service. A substantial number of BIC women and men served in MCC service projects.[32]

In the first postwar decade, these emphases continued, now often named the "peace witness." Peacetime conscription systems, put in place in the United States from 1948 to 1972, helped sustain community involvement. Peace conferences, literature, and draft counseling figure prominently in the pages of the *Visitor*. Gradually, the Brethren in Christ changed their thinking on participation in electoral politics and in other aspects of public life. BIC literature increasingly connected peace issues to social justice concerns, especially after the rise of the civil rights and antiwar movements of the 1960s and 1970s. However, statistics on BIC drafted men indicate that between 1951 and 1957, close to half chose military service. Among those choosing military service, very few registered as noncombatants. In a paradoxical response, a 1958 General Conference decision revoked the requirement of conscientious objection for membership in the church.[33]

Other related areas of BIC community life were also in flux. In the 1950s, the church retreated, sometimes in piecemeal fashion, from a variety of nonconformist practices—plain dress and prohibitions on the use of musical instruments in churches and on the purchase of life insurance policies by individuals. At the same time, a major reorganization of church polity further central- ized church structures. Individual church congregations, each led by one paid minister, began to replace the district system of multiple unpaid ministers. Six conferences and six bishops replaced the more than thirty districts and nearly thirty bishops. This was also the decade when the Brethren in Christ joined the two coalitions outside the Anabaptist family: the National Association of Evangelicals, established in 1942 to represent many conservative Protestants, and the National Holiness Association.[34]

These decisions and events did not end the BIC peace witness. Some BIC lead- ers vigorously promoted the peace witness, even within evangelical circles. Some Brethren in Christ welcomed new issues raised in the turbulence of the 1960s and 1970s as means to deepen the peace witness. But the belief and its practice divided more than united the community. The peace witness and divisions over it posed a threat to a major goal—the recruiting of new members. In addition, the decisions of the 1950s made the Brethren in Christ less distinct from main- stream society in personal appearance, economic lifestyles, sense of citizenship, and especially in emphasis on the individual. As more of daily life slipped be- yond the reach of the corporate body, the individual soul seemed increasingly destined to wend its own way to heaven. This loss of the visible, separated com- munity paralleled, however, a steady growth in membership numbers.[35]

In the last decades of the twentieth century, the BIC course remained di- vided and unclear. A 1998 doctrinal manual included appeals for nonviolence, for "active peacemaking," for nonconformity, for simplicity, and for conscien- tious objection to participation in war. It gave no indication, however, of the importance of these tenets for membership. Some BIC church members con- tinued to participate in new ventures of the Historic Peace Churches, includ- ing the New Call to Peacemaking and Christian Peacemaker Teams. Numer- ous writers—church leaders, academics, and lay people—continued to call the BIC community to peace action, nonconformity, and simplicity. Academics in particular offered measured criticism of the loss of Anabaptist values. But whether these voices reached the members of this still small but growing de- nomination remains to be seen.[36]

Many new members have only limited knowledge of the BIC community's history and traditions, and, as we will see throughout this study, many estab- lished members seem forgetful themselves. Such BIC "historylessness" is cen- tral because the community's history and that of other religious groups show that new members sometimes most actively and vocally embrace nonconform- ist requirements.[37] The conception embraced by some Brethren in Christ of salvation as an afterlife reinforces this amnesia—to them, the future seems more compelling than the past. Perhaps BIC forgetfulness has been reinforced by the community's history, which has been entangled from its beginning with that of a nation fixated on the pearly gates of economic expansion.

Whatever its future, the community's past demonstrates persistence as well as change. The Brethren in Christ worked long and hard at approximating their vision of a redeemed people. They also helped to form the core of an ongoing pacifist presence in North American society. Furthermore, issues the Brethren in Christ addressed between 1914 and 1958—violence; the relationship between individuals and communities, and between women and men; the requirements of neighborliness and social concern in a world capable of massive destruction—remain among the most pressing in the early twenty-first century.

Their future vision will necessarily reflect the changes of the larger world—evolving systems of production and consumption, war and oppression, changing social relationships, and the experiences of other small communities struggling to define themselves. That larger context is especially important whenever a small community challenges powerful understandings that have united humans, often violently, over long periods of time. And, of course, that larger context makes up the real setting in which BIC people live on a daily basis—in the world, even as they seek to create a new one.

Brethren in Christ in the Mennonite Mosaic

When war broke out in Europe in 1914, the Brethren in Christ hovered on the edge of a complex Mennonite world.[38] Like the Brethren in Christ, most Mennonites drew boundaries not only between themselves and the larger world, but also among themselves. Ethnic, denominational, and national lines crisscrossed Mennonite groups, often oriented toward local congregational life.[39] A variety of groups that have come to be called "Old Order"—Amish, Mennonite, River Brethren—shared histories with "progressive" Mennonites and Brethren in Christ but followed plain paths that led to increasingly distinct social and cultural groups. All of the progressive groups, in differing ratios, maintained certain old symbols of plainness as they accepted technological, intellectual, and institutional changes alongside many other Americans. Mennonites in general and their scholars in particular continue to debate the significance of those adaptations. Were they evidence of assimilation to a powerful core America? Were they a more complex cultural interchange that allowed for the persistence of distinctive beliefs and practices? What is clear is that BIC and Mennonite responses to World War I combined elements of small, decentralized communities with instances of increased coordination between new bureaucratic structures.[40]

In the next fifty years, Mennonites and the Brethren in Christ worked mightily to respond to warfare of horrific violence. They greeted World War I somberly, knowing the costs that war exacts on pacifists. What they could not know was that the mobilization of technology, materials, and humans would eclipse old verities and ways of living. Gerlof Homan's study of Mennonites in World War I provides a context for the experiences of the Brethren in Christ. The Mennonites' disparate and often conflicting official responses to mass mobilization resulted in traumatic experiences on the home front and in military camps. Those experiences also reflected the confusion of the national mobilization, as well as the intimidation of Mennonite leaders by government investigations, the harassment of dissenters by vigilantes, and the decisions of individual military officers in camps. Nevertheless, many Mennonites on the home front and in military camps took stands to express their nonresistance.[41]

The war effort brought unprecedented cooperation between business and government, which encouraged bigness and centralization in the economy of the postwar years. The peace churches also learned the advantages of centralized efforts in their negotiations with government and military officials for exemptions for conscientious objection. Under the aegis of the Quaker's American Friends Service Committee, Mennonites and one BIC man participated relief efforts in war areas, establishing the principle of a positive humanitarian contribution and, undoubtedly, responding to pressures of war mobilization.[42]

In the years between the world wars, a powerful group of Mennonite leaders emerged. They combined appreciation of higher education, ability to strike a balance between Mennonite-style fundamentalists and modernists, and deep commitment to maintain a distinctive Mennonite identity as the group encountered social and economic change. Perry Bush charts that change most extensively; he addresses the collective, dynamic, and productive efforts of leaders from the 1930s through the 1970s. Other historians have focused more narrowly on towering men who filled key positions in Mennonite colleges and on the Mennonite Central Committee. Albert Keim's biography of Harold S. Bender, one of the best-known Mennonite leaders outside the community, portrays an intellectual who used history and tradition to recast the role of Mennonites in the modern world. Bender spelled out a new "Anabaptist Vision" in his seminal 1943 essay and in his whirlwind of activity from 1920 to his death in 1962. He worked to create a usable Anabaptist past and a sense of Mennonites as an international community. At the center of his vision was "the ethic of love and nonresistance," which he described as "the most radical departure" from Protestantism. During World War II, Bender worked alongside other powerful leaders to implement new structures. He helped to design the Mennonite CPS camps, which not only housed four thousand Mennonite conscientious objectors but also educated the next generation of academic and administrative leaders. In addition, Bender contributed substantially to the MCC Peace Section, set up in

1942 to promote and expand the peace witness, and to MCC international volunteer and relief efforts. MCC international volunteers formed a second group of leaders, who emerged in the late 1950s—ecumenical, prophetic, and ready with a new intellectual formulation. All of this facilitated Mennonite conversations with a variety of social groupings, including the civil rights movement and the Vietnam antiwar movement.[43]

Bender personifies a group of leaders who were not afraid to use power and who dominated institutional life.[44] Their ideas and actions had substantial impact on numerous BIC men in Civilian Public Service and in the postwar alternative service program. BIC women and men in MCC voluntary service assignments, on committees and boards, and in new Mennonite ventures in mental health and disaster service also joined in collective efforts sometimes termed "Mennonite and Brethren in Christ."[45]

Throughout these same years, the Brethren in Christ had their own powerful leaders. Two men in particular provided the BIC community with its own usable past and charted new avenues for nonresistance. Ernest (E. J.) Swalm in Ontario and Christian (C. N.) Hostetter Jr. in Pennsylvania provided charismatic leadership that responded to the needs of the smaller BIC community. Until World War II, neither moved in the intellectual, ecumenical, or international communities that Bender and other Mennonites leaders did. Both served as bishops and filled key positions in the General Conference. Hostetter was president of the BIC school, Messiah College, from 1934 to 1960. Swalm, a powerful orator and storyteller, wove his experiences as a conscientious objector in World War I into his traveling church evangelism. In 1938, the denominational press published his account, Nonresistance under Test. Many Brethren in Christ equated nonresistance with Swalm's story, pleased that it could draw large audiences. Both men worked extensively in the World War II and early postwar peace coalitions. Swalm chaired the Canadian Conference of Historic Peace Churches; Hostetter chaired the Mennonite Central Committee.[46]

Like Mennonite leaders, both men were comfortable wielding power and moving into ecumenical circles. For Hostetter in the 1950s, that meant representing the Brethren in Christ both on the Mennonite Central Committee and in the National Association of Evangelicals (NAE).[47] Histories and sociological studies make clear that Mennonites, like the Brethren in Christ, have been influenced by successive irruptions of American revivalism, especially since the second half of the nineteenth century. But although there was cooperation between the National Association of Evangelicals and Mennonites, only smaller Mennonite groups and the Brethren in Christ joined the organization. In the 1950s, Hostetter worked with Mennonite leaders to communicate the peace witness to the National Association of Evangelicals. Perry Bush argues that the Anabaptist perspective influenced a group of "Young Evangelicals" in the 1970s; most evangelicals, however, remained unengaged and even hostile to Anabaptist messages of peace and nonconformity. That did not end the evangelical appeal to many Mennonites; nor did it end BIC membership in the National Association of Evangelicals. In fact, numerous BIC leaders served in leadership positions of the coalition.[48]

Sociologist Calvin Redekop argues that evangelicalism has always had a stronger influence on smaller Mennonite groups partly because they are small, having few like-minded people with which to engage. Perhaps these small groups, the Brethren in Christ included, have also used evangelical identities to challenge the Mennonite churches that dwarf them. Regardless of BIC motivations, evangelicalism deeply influenced the community in the postwar period. Amorphous and dynamic, evangelicalism has consistently been entwined with American nationalism. In that sense, Redekop contends, evangelicalism, whatever else it might offer individuals and churches, denotes an acceptance of the dictates of the twentieth-century world, a world dominated by American economic and military power.[49] The challenge to peace churches is obvious. More difficult to uncover is the way in which new religious strands appeal to ordinary people facing the complexities of daily life.

In the period of this book, the daily life of many Brethren in Christ and Mennonites included the church community at its center but also involved life in families, at school or in a job, and with neighbors. Leaders from both groups reiterated that nonconformity and nonresistance was legitimated by consistent practice in these settings. Leaders and doctrinal statements laid out guiding principles. In their daily lives, ordinary people were the final arbiters of practice. Guy F. Hershberger, a leading Mennonite social thinker in the 1930s and 1940s, suggested that the acceptable use of force for nonresistant people resided "somewhere between spanking and serving on the police force."[50] Scholarly evaluations also note, sometimes indirectly, how little we know about the daily applications of nonresistance. Sociologists Leo Driedger and Donald B. Kraybill, for instance, write that "although Mennonites spanked their offspring, sometimes beat their cows, and hunted game for sport, their rejection of force had sweeping implications for many social involvements."[51]

CLAIMS OF THE EVERYDAY

"The missing element in social awareness of the nature of human experience through history," writes Quaker sociologist Elise Boulding, "is an image of the dailiness of life—of the common round from dawn to dawn that sustains human existence."[52] That missing piece is important, not simply because it is missing but also because the daily round is a key arena where one can see how the structures of society are maintained by thousands of ordinary people. Here one also sees how those same people sometimes live in ways that challenge those structures, becoming players in the processes of change. Finally, one can examine how beliefs are transmitted, reshaped, or discarded.

After World War II and with increasing intensity after the 1960s, American social and cultural historians turned their attention to ordinary people and everyday life. The actions of thousands of nameless people, when quantified, became significant. Habits and attitudes became as important as beliefs and events. The attention to ordinary people also often meant a focus on immigrants, racial minorities, women, and religious minorities—people brought into more active participation in public life by the social changes and movements of the postwar world. Interdisciplinary influences turned historical attention to what did not change as well as to what did, paralleling late-twentieth-century popular interest in small local cultures. Taken together, these approaches produced studies that added new strands and sometimes challenged overarching historical explanations.[53] For instance, American slavery became not simply a political, legal, and economic system but one that depended on "tens of thousands of individual acts of personal domination." At the same time, slaves and immigrant laborers became key builders of the American economy and polity as well as shapers of its ideology and culture.[54] In similar ways, minority ideas, such as pacifism, became influences on the larger society, even as that society helped to shape the form and content of those ideas.[55] The BIC community, in the process of living out and transforming its nonresistance, offers examples of the importance of the mundane and the ordinary in that process.

A number of these examples, explored further throughout the book, point to contrasting strands of BIC life in the first half of the twentieth century. One example—the passing of nonresistance from one generation to the next—reinforces interdisciplinary studies that see change as multidirectional and dependent on an intricate interchange of ideas, structures, ideologies, habits, and contingencies. Contemporary authors during the world wars, as well as people looking back to those years, often fault the BIC church for inadequate attention to peace issues, a common complaint among all the peace churches. Certainly, lapses in nonresistant practice on farms, in factories, and before local draft boards substantiated the charges. At the same time, the fact that a substantial number of BIC people continued to take their nonresistant practice very seriously also requires explanation. One BIC woman, looking back, struggled to explain the process of learning to be nonresistant in the 1920s and 1930s. She finally chose the word "caught." Her word choice echoes other descriptions of nonresistance—"an overriding sense" or "the art of give and take."

These sources suggest that nonresistance was often learned by absorption, not didactics, and that an important setting for such learning was the home. Others remember, often less positively, another arena for learning about nonresistance—church discipline imposed upon members who violated a BIC position on participation in war.

During World War II and in the 1950s, the Brethren in Christ worked toward a more rationalized system of teaching peace: literature, conferences, and draft counseling. They moved toward encouraging a peace witness among members rather than requiring it. The results were disappointing. In the 1950s, the percentage of conscripted BIC men who chose military service continued to grow. At the same time, however, some members began to practice their peace witness as humanitarian service. The profiles of Nelson Hostetter and Elsie Bechtel, who chose to volunteer in service projects, show a lifelong commitment to an evolving peace stance. But these are only two individuals, and Hostetter left the Brethren in Christ to join the Mennonite Church, which he viewed as more committed to countercultural values. The excavation of this complicated picture is the task of this book. Two studies suggest the importance of everyday life in that dissection.

Theologian Theodore Grimsrud's categorization of the ethics that informed the choices of conscientious objectors during World War II establishes the centrality of everyday practice—the "servant" ethic—for those emerging from nonresistant traditions. In these communities, "day to day practice" and "internalized habits" learned early in life made obedience to a corporate stance more important than intellectual formulations based on logic and argumentation and accepted by individuals.[56] Grimsrud uses the observations of Richard C. Hunter, a conscientious objector from a Methodist background, to illustrate the servant stance. Serving in a Mennonite-run CPS camp, Hunter at first found it difficult to accept the validity of convictions that were "never verbalized" by fellow conscientious objectors. He gradually, however, came to admire "the strength and character of an organized culture." One day he witnessed a work crew, led by an Amish man, begin a day's assignment and then discover that the work was the first stages of what would become a military base. With little discussion or interest in publicizing the event, the men simply put down their tools and left. "When conviction called for action," Hunter noted, "it was taken quietly and effectively."[57] Grimsrud identifies key features of that culture: communal values and authority, values understood as practice, transmission of values by example.[58]

Some of the best work detailing the practice of such a culture appears in studies of Old Order Anabaptists, who in the early twenty-first century continue to reject many of the accouterments of modern life and to define their religious devotion as visible practice. The context of these communities differs from that of the Brethren in Christ before 1960. The attention paid by scholars of these groups to change, diversity, and complex interaction between a small community's values and the realities of the invasive larger society, however, is instructive. Summarizing their study of four Old Order groups, sociologists Don Kraybill and Carl Bowman suggest that countercultural persistence lies in values that venerate tradition rather than the future, the group rather than the individual, and habitual practice rather than rationalized ideas.[59] That persistence, however, constantly interacts with the larger society to produce what Kraybill describes elsewhere as "a common public front," which masks "enormous variation in everyday practice."[60] That variation suggests that if daily life is the medium in which countercultural ideas persist, it is also where the world invades. Among the Brethren in Christ, it was families, gender roles, and geographic dispersion that brokered that persistence and that invasion.

Vast economic and political changes have altered daily life in the modern world. But the family and the home, though changing themselves, remain at the center of daily experience. With the exception of the communal Hutterites, most Anabaptist families have consistently resembled those of the larger society.[61] Obviously, those families teach values and expectations to their members. But as historian Elizabeth Jameson illustrates with her analysis of the relationship between Jewish religion and a Jewish homesteading family, teaching is much more than simple transmission. Families also *interpret* the religion, as they encounter new realities and as they choose which religious practices are "malleable" and decide how to shape them. Daily practice, then, is shaped by religious beliefs interpreted by the family.[62] That interpretation, however, takes place through the inevitable conflicts that arise among different family members.

Quaker sociologist Elise Boulding describes the family setting as an important one for the practice of peace. She also notes, however, that pacifist families often have failed to meet the special demands placed on their members. They were sometimes incapable of responding to childhood aggression and passing on perfectionist goals to their children and youth. Lurking at the edges of BIC nonresistant practice was the fear that the "war nature" was present in families or in the church, not simply in the world.[63] Domestic violence and abuse directly linked questions about nonresistant practice to the home. Families also negotiated other issues. Which family members would carry which burdens of nonresistant practice in wartime? How much discussion of the belief would be permitted in the family?[64]

Within the family and well beyond it, gender often shaped the daily practice of nonresistance. Massive literature produced in the last thirty years focusing on the experiences of women demonstrates that sexual differences and cultural values assigned to those differences shape every aspect of human existence. A sexual division of labor and the lower value assigned to women's labor has worked its way into every social institution from the family to international warfare. "War," argues essayist and social critic Barbara Ehrenreich, is "one of the most rigidly 'gendered' activities known to humankind."[65] At the same time, mutuality between women and men and women's own expression of value and power have also shaped history. Because nonconformist Anabaptists have largely borrowed their gender expectations from the larger society, and because the nature of particular wars shapes pacifist responses, the experiences of nonresistant women often parallel those of other pacifist women and women engaged in war efforts.[66] Rachel Waltner Goossen provides an important study of gender and conscientious objection, focused on the approximately two thousand women connected to Civilian Public Service. These women were staunch conscientious objectors themselves, not simply camp followers, and key players in the formation of nonconformist subcultures. In the same years, patriots used gender roles to question the manhood of male conscientious objectors. In turn, Frances Early's work on feminist pacifists notes a socialist male conscientious objector in World War I who described religious objectors as "effeminate." The gendered nature of pacifist subcultures in daily life and in families has yet to receive adequate attention.[67]

Certainly, by World War I the Brethren in Christ had consciously and unconsciously assigned plain dress as the special province of women. The covered female head, in particular, symbolized the unequal status of women and men in the structures of the BIC church. Formal district leadership was reserved for men, as were most positions in church structures beyond the district. After the mid-1960s, women slowly joined the ranks of elected delegates to the General Conference.[68] Informally, women undoubtedly helped to define and maintain the boundaries of nonconformist and nonresistant practice. When it came down to final definitions, however, men made the rules and administered discipline. Nonresistance, then, reflected not only the goal of peaceful living in a new kingdom but also unequal power among the people pursuing it. As Calvin Redekop points out, among Anabaptists "structural restraints of power" focused on the state. Within marriages, families, and communal life, ethical standards for the use of power were much less developed.[69]

Dress and discipline were only the conspicuous aspects of the massive work of maintaining community life. A closer look at nonconformist groups, however, demonstrates that despite that inward focus, all of them participated with neighbors outside their communities. Over time, American Anabaptist settlement patterns have varied; in many cases the pattern has interspersed Anabaptists with a variety of neighbors.[70] Certainly that was true for the Brethren in Christ. In addition, many of these groups actively cultivated relationships with neighbors. Again, work on late-twentieth-century Old Order groups is instructive. Even the most spatially separated and communal Hutterites sometimes joined agricultural organizations and volunteered in local social-service organizations. Local economic culture, neighborhood events, and "daily gestures of friendship" connected nonconformist communities to local public life. Farm auctions and yard sales, natural disasters, volunteer fire companies, and labor exchanges suggest the avenues.[71] In the first half of the twentieth century, the Brethren in Christ, like these Old Order groups, were scattered across many regions and two nations. Some lived in areas densely populated by community members or other Anabaptist groups; other migrating groups lived in small, seemingly isolated communities. Of course, both worlds abounded with neighbors. Those neighbors only occasionally presented themselves as tempters or persecutors. Even more rarely were they the monolithic sort of Americans that twentieth-century Anabaptists decry—individualistic, consumeristic, militarized, and secular.[72] Indeed, in the daily world of most Anabaptists, the entanglements of mainstream values were often hidden. In this world, neighbors shared many goals with the plain people.

Even in the intense and, in many ways, atypical days of the world wars, nonresistant people shared the fears and the joys of collective effort with those mobilized for war. BIC people met neighbors involved in the war effort who openly admired their stance.[73] The corporate peace witness persisted in this small world of neighbors, as well as in the larger world of war, nations, and greed.

SMALL COMMUNITY LIFE IN AMERICAN SOCIETY

The Brethren in Christ might profitably be compared to many communities beyond those in the Anabaptist grouping. In the first half of the twentieth century, ethnic Norwegian farmers in Wisconsin maintained a rural culture distinct from those of neighbors; Italian immigrants worried about the ways in which public education drew children away from the family; African Americans and Japanese Americans faced repressive social policies and vigilante violence that often increased during war periods; and workers who struggled for a more equitable society in the 1910s and 1930s failed to tell their stories to the next generations.[74] The Brethren in Christ might also be placed in the context of modern American religious history. In addition to the blending of Anabaptism and revivalism, BIC thinking was influenced by fundamentalist, dispensational, and premillenial ideas, beginning in the late nineteenth century.[75] Taken together, these strands have placed the Brethren in Christ in a shifting conservative configuration throughout the twentieth century and into the present. That configuration is cut through with "cross clefts and crisscrossing."[76] The persistent BIC peace witness illustrates the messiness. That most radical of their beliefs make comparisons to groups that have self-consciously embraced countercultural beliefs particularly fruitful. Also, the practice of peace sometimes linked the Brethren in Christ to champions of justice, to modernists, and to atheists, when those groups saw peace as a route to a better world. The Brethren in Christ were hardly unique in claiming a separated community as an identity, one that gave meaning to their lives, modeled a better way, and indicated divine approval. They shared two important and recurring American dreams with other such communities. First, they dreamed of transforming the world, even while being dismissed as "peculiar" or utopian. Second, they dreamed of joining like-minded people in communities intent on putting countercultural beliefs into practice.[77] Claims to "outsider" status may be widespread in a competitive society, but willingness to pay material costs is more limited.[78] A brief look at three "costly" communities in the nineteenth century provides a time span and a non-Anabaptist lens by which to consider how "the claims of the commonweal" sometimes fostered and sometimes pulverized small communities and local cultures.[79]

The Brethren in Christ have rarely compared themselves to the Church of Jesus Christ of Latter-Day Saints (Mormons) or to the community established by John Humphrey Noyes at Oneida, New York. Yet the experiences of these groups, both established in the 1830s, help to illuminate both the common struggles of countercultural communities and the unique issues of a nonresistant one. In his study of the relationship between Mormons and the larger society, sociologist Armand L. Mauss suggests a model for understanding new religious groups. His model applies particularly to those that begin as "conspicuously deviant and unpopular" but persist and, as in the case of the Mormons, grow rapidly. Throughout the nineteenth century, Mormon beliefs offended many other Americans. Polygamy and a modern prophet who claimed divine revelation and instituted theocratic structures were the most visible markers of nonconformity. Communal values and experiments also challenged the image of American individualism. Many Americans, sometimes backed by military and judicial power, were outraged and intolerant.

Throughout the nineteenth century, Mauss argues, Mormons endured persecution and attracted members as a counterculture. That countercultural stance, however, had its limits. Those limits, although imposed by federal coercion, were also shaped by Mormon leaders. Between 1900 and 1960, Mormons devised a new collective identity as patriotic, law-abiding, model American citizens. Mormons continued to call themselves a "peculiar" people, but by the 1960s they resembled broad swathes of American society. Mauss's model, however, does not posit unilinear movement. Mormons, he says, found it necessary to respond to the "predicament of respectability." They responded not only theologically—rehabilitating modern prophets—but also with more religious education and more service opportunities. "Peculiar" people, Mauss suggests, seesaw between countercultural values and the values of the larger society. Mauss may be downplaying important persistent communal sentiments among ordinary Mormons.[80] Nonetheless, his picture of Mormon leaders approximates Bush's analysis of Mennonite peace leaders in the twentieth century—a pattern of jarring clashes between nonresistant people and neighbors during World War I, followed by the reworking of the nonresistant doctrine as a higher patriotism, expressed in humanitarian service and careful negotiations with government and military officials in World War II. During the Vietnam War, more radical resistance to conscription claimed the authority of an Anabaptist heritage even as it joined the larger antiwar movement.[81]

Although BIC leaders sometimes moved among high government or military officials during negotiations, more often the Brethren in Christ involved themselves in small affairs of the neighborhood. Again, a group not obviously like the Brethren in Christ provides a useful point of comparison. As Christian perfectionists, the nineteenth-century New York Oneida Community aimed at creating a small society as a model for a disordered larger one. As with many utopian communities, rearrangement of domestic relationships was an important part of the new community. Concerned about the exclusivity of monogamous marriage, Noyes set up a system of sexual relations that was to reflect "a heart . . . free to love all the true and worthy." Noyes called the arrangement "complex marriage"; his earliest neighbors in Vermont charged him with adultery. When the community moved to New York, members used neighborliness to disarm neighbors shocked by their radical practices—or perhaps, more unconsciously, outraged at the hubris of people who claimed to be models. In New York, however, the community carefully cultivated neighbors with visitation, respectable demeanor, civic activism, and contributions to the local economy.[82]

Both the nineteenth-century Oneida Community during the Civil War and twentieth-century Mormons in the world wars chose a way of cultivating neighbors that was not available to the Brethren in Christ—supporting wartime mobilizations.[83] The religious groups used wars, as have many excluded social groups, to become good Americans. In contrast, in times of war the Historic Peace Churches worked with another group of neighbors—a devoted, shifting group of peace advocates who claimed religious and secular pacifism, antimilitarism, internationalism, and activist nonviolence. Histories of peace advocates usually include nonresistant religious groups, but often in a peripheral way. Yet similar concerns spanned the spectrum of groups insistent on pursuing alternatives to violence. For example, all Protestant pacifists, not just those in the Historic Peace Churches, initially emphasized obedience to biblical injunctions against war. Among all these pacifists, humanitarian service "provided the transition from nonresistance to modern pacifism." Most peace advocates moved slowly to connect structural injustice to issues of peace. Nonresistant Anabaptists seldom led the way. Nonresistant groups did, however, make up a substantial portion of the core of absolute pacifists who endured in the ebbs of particular antiwar organization, even as they distinguished their biblical pacifism from that influenced by modernist thought or secular pacifism. Their creation of model communities, a strategy sometimes advocated by other pacifists, also provided alternative routes to social change when the claims of utilitarianism seemed false and promises of social betterment failed.[84]

In their persistence and corporate life, nonresistant communities embody traditions of peace that outlast wars, traditions that might be labeled an "intergenerational" peace movement. Much of the history of the larger peace movement is a story of activists and organizations. How peace advocates have interacted in families and more local settings is less clear. Certainly, many have worked tirelessly for goals that they understand will be realized only well after their own lifetimes.[85] Once again, attention to gendered experiences in the peace movement has yielded new attention to peace cultures that addressed everyday interactions. Histories of the women's separate peace organizations show women who conceived of peace as a culture. Their emphasis on daily practice and intergenerational continuity, not always at the forefront of antiwar movements, again suggests points of comparison for evaluating nonresistance.[86]

Although all peace groups strove to survive, all of them sometimes lost members or their pacifist stance itself. Radical peace activist A. J. Muste watched his son volunteer for military service in World War II. The grandson of BIC member Jacob Eisenhower became supreme allied commander in Europe in World War II.[87] Studies of Mennonites who chose military service and subsequently were expelled or voluntarily left the community thus provide another angle for considering peace history.[88] Similarly, American religious groups that lost the peace witness yield clues for understanding the BIC experience. Shirley Hershey Showalter's introduction to a collection of essays that include such groups summarizes the case studies. She contends that practice, stories, history, and tradition must be valued over intellectual formulations, creedal statements, and orthodoxy. But, she continues, the old stories that represent history, experience, and practice must be made new if they are to persist.[89] Showalter's formula is not an easy one to execute; certainly the Brethren in Christ found it difficult. After two hundred years of the practice of peace, worried members often seem most adept at explaining its demise.

Thomas D. Hamm's study of Quakers over the nineteenth century provides an important comparison for the BIC twentieth-century experience. First, although ethnically and theologically different, the BIC and Quakers shared pacifism, self-designation as plain people, and an encounter with revivalist holiness teachings. Second, both provide stories of interaction between a "peculiar people" and the world. In both cases, "the world" was not simply mobility, social and economic change, or the nation-state, though all of those factors were important. For both groups, the world's most potent challenge drew on their history while denigrating their traditions. Hamm's detailed study uses the Quakers as a microcosm of American Protestantism. He shows the power of mainstream evangelical formulations to fragment Quakerism, drawing a large branch of them into the dominant religious discourse of revivalism, individual conversion, a certain brand of biblicism, and American nationalism. In an intricate weaving of issues, those unique to Quakers and those they shared with many other Americans, Hamm details a process that left the largest group of Quakers bereft of their peace witness and almost indistinguishable from other evangelical Protestants. Revivalism appealed to Quakers' sense of their fiery origins in England. Sanctification promised speedy help in reaching a traditional goal—perfection in daily practice—in a quickly changing world. But joining this holiness revivalism brought new neighbors who were unfamiliar with salvation as disciplined lifelong practice and unimpressed with the value of being a small "peculiar" people of peace.[90]

Although this book examines the persistence of nonresistance among the Brethren in Christ, it does not assume the survival of a BIC peace witness. Such witnesses are dynamic but also tenuous. The interaction of persistence, change, and loss is vital for understanding how one group both succeeded and failed in living together. We know something about the agility with which intellectuals weave new dreams that sustain and transform old commitments. We know much less about the communities that have implemented or rejected those dreams. This study, therefore, turns to a consideration of nonresistance in one twentieth-century community.

CHAPTER ONE

Nonresistance in World War I

cℐ⌀

Neighborliness, friendship, kindness, sympathy—these are made of
stuff which no chemistry of war can crush.

In 1914, Europe awakened its sleeping dogs of war. Their rampage would eventually draw sixty-five million people into the world's militaries. Ten million people would be killed; twice that number would fall wounded or maimed. The slaughter of the Great War would yield a military stalemate, political instability, and despair.

In Pennsylvania, George Detweiler heard the first rumblings of this cataclysm and worried. He was editor of the *Visitor*, the monthly magazine of the Brethren in Christ. On August 10, 1914, six days after Britain joined the war, Detweiler wrote, "The dogs of war are set loose once more in Europe." He wondered how far the war would spread. Jabbing at the optimism of progressive peace advocates, he asked, "O where are the signs of the universal peace that has been heralded as being almost here?"[1]

On a farm in nearby Lancaster County, another member of the BIC community heard the same rumblings. Fifteen-year-old C. N. Hostetter Jr. wrote in his diary for August 13, 1914, "At the present time sugar is 8½ cents. War in Europe."[2]

Although neither Detweiler nor young Hostetter knew it at the time, the Brethren in Christ were about to be drawn into a tumult that would mark their lives, reshape their church, and raise questions that are still being pondered by the children and grandchildren of their generation.

Those questions centered on nonresistance and on the nonresistant position prescribed by BIC leaders. The Brethren in Christ were forbidden to enter

military service or to participate in national efforts to mobilize civilian populations in support of the war. During World War I, many in the BIC community
lived by those prescriptions in military camps and on the home front, sometimes at a cost. Others, however, joined the war effort. In both cases, nonconformist beliefs of separation and nonparticipation influenced their decisions.
The BIC community's ideas on discipline, roles for women and men, and neighborliness also shaped nonresistance, as did pacifism, premillennialism, and patriotic appeals. The service-oriented peace witness, therefore, reflects not only
the massive changes wrought by World War II but also the BIC community's
ongoing work of shaping particular ideas, always in interaction with the larger
society. All of these BIC experiences closely paralleled those of many Mennonites. Certainly, the Brethren in Christ drew on the ideas of the larger grouping;
sometimes they coordinated efforts. But the small BIC community thought in
their own particular terms.[3]

The World War I years brought considerable urgency to the work of shaping BIC ideas about nonresistance in both Canada and the United States. Conscription laws began affecting BIC men north and south of the border at about
the same time, in the second half of 1917. In both countries, conscription raised
issues different from those anticipated by BIC leaders. In the past, Canada had
granted legal exemptions from military service to certain nonresistant groups,
including the "Tunkers," a common name for the Brethren in Christ in Canada.
So Canadian BIC leaders responded first to the issue of military service by passing
resolutions in 1912 and 1913 that tried to protect the earlier legal exemptions. In
the United States, in the very week Congress passed the 1917 Selective Service
Act, the annual BIC General Conference issued a statement spelling out the
nonresistant position. Meeting in Kansas, the conferees also drew up a membership certificate for conscripted men to use. In the next issue of the *Visitor*,
Detweiler noted that General Conference had not authorized BIC contacts with
the U.S. government; the church had already established its nonresistant cre-
dentials. The BIC leadership in both the United States and Canada supposed
that earlier contacts with national governments would suffice. They instructed
their young men to register as conscientious objectors, assuming that as such
they would be completely exempted from military service. Their assumption
proved wrong. Consequently, young BIC men in both nations registered and
entered military training camps without a clear understanding of what to do
once they arrived.[4]

If the BIC church provided only limited instructions to conscientious objectors, government officials implementing the conscription law did no better
for military camp officials. The secretary of war, Newton D. Baker, purposely
kept definitions of conscientious objection vague, hoping to thin pacifist ranks.

Local draft boards made their own decisions, sometimes without regard to national law. Neither nation's conscription laws initially provided conscientious objectors with alternatives other than noncombatant military service, which was unacceptable to most nonresistant groups because it supported the war effort. Consequently, from mid-1917 through the end of the war in November 1918, conscripted BIC men practiced nonresistance in confusing, often intimidating, and lonely settings.[5]

BIC families and church leaders in Pennsylvania and Ontario visited military camps and made contacts with government officials and military officers. District, state, and provincial councils—not General Conference—authorized these efforts. The General Executive Board and the *Visitor*, however, attempted to spread the news of local actions and concerns to the larger BIC community. Documented Canadian conscientious objectors were granted leaves of absence and sent home after no more than two months in camp detention or in military prisons. But most American men remained under military supervision until their discharges after the Armistice in November 1918.

On the home front in both Canada and America, nonresistance required BIC women and men to respond to a variety of issues related to war mobilization, including war bonds, saluting the flag, and agricultural profits brought by increased wartime prices. Both branches of the church encouraged contributions for the relief of civilians in war areas, explicitly tying the contributions to their position against war.

At the same time, specific experiences in military training camps and on the home front were shaped by the broad contours of mobilization in North America. In the United States, civil and military leaders who hoped to mobilize the population with nineteenth-century ideals of voluntary collective effort and informal power also encouraged emotional appeals and tolerated vigilante actions that targeted dissenters. The relief efforts of nonresistant people responded to war victims but also served as a vehicle for nonresistant people to express national loyalty and to reassure angry neighbors.

If old ideals helped to power the war effort, the scale of mobilization eclipsed the individual, and the massive slaughter bred a sense of meaninglessness in daily life for many. In his study of the cultural impact of the war, literature professor Paul Fussell argues that the postwar society "commemorated" the war by mimicking army life's imposition of uniformity. Mass production and mass media would feed that regimentation. In their own small way, the Brethren in Christ and other nonresistant churches would also centralize their efforts to maintain a peace witness. The Brethren in Christ would draw on photography—a troubling media for nonconformist groups—to picture the suffering of war victims and encourage contributions for relief efforts. New questions about the meaning of human existence and changes in economic structures raised issues from which no community at that time could emerge untouched.[6]

Nonresistant Thought and Practice on the Home Front

Between the 1880s and the 1930s, the Brethren in Christ passed resolutions on a variety of issues growing out of their understandings of nonresistance and nonconformity. BIC histories describe prohibitions by General Conference or other councils of military service, police work, jury duty, and participation in electoral politics or labor unions.[7] Sometimes, however, the BIC community found these issues too complex for simple proscriptions. An 1889 General Conference resolution, while abjuring participation in elections on nonresistant grounds, excepted voting for Prohibition, as a "moral" rather than political question.[8] A 1904 decision prohibiting labor union membership came only after two years of extended discussion in General Conference.[9] The closing "Expression of Faith and Resolutions of Thankfulness" of the 1913 General Conference addressed the injustices of industrialism as much as it condemned participation in organized labor. Heralding first "the gentler and more potent ministries of peace" expressed in "arbitration . . . of industrial and international disputes," the statement went on to "deplore the unjust wages and living conditions which prevail in many industrial centers, and we plead for a wage rate that shall guarantee to labor, its just share of the comforts and conveniences produced by its own industry." Holding "industrial slavery" responsible for the "traffic in vice," the authors also connected these injustices to "the insidious encroachments of leisure, luxury, and extravagance."[10]

The mixing of progressive sentiments with nonresistance did not end with World War I. Eli M. Engle, a prominent BIC minister, probably wrote the 1926 piece entitled "The Way to World Peace," which articulated many themes of the larger peace movement. He cataloged the destructive new technology of World War I, condemned "narrow nationalism," and attributed increased "race hatreds and jealousies" to the war. In addition to condemning war, Engle called for "preparing adequately and intelligently for peace" by first "build[ing] machinery for world peace" and then by encouraging popular support for international peacekeeping. The World Court was to be supported by "every peace-loving citizen of our land." The League of Nations provided another "true instrument for peace."[11]

International bodies, however, were not the only arenas for nonresistant practice. Two Ontario church leaders in the early twentieth century thought nonresistance should inform broad areas of daily life. Fred Elliot, who helped draft a petition for BIC community military exemption in Canada during World

War I, questioned the nonresistance of people who were "combative in their families, their neighborhoods, and their churches whenever their wishes were crossed." He continued, "While hurting no one's bodies, they often deeply wound their souls." Similarly, Charles Baker advocated practicing nonresistant virtues—humility, generosity, kindness—in the treatment of animals, family members, neighbors, and "the whole human family."[12]

Interactions with this whole human family, however, sometimes revealed a disjunction between official BIC positions and daily life, especially in times of war. The South African, or Boer, War elicited a Canadian joint council statement against war; at least one BIC member who served in the army was "disfellowshiped." But during the war, Charles Baker's daughter Lillian remarked in her diary about going to a train station with friends to greet a local man who was returning from the war.[13] Apparently daily life entailed less isolation than official boundaries encouraged.

The U.S. Civil War revealed similar fissures in the BIC community south of the border. In that war, according to its records, the BIC church officially communicated its nonresistant stand to the national government. Family stories describe BIC men hiring substitutes or paying annual fines in order to receive exemptions.[14] But during World War I, the *Visitor* published the obituaries of three Civil War veterans, suggesting BIC connections to men who fought in the war. One obituary described the "faithful" military and church service of one veteran; another detailed the solemnity of soldiers participating in a funeral presided over by BIC church elders.[15] Even if these veterans were only peripherally connected to the BIC community, in death they were included in community news, and they drew nonresistant Brethren in Christ into the great events of the day. The larger BIC community of kin, church attenders, members from other churches, and children who had left or not yet joined the church always surrounded and influenced the tiny core of official BIC members. The people who looked on at baptisms were important, but so were the ones who attended funerals.

The impact of war increased with World War I, which internationalized what the American Civil War had instituted nationally—the mobilization of entire societies to prosecute total war. From August 1914 to April 1917, the Brethren in Christ in the United States analyzed war and peace without the threat of imminent conscription or restriction of civil liberties. But this changed when America entered the war in 1917. For the Brethren in Christ, the war brought anti-German sentiment, constriction of civil liberties, and harassment growing out of aggressive campaigns to elicit voluntary participation. In April 1917, the United States established the Committee on Public Information, a propaganda agency. Congress passed a series of laws restricting the rights of the foreign born and those opposing the war, including the Espionage Act in June 1917 and the Sedition Act in August 1918. Canada passed in September 1917 the Wartime Elections Act, which disenfranchised conscientious objectors and people who spoke German. Both countries encouraged home-front mobilization with campaigns to sell war bonds. Laws, campaigns, and their emotional presentation magnified a general atmosphere of wartime fervor.[16] This fervor exacted a price from dissenting minorities, but it also pushed nonresistant groups to find peaceful ways to contribute to the larger world, even as they attempted to maintain their centuries-old stance of dissent.

In notes for a sermon probably preached sometime during the war, Eli Engle seems to have built on General Conference's 1917 statement on "nonresistant principles."[17] He articulated the cardinal tenets of nonresistance. Drawing on the Beatitudes, Engle defined nonresistance as the imperative to abjure all force in response to power. Individuals should "meet abuse with blessing, persecution with endurance, slander with gentle words." Nonresistance required children to respect fathers and mothers and, in its most passive aspect, wives to submit to husbands. Members of the BIC church must practice the virtues of forgiveness, humility, endurance, and most importantly, "maintain the unity of the spirit." Nonresistance must also be applied in business by honest practice, by reimbursing an opponent above the legal requirement, and above all by never seeking redress in court. Finally, Engle argued that biblical injunctions implied a duty to disobey authorities who violated their own divine callings by, to give the chief example, conscripting men for military service. Engle in conclusion argued that both the means and ends of militarism were flawed, because they relied on "brute force, and the flower of manhood is wasted on battlefields, in prison pens and camps; [and they] also [cultivate] the spirit of savagery."[18]

In the *Visitor* throughout the war, similar classical statements of nonresistance mixed with premillennial voices. These latter understandings often viewed World War I as an event fulfilling biblical predictions of the end of the world. Some writers even welcomed militarism as preparation for the final battle between God and Satan at Armageddon.[19]

Another explanation pointed to war as judgment, part of a preordained divine plan to avenge national sins. The catalog of national sins thus avenged by God in war drew upon fundamentalist and anti-imperialist sentiments. In this evaluation, no nation was exempt. The United States had been punished for slavery by the Civil War; now, although not yet involved in the Great War in 1915, America now tempted God with its murder rate and materialism. Germany too had yielded to materialism and, even more importantly, had to answer for scholarly criticism of biblical texts. The war exacted punishment also on Britain, Belgium, Russia, and Turkey, who had oppressed people at home and abroad.[20]

A. C. Rosenberger of Souderton, Pennsylvania, provided one of the occasional *Visitor* articles that connected social and economic analysis to active nonresistance. Armageddon, he argued, would combine economic greed with class and race oppression. He held political elites responsible for wars in the twentieth century, because these elites forced common people to work for them in times of peace and die for them in times of war. Many factors contributed to the outbreak of war: autocracy, militarism, national claims of divine sanction for military success, and especially the heavy taxation that had powered arms buildups. Finally, he turned to the lack of equality as a root cause of war. "It is only when we realize that our brother and sister have equal rights and we respect those rights that we are in divine order. We are placed in this world as free moral agents and we must select our own destiny. We can go on abusing the rights of others and make ourselves masters of men and positions but the day will come when we will be called into judgement." Although he despaired of world peace and reminded nonresistant people to avoid all participation in violence, he also insisted in "the believer's duty to take a firm stand against those who produce wars; and with all our reasoning powers to persuade men not to take up weapons."[21]

Rosenberger's analysis, although not typical, resembled those of a number of other articles. John Garman, of Harrisburg, Pennsylvania, undoubtedly addressed calls for military preparedness when he criticized the idea that military buildup preserved peace. He also called for action. "Christian citizens" should communicate to their representatives that they would not pay taxes for "something that is so dangerous to Christian principles as a large army." Detweiler repeatedly intertwined news on European peace activism or imprisonment of conscientious objectors with accusations that war hurt revival meetings and led to vice. He quoted from a long article on the peace work of a Baptist minister in Sweden; the article argued for a "radical peace movement," using the "toughest of weapons—a passive resistance." Common people willing to die for peace must take the lead against militarists, replacing ineffective diplomats, congresses, and resolutions, answering "the stabbing, armor plated, barb wire piety of our day." Militarists, the article contended, cunningly linked peace efforts to antireligious socialism. In contrast, the Swedish pastor held up Finnish passive resistance as both effective and an example of Christian morality, a morality that prohibited killing even in national self-defense.[22]

However diverse the analysts who addressed war and nonresistance in the *Visitor,* they were similar in one respect—almost all were men.[23] In the early decades of the twentieth century, the magazine provided an important medium in which women could "preach and prophecy" publicly, but few female writers addressed nonresistance directly.[24] At the time, nonresistance narrowly defined—police work, jury duty, military service, voting—fell mainly in areas that men dominated. Increasingly, however, the BIC community, and a number of women in particular, pushed to broaden that definition to include the production of food and clothing and the care of the sick, orphaned, and elderly. Yet many women continued to view nonresistance as a man's issue.

These women tended to focus on nonconformist dress more than on nonresistance. Plain fashions were part of the BIC community's nonconformist self-definition. Legislation on nonconformist dress, like that on nonresistance, tended to focus on prohibitions against fashionable attire and therefore to separate the group from the larger society.[25] Women's writings on the subject, however, are much more complex, describing "plain" appearance as an important visible symbol of group identity or, for converts, a new identity. In either case, women sometimes claimed plain dress, particularly women's head coverings, as a symbol of deepened spirituality, a means to gain spiritual equality with men, or an expression of simplicity that freed resources to be shared with others. An analysis of the variety of meanings women assigned to plain dress would require a study in itself.[26]

Two examples, however, show that women also perceived nonconformist dress to be central to their public roles in the community. In 1916, Rozella Boyer, who would turn fifteen in that year, wrote a letter to the *Visitor* about her struggle with nonconformist dress in a Dayton, Ohio, high school. Initially, she had refused to wear a head covering. But "then the glory came," after which she was willing to wear one in the school, where she estimated more than a thousand people a day would see her. Sometime in the next two years, Boyer quit high school over war-related pressure to salute the flag, something she thought inconsistent with her nonresistant beliefs. Apparently Boyer never felt moved to write to the *Visitor* about this decision, as she had of her struggle over wearing the head covering. Instead, it became a story passed down through the intergenerational family.[27]

In another example, Mrs. Girvin Sider connected dress, rather than nonresistance, to increased social concern. Writing from Wellandport, Ontario, in 1914, Sider complained of unnecessary consumption, including unhealthful corsets and "many changes of dress which belong to the world." Without such consumption, there would be much more money for the poor, "who have not the comforts of life," and for spreading the Christian gospel. Sider predicted a day of judgment in which "heathen, and widows, and homeless children, will rise up and condemn us for the way we have spent God's money."[28]

Another reason women skirted nonresistant topics may be that in the home, where their roles usually placed them, nonresistance seemed difficult to apply, even for church leaders. When Guy F. Hershberger, a Mennonite apologist for nonresistance, defined the limit of acceptable use of force between spanking a child and joining the police force, he may well have placed the boundary in the home.[29] Neither women nor men wrote much concerning this nebulous area during World War I. One anonymous writer in the *Visitor* asked, "Where will we draw the line?" How could people claim spiritual holiness, which would include nonresistance, when husbands and wives exhibited jealousy or spoke bitterly to each other? Might hired help observe those same people beating animals in anger?[30] Another letter referred to a religious cleansing of "the war nature" in individuals.[31] Yet a third writer compared the current war spirit to Christian people involved in spiritual "warfare" against sin. Both secular and religious battles had tendencies to make individuals "hard and critical" or "stern and impatient," rather than compassionate.[32] A prescriptive list for boys admonished, "Never call anybody bad names, no matter what anybody calls you," and "never be cruel."[33] None of these general statements explicitly connected nonresistance to the home, but they suggest concern about violence and aggression in daily life.[34]

Particularly in local BIC church districts, the cardinal virtues of nonresistant neighborliness often eluded the Brethren in Christ. The ideal was "the weary pilgrim[,] . . . greeted of the saints with a lovely hand shake of peace, and . . . with a kiss of charity."[35] But not uncommon were comments such as a plea from the General Executive Board to districts to settle their own conflicts, in order to save the committee time and money.[36] One article, entitled "Undue Officiousness," provides a graphic list of the nature of group conflict: publicly opposing official group decisions, "electioneering on behalf of a friend, or relative," trying to depose committee members set in place by General Conference, and providing visiting evangelists with list of "unreliable" church members.[37] Two other articles described BIC community members as easily offended and refusing to speak to each other, given to holding grudges and backstabbing, and revengeful, stingy, and concerned only with personal interests.[38] In retrospective private interviews, individuals sometimes provided even more concrete details of group conflict: BIC leaders often perpetuated conflict with their interventions, favored family and friends, and proved vindictive when crossed even on small matters.[39]

Some of the sense of conflict in the BIC community might have come from the idea, articulated in the official 1917 statement on nonresistance, that nonresistance was supposed to mean unity within the church. Many writers made that point during World War I. Two accounts equated peace with unity in the church and lack of unity with murder.[40] In an article peppered with scriptural reference to peace, Lillian C. Baker argued that "to follow after the things which make for peace, forecasts unity."[41] Another woman pointed to one of the sticking points in such an expectation—"There is much difference in the teaching of some doctrines and this has a tendency to cause grievances of a serious nature." She added that visiting preachers should avoid "dividing the members where there once was peace."[42]

Regardless of the community's small size and relative homogeneity, social differences and the accommodation of minorities remained troublesome issues in BIC corporate life.[43] Describing the 1914 General Conference, Detweiler seemed relieved at the smoothness of proceedings. Discussions had been "amicable . . . and when decisions were made there was acquiescence, or, possibly better, submission, on the part of the minority, as it is always to be remembered that the minority is not necessarily in the wrong, and what is defeated today may be accepted tomorrow."[44] As editor of the BIC magazine, which accommodated diverse and sometimes contradictory voices and criticisms, Detweiler was in a prime position to feel the tensions.[45] Different nonresistant stances, including a variety of positions on conscientious objection to military service, were apparent but not openly discussed in the *Visitor*.[46]

During World War I, Detweiler noted with regret that denominational lines had divided "plain" people.[47] Those divisions might have seemed particularly troubling as the tiny BIC community faced the daily pressures on the home front and in military camps of nations at war. In the first *Visitor* published after the United States entered the war, Detweiler wrote pointedly about the imperatives of nonresistance. He noted the imprisonment of British conscientious objectors, who had demonstrated "that it takes more courage to keep out of the bloody business than it requires to go into it. We'll soon find that out over here."[48] In the next year and a half, the Brethren in Christ did find this out, as they confronted conscription laws, government muzzles on dissent, vigilante patriots, and the ambiguities of wartime economics.

Just as reflections on war and peace in the *Visitor* demonstrate that nonresistance meant different things to different people, so the choices and actions of BIC community members defy simple explanations. Events, beliefs, and the institutional setup of the church all conspired to make everyday life difficult for nonresistant people.

The diaries of four BIC community members in the World War I years reflect daily rhythms determined mostly by the seasons, by school and work, by social life in the BIC community and in the neighborhood, and occasionally by spiritual experiences.[49] At the edges, however, events of the larger world affected the Brethren in Christ much as they did other Americans. Writers in the *Visitor* noted, often tangentially, the impact of the war. Authors recorded feverish industrial production, coal shortages, the presence of military personnel on trains, and war-related delays for missionaries hoping to travel overseas.[50] Above all, the influenza epidemic, associated with the war in many minds, touched the BIC community, sweeping away loved ones.[51]

War mobilization not only took place before the eyes of the Brethren in Christ but entered the language and thinking of the community's members. The editor wondered, for instance, whether community members who failed to renew their *Visitor* subscriptions were "slackers," a term often used for draft evaders. Military discipline apparently appealed to many writers, who noted parallels between life in the military and life in the BIC community—both required high levels of commitment, established corporate goals that overrode individual wishes, and imposed disciplinary measures for unruly members.[52]

Other home-front experiences, however, grew directly from the community's German ethnicity, from its nonresistant position, or from a combination of the two. In April 1916, S. R. Smith, secretary of the General Executive Board, began issuing warnings about the annual General Conference to be held that June in Ontario. Trouble might arise at the Canadian border because of German surnames, accents, or descent.[53] Even more serious trouble might arise from undercover officials, who might hear "indiscreet" statements about the war or about the British during conference discussions. Elder Fred Elliot called on BIC community members from the United States to be aware of public tensions in Canada, as growing numbers of Canadian soldiers were wounded or killed in combat. He cautioned against "thinking audibly" about the war. If it was necessary to comment on the war in a prophetic sermon, such general terms as "world crises" should be used.[54] After a flurry of negotiations with Canadian officials, an announcement that General Conference had been moved to Lancaster County, Pennsylvania, appeared in the magazine with no explanation.[55] Other contemporary sources suggest the difficulty of practicing nonresistance when societies mobilize for total war. In April 1917 Detweiler obliquely recognized the problem by mixing his own musings with a reprint from the Mennonite Church *Gospel Herald*. The ideal nonresistant person must live a "consistent life," which he defined as willingness to take financial loss or to emigrate to maintain the peace position.[56] In fact, financial gain proved to be the real challenge to consistent practice.

Enos H. Hess, a faculty member and administrator at Messiah Bible College, a BIC school in Pennsylvania, suggested in the *Visitor* that people whose citizenship was heavenly, not national, should not benefit from high wartime prices for farm products. Although a few other people also addressed the issue, Hess's analysis raised important questions about total war mobilization, questions that pacifism would need to face throughout the twentieth century.[57] While acknowledging that the war had also brought higher costs for farm supplies, he argued that profit beyond those costs was "blood money" and should be given for "Christian advancement." His practical suggestions pinpointed daily patterns and the nature of social life: buy fewer clothes, avoid substantial business expansion, forgo the purchase of an automobile, do not replace a Ford with a Cadillac. Hess even argued, "There are few people that set better tables of greater variety then we. A little less variety and pie and cake would not be amiss"—a challenge to people who often expressed hospitality in terms of food. Hess reported that twenty people at that year's General Conference had pledged to give agricultural profits to the church.[58]

A year later, a letter to the General Executive Board from J. N. Hoover, bishop in the Miami district of Ohio, echoed and broadened Hess's concerns. Hoover expressed disappointment that the 1918 General Conference had not addressed the broad impact of war on the lives of nonresistant people. Hoover insisted that "we as a people" must address "at least some of the conditions as they really are." He understood that total mobilization touched many areas of life. He was concerned that investments, agricultural profits, and even relief work in war zones might actually contribute to the war effort. Militarism, he argued, pervaded a variety of organizations. At the same time, he called on "Christians to relieve suffering whenever possible, regardless of what has caused the suffering."[59] General Conference in 1919 called for relief aid but did not address Hoover's description of pervasive militarism;[60] attention to the structural ramifications of war and militarism was not sustained. These issues, however, would arise again in the next war; in World War II, for example, opinions would differ on whether BIC men should accept draft deferments for "essential service" on farms.

Other aspects of mobilization on the home front were easier to address than the farm economy or general militarism. Saluting the flag and buying war bonds represented straightforward symbols for the nonresistant BIC community. Refusing to participate in these activities sometimes elicited hostile responses from neighbors and exacted a price for individuals. Detweiler noted, "Some of our brethren have had tests along the line of flag reverence," particularly at workplaces. But apparently, even here members made different choices. In the same article, he chided other members for wearing replicas of flags as pins and for displaying them on cars.[61]

Memories of the war years corroborate both responses. As mentioned earlier, Rozella Boyer dropped out of high school to avoid saluting the flag. Her older brother Clarence, who worked in an envelope factory, also refused to salute the flag. An otherwise friendly boss felt compelled to fire him, because coworkers suspected him of being a German sympathizer.[62] On the other hand, Elizabeth Engle Heise, an elementary student in Lancaster, Pennsylvania, remembers the war as the period when she began saluting the flag in school, arm outstretched. A Saskatchewan child in the war years remembered being part of patriotic expressions and later honoring those who had died in the war. In 1918, Kenneth B. Hoover, a first grader in Kansas, recited the rhyme, "Kaiser Bill went up the hill/To take a shot at France/Kaiser Bill came down the hill/ With a bullet in his pants."[63]

One writer in the *Visitor* described people who bought war bonds as bloodying their hands with a "sword fund." Numerous Brethren in Christ refused to buy war bonds; others refused to contribute to government-related relief agencies.[64] Refusing to buy bonds forced Ohmer Herr to leave a much-loved job teaching woodworking.[65]

I. J. Ransom, son of a British army captain, voiced objections to war bonds from his vantage point on the edge of the BIC community. He had once been involved in attempts to start a BIC mission in Toronto. By 1917 he was a Baptist minister, but he stayed in contact with the BIC community. He compared being among "'plain' Christian people" to entering an oasis where he could talk to church school students about the peace expressed in the Beatitudes. This oasis took one out of the "clatter of war" into "sweet enjoyments with saints of former days," where no one sold Liberty Bonds but instead gave money to spread the "Gospel of peace." The Brethren in Christ, he contended, had no love for German militarism, nor did they countenance that nation's atrocities, but they had a better response than war.[66]

Nonresistant people sometimes contributed to war relief because aroused neighbors had questioned their patriotism. But most appeals to relieve suffering in war areas did not explicitly mention such pressures. In fact, BIC interest in war relief had arisen well before the United States entered the war. Many Americans worried about the Christian Armenian people deported from the Turkish-Russian war zone. But the Brethren in Christ had a personal connection in Meshack P. Krikorian, an Armenian who had graduated from the Bible department of the Messiah Bible College in 1915. Krikorian's relief efforts in 1916 aroused the Brethren in Christ and resulted in an unofficial day of prayer for the Armenians and a fund for donations. By 1922, Krikorian had been ordained as an elder in the BIC church and was listed as doing relief work for his homeland.[67]

The General Executive Board began organizing an official war relief effort in the second half of 1918.[68] But as with Armenia, individuals had already begun responding to war-ravaged Europe. In the summer of 1917, T. A. and Mary J. Long wrote to the *Visitor* about "Brother" Long's appeal for money for the starving widows and children in Belgium. Instead of giving a Sunday morning sermon, Long had read aloud a letter about the suffering and had contributed one dollar. The result was a fund of six dollars.[69]

In 1918, the General Executive Board sought to establish its own fund, by issuing a pamphlet entitled *An Organized Effort For the Relief of Sufferers in the*

War Stricken Countries. The pamphlet offered two rationales for participating in relief efforts. First, the Brethren in Christ had always carefully avoided contributions to the war effort but had "repeatedly proven their willingness to give liberally to alleviate suffering wherever they can conscientiously do so, without fear of violating the spirit of the Gospel, and the tenets of the Church." Second, the BIC community included not only conscientious objectors in military camps but also "friends in trenches" in France. Relief contributions expressed Christian sympathy for those beyond one's own family but also provided an alternative for people not able to tend a loved one's grave. These rationales clearly connected the BIC community to people on active military service.

Subsequently, the focus of the pamphlet returned to a nonresistant theme—giving to this relief appeal was superior to buying war bonds, because there was no thought of return. Recognizing that "new conditions bring new responsibilities," the authors scolded the BIC community for being slow and indifferent to a "shattered world." In conclusion, the board urged the BIC community to give to relief without cutting back on giving to the "Foreign or Home Mission work or any other church institution"—a theme that would be reiterated during World War II.[70]

At about the same time that the pamphlet was published, the General Executive Board endorsed the Quaker's American Friends Service Committee. Its relief programs provided a channel for "non-resistants or Conscientious Objectors." Mennonites had already contributed forty-six thousand dollars. Detweiler published excerpts from a news bulletin received from American Friends Service Committee on relief work in France. The account echoed themes important to BIC sensibilities. Relief work was social but also very personal; relief workers fixed houses but also, and more importantly, mended hearts. "Neighborliness, friendship, kindness, sympathy," the bulletin argued, "these are made of stuff which no chemistry of war can crush." Furthermore, the Quakers' work had the commendation of the Red Cross and of President Woodrow Wilson. Vernon L. Stump, who succeeded Detweiler as editor, ran American Friends Service Committee bulletins throughout 1919.[71]

The BIC pamphlet on relief efforts elicited a 1918 letter to the *Visitor* from Mary Zook of Missouri. She urged BIC women to take the lead in producing bedding and clothing for relief, as they had earlier produced two hundred quilts for famine victims in India. After having received the church pamphlet, Zook had meditated, particularly on its photographs, and had come up with a plan for the sisters of the church to make comforters, perhaps not "beautiful but warm and substantial." Then she found a coat set aside before its usefulness had ended. She washed and ironed it, making it presentable. "Sisters," she wrote, "let us hunt out the corners, or if you want to get new material all the better, but let us go to work." As she saw it, BIC districts should collect the goods and send them to a central point. "From there, as the brethren would arrange, I am sure the railroads would ship such goods free if it would be labeled, 'For the suffering refugees.'" Districts should report production figures in the *Visitor*. Zook guessed that people "outside the Brotherhood" would want to partici-pate if informed of the program.[72]

Two months later Zook wrote again, asking for information on how many comforters had been produced. She herself had three ready to ship and had written personal letters to "stir up" other sisters. She added, "Someone must take hold of this work and try to get others interested in this matter. I am intensely interested." The thought of people without homes as winter ap-proached touched her "sympathies to the very depths," and she hoped such thoughts would do the same for others, previously uninterested. She had re-ceived mail from "a brother in Pennsylvania (a stranger to me)," also interested in relief, who planned to travel to France as a relief worker. He had encouraged Zook's work and suggested the American Friends Service Committee head-quarters in Philadelphia as a collection point for relief goods. Still pressing others to join the work, she gave the address and urged that each package be marked from "the Brethren in Christ Church," with a request that the head-quarters notify the "Board" and instruct it to notify the *Visitor*.[73]

Zook's plan never again appeared in the pages of the *Visitor*, perhaps be-cause the General Executive Board began organizing official women's sewing circles. In the instructions to these sewing circles, the board's secretary, H. K. Kreider, described the motivation for producing goods as an act of compas-sion but also as proof of BIC "loyalty to the [governmental] authorities." This rationale directly linked women's work to the simultaneous attempts to prac-tice nonresistance and to appease a society mobilized for war.[74] During World War II, a group of men and women from the Pennsylvania's Rapho district would argue unsuccessfully for official BIC recognition of women's sewing for relief as an equal and positive corollary to the peace witness of conscientious objectors. Periodically, someone would note the centrality of women's contri-butions in the BIC community. But the necessity of enlisting women to help maintain this tenet of the BIC church never received sustained attention.

Soon after the United States entered the war, Detweiler advised that "our words be few and the few well considered" to avoid the appearance of disloy-alty. Nevertheless, throughout the war individuals from the BIC community continued to articulate their understandings of nonresistance.[75] In September 1918, Seth Adams wrote to the *Visitor* from Michigan: "Some of my shopmates ask me whether I am praying that this country would win in the war, this dreadful war of hatred and strife and murder among mankind. I told them that I pray that men will beat their swords into plowshares and their spears into pruning hooks." Adams had joined the Brethren in Christ five years earlier. He acknowledged that he had difficulties in his new life but felt a sense of divine guidance in his "walk." His walk clearly included nonresistance. He empathized with "the brethren" consigned to military camps, guessing that they might be asked questions similar to those his shopmates asked him. The answers, he asserted, required knowledge of the scriptures.[76]

Adams's BIC community in southeastern Michigan was a small one, distant from other concentrations of Brethren in Christ. It included converts, such as Adams, from nonagricultural occupations.[77] Yet throughout World War I and into the early Cold War years, important demonstrations of nonresistant belief would arise from this tiny BIC group. Some of these actions are among the clearest examples of staunch nonresistant practice, though not the best known.

Nonresistance in the Military Camps

For young BIC men conscripted under 1917 and 1918 legislation, conscientious objection dramatically raised issues about the nature of nonresistance. It also raised questions about whether a dissenting way of life could be explained to the larger society. For these young men, nonresistance required individual decisions and actions, some of which would influence corporate church life and shape BIC thinking in the next war.[78]

Despite the variety of positions among the Brethren in Christ, two basic understandings of conscientious objection emerged in World War I and persisted into the next war. One group of BIC men refused to wear uniforms and often refused to work under military supervision. One of these men, Harry L. Brubaker, justified this position shortly after his discharge, using the life of Jesus as his model. Brubaker argued that he could not take part in any way in an "organization, whose ultimate end was to defeat the enemy." That included work in military hospitals, which simply expedited the return of men to battlefields.[79]

The second group of BIC men chose to accept noncombatant service. Many worked in military hospitals, believing that killing was forbidden but relieving suffering, even within military structures, was not. Distinctions between these two approaches, however, sometimes blurred. A man might refuse to wear a uniform but agree to work in the medical corps, for example. Military coercion sometimes determined choices; some individuals were forcibly dressed in uniform.[80]

By focusing on the daily lives of BIC people and on their relationship to the larger society, it is possible to identify additional questions about the experiences of conscientious objectors. For example, how did their individual experiences interact with the corporate life experiences of the BIC community at home? General Conference passed resolutions, the General Executive Board issued statements, and the *Visitor*'s editor ran articles advocating conscientious objection and even condemning noncombatant military service. But obituaries, passing comments in articles, and retrospective accounts make clear that the BIC community was intimately connected to many men who chose to do combatant military service.[81] Apparently, BIC conscientious objectors rarely made decisions based on clear directives from the BIC community. Subsequently, the community would need to devise structures to encourage compliance with BIC standards while also allowing erring members to be reincorporated.

Family connections undoubtedly muted nonresistant expression. Among obituaries of men who died in military service, only one expressed disapproval of the military connection. Others often carefully noted a religious conversion experience. Some of the casualties were listed as official members of the BIC church; others had been less formally connected to the church. An editorial announcement and later obituary noted the death of Samuel Andrew Zook in the Argonne Woods, France. Samuel, the son of a BIC elder, had written to his mother, "It looks as though I shall be called upon to do what I had hoped I would never need to do but I go willingly because I feel it is my duty. If I must die, I want you to know I am ready, and, not because I am a good soldier." Probably Zook had left the Brethren in Christ; a Methodist Episcopal minister officiated at his memorial service. But the editorial attention given him suggests a close connection with the BIC community.[82]

Conscripted conscientious objectors undoubtedly recognized that their positions contrasted with those of their BIC contemporaries who had been deferred or willingly served. That dissonance might help to explain one retrospective evaluation of war experiences faulting the BIC church for inadequately teaching nonresistance to its young men and then neglecting them in the military. Ten BIC conscientious objectors surveyed by Ray Bert in 1970 remember written literature on nonresistance, which some of them had read before the war. But almost none remember teaching or counseling on the tenet.[83] Clarence Byer and Edgar Heise, who were conscientious objectors, and Paul Engle, who had enlisted, made similar points.[84] Byer's son remembered his father's story that papers written by his bishop in support of Byer's conscientious objection status had been stolen while he was at Fort Riley, Kansas. Byer wrote to the bishop requesting replacements but never received them.[85]

Although their efforts were slow and disjointed, BIC leaders across the country did take steps to support conscientious objectors during the war. But they had not anticipated the actual provisions of the new conscription laws. In 1917, the joint council in Ontario appointed two men to meet with Canadian government officials. A third man, D. W. Heise, spoke on behalf of many Canadian conscientious objectors at military disciplinary proceedings.[86] Just across the border, D. V. Heise wrote to the Pennsylvania BIC leadership asking about its experience with "exemptions." What appeals were available? A "young Brother," probably a tenant farmer on Heise's land, was "very anxious" about appearing before an "examining board," so Heise hoped for a quick response.[87]

BIC leaders in other parts of the country also were facing conscription questions. Leaders from California, Pennsylvania, Kansas, and Indiana corresponded in June and July 1917 about how they could quickly produce membership certificates for draft-age men, as authorized by the May 1917 General Conference. They also discussed how to care for the newly converted who were not yet members. California BIC bishop C. C. Burkholder took steps on his own to print the first membership certificates for conscientious objectors.[88] In November and December, the General Executive Board recorded steps being taken in Pennsylvania to visit and in other ways support BIC men at Camp George G. Meade, Maryland. The board wrote a notice encouraging other districts to do the same. The board consulted Frances Brubaker, who had corresponded with her son Harry in camp.[89] BIC leaders visited Camp Meade periodically, perhaps as early as October 1917, but little documentation exists of official church visits to other camps.[90] Only BIC men who were in camps near southeastern Pennsylvania or in Ontario later recalled visits from church leaders.[91]

At the April 4, 1918, Pennsylvania State Council gathering, Donegal district petitioned the council to do more for the young men. The petition focused on the dangers to conscientious objectors, isolated "from the home congregational teaching and spiritual instruction" and that isolation might "draw them away from their stability in Christ and the faith and doctrine of the church." The petition also mentioned President Wilson's recent order on conscientious objectors. The order had offered only the objectionable noncombatant military service, but the petition made no comment on this.[92] (By this time, the Brethren in Christ were probably becoming more careful in public statements, particularly in print.) The gathering set up a committee to oversee official visits and to send BIC literature.[93]

Despite these attempts to respond, little went smoothly. Exactly a year after a BIC membership certificate had been drafted, the General Conference secretary, C. N. Hostetter Sr. noted in a letter that some BIC leaders were still unclear about how to use certificates or were even unaware of their existence. Perhaps his letter was connected to a complaint from Paul B. Baum of Aurora, Illinois, about a lack of action by the BIC community in support of its conscripted young men. The only step Baum had heard of was the membership certificate, and he had not received one. He had been in contact with "other non-resistent members and I find they are doing all within their behalf to keep their young men from entering this war."[94]

Despite tenuous communication with other members of the BIC community, conscientious objectors in the camps welcomed contacts with the church and longed for their home communities.[95] Their own correspondence sometimes expressed a longing for the warmth of BIC religious expression.[96] Harry Fishburn, in a Virginia camp, wrote to Ethan Kreider, "I grow homesick to hear the true Word preached." Both "a flood of glory" and "a longing" came when Fishburn read Kreider's account of a revival service.[97] At the same time, BIC conscientious objectors had many contacts with people beyond their small community. The nature of those contacts suggests how the Brethren in Christ understood their relationship with the larger society.

The inability of nonpacifists to understand the nonresistant position is a key theme of several accounts. Many of the men faced coercion and threats and had heard of much worse. Ernest J. Swalm and Earl M. Sider, both inductees from Ontario, recalled sensing that their farewells to their families might be final ones.[98] Edgar Heise remembered that when he registered in Kansas, the person who interviewed him repeatedly kicked his shins under the table.[99] In a contemporary account, Samuel Wenger described the initial response of camp officials to his conscientious objection as "bitter rebuke and hard-heartedness." He described enduring pressure to put on a military uniform and to accept work. But with divine aid he had refused, "in the p[r]esence of my commanding officers and in the face of punishment." Throughout his time in camp, he heard stories about the mistreatment of other conscientious objectors.[100] Wenger's older brother Rolla Leroy was court-martialed and sentenced to fifteen years in prison. He served nine months of the sentence at Fort Leavenworth, Kansas.[101] John Henry Heise and Charles Wright, of Ontario, were sentenced to hard labor at a prison farm in the northern part of the province. After a number of weeks, they were released through the efforts of BIC leaders.[102]

Other accounts describe military leaders who eventually came to respect conscientious objectors.[103] Swalm's account of his court-martial and brief imprisonment in Ontario serves as the best-known example of triumphant resistance, but there are others. Harry L. Brubaker remembered that a guard, in the process of moving a group of conscientious objectors out of a building for exercise, politely waited for Brubaker to finish praying on his knees. Brubaker described two of the guards as "good friends" of his. One guard apparently grew attached to the conscientious objectors, devising justifications for joining the group at meals.[104] Harvey and Naomi Lady described an unnamed conscientious objector who had initially been treated with contempt but later with respect.[105]

One genre of stories describes scoffers who were silenced when conscientious objectors quoted biblical passages. Such stories suggest the ongoing authority of the Bible, both for those at war and for those resisting the war. In other stories, the silence may have had more to do with amazement than with anything else. When O. B. Ulery refused to buy war bonds, the campaigner asked him how he would respond if the kaiser's army came marching down the street. Ulery replied with his own question: "And what do you think that German regiment would do if I jumped up and shouted 'Glory, Hallelujah' at them?"[106] When Walter Taylor defended his conscientious-objector stand, someone argued that all citizens must serve militarily. Taylor responded, "If you were going to blot out sin with cannon and sword, where would you begin?"[107]

Despite the hostility of their fellow citizens, nonresistant people conceived of themselves as expressing the highest form of patriotism. Throughout the war years the BIC community took part in national expressions of unity, publicizing Thanksgiving proclamations and calling for participation in a day of prayer. Woodrow Wilson's moralism appealed to the Brethren in Christ, as did his initial calls for neutrality. Even after the United States entered the war, Detweiler expressed gratitude for American liberties and supported a qualified obedience to government.[108]

As noted earlier, one of the key ways in which the BIC community demonstrated concern for the larger society was through relief work. Contributions for relief of "war sufferers" were channeled through the Non-Resistant Relief Organization in Canada and American Friends Service Committee and the American Relief Board in the United States. BIC conscientious objector C. Benton Eavey asked his draft board for a furlough from Camp Lee, Virginia, to do relief work in Europe. Eavey, a faculty member at Messiah Bible College, had apparently decided to make the request after consulting with BIC leaders.[109] The draft board granted his request. V. L. Stump published in the *Visitor* a report about the work of the Friend's Reconstruction Unit in France: "Most of you know that we have a representative on the field in the person of our dear and worthy brother, C. Benton Eavey."[110] (He undoubtedly was also the unnamed man who corresponded with Mary Zook, encouraging her interest in production of relief goods.)[111] From late 1918 through mid-1920, Eavey worked in France. In a factory, he produced house parts to send into areas where homes had been destroyed by the war. Later, he distributed chickens and rabbits to families in twenty-four villages. In reports written for the *Visitor*, Eavey connected his work with the BIC community's contributions. He expressed the hope that some in the church would be interested and support him with prayers, despite the fact that he was not serving under the auspices of the Brethren in Christ.[112]

Eavey's work, which he described on a 1946 questionnaire as "love in ac-

Mabel Wengert Eavey and C. Benton Eavey. C. Benton Eavey, a BIC conscientious objector in World War I, was furloughed from Camp Lee, Virginia, to do relief work with the Friend's Reconstruction Unit in France. *(Courtesy of the Brethren in Christ Historical Library and Archives)*

tion," prefigured what many other BIC young people would do during and after World War II. To the next generation, his experiences and evaluations would suggest new formulations of the BIC peace witness. His work enlarged BIC social concern beyond proselytizing. As Eavey described it, religious work could not be done "except that our material activities are an expression of practical applied Christianity." It thus served as an expression of religious faith.

Eavey found his initial work boring and longed to get to the real war zone. When he did, he described the destruction graphically, asking his readers to imagine fleeing from their homes and returning to rubble, the animals and machinery gone.[113] In a much less polemical piece after he completed his relief service, Eavey described French social mores affectionately. He was obviously charmed by "their extreme politeness" across class lines; their slow daily pace, amenable to conversation; and their affectionate families, dominated by strong women who were not suffragists but often managed family businesses.[114] Sometimes Eavey seemed to think that he should be sharing the gospel, as the BIC community would expect of him. At other times he thought the work of meeting human needs apart from emphasis on the spiritual was a worthy cause.

Perhaps he had received few letters from home, because in his last letter of 1919 Eavey wrote of uncertainty that others were interested. In fact, he had questions about the work himself, although he assured readers that their donations were well administered by American Friends Service Committee. Donations for war relief in Europe did drop off soon after the war ended. The BIC community turned to the human needs of people on continents to the south and east, more promising areas for proselytizing than Roman Catholic France. Twenty years later, Eavey would describe his relief work as valuable, though by then he was teaching at evangelical, and decidedly unpacifistic, Wheaton College in Illinois.[115] How he put together his BIC nonconformity and nonresistance, his relief service under Quakers, and his draw to a leading evangelical institution would be instructive. He would not appear as a peace leader in the next war.

Many BIC young people in the next generation, though not necessarily aware of Eavey, would follow in his footsteps. They might have heard other stories of nonresistance, as this small dissenting community wrestled with its identity amidst a larger society at war. Swalm had told his story many times by the 1940s. During World War I, he had experienced conscription, court-martial, imprisonment, and finally release. He became a BIC minister, a bishop, and a popular evangelist who traveled widely in the community. As one woman remembered, "He was in all of the churches and knew everything about everybody."[116] The church press published his *Nonresistance under Test* in about 1938. In his retrospective accounts, he expressed affection for and confidence in his family and his church community. He recalled visiting his mother's grave and embracing his sobbing sister before leaving with his father for induction. Earlier his father had cried as he said, "Though it would be very hard for me to lose my only son, and it would mean a lot, I'd rather know that you honored your convictions if it cost you your life, and I must spend the rest of my days without you." At least three BIC leaders had aided him throughout his ordeal. D. W. Heise, who spoke at his court-martial, wrote to Swalm's father, "I am on the go almost night and day this week on behalf of our boys."[117]

Connections to people outside the BIC community provide another key component of Swalm's story; in later years, he described this aspect of his account as the part he "loved" to tell.[118] After his court-martial, he arrived at a prison in St. Catharines, Ontario, where the governor turned out to be the grandson of a "Tunker." The prison turnkey, Garley Clinch, was initially hostile to his eighteen conscientious-objector charges, but eventually he requested that they sing gospel songs for him. Clinch died in the influenza epidemic. His last words, "I am glad I ever met the conscientious objectors," suggest that despite their minority status, adherents to nonresistance had the power to draw others to them.[119]

The story of Melinda and Walter Taylor, of Lapeer County, Michigan, parallels some of Swalm's themes and adds others. In a 1939 issue of the *Visitor,* Melinda Taylor described the ill treatment of her husband during World War I. He had refused to buy war bonds and had taken a conscientious-objector position in response to conscription.[120] An angry mob knocked him unconscious, cut off his hair, and rubbed "ill-smelling stuff" on his head, leaving sores and scars. Melinda later described her fear when the crowd took her husband away in a car. Earlier, when a large rock crashed through a window, narrowly missing her son, she had wondered, "Would they kill the boy?" A member of the "Vigilent" Board tried to convince others in Lapeer County to refuse to sell to, buy from, or work on the Taylor farm. Threshers were intimidated or stayed away from the farm at harvest because they disagreed with the family's nonresistance. Melinda and Walter considered emigration, a long-standing Anabaptist tradition during persecution.[121]

Melinda found the experiences not only frightening but also humiliating. Sometimes they brought tension into her marriage. Walter had offered to give money to the Red Cross instead of buying bonds, but this compromise bothered Melinda. Perhaps, like other Brethren in Christ, Melinda was unsure where to draw the line. "I thought a moment. . . . I decided that if it was right for us to give to the Red Cross, the Board would accept our offer, and if it was not right for us to give in this way either, the Board would reject our offer." When the board did reject the offer, Melinda was saddened at first but then thankful, "for we had made a fair test, and the Lord was leading." She mentioned later that they did give to the "Relief fund, and we were glad to do it to help relieve the suffering." The singing of her children, worship with the hired girl (a "young sister"), and prayer cheered her in these hard times.[122]

The Taylors' story is not only about persecution. It includes examples of neighborliness and support from people other than the Brethren in Christ.

Mennonites and "the brethren at Mooretown" had talked of coming to help the Taylors with threshing, but the timing was wrong. Local men who worked for the Taylors warned them of attempts to organize a boycott. Another neighbor, who exchanged farmwork with the Taylors, came in secret to warn them of a crowd that hoped to waylay Walter when he returned from registering for the draft. Many of the neighbors "were quite indignant" about his mistreatment. In fact, Melinda thought it better that those neighbors found out about the crowd attack only after the fact, or there might have been a different kind of trouble. "However," she concluded, "it brought the people to thinking more seriously of life, also convictions to live better lives." She gave examples of individual transformation, so important in BIC thinking. One farmer described Walter as doing more than all the churches put together, because they had whole groups behind them, whereas Walter stood alone, "being isolated from our church people."[123]

Eventually, the Taylors held an auction and moved away; the connection to the war events is not clear. The Taylors' main antagonist, a prosperous farmer and stockholder in the Farmer's Elevator, also moved away. He moved, according to Melinda, because he could no longer get people to help him on his farm. Neighbors, in contrast, turned out in force at the Taylor auction and later held a farewell gathering for them. A "Catholic couple" attended; the man surprised the Taylors by rising to say, "When I heard what they done to Walter, I said he had more religion than I."[124] Melinda's nephew would choose combatant military service during World War II.[125]

The experiences of Brethren in Christ during Word War I show that nonresistance was an important community belief. Not all members, however, took a nonresistant position in response to war mobilization, and few addressed its application in daily life. Furthermore, many influences—conservative theologies, the larger pacifist movement, national loyalties, gender roles, community conflict, and local neighbors—shaped their understanding of nonresistance and led to elaborations that did not always reflect the BIC church's formal statements. Although primarily men elaborated on nonresistance in writing, various members of the BIC community practiced nonresistance as they attempted to avoid participation in the war mobilization and joined pacifist relief efforts. Many BIC individuals acted alone or felt isolated from the community during the war. But most understood their actions as part of a corporate position and often connected those actions to emotional expressions of evangelical beliefs. Neighbors and coworkers sometimes responded with hostility but at other times tolerated or even admired the BIC community's position. Nonresistant practice in the next war, then, grew not simply from ideas of separation but from the experiences of a community woven into American society.

CHAPTER TWO

Nonresistant Thought and Practice in

the 1940s and 1950s

⚬℘⚬

That the youth of our church may be established in
these great doctrines of the word.

For the Brethren in Christ, nonresistance was both a response to war and a guide for daily living.[1] As such, it had to be applicable in many different situations. The result was a wide variety of sometimes conflicting definitions. This variety arose, in part, as the BIC community responded to ideas, events, and trends in the larger society. Interactions with neighbors also influenced the definitions. Even internal community tensions only indirectly connected to nonresistance affected the belief. In addition, nonresistance continued to combine passive and active elements. It drew on nonconformist ideals of separation from society, on a variety of intellectual currents, and on contemporary attitudes that valued individualism and denigrated smallness. Nonresistance also reflected the BIC community's division of labor between men and women and its uncertainty about how to accommodate diversity within the group. Taken together, these elements intensified the complexity of nonresistance already evident in World War I.

When Germany invaded Poland in September 1939, Canada joined the war. The United States remained unencumbered but not uninvolved. As in World War I, Canada avoided as long as possible the inevitable conflicts of conscription. In the United States, President Franklin D. Roosevelt gingerly challenged his country's isolationist sentiments. The Wehrmacht's advances, however, had elicited new conscription systems in Canada and the United States by 1940, well before the Japanese attack on Pearl Harbor. The armed hostilities of World War II lasted for six years. The mobilization, death, and destruction of these years far outstripped those of the Great War.[2]

In response, the Historic Peace Churches mounted their own programs on behalf of peace. Their united efforts brought about creative new expressions of nonresistance, such as Civilian Public Service (cps) and relief work. But conflicts also arose over the meaning of nonresistance. These conflicts soon threatened the very identity and cohesion of the small bic community. Amidst the turmoil of a world at war, the Brethren in Christ struggled to formulate a definition of nonresistance that could encompass all the perplexities of their lives. In their intellectual formulations of nonresistance, they drew on those of the larger Mennonite community. In the new peace programs, the Brethren in Christ worked side by side with Mennonites. However, although they joined such organizations as Mennonite Central Committee (mcc), bic leaders worked to maintain a distinct identity.

Church Teaching on Nonresistance

Many Brethren in Christ who were young in World War II remember little bic church teaching on nonresistance in the 1920s and 1930s. One asks, did we fail to listen? They do remember, however, that nonresistance was "an overriding sense," that they assumed all bic members were nonresistant, and that a few key preachers promoted the doctrine. Above all, people associate nonresistance with E. J. ("Ernie") Swalm's story of his World War I experiences as a conscientious objector. Many Brethren in Christ had a copy of his book, *Nonresistance under Test,* in their homes.[3] Esther Tyson Boyer recalls being very impressed as an adolescent that the people who came to hear Swalm's story filled a large high school auditorium in Souderton, Pennsylvania.[4] Harold Heise asks, "How can we forget . . . the mighty eloquent way he defended the Peace position?[5]

The start of World War II and the passage of new national conscription laws in 1940 and 1941 brought, in Gerald N. Wingert's words, "a flurry of indoctrination." Others note that it was a time when the bic community joined with other peace churches in exciting peace conferences. But a number of people also remember the teaching on nonresistance for the sectarian aspects of its presentation and content. For example, some who question or no longer accept nonresistance remember it as being dictated or presented dogmatically.[6] Others, such as Robert D. Sider and Paul S. Boyer, both elementary school children in the 1940s, are no longer official members of the bic church but still value their nonresistant heritage. They describe nonresistance, however, as primarily a plank in the edifice of separatist nonconformity.[7]

Contemporary accounts in the 1940s also complained of inadequate teaching on nonresistance and lack of support for conscientious objectors. In 1940, V. L. Stump castigated in the *Visitor* the BIC community for "an utter lack of any organization or definite plans" in World War I and charged that Episcopalians, Methodists, and Congregationalists did more for conscientious objectors than did the Brethren in Christ.[8] BIC men in Civilian Public Service also indicted church teaching as they responded to a questionnaire that was published in 1945. Ninety-one percent of the sixty-six respondents answered "yes" to the question, "Do you think that the principle of nonresistance and its practical application to the world today, including its political, economic, and more moral implications, should be given greater emphasis in the church's educational program?" Some respondents argued that the Brethren in Christ in general and their church schools in particular did a worse job of teaching nonresistance than did other churches. Two called for teaching to be analytical, not dogmatic.[9] In 1945, BIC leaders in Ontario's Wainfleet district took the charges against leadership seriously and apologized to the district for the "failure in their administration" to adequately teach the church's stand against work in war industries.[10]

Such criticisms led to a new emphasis on nonresistance: more literature about it in BIC schools; participation in an intercollegiate peace organization; peace conferences in the United States and Canada; and, after demobilization, CPS conventions.[11] World events during the 1940s and 1950s also focused the attention of the BIC community on nonresistance. Like all North Americans, pacifist people lived through atypical events that remain today etched in their memories. These memories serve as important historical sources on nonresistance, particularly its daily practice and its lasting influence. The reflections, however, like many described by oral historian Studs Terkel, are more "a memory book . . . than one of hard fact and precise statistic." The memories are of "pain . . . [and] exhilaration[,] . . . a fusing of both . . . long-ago hurts and small triumphs[,] [h]onors and humiliations."[12] Much nonresistant thought as it existed at midcentury, however, has been forgotten, including the BIC community's own ongoing struggle to define adequately nonresistance.

NONRESISTANCE AND WAR

From the 1920s through the 1950s, official BIC statements on nonresistance emphasized and elaborated on many of the same ideas that equivalent statements had advanced in World War I. They show a deep affinity to statements by Mennonites. In fact, from the 1890s on, the Brethren in Christ drew on Mennonite publications.[13] A brief section in the church's 1924 constitution defined nonresistance as "abstain[ing] from the employment of carnal forces which involve the taking of human life," on the basis of the "tenets and principles of [Christ's] government," in sharp contrast to earthly governments. The latter were owed prayer, taxes, and obedience but not political participation. In 1939, a BIC statement on nonresistance insisted that in cases of conflict between earthly and heavenly commands, the response should be "passive resistance . . . even at the expense of . . . life." Individuals were never to retaliate; they were to "exercise a positive ministry of love," expressed in service, sacrifice, "fidelity, courtesy, tolerance, and sympathy." Within the BIC community, non-resistance translated into "unity, love, fellowship, peace and harmony." A 1961 article offered few details on nonresistance, asserting instead its wide scope as "both a doctrine and a way of life." This later statement of nonresistance maintained the distinction between allegiance to earthly governments and that owed to the heavenly government.[14]

All of these official BIC documents also included statements on nonconformity, or separation from society. These statements supported the view that nonresistant people should remain aloof from the larger world. Within these official tenets, however, elaborations on nonresistance exhibit countervailing sentiments. Service and neighborliness, for example, suggest outward-looking attributes. Furthermore, both the 1939 and 1961 statements reflect influences from the larger society, although from different ends of the ideological spectrum. The 1939 statement explicitly distinguishes nonresistance from "anarchy, non-violent coercion, [and] modern pacifism." This desire to distance nonresistance from pacifism and its connection to religious modernism suggests the influence of fundamentalism.[15] Although the BIC community had at times expropriated ideas from both premillenialists and pacifists, during the cultural conflict of the 1920s the community reflected the conservative end of the spectrum. But by two decades later, as shown in the 1961 statement, a shift had occurred in language, slight but telling. Rather than owing the state prayer and obedience, nonresistant adherents must give "such loyalty and service as will enhance [our] testimony of peace and good will toward all men." Rather than grant the state the right to wield unchecked power outside the community, the statement suggests that state actions be measured against the goals of the peace position.[16] Here we see the influence of the coalition of peace groups that ran alternative service programs for conscientious objectors in World War II.

Other official BIC statements stressed traditional themes: the biblical basis of nonresistance, with its limitations on loyalty to government, as an expression of separation from the world and its abjuring of violence.[17] But within such statements, as well as other writings by BIC leaders and rank-and-file members, we

C. N. Hostetter Jr. overlooking the Civilian Public Service camp at Colorado Springs, Colorado, 1941. On the back of the photograph someone, probably Hostetter, wrote, "Oh, C.O. camp; oh, C.O. camp, how often would I have gathered thee as a hen gathereth her chicks." *(Courtesy of the Brethren in Christ Historical Library and Archives)*

sometimes find these themes paired with sentiments of neighborliness and good citizenship. For example, limited loyalty to government was sometimes transformed into a responsible patriotism that rejected war enthusiasm as harmful to the long-term welfare of the nation. Repudiating retaliation meant not passivity but a more effective means than violence for dealing with evil. Nonresistance obligated one to cooperate with and serve neighbors.[18]

In the World War II years, these active themes accompanied new sources of authority that supplemented biblical injunctions. Four established male leaders—O. B. Ulery, an Ohio bishop; C. N. Hostetter Jr., a Pennsylvania bishop and president of Messiah Bible College; E. J. Swalm, now an Ontario bishop and evangelist; and Henry G. Brubaker, minister and president of Beulah College, a California BIC school—emphasized doctrinal nonresistant articles of faith. They also defined the tenet as one they could defend with logical argument and express in service to humanity. The appeals of these established BIC leaders stressed engagement with the larger world.

In a pamphlet entitled *Can a Christian Fight?* Ulery based his arguments mostly on biblical citations, and he tightly linked nonresistance and nonconformity. But like the other leaders, he enthusiastically supported the new programs of

Civilian Public Service and relief work, particularly in the Ohio-Kentucky state council, which he dominated.[19] Hostetter, employing biblical authority, also provided philosophical defenses. War, like slavery and the liquor trade, was a great social evil that violated not only love but also truth, the "human personality," property, and the mission of the church. Those advocating nonresistance could respond to common criticisms of pacifism by permitting the use of nonlethal force and by demonstrating that tyranny could be destroyed from below by a mass of adherents willing to die for others. In this rationale Hostetter echoed the cardinal tenets of the philosophy of nonviolence. Nonresistance, which he defined as "love applied in daily living," also offered a concrete program of social care of the hopeless, sick, and hungry. Hostetter, more often than these other leaders, defined nonresistance as a corporate belief to which individual desires might need to be sacrificed.[20]

Swalm based his own appeal on his storytelling and oratorical skills, stressing the heroic, positive program of the "great neglected doctrine" lived out in the World War II years by the "splendid young men" in alternative service programs. Nonresistance, he argued, must be intelligently reinterpreted each generation.[21] In 1949, Brubaker appealed to history in describing peace as the highest cultural expression of any society. The peace witness, he argued, had great potential for addressing enemies, race barriers, nationalism, and human annihilation.[22]

Because periods of war stimulated discussion of nonresistance more than did daily life on the farm, the years between 1939 and 1958 yield many voices beyond those of established BIC leaders who championed the doctrine. Younger writers drew on the traditional planks of the tenet. They argued that biblical authority, especially Christ's words and life, made clear that individual salvation must precede social improvement.[23] Some stressed nonconformist sentiments: they were pilgrims in a foreign land; they would stand fast when other pacifists weakened under public pressure; they would pray rather than write letters to governmental leaders.[24] Sacrifice of money, prestige, or even life strengthened rather than threatened their commitment to nonresistance. They saw nonresistance as a gift and a privilege given to them by God, not as a constitutional right granted them by the government.[25] These almost mystical ideas had practical ramifications. For example, BIC community leaders wrote letters of appreciation to national governments thanking them for granting alternative service to conscientious objectors. Brubaker interpreted the requirement that the Historic Peace Churches, rather than the U.S. government, bear the cost of administrating Civilian Public Service not as discrimination against a minority but as something the community should "gladly and willingly bear."[26]

Two prolific young writers who drew on traditional themes also felt compelled to look beyond those themes when they defended nonresistance. Jesse W.

Hoover and Wendell E. Harmon, both of draft age in World War II, wrote columns in the *Visitor* and the *Sunday School Herald* in the 1940s. Much as C. N. Hostetter Jr. had done but in more detail, they emphasized nonresistance as an effective alternative to war. They advocated active service and addressed difficult challenges to these beliefs.[27] Hoover and Harmon exhibited talent and education in their writings, but like other leaders, they needed to respond to challenging questions from the BIC community's own youth. For example, in 1940, five men and six women from Beulah College in Upland, California, attended a student association rally uniting five holiness-related schools. A report on the session entitled "My Attitude toward Military Service" promoted conscientious objection in response to conscription but also noted the discussion of questions such as the validity of defending democracies against dictatorial takeovers.[28] In the same year, students at Messiah Bible College who participated in a lively Bible conference forum on nonresistance raised similar questions. For example, could a conscientious objector at least sympathize with one warring nation?[29] Ray M. Zercher, a young artist chafing at nonconformist strictures in the BIC community, remembers needing more of a philosophical rationale for the peace position than traditional nonresistance provided.[30] Harold S. Martin argued that conscientious objectors who refused to cooperate in any way with the conscription system, which included a rejection of serving in Civilian Public Service, were "the most misunderstood" of men opposed to the war.[31] Although younger members asked hard questions, editors and writers drew on a multitude of surprising sources to support nonresistance. The Messiah Bible College periodical, the *Clarion*, quoted from Benjamin Disraeli, Edgar Faure, and other political and intellectual figures about the horrors of war.[32] Arthur Musser's article in the *Clarion*, later reprinted in the *Sunday School Herald*, noted that Lao Tzu had practiced nonresistance in the seventh century B.C.E. and that Socrates had challenged the power of the state over individual conscience well before the Christian era.[33]

In this milieu, Hoover and Harmon's columns became settings for wide-ranging discussions about the response of nonresistant people to international issues. These discussions drew on a variety of authorities. Hoover sometimes quoted isolationists or other voices against war or peacetime conscription that had appeared in the secular press.[34] He once argued that modernists, in their social concerns, were more fundamental than "so-called 'fundamentalists.'" If the social gospel compelled "a greater sense of responsibility for our fellowmen," he asked, "who can deny its legitimacy?" Similarly, he faulted extreme dispensationalism—the idea that God employed different ethical standards in different historical periods—for rejecting the Sermon on the Mount.[35] Harmon suggested that in the event of an invasion, "nonviolent techniques" were acceptable. The real goal, however, required longer-term thinking in a slow process that was necessary to build peace.[36]

International events also shaped Hoover and Harmon's writings. Even in the early stages of World War II, Hoover ran articles addressing Hitler and national socialism.[37] By the end of the conflict, war guilt—Japanese, German, and American—was an even more central question. Harmon argued that all humanity stood responsible for the Holocaust; that military occupations of Germany by victors after both world wars created rather than solved problems; and that Americans tended to emphasize Japanese atrocities while ignoring American responsibility for the incineration of Hiroshima and Nagasaki.[38] Hoover described those bombings as a new chapter in the ferocity of war, which allowed "roast[ing] people alive by the thousands and hundreds of thousands" and represented "the most sadistic forms of intimidation and revenge."[39]

In the postwar years, nonresistance extended its criticism to Cold War rhetoric and continued to borrow from other peace advocates. In a *Visitor* section entitled "News Gleanings," one item noted that the United States and Great Britain had built airfields in, and were transporting weaponry to, nations in the eastern Mediterranean. The author wondered presciently, "How would we be behaving if the Russians were doing the same in Mexico, Cuba and Venezuela?"[40] C. N. Hostetter Jr. publicized in the *Visitor* a statement from a 1950 ecumenical conference supporting "non-violent action, such as Gandhi has demonstrated." He commented that "Mennonite and Brethren in Christ representatives ... [had] decided there was much value in our continuing some association with this conference."[41]

Nonresistant ideas appeared not only in BIC magazines but also on school campuses and at Bible and youth conferences. Hoover not only wrote but also spoke at numerous BIC gatherings, where he advocated "nonviolent techniques."[42] A 1941 youth group curriculum for a Memorial Day program employed standard antiwar imagery—the meaningless butchery of World War I—and ended with a sentence prayer, "Strengthen the spirits of all who believe in peace."[43] Shirley Lenehan, a student at Messiah Bible College, criticized the news media for its many heroic war stories that ignored the losses endured by many families.[44] A sermon at a BIC youth conference in Grantham, Pennsylvania, argued that Christians always had a greater responsibility for the material needs of enemies and the "poor and needy" than did non-Christians. That humanitarian service, the speaker argued, could directly replace the violence often visited on the less fortunate.[45]

Although most advocates focused on nonresistance expressed in service, occasionally the issue of political participation arose.[46] Harmon surveyed CPS men in the mid-1940s. His questionnaire included an inquiry about the importance

Wendell E. Harmon. Harmon served in Civilian Public
Service from 1941 to 1945. In his column "Peace Periscope"
in the *Sunday School Herald*, Harmon argued that all
humanity stood responsible for the Holocaust, that
military occupations of Germany by victors after both
world wars created rather than solved problems, and that
Americans tended to emphasize Japanese atrocities while
ignoring American responsibility for the incineration of
Hiroshima and Nagasaki. *(Courtesy of Wendell E. Harmon)*

of "the political, economic, and moral implications" of nonresistance in "the
church's educational program." Ninety-one percent of the men who responded
argued that such nonresistance should be given increased emphasis. One of the
responses directly challenged political aloofness—"If non-resistance includes total
abstinence from governmental participation, then I do not agree with it."[47] A
1947 article for youth on nonconformity contended that BIC doctrine neither
advocated nor forbade voting.[48] When the possibility of postwar conscription
emerged, Messiah Bible College and two Pennsylvania BIC districts sent letters to
the U.S. government protesting such an expression of militarism.[49]

Despite these brief forays into political participation, nonresistance increasingly became synonymous with service. The refusal to participate in war became linked with the promise to work on behalf of others. In late 1940, Erwin
Thomas responded to a Messiah Bible College campus poll that asked, "What
would you do if called to fight?" He indicated that he would present himself as
nonresistant, then proceed to say what he would do to help "the suffering and
wounded" rather than what he would not do.[50] The Dauphin-Lebanon district
council decided that sermons on nonresistance should be accompanied by financial offerings for relief services.[51] Articles by Miriam Bowers and Elsie C.
Bechtel, both of whom later volunteered as relief workers in postwar Europe,
made two of the strongest statements connecting active service and the stand
against war. Bowers coupled her opposition to "having even the smallest part
in this revolting butchery called 'war'" with the belief that "a positive life of
service" translated "the path of non-violence . . . into daily life."[52] Bechtel argued that service met not only the needs of war victims but also a human
desire to work collectively for a higher good.

Collective effort transcending the individual, she astutely noted, was one of
the appeals of war efforts. Peace service could answer that challenge of war.[53]
With more enthusiasm than accuracy, Harmon described the Brethren in Christ
as "in the vanguard" of CPS men doing service work in state mental hospitals.[54]
Hoover described nonresistance's potential as "breathtaking progressivism" that
was "almost radical."[55]

The Brethren in Christ in the World War II era may have had an unrealistic
sense of the transforming power of service. They certainly lacked an analysis
of war's connection to political and economic structures. But they cannot be
faulted for parochialism or separatist complacency. Yet as in World War I, members conceived of nonresistance as a way of life that addressed intimate relationships as well as the events of a world at war.

Nonresistance and Daily Practice

In the edition of *Nonresistance under Test* published in 1949, Swalm noted the
ironic fact that the current emphasis on peace issues was "one of the by-prod-
ucts of war."[56] In his columns just after the end of the war, Harmon anticipated
the problem of maintaining a concrete peace program without the impetus of
war mobilization.[57] His concerns were not misplaced. During World War I,
BIC community members had found it harder to practice peace in their neighborhoods, in their church, and in their families than to respond to war periods. Public writers, seeming to sense the difficulty, usually chose other topics.
But memories and reflections on nonresistant practice often describe its application in ordinary daily life as its most powerful expression.

Most writers throughout these war years agreed that to be consistent, non-resistance had to be practiced in everyday life. Even Messiah Bible College's unauthorized school paper, *Flash,* which focused on student social life, devoted a sizeable article to an address, "Non-Resistance in Theory and Practice." To be effective, the orator contended, nonresistance "must be practiced in our daily life."[58] In a very different setting, one respondent to an early 1940s survey of church leaders argued that it was not more effective teaching that was needed but "examples of fairness and good peaceful living . . . from the highest officia[l] to the least of the laity."[59] At the end of the World War II period, C. N. Hostetter Jr. told conscientious objectors leaving for alternative service in Peru that "the cry of our day is to interpret Christ in everyday life."[60] Ross Nigh, a drafted conscientious objector who served in Canada's Alternative Service Work, described "warm testimonies" of BIC community members as people "fortified by consistent lives."[61]

What exactly did this consistency entail? For youth, one article contended, nonresistance should mean rejecting verbal or physical retaliation and even "a pugnacious spirit, which always insists on 'sticking up for our rights.'"[62] In one issue of their school periodical, Beulah College students discussed nonresistance in the home, at school, in recreation, and toward enemies. In home and at school, nonresistance meant harmonious relationships built on forbearance—or, in an important phrase of the period, "going the second mile." Evelyn Raser argued that a nonresistant position was an "outward expression of an inward possession." Other writers tied daily nonresistance to larger issues.[63] Ira Lehman, who served in Civilian Public Service, argued that people in the larger society who castigated conscientious objectors as cowardly might not be exhibiting intolerance so much as responding to prewar everyday inconsistencies. His examples of inconsistencies included driving recklessly, using the courts to defend one's rights, and ignoring race prejudice at home while sending missionaries overseas. Nonresistance, he concluded, could be proclaimed to those at a distance but must be lived for those nearby.[64] The most sustained discussion of nonresistance in daily life came from men and women participating in CPS work in state mental hospitals. They argued that daily practice of nonresistant principles brought remarkable changes in the residents of those institutions.[65]

Written sources from the period are few, and their analyses of nonresistance in daily life are brief. A number of retrospective reflections on nonresistance, on the other hand, focus on life in rural farm neighborhoods as a central arena for practicing the belief. Individuals describe both "defenseless" responses to wrongs and active peacemaking in local communities. For some, avoiding legal redress best symbolized nonresistance.[66] Allyne Friesen Isaac's biographical article on her parents valued both her father's warm welcome of returning BIC men who had served in the military during World War II and his refusal to sue a man who had given him a bad check for six hundred dollars on a cattle sale. Her father argued that all people, not just coreligionists, should be treated as family.[67]

Farm life offered ample opportunity for conflicts requiring "the second mile." In a forum on E. J. Swalm's legacy, Lester Fretz recounted Swalm's allegory of a peaceful resolution to a boundary dispute. Perhaps Fretz was remembering his own experience with an irate neighbor.[68] Fretz had grown up in a BIC family on a substantial farm near Stevensville, Ontario.[69] To illustrate how nonresistance had been conveyed within his family, Fretz told how his father once sent him and his brother to cut, rake, and bale the hay field of a farmer with whom they would split the crop. The field had a poor crop, hardly worth cutting. The hay bales were far apart, so Fretz decided to take his family's two-thirds of the crop from one side of the field rather than leaving every third bale. He reasoned that the other farmer would have less driving to pick up his share of the bales. As Fretz remembers the event, the farmer left his bales to deteriorate in the fields for two months before picking them up. Sometime later, he flagged down Fretz and his father on the road to castigate them for leaving him the worst hay of the field. Fretz remembers the man cursing and saying, "Howard, I never would have thought your family would have acted like this. I thought you were more uprightly than this." Fretz recalled, "My dad just sat there and said, 'We'll make it right.'" After the man left, Fretz's father had him take the year's best alfalfa hay to take to the farmer as a replacement. Fretz was deeply moved by the memory of his father's generosity. But he also recalls that when he delivered the alfalfa hay, "he was in the mow and I was throwing the bales in, I threw them real hard. I tried to hit him."[70]

Mildred Byer Charles recounts a similar story about her husband's family. Her father-in-law's response to a theft had "nothing to do with the war" but best expressed her understanding of nonresistance. During the 1930s, finances were tight, but the Charles family saved enough money to buy a car, "and this was something tremendous." Quite soon, however, the new car disappeared. Jacob Charles was sure he knew who had taken it; the suspect had been on the farm asking questions and later drove an identical car. Jacob never pressed charges, telling his family that someone who had resorted to theft must have had greater need than they had. The Charles family went back to traveling with horses for "a long time" before they saved enough to buy another car. Charles concludes, "To me that's nonresistance in real life; that's the real test right there."[71] Gordon Schneider, on the other hand, notes that his father's "soft touch" encouraged requests for loans that were never repaid. "My mother would shudder every time a strange car drove in the driveway."[72]

Cornelius and Frances Lady family, Abilene, Kansas, 1941. L to R (front row): Martha, Ruth, Frances, Mary Olive; (back row): Cornelius, Myron. Martha and Mary Olive Lady remember their parents' relationship as an expression of nonresistance. (*Courtesy of Mary Olive Lady*)

Besides illustrating concrete understandings of nonresistance, these stories also suggest that these farms were more prosperous than those surrounding them.[73] Prosperity and careful regulation of neighborly relations undoubtedly resulted in an element of prestige in local settings. Perhaps that prestige cushioned the neighborhood's response to the BIC nonresistance. But it might also have made it hard for the Brethren in Christ to suddenly take an unpopular position during war mobilization. Church historian Martin E. Marty has written that "the *historic peace churches* . . . were used to suffering in wartime."[74] Yet these stories reveal people who were woven into their neighborhoods and who were uneasy with disruptions to those neighborly relationships.

The active mending of relationships was another important element of nonresistance.[75] Several deceased patriarchs—the examples given are always men—were remembered for their skills as neighborhood peacemakers.[76] Martha Lady and Mary Olive Lady, secondary and elementary school students during World War II, remember particular incidents in which their father mediated disputes. As a farmer, he had reconciled two feuding partners with whom he shared labor and equipment. In the extended family, he had helped smooth tensions over the division of the estate.[77]

Such peacemakers were important in families and even more so in the BIC church, where small-group conflicts were frequent. Responses to a mid-1940s survey of church leaders often blamed such lapses on family life. A list of complaints against the home included the following: parents who criticized the BIC church in front of children or assumed children would absorb beliefs by osmosis; families who ignored BIC doctrine in the home or were openly antagonistic to church doctrine; and parents who were "loath to have [their children] distinctly different than those whom they associate with."[78] Ministerial criticism of families might have been self-serving. But ordinary members also reported that nonresistance was chiefly imparted in the home. As one respondent contended, he learned nonresistance only at home—the BIC church had forgotten the tenet.[79]

In homes, nonresistance was often implanted in young minds by example, not by instruction. In other words, peace was practiced, not talked about. Jeanette Dourte summarizes a widespread sentiment: "I think I 'caught' it rather than learned by teaching." Maynard C. Book describes nonresistance as "learning the Art of Give & Take as children growing up."[80] Martha and Mary Olive Lady say that their understanding of nonresistance grew out of observing their parents' perhaps atypical marital compatibility. The Lady sisters describe their father as "a gentle man" who liked animals and children and was hurt by the abuse of either. They remember their mother, on the other hand, leading a panel at church on nonresistance. It was to her that they turned with questions about war after the bombing of Pearl Harbor.[81]

An emphasis on gentleness in males, however, shows up in other accounts as well. Men's association with nonresistance, then, grew not just from their nonparticipation in military life, electoral politics, or the courts. Nonresistance also allowed men to assume gentle or nurturing roles in the BIC community. For example, E. Morris Sider's father, Earl Sider, combined the public experiences of a conscientious objector with an unassuming manner and forbearance in the BIC church he pastored. The elder Sider's experiences as a conscientious objector in World War I "took on mythic proportions" as a family story. "It was such a dramatic story[;] . . . here our father was in jail, in a far off city— Toronto was a far off city for boys." Incidents in which his father was forcibly dressed in military uniform and threatened with execution "became larger in my mind than probably really warranted." But Morris also describes his father as "a model of peace in all aspects of his life," including his role as pastor. On occasion, an unhappy but vocal minority in Earl Sider's congregation would criticize him in public prayers and testimonies, and spread gossip about him. Morris remembers that his father never responded unkindly or vindictively. When Morris asked his father why he did not enlist the district bishop to quiet the dissidents, his father responded, "The situation is bad," but "I can't do what you're suggesting because I love these people, they're my people."[82]

Numerous retrospective accounts connect nonresistance with a father's gentle temperament. Beth Ulery Saba describes her father's gentleness in caring for his dying father and in helping with a sister-in-law's sick baby girl, whose father was away from home in Civilian Public Service.[83] Ivan Byers remembers that his father was intrigued by the mysteries of the natural world and astonished that others could enjoy hunting.[84] Naomi Heise Marr describes how her father literally turned the other cheek when someone struck him.[85] A number of women report that their husbands' alternative service seemed to draw from the men's gentleness, generosity, and care for the less privileged. Conversely, some who reject or question the nonresistance of their childhood point to more dogmatic or combative actions by men.[86]

Women, particularly mothers, are less often noted for their gentle and nurturing attributes. This discrepancy perhaps results from a combination of a presumption that women would exhibit a pacific nature and of women's common role of dispensing justice in the home. E. Morris Sider contrasts his father's patience to the demeanor of his mother, who "wanted us to jump when she said jump" and who issued many more spankings than did his father. Leone Dearing Sider recalls that mothers often had to be disciplinarians in their husbands' absences. Her husband Morris's father, for instance, left home for lengthy periods of time on evangelistic travels.[87]

Other accounts point to women's pivotal role in imparting nonresistant beliefs. John Hensel lists his mother and wife as the important influences in his registering as a conscientious objector. Another man describes his mother searching scripture with him to help him come to a conscientious-objection position. She "was the promoter of Peace in our family," the one who recounted stories of nonresistance. It was Paul Carlson's mother who forbade him to build model war planes, which annoyed him. Drawing an important connection, Carlson also remembers feeling embarrassed by his mother's plain dress.[88]

Contemporary and retrospective accounts consistently paired nonconformist dress with nonresistance. Although the issue of dress affected both sexes, it invariably weighed more heavily on women. One response to the leadership survey pointed to mothers who were "brawley and cross" even while wearing plain clothes. To attain the perfection espoused by Wesleyan holiness, one respondent averred, "mothers especially must be Godly." Another argued that male ministers who disregarded dress codes themselves led the "weaker vessel" to follow in putting on "worldly dress."[89]

Thus BIC women learned to see that their particular role in the community was to maintain nonconformist appearance standards. Four women whose recollections we have indicate that nonconformist dress, not nonresistance, was the primary concern for young women at midcentury.[90] BIC women could be disfellowshiped for violating appearance codes, just as the men could be disfellowshiped for military service.[91] In 1940, the Canadian Nonresistance Committee set up standards that conscripted young men had to meet in order to be given BIC membership certificates. The standards were presented in terms of who would not receive such certificates: those who did not attend church; those who participated in a variety of proscribed social, economic, and political activities; and those men *and women* who violated dress codes.[92] The statement may have included women in the item on dress because of a concern that nurses might face conscription or simply as a reflection of their roles as important symbols of nonconformity.

Nonconformist dress also affected men, some of whom remember embarrassment at not wearing ties in formal public settings. Describing the Ontario BIC community in the 1930s, Dorothy Sherk remembers, "Most of the young men weren't joining the church because it was a lot of fussing over things that didn't matter." The necktie was the example she gave.[93] Although symbols of nonresistance and nonconformity intertwined for the entire BIC community, women seemed more likely to consider the plain dress as either a cross to bear or a badge of religious fervor.

Since women carried on much of the work of the BIC church and dominated it numerically, the aspects of nonresistant practice that they chose to emphasize are important. Some women strongly connected nonresistance with active relief service. After the war, a number of women who wrote about peace did volunteer in relief work in Europe and Mexico.[94] Looking back, they remember wanting to take visible stands as women, stands that would, in Bechtel's words, test the BIC community's theory that "love is the greatest thing in the world."[95] This emphasis on service continued in the 1950s. The 1953 church peace conference, though dominated by male speakers and the issues of male conscientious objectors, included one woman, Eunice Lady Wingert, speaking on relief work in Japan and Korea.[96]

Women who volunteered as relief workers were not the only ones who addressed nonresistant practice. In 1952, Grace Herr gave a speech on nonresistance in an oration contest sponsored by the Messiah College Peace Society. Herr focused on "be[ing] consistent in the little daily conflicts that arise." Those conflicts, she argued, are "the seeds of war." On her way to this relational form of nonresistance, Herr passed through an economic analysis, which associated war with the greed that also expressed itself in consumerism, large corporations, and "bosses in the factories." The heart of the matter remained "deep within the lives of individual men." Herr embedded war in economic systems—a connection pacifists in general were only beginning to grasp. Nevertheless, she set forth a personal and individualistic solution.[97]

Other women focused on nonconformist issues. Anna Verle Miller, in a 1945 article, discussed separation from the world in social settings, as well as plain dress, but did not consider nonresistance.[98] Looking back, Miller remembers her father encouraging "young men to follow it [nonresistance]."[99] In 1993, Ruth Herr Pawelski mourned the loss of distinctive BIC community practices. To symbolize this loss, she chose footwashing and women's head covering. The latter was an important aspect of women's plain dress, symbolizing their submission to male leadership.[100]

Although women were active in nonresistant practice, male leaders seldom drew on women as public symbols of a belief that was supposed to be central to the life of the BIC community. Ross Nigh, writing in 1993 on the BIC community's identity, connected men to nonresistance and women to nonconformity—expressed as simplicity, one rationale for plain dress. Looking back over his life, he recalled E. J. Swalm for his nonresistance and his own grandmother for her critique of consumption.[101] These gender divisions seemed natural, not something for official nonresistant statements to note explicitly. But gender roles provided two experiences of BIC nonresistance, just as military service creates two different experiences of American citizenship.[102]

Other divisions within the BIC community sometimes turned into open conflict.[103] E. Morris Sider, who describes his father's nonresistant response to a contentious group in the church, admits that he himself could not have taken so accommodating an approach. Sider's choice of an academic career, as opposed to one in the ministry, was in part an acknowledgment that his father's accepting response was beyond his reach. He describes nonresistance in the BIC community as an "intermediate" level between international and family peace. To illustrate the absence of peace at that middle level, he quotes his university thesis advisor on the BIC community's peace position: "I know your people. . . . They wouldn't take a gun and go to war and kill somebody with a bullet; what they'll do is get up in council meeting and shoot each other with words."[104] BIC community members themselves can be just as blunt. Millard Herr recalls, "My church was always putting up resistance to something. . . . It seems the church believes in nonresistance when dealing with the nation and war but not when managing its internal affairs."[105] Dorothy Sherk remembers group conflict as community failure; intolerance, she maintains, was more likely inside than outside the BIC community. "In-house fighting in Bertie [district]" made her question nonresistance, which she believed must include "peace and harmony" with one's closest neighbors.[106]

Time and again during World War II the inability of the BIC community to reach or maintain uniformity on definitions of nonresistance, in particular, created conflicts. James Alderfer, who served as an army medical officer from 1946 to 1949, remembers receiving no criticism from BIC community members in California; in Pennsylvania, however, he became the focus of conflict between a BIC bishop and a minister. The bishop did not want Alderfer to take Communion while in uniform, but the pastor "insisted otherwise" and prevailed.[107] Clara Gibboney Kritzberger had an older brother in Civilian Public Service and three brothers-in-law in military service in the Pacific during World War II. She remembers vividly an incident of those years, one that her sisters have recounted many times, in which their husbands, in military uniform, were confronted by a member who told them they were unwelcome in the BIC church.[108]

Wendell E. Harmon recalls one pastor's support when his conscientious-objection stand "was maligned by a few people in the Upland, [California,] congregation whose sons had taken the military route." That same pastor, however, in 1942 opposed the General Conference's decision to disfellowship members who served in the military. Thereafter General Conference never again appointed the pastor to any of its committees; his wife interpreted this as a response to his 1942 statements.[109] Harmon and his wife, Frances, returned to the Upland BIC congregation after doing CPS work in a state hospital. Looking back, Frances argues that the BIC community missed an opportunity to encourage understanding between those who chose alternative and those who chose military service. "Emotions were pretty high then[,] . . . so you didn't do anything that would make it more hurtful to yourself." An attempt at "assimilation" might have improved relationships that "never were really very deeply healed."[110]

Although, looking back, BIC members assume the importance of unity and healing, both proved elusive within the Brethren in Christ. Difficulty in dealing with divisions over military service beset Mennonite congregations as well.[111] But for the Brethren in Christ, conflict over nonresistance interacted with their position in the larger society and with corporate authority within their community. That convergence presented new challenges to the unity of the small BIC community.

NONRESISTANCE IN AMERICAN SOCIETY

Not only gender roles and disagreements affected the practice of nonresistance. Three other factors helped to explain why BIC people had different ideas about nonresistance, particularly in the BIC community and in the home. First, the Brethren in Christ, who were scattered geographically, lived in a variety of larger worlds. The contemporary record challenges the idea that the BIC community was isolated and enclosed, although that perception is central to many memories of the 1940s and 1950s. Second, the intractable question in Western culture of how to relate the individual to the group—and the connected question of how to tolerate differences while maintaining boundaries—bedeviled nonresistant beliefs and practice. Third, the BIC community was in a constant struggle to define itself, survive, and grow under the shadow of the vast American society.

Borrowing from Larger Societies

At many different levels, the Brethren in Christ were connected to local, regional, national, and international religious and ideological groupings. These connections were not simply results of impersonal social and economic trends. Writings from 1939 to 1954 demonstrate a variety of ideological affinities, institutional requirements, nationalist sentiments, and social concerns that tied the small group to larger ones. Mobilization for total war, hot and cold, undoubtedly increased the church's contacts outside the BIC community. But these new contacts only accentuated well-established patterns of borrowing from the world to create a unique community.

In a 1946 *Visitor* editorial, in a piece he entitled "Democracy and Discipline," Jesse W. Hoover explicitly tied the BIC community to the national society. Hoover criticized the growing centralization of power in the postwar United States. Whereas proponents of centralization contended that it increased efficiency, Hoover argued that it challenged democracy. Moves to increase centralization in the BIC church reflected this trend of the larger society. Although the influence of the larger society was a natural one, it was one the BIC church had to analyze before accepting. The underlying ideology of centralization, Hoover argued, was a belief that discipline and democracy were inimical. Using biblical passages describing early Christian church organization, Hoover argued that voluntary association and democratic methods could lead to consensus stronger and more disciplined than that produced by centralized power.[112] In his advocacy of democracy, Hoover searched for a means to mediate differences within the group.

At the level most directly related to nonresistance, the BIC community increased its cooperation with the other Historic Peace Churches, especially with Mennonites.[113] Similarly, the peace position knit the small, evangelical BIC community to the more mainstream Church of the Brethren and the Religious Society of Friends. BIC writers drew on all of these groups to build their peace witness.[114] Reporting on his attendance at a seminar on peace issues at Pendle Hill, a Quaker center near Philadelphia, Hoover noted that although some approaches discussed were different from those of the Brethren in Christ, "the

exchange of viewpoints, ideals, and purposes did have a wholesome and stimu-
lating effect."[115] From 1940 to 1965, E. J. Swalm and C. N. Hostetter Jr. provided
leadership in coalitions of peace churches.[116] The impact of these coalitions
reached beyond BIC church leaders. Individuals who grew up in Ontario remember anticipating the annual gathering of the Conference of Historic Peace
Churches with as much enthusiasm as they had BIC annual gatherings.[117]

The commitment to pacifism also connected the small BIC community to
pacifist expressions beyond those of the Historic Peace Churches. BIC leaders
periodically had contact with such groups as the Fellowship of Reconciliation
and Peace Now.[118] Conscientious objectors from around the world and from
different ideological backgrounds were of interest to the BIC community.[119] Noting the special hardships of conscientious objectors in Civilian Public Service
who did not come from Historic Peace Churches, Swalm reported telling one,
"It is men like you who add dignity to our cause." To this the man responded,
"You are mistaken, this cause had the dignity; I am only sharing in it."[120]

Any movement by evangelical or mainline Protestants that had the effect of
lessening their support for war was welcomed.[121] Individuals and groups, contemporary or historical, that made even oblique antiwar statements or advocated nonviolent approaches to conflict were recognized as giving validity to
nonresistance: Mohandas K. Gandhi, Henry Wallace, the National Association
of Manufacturers, Flavius Josephus, Charles Wesley, Dwight L. Moody.[122] Isolationists in the 1930s and early 1940s were warmly commended. The *Visitor* hailed
Idaho senator William Borah, a leader among isolationists, as a "great states-
man" when he died.[123] In 1948, an extended article extolled the power of popular
protest to avoid armed conflict in the 1905 separation of Sweden and Norway.[124]

In the same years, the Brethren in Christ did have some misgivings about
borrowing from the larger society. In 1942, Hoover criticized Gandhi's nonviolence as an eclectic blend of religions and secular ideas.[125] In the same year,
the Oklahoma joint council carried a motion to question General Conference
about "the advisability of admitting members from other denominations whose
doctrines are not based on the Word of God, into the C.O. [conscientious ob-
jector] camps."[126]

The BIC community extended its boundaries by borrowing not only pacifist views but also other religious expressions, including those of holiness
groups, the Moravian mission impulse, the American Bible Society, and the
Waldensians in Italy. (Ironically, during the same years, the BIC church practiced closed Communion, which excluded people outside the Brethren in
Christ.) The German Lutheran pastor Martin Niemöller was the focus of several articles in BIC periodicals.[127] Diaries and biographies show that not only
editors and leaders were drawing from groups beyond their own.[128] In her di-

ary between 1940 and 1944, Irene Frey Hensel of Harrisburg, Pennsylvania, recorded visits to a Church of Christ, a Church of God, a Lutheran church, an evangelical church, a Colored Baptist church, and the Salvation Army.[129]

The Brethren in Christ not only cooperated with other religious groups but also made forays into civic life. The memories of people who were youths in the 1940s and 1950s often focus on how nonconformity excluded them from participation in school and community life. But church-related literature turned periodically to the issue of citizenship. In the 1930s, one Messiah Bible College social science course was "Problems in Democracy," its objective described as "developing civic virtues" in "an intelligent citizen."[130] In 1939, H. G. Brubaker argued that Christians had to be good citizens, particularly in democracies.[131] His discussion did not detail what that might mean. BIC-developed youth curricula in the 1940s included lessons on "National Life," "Christian Patriotism," "The Christian Citizen," and "The Church and the Community." (This last topic suggested a survey of neighborhood needs in order to deepen a sense of responsibility for all people, not just for a small group.)[132]

Those addressing citizenship carefully articulated the limitations of obedience to governments and described religious conversions as civic contributions. But one lesson also argued that the BIC community should be loyal to the nation; it urged not "a blind, unreasonable, or sentimental type of patriotism" but support for "principles and ideals which inflamed the hearts of the founders of our free country."[133] Patriotic statements, particularly ones noting religious freedom, appeared in all the church periodicals.[134] At the end of World War II, Wendell E. Harmon noted that the war had made questions of relationships to neighbors, humanity, and the nation increasingly urgent.[135]

As the Brethren in Christ interacted with ideas from other groups and with world events, they shaped what they borrowed by adding nonresistant sentiments. For example, a statement from Pennsylvania's Rapho district argued that postwar conscription would not only challenge nonresistance's opposition to military participation but also "seriously degrade our national life . . . and standards as set forth in The Constitution."[136] The end of war in Europe elicited a prayer meeting in the Grantham, Pennsylvania, congregation. Anna Lane Hostetter, who attended, recorded no jubilation in her May 8 diary entry. Rather, she wrote, "Mussolini and his mistress were shot—she is only 25. . . . They were kicked, spit upon, etc. and hung up by their heels after death. A number of people were at the meeting—town people."[137] Similarly, Jesse W. Hoover's editorial entitled "Victory!" was sober. "The waging of war does not propagate peace," he warned. Rather, "each war has initiated another more terrible." He asked whether the airmen bombing Berlin had given thought to the babies of the city. He professed thankfulness for the freedom, tolerance, and religious heritage of the nation but castigated the "fanatical patriotism" that gave little thought to the nation's welfare in times of peace.[138] Hoover also printed an article suggesting that the Historic Peace Churches would be leaders in "carrying the hope of human progress," being "humane in emphasis and democratic in method."[139]

In many areas of life, however, the small BIC community's attitudes reflected those of the larger society more than they heralded international progress. Comments on race relations in the United States or the persecution of Jews mirrored general American prejudices. A *Visitor* article on America's race problem, for example, began by deploring racism but ended by condemning interracial marriage.[140] BIC periodicals consistently condemned national socialism in Germany.[141] But articles also expressed sentiments that construed Jewish people as outsiders and a problem.[142]

Although mainstream news sources reported political events of the day, attention to these events undoubtedly varied by individual and by family. In a 1977 interview, Nelson, the oldest son of C. N. Hostetter Jr. remembered little reading material in his home other than the *Visitor*.[143] In contrast, Mary Olive Lady, in elementary school and high school in Kansas during those same years, remembers reading articles and editorials from the Abilene and Topeka newspapers, to both of which her family subscribed.[144] The Messiah Bible College *Clarion* ran columns debating America's response to German refugees in 1941 and the merits of presidential candidates in 1944.[145] Despite disapproval of some of Franklin D. Roosevelt's public and private practices, BIC people joined the national outpouring of grief at his death.[146] Interest in World War II leaders extended beyond national boundaries. Walter Winger can remember no Brethren in Christ who did not express some degree of admiration for Churchill and recalls that E. J. Swalm, with his oratorical skills and excellent memory, was able to recite Churchill speeches verbatim.[147]

This integration with the larger society went beyond a simple awareness of current events, however. A community that demanded high levels of discipline, commitment, and sacrifice from its members easily fell into admiration of similar qualities in military life. In World War II, as in World War I, militarism itself soon infiltrated the language and imagery used by the Brethren in Christ. Direct comparisons to war mobilization supplemented analogies of Christian warfare and victorious living, present not only in war periods.[148] Blackouts and the omnipresence of military personnel and equipment in San Francisco drew William Hoke's mind to "spiritual battle."[149] In 1940 and 1951 (the second year of the Korean War), writers compared a religious call to conscription; one writer in Saskatchewan argued that the BIC church should "conscript" youth for service.[150] Numerous didactic anecdotes illustrated spiritual power in time of war:

the power of prayer to deflect bullets; the death of atheism under military fire; and conversions of dying soldiers.[151]

Militarism influenced the Brethren in Christ not only through the press or general mobilization. There were also more direct connections with the military. MCC leaders—including Jesse W. Hoover—worked with General Lewis B. Hershey, the head of the U.S. Selective Service. Dwight D. Eisenhower, supreme commander of Allied forces in Europe, was considered one of the BIC community's kin.[152] Eisenhower was a grandson of Jacob Eisenhower, a BIC minister, and a first cousin of Ray I. Witter, a well-known BIC evangelist and member of the General Conference Peace, Relief, and Service Committee in the 1940s and 1950s. General Eisenhower's kinship parallels much less famous family mosaics that connected nonresistant Brethren in Christ with others in the BIC community who participated in the military. As in the larger Mennonite grouping, an estimated 50 percent of BIC drafted men served in the military.[153]

The evidence of diaries, obituaries, minutes from all levels of church polity, alumni news in school periodicals, and retrospective accounts suggest that most BIC families or communities had relatives or friends connected to the military. Some church members lost members of their immediate or extended families in the war; some lost friends.[154] Some individuals who would later be strong BIC advocates of the peace witness fought in World War II.[155] Some extended families that combined conscientious objectors and men in the military worked together to get through the war years. Ruth Hilsher Hoover, for example, describes being driven by her brother-in-law, in military uniform, to a CPS camp to visit her fiancé, David Hoover.[156] For some BIC members, maintaining a conscientious objection stand brought pain in their families. This was most often true in families in which individuals, usually recent converts, were the only adherents to nonresistance. John S. Kohler of Mansfield, Ohio, describes "verbal abuse" from his immediate family when he participated in Civilian Public Service.[157] But even longtime BIC families felt tension over choices made during the war. One woman who served in Civilian Public Service with her husband remembers, "I had an uncle who was a minister in another denomination, and he was, in a way, the most critical of [us] as anybody, at least, maybe it was just more poignant because it was someone you loved."[158] Some BIC districts officially called for efforts to stay in touch with both conscientious objectors and soldiers.[159] Pennsylvania's Donegal district, for example, published *Donegal Tidings*, a newsletter with items for and about CPS and military men.[160] In 1946, Messiah Bible College's paper noted that the student body welcomed back men from alternative service and from military service both.[161]

Because of this complex mosaic of interconnections, all nonresistant beliefs and practices had to be reformulated, not only within a society mobilized

for war but also within the BIC community itself and within BIC families divided by the war. Consequently, tensions emerged within the Brethren in Christ
as well as between the community and the larger society. Those tensions were
heightened by the fact that nonresistance was seen not simply as an individual
belief; it also was to have a corporate expression. In the coming years, the BIC
community would struggle mightily with knotty questions of individual choice,
group uniformity, and toleration of differences.

The Individual and the Group

Among BIC leaders in the 1940s and 1950s, C. N. Hostetter Jr. was the most
eloquent proponent of the idea that nonresistance was a corporate expression.
In a sermon at the 1943 General Conference, he addressed "meeting today's
crisis" and used the biblical story of Esther, who defied Persian law and "gave
herself in utter self-surrender and saved her nation." In the modern world,
Hostetter argued, "the individual must be willing to surrender his personal
rights for the good of the group."[162] His brother, Henry N. Hostetter, made a
similar point in an evaluation of Civilian Public Service. The corporate nature
of the experiment, he argued, gave the program more impact than if conscientious objection had "remained an individual matter."[163] E. J. Swalm enumerated the costs of maintaining the nonresistant stand, costs that included "the
crucifixion of personal ambitions."[164]

These ideas of church leaders were disseminated in BIC educational programs and magazines. One program in a youth curriculum held up a biblical
character who was quiet and unassuming as the model for overcoming evil
with good in the home, school, neighborhood, and workplace. In another, young
people were urged to consider issues as a group.[165]

Jesse W. Hoover also advocated corporate nonresistance, but he struggled
with the complications of the issue in successive editorials of 1944. Apparently,
he was responding to tensions over attempts to define corporate nonresistance
in 1942 and 1943 General Conference legislation. Hoover noted that in a nation
with religious freedom, all church participation was voluntary. But at the same
time, he rejected "popular church bodies who have no creed but individual
convenience," and he argued that the family and the BIC community had the
right to do all in their power to mold individuals. Equating the right of a voluntary group to protect "corporate purity and unity" with religious intolerance was unfair. Furthermore, "those who plead for unrestricted rights of individual opinion and personal variation within the group are pleading for
anarchy." In other editorials, he argued that group beliefs should be maintained even to the point of "breaking fellowship with recalcitrant persons." He

buttressed this contention by noting in the larger society an "almost overwhelming influence in the rousing of hatred, and such powerful social and patriotic pressure in the direction of militarism."[166] Hoover's clear-eyed analysis pointed out what historians would carefully document half a century later—the joint efforts of military, political, intellectual, and cultural leaders to "sell" the war by presenting "only positive aspects." Michael Adams describes World War II as "one of the most censored events in modern history."[167]

In discussions of the disciplining of individuals who violated the church's stand on military service or military-related work, the intergenerational survival of nonresistance was part of the issue. In order to preserve nonresistance, young people "must make up [their] minds" to be conscientious objectors or not to be. "There is no middle course to follow," Clarence Musser said at a youth conference. But Musser also urged "tolerance toward others."[168] A 1943 editorial by Jesse W. Hoover argued that whenever pacifist groups made adherence to nonresistance optional, the belief declined and eventually disappeared.[169] At Donegal district's special council meeting in 1944 to decide on discipline for BIC members who entered military service, the bishop described how Mennonites in Germany had lost their "non-resistance and peace testimony by compromising in various ways."[170] Historians have since made similar points in studies of religious groups whose traditions of pacifism disappeared.[171]

At the same time that BIC writers defended or advocated the importance of corporate life, they championed the centrality of individuals. The most civilized societies, H. G. Brubaker contended, were those who protected the *"individual human soul."*[172] C. N. Hostetter Jr. listed war's violation of "the sacredness of . . . human personality" as a rationale for nonresistance.[173] Harmon noted that although Americans rejected "collectivism, socialism, and communism" as threats to the individual, they accepted a war machine that also threatened the individual.[174] Many descriptions recognized the supreme importance of conscientious objection as an individual conviction. A selected article put it most bluntly—conscientious objectors emerge not from movements or even "peace sects" but from "an inner conviction."[175] Among BIC youth curricula that often championed the higher good of corporate life, one lesson listed "cooperative collectivism" as a "dangerous substitute" for "conscientious individualism."[176] Faithe Carlson remembered her son spending hours studying the church's stand on nonresistance before coming to his own conclusion.[177] When men in Civilian Public Service were asked if they had chosen alternative service because of personal beliefs or because the BIC church advised the position, 74 percent chose the former and only 21 percent the latter.[178] The concept of "inner personal salvation," sometimes heralded as an antidote to religion as ritual and visible form, increased the centrality of individual authority.[179]

On a complementary issue, C. N. Hostetter Jr. argued that nonresistant people were tolerant. Although they unabashedly pronounced war wrong, they recognized sincere beliefs among people who fought wars.[180] One man evaluated as perhaps "too stern" his congregation's disciplining of a young man who had joined the crew of a commercial shipping company. (Shipping in the war years was associated with delivery of military goods.)[181] Dorothy Sherk remembers E. J. Swalm's contention that as he got older, he let more people into heaven, including those in the military.[182] New contacts in the CPS coalition effort required a sentiment that participants in that program often voiced—a growing appreciation of people with ideas different from one's own.[183] Realism about the lack of uniformity in BIC church practice undoubtedly also informed the appeal to tolerance. In a 1947 *Visitor* article, BIC minister John A. Climenhaga pointed out that the BIC community did not agree on any number of issues, including nonresistance; in an attempt to deal with that intractable reality, he entitled his discussion "Unity in Diversity."[184] Furthermore, the pragmatic goal of keeping and recruiting members affected decisions on the importance of a firm position on nonresistance.

Small-Group Identity

During World War II, the Brethren in Christ wavered between holding their smallness as a badge of virtue and worrying that it reflected poorly on their claim of ideal Christianity.[185] Carlton O. Wittlinger's appraisal of minority status in the last year of World War II argued that neither mass appeal nor minority status conferred righteousness. After all, he noted, national socialism had been a minority group that triumphed.[186]

The issue of size, however, was never simply about attracting outsiders. In America's competitive religious marketplace, the next generation had to be retained.[187] In the 1930s, C. N. Hostetter Jr. had warned that the BIC community's youth required constant attention. Any program designed for them, he argued, must always make clear that they were contributing to the entire community and "that youth's part in that program is not an independent movement apart from the group."[188] In 1946, Wendell E. Harmon likewise argued that the small, scattered BIC community, pressed upon by powerful external forces, would have difficulty maintaining unity, especially among the young. Perhaps a special youth conference would unify young people by showing them that their problems were corporate, not personal. Harmon contended that one group in the community did feel a sense of unity—the men in Civilian Public Service, who had joined in an important corporate effort.[189]

But some Brethren in Christ believed that the community's strict enforcement of corporate life was driving away potential members. One response to the leadership survey argued that in the early part of the twentieth century, the BIC church had lost two generations because it had resisted the institution of Sunday school. The BIC community's rigid dress code of the 1930s was blamed for other departures.[190] Dorothy Sherk still mourns the death of her brother on his last training flight in the Royal Canadian Air Force. Her brother, she explains, along with many other young men, had not become a church member because of its emphasis on small matters, such as proscribing neckties.[191] Although comparisons with "progressive" and Old Order Anabaptist groups in the late twentieth century suggest almost the opposite, the perception of a need to accommodate youth was a powerful engine of change among the Brethren in Christ.[192]

During and after World War II, the identity of the small community was challenged in yet another way as the Brethren in Christ joined with much larger groups to fund and administer new institutionalized expressions of the peace witness. At the beginning of the war, in reports on his attendance at Mennonite and other peace group meetings, H. G. Brubaker repeatedly referred to *four* Historic Peace Churches, giving the Brethren in Christ the same stature as the three other bodies.[193] But others increasingly identified the BIC community as Mennonite. Leaders of the tiny community worried about and searched for ways to maintain a separate identity. The correspondence of the BIC Peace, Relief, and Service Committee makes this clear—BIC candidates volunteering for the Mennonite Central Committee were to be authorized by the BIC committee before being considered by MCC.[194] The BIC concern was not groundless. In Elsie Bechtel's diary and letters home from her relief work in France, she always referred to herself as Mennonite, never as Brethren in Christ. Miriam Bowers also did not remember thinking of herself as Brethren in Christ during her relief work.[195]

In the 1940s and 1950s, the Brethren in Christ struggled to define nonresistance in ways that adequately responded to a world at war and to a larger society that continually impinged on their small community. At the same time, these emerging definitions had to confront internal community conflicts and divergent expectations. The resulting formulations of nonresistance were sometimes inconsonant and seldom without discord. Yet they were also creative and powerful enough to inspire women, men, youth, and children to take dissenting public positions in a society mobilized for war.

CHAPTER THREE

Nonresistance and Home Front Life

❦

Citizens could have differing convictions and yet be worthy citizens.

War hysteria was high in Canada during World War II. Everyone over 16 years of age was required to register on a certain day in August, 1940. It so happened that I was travelling through the BIC churches in Ontario with our Ladies' Quartet from Ontario Bible School.

That day we were in the Houghton, Ontario area. . . . Germany was our "enemy." Swalm (formerly Schwalm) is a German name and I wasn't sure what this registration was for. I was very apprehensive since I was away from home and my parents. Of course, my worst fears were unfounded.

Lela Swalm Hostetler
Duntroon, Ontario

We were walking toward the house upon our return from a Sunday afternoon wedding. Cousins Milton and Laban Byers were hurrying toward the barn for evening chores, but they stopped to share the news about the bombing of Pearl Harbor. . . . The hope of peace for the world seemed to explode around us—life would never be quite the same again!

Alice Grace Hostetter Zercher
Washington Boro, Pennsylvania

Perhaps we all remember where we were when we first heard of the bombing of Pearl Harbor. As I recall, I was on my way home from having given a program with a male quartet I sang with for a few years. . . . I heard the news on the car radio just I turned into the lane at home, I said to myself, *This will probably have a radical impact on my life.*

Ray M. Zercher

Mount Joy, Pennsylvania

I was hired, as a teacher, for my first job, I told the superintendent, who was interviewing me, and teachers were very hard to get then, that my husband was a conscientious objector and he was scared to death to hire me. And then he said, "Don't ever say anything about that, please. . . . If one of my board members would find that out, I would be in a lot of trouble." So, you know, it wasn't a good feeling. . . . [Y]ou know, those were times . . . when everybody was having their own scary times.

Frances Harmon

Upland, California

During World War II, the Brethren in Christ shared many experiences in common with millions of other North Americans. A sense that the world had irrevocably changed, mobility, overwork, scarcity of time, intrusion of public concerns on private life, and an intense desire to be reunited with loved ones connected peace and war efforts. Stories of real courage, sacrifice, and loss that the war entailed are enshrined in family stories and popular conceptions across North America.

However, some people who lived through the war, as well as scholars with a skeptical bent, have labored to convey less savory aspects of the war years. Veteran and scholar Paul Fussell suggests that World War II, like the Great War, was a battle of machines, media, and mediocrity against humanity—a battle that humanity lost. The consensus in America, according to historian John M. Blum, was to win the war as quickly as possible while sustaining a booming economy. Although in many ways the Brethren in Christ remained "different from people who supported war," any resulting hardships pale in relation to the intolerance and violence visited on racial minorities when their presence and aspirations were not conducive to the prosecution of a pragmatic, materialistic war.[1]

The Brethren in Christ who wrote on nonresistance in the 1940s and 1950s did so not in isolation but in response to this larger world. World War II in particular brought the weight of world events into the daily lives of ordinary women, men, youth, and children in the BIC community. From day to day, these community members defined nonresistance not only in words or in intellectual formulations but also as practical responses to the war economy, government programs, coworkers, neighbors, and classmates.

What were these nonresistant responses on the home front? The picture that emerges from contemporary articles in BIC magazines, correspondence, and especially memories recorded in writing and recalled in oral interviews is of a BIC community that was neither unified nor neatly bounded.[2] Different people made different choices about how to respond to the war. Often, however, the peace witness elicited discipline and commitment from adults and children, who took lonely stands in their attempts to translate nonresistance into the consistent daily practice for which many yearned.

Even before war began, members of the BIC community paid attention to events in Europe. Looking back, individuals who were in their teens to mid-twenties during the war remember their fear of Adolf Hitler's rising star in the 1930s as a defining experience.[3] Writers in the *Visitor* consistently condemned Germany's national socialism. The Brethren in Christ, like other groups interested in biblical prophecy, worried that Hitler was the Antichrist.[4] The fervor of the German people, however, appealed to some. One member of a missionary family, returning home through Germany in 1938, noted the activity and enthusiasm of that nation's youth. He suggested that the BIC community emulate German loyalty while substituting God for Hitler.[5] But when the war began, the BIC community found little cause for rejoicing. In mid-1940, Bishop O. B. Ulery of Ohio wrote, "Relief efforts seem so futile beside the terrific destruction." He added, "It just seems the whole world, political, industrial and religious is so confused and filled with strife, that it is difficult to make any plans for permanence."[6]

Canada joined the war more than two years before the Americans did, but the Japanese bombing of Pearl Harbor in December 1941 made the war seem closer to people in both nations.[7] Contemporary records and individual memories show that in both nations public affairs intruded on private. Life in general picked up tempo.[8] Food and gas rationing, the effective end of unemployment, scarce consumer goods, air raid drills, and travel restrictions affected rural and urban members of the BIC church alike.[9] Although some recollect that rationing did not have a major impact on farming people, others point to the difficulties it posed in obtaining farm labor, feeding harvest crews, or obtaining farm machinery.[10] Food rationing created shortages in BIC benevolent institutions.[11] Gas rationing sometimes lowered revival meeting attendance and affected other BIC gatherings, notwithstanding, as Jesse W. Hoover noted, the benefits to church life of more walking and less driving.[12] From 1943 to 1945, government regulations restricted attendance at General Conferences to delegates and church officials.[13] Numerous missionaries either could not return home on furlough or could not travel to international mission assignments.[14] Conscription drew men from the BIC community into Civilian Public Service

(CPS), the military, or essential farm labor. Consequently, the percentage of young women in BIC schools grew.[15] Male students below draft age competed to see who could hitchhike the farthest on school breaks; female students, without "the right characteristics to hitch-hike, just didn't go home."[16]

The absence of young men was even more marked in the workplace, especially in factories.[17] BIC women, like women across the nation, assumed the tasks men left behind. In mid-1941, John M. Wolgemuth became the first conscientious objector from Lancaster County, Pennsylvania, to leave for a CPS camp. He worried about who would run his thousand-chicken poultry farm. His answer was that his sister Rhoda, with the help of a young neighbor boy, "could do the job well."[18] Jeanette Frey Dourte, whose fiancé was in alternative service, helped another BIC woman operate her brother's dairy herd-improvement business when he left for military service. Betty Grove ran the family ice and coal delivery business while her husband was in Civilian Public Service.[19] Many other women carried on farm work while men in the family were gone.[20]

The effects of the war quickly entered homes as well as the workplace. Mary Olive Lady and Morris Sherk, both schoolchildren when the war began, remember that the war years launched their interest in reading newspapers and following world events.[21] For some, the military presence was next door. Lady and her sister Martha lived near Fort Riley, Kansas. Brothers E. Morris and Harvey Sider lived near an Ontario military airfield.[22] Looking back, BIC people remember keenly the deaths of high school classmates and neighbors who went to war.[23] The death of a loved one in the military touched BIC families as well.[24]

The war also brought racism and xenophobia into the open. Two women in California, as well as Clara Meyer Eberly in Grantham, Pennsylvania, recall hatred of Japanese American neighbors.[25] Clarence H. Sakimura, who became a BIC conscientious objector after the war, saw his parents lose their flower shop and truck farm in Gardena, California. They became family number 5,314 in the internment of 112,000 Japanese Americans.[26]

Although members of the BIC community shared certain experiences in the war years with other Americans, their nonresistant stance quickly set them apart. Beulah Heisey, who was fifteen in 1941 and lived at a distance from other nonresistant people, remembers the war years in Centre County, Pennsylvania: "I felt it to be lone[l]y to walk this different lifestyle."[27] Judson Hill of Wheeler, Michigan, spent over four years in Civilian Public Service. For him, "it was a time of being watched where ever I went & what ever I did."[28] Writing for the *Sunday School Herald* in 1944, Donald Engle, also in alternative serve, described feeling shaken when he had to head a line of conscientious objectors—young men not in military uniform—as they walked though a train from their coach to the dining car.[29]

Other Brethren in Christ found the war years difficult but exciting. Geraldine M. Wenger, who took her brother's clerking job for the Pennsylvania Railroad when he left for Civilian Public Service, says that her most vivid memory of the war years "centered around my twin brother who was drafted as a conscientious objector. It was hard for me to see him go to camp. It was the first time in our lives that we were really separated by any distance and for an unknown length of time. But I was proud of him for the stand he took."[30]

Wenger's new job and her admiration of her brother illustrate how the war mobilization intertwined with nonresistant support for Civilian Public Service, creating an alternative culture in the war years. The Brethren in Christ mounted their own efforts, borrowed ideas from the bigger Historic Peace Church coalition, and increasingly wove their efforts into those of the Mennonite Central Committee.[31] The significant contributions made by ordinary BIC women, men, and youth, however, were most often organized in district settings: they wrote letters and visited alternative service camps; they devised district quota systems to fund the program and to contribute monetarily to relief work; and they contributed food, clothing, and live animals for relief efforts in war areas. Married women joined their husbands in CPS work, particularly in state hospitals. Young men and women volunteered for a variety of newly emerging volunteer service programs.

Despite an increased focus on nonresistance in BIC church magazines during World War II, some war-related issues were given scant coverage. For example, the farm economy, though central to BIC community life, received less attention than it had during World War I. Discussion of wartime agricultural profits was virtually absent. A 1942 official Mennonite Central Committee (MCC) statement condemned profiteering but used industrial gains as its example. Minutes from the Pennsylvania BIC state council commended the contribution of profits to denominational institutions.[32] Similarly, few people wrote about flag veneration as a problem for nonresistant people.[33]

The issue of war bonds, on the other hand, which had proved so problematic in the previous war, received attention early in World War II. In 1941, the BIC Peace, Relief, and Service Committee issued certificates recognizing contributions to alternative programs.[34] This gesture, intended as a substitute for war bonds, did not simplify matters for the BIC community. Correspondence in 1942 noted that in some areas, especially Ohio and Indiana, coworkers pressured Brethren in Christ to buy bonds. Dorothy Meyer Baldwin, who worked in a garment factory in Chambersburg, Pennsylvania, remembers being asked why she would not buy war bonds.[35] In mid-1942, the MCC executive secretary, Orie Miller, pushed the organization to create government-approved civilian bonds that would fund relief work.[36] The *Visitor* announced the "Civilian Bond

No. 2439

CERTIFICATE

$5.00

Relief and Service Committee of the Brethren in Christ Church

2001 Paxton Street
HARRISBURG, PENNSYLVANIA

This Certifies that Miss Mary E. Heisey

has contributed the within stated sum to the Brethren in Christ Church to be used in Civilian Public Service, in relieving suffering, in creating good will and in making Christ known as Prince of Peace.

CONTRIBUTOR'S STATEMENT OF PURPOSE

This contribution, made in addition to my normal giving, is in consideration of tragic world need, of the sacrifice of life and money which many are making in war and of my desire to support constructive service to humanity. This contribution is intended as an *alternate service* to war, in which my conscience does not permit me to engage. I give it voluntarily, asking neither interest nor return of principal.

....
Signature

In witness whereof the Relief and Service Committe of the Brethren in Christ Church issues this certificate

on this ..15th.. day of ..Feb...A. D. 1943....

....
Signature of Local Relief and Service Agent

....
Signature of Relief and Service Committee Treas.

Certificate issued by the BIC Peace, Relief, and Service Committee to recognize contributions from nonresistant people during World War II

Purchase Plan" in July of that year.[37] In December, a Beulah College periodical urged nonresistant people to buy these civilian bonds before being pressured to do so.[38] Canadians had also worked out a government-authorized program of "non-interest bearing certificates."[39]

Civil defense programs and the Red Cross proved thornier problems for the BIC community. Such programs were less amenable to alternatives than were war bonds and therefore elicited more diverse responses from the BIC community. In 1942, at the request of the Pennsylvania Department of Education, Messiah Bible College joined the village of Grantham in instituting a civil defense plan. Apparently, the BIC community there felt it could participate while adhering to the "philosophy of Love."[40] Meanwhile, in Kansas, Mary Olive Lady's father was in charge of enforcing blackouts during air raid drills. She remembers that he felt uncomfortable in this civil defense position but participated anyway.[41] In 1942, Jesse W. Hoover reported the formation of Church Service Units and urged more groups to define their own emergency service plans, not under the aegis of the nation's civil defense program.[42] In the same year, about forty women connected to Messiah Bible College sewed for the Red Cross.[43] By 1943, Canadian conscientious objectors on farms and in industries in the Alternative Service Work program contributed a certain amount of their earnings to the Red Cross.[44] But a year earlier, one Pennsylvania BIC district had promoted the civilian bond system as a response to war bonds and Red Cross contributions.[45] Evaluations of the Red Cross's connection to military efforts differed. Its relief efforts, like those of the United Nations Relief and Rehabilitation Administration (and even those of pacifist groups), often required close cooperation with military forces.[46]

In the workplace, both women and men faced questions about the nature of nonresistance. A 1943 General Conference ruling on war work prohibited participation in the manufacture of war materiel.[47] Additional sources show that people were aware that the war effort touched many other areas of work as well. An article in the *Visitor* noted, "Our corn and wheat—the clothing we produce—the taxes we pay—the natural resources we preserve—all contribute to the war effort."[48]

In 1939, Ontario's Wainfleet BIC district petitioned the Canadian Nonresistant Committee to issue statements in seven areas, including growing food "expressly for the supply of military men" and working on the construction of airports to be used by the military.[49] No response to these comprehensive occupational questions is on record. After the war, one man who had served in Civilian Public Service likened Brethren in Christ, "who drove large machinery to build air ports and camps, and some who worked in strict defense work," to those who had done military service. Such work stood in contrast to his own commitments, expressed in alternative service. But then he equivocated—both military service and war work should be left "in the hands of God."[50] Individuals, however, had to make occupational decisions here and now.

Only a few nurses, almost all of them women, remember mobilization pressures in school or the workplace. Irene Wagaman Engle recalls that all of her classmates in nurse's training were in the "Cadet Nurse Corps," a program that included tuition remission by the federal government. Engle's parents did not permit her to participate, instead covering her costs themselves. Martha Lady, who worked on a master's degree in nursing in Cleveland between 1949 and 1952 and then trained as a midwife in Kentucky, recalls much talk about the drafting of nurses. She decided that she would not participate in the military. She does not, however, remember the BIC church addressing the question.[51] Clara Meyer Eberly, who became a nurse and midwife during roughly the same years, also remembers coworkers going into military service.[52]

In fact, substantial concern surfaced in the BIC community about the connection of nurses to the military. As early as 1939, the Ontario Joint Council adopted a recommendation to draw up rosters of men ages eighteen to forty-one and of all BIC nurses and women in nurse's training.[53] Apparently, the council was concerned that nurses might be conscripted. In 1941, the *Visitor* reprinted an article from the Mennonite *Goshen College Record* urging women—"nurses, teachers, homemakers or secretaries"—to strengthen their nonresistant commitments. The author argued that although much nonresistant teaching focused on men, "we of the opposite sex need a little attention also." Drawing on a *Pacifist Handbook,* the article predicted, correctly, an increase in the number of women serving as nurses or in other noncombatant roles in the military. Female conscientious objectors would "suffer most at the hands of their sisters. Theirs will be the task of withstanding the emotional hysteria which hides so many of the more subtle horrors of war."[54]

In 1942, O. B. Ulery wrote to Orie Miller of Mennonite Central Committee that BIC nurses were being pressured to fill out Red Cross forms pledging military service if called. Ulery, who had encouraged nurses not to sign the forms, reported that those in nurse's training were being told that they could not graduate without doing so. Miller had not heard of this problem but passed the letter on to "Brother Jesse" [Hoover].[55] A 1943 Peace, Relief, and Service Committee report noted the "likelihood of some measure of conscription of women." The next year, this BIC committee described the War Manpower Commission's institution of a nurse classification system. The commission told the National Service Board for Religious Objectors, the largest pacifist coalition negotiating with the national government throughout the war, that the program was a voluntary one. But the form for nurses did not make that clear.[56] In her 1945 diary, Anna

Lane Hostetter noted the possibility that nurses might be drafted. She recorded that she and her husband, C. N. Hostetter Jr. met with a gathering of the Mennonite Nurses Association, which included about fourteen of "our girls."[57] The founders of the association, as well as its constitution, explicitly tied its purpose to conscientious objection.[58] In a 1944 editorial on women in the military, Jesse W. Hoover focused on the nursing profession. Insisting that nurses in the military should never expect simply to do medical work, he reminded readers that these nurses had to take an oath to follow military commands. In addition, he pointed to "the degeneracy and immorality and debauchery" of the military, revisiting World War I themes that tied war to sexual immorality.[59]

Men in medical school faced similar problems, which were exacerbated by conscription. James Alderfer, studying medicine in 1942, wrote to H. G. Brubaker, of the Peace, Relief, and Service Committee, about selective service requirements. Medical students had been instructed "to apply for a commission in the Medical Administrative Corps." If they did not, they would be conscripted for active duty. A lawyer from a "Friends Church" had advised him as a conscientious objector not to apply for the commission, but Alderfer needed additional advice on how to proceed. He also asked whether Brubaker knew of a way to be exempted from taking a required military service course. Brubaker's answers, if available, would be instructive. Alderfer eventually served in the military medical corps and today retrospectively expresses no conflict between conscientious objection and medical work in the military—an important dividing line in the BIC community.[60]

BIC medical students who did refuse all participation in the military faced discrimination for their conscientious-objector stand. A dean of Temple Medical School in Philadelphia indicated that he would not have accepted Harold Engle as a student had he known Engle was a conscientious objector. After completing medical school and residency, Engle practiced medicine in Palmyra, Pennsylvania. From 1945 to 1968, the medical director of a hospital in nearby Hershey did not permit Engle to refer patients to the hospital, apparently because of Engle's conscientious-objector position. The prohibition did not seem to affect Engle's practice adversely, however, and a new director in 1968 brought Engle to the hospital, where he eventually became chief of staff.[61] Alvan Thuma, another BIC member, was accepted as a medical student at Hahneman Medical College in Philadelphia in 1944. Hahneman was known as one of the few medical schools that would accept candidates not willing to join the military.[62]

A variety of other jobs also raised concerns, and some Brethren in Christ paid an economic price for eschewing work connected to the military. O. B. Ulery had bought a tool-and-die business just before World War II. When he refused to take a government contract producing war material, the government reportedly closed his business.[63] Charlie B. Byers, bishop in Pennsylvania's North Franklin district, supported himself by working in another member's lumber mill. In 1943, Byers left the mill and set up his own cabinet-making business, in part to have more flexibility in his work schedule but also because the mill had begun producing war-related products.[64] The range of decisions the BIC community made is also evident in the example of Raymond Hess of Souderton, Pennsylvania. He chose to leave a factory job upon realizing that all of the work of the firm came from military contracts. He moved to his father-in-law's peanut butter and cheese factory. Hess's former position, however, was filled by the son of a BIC bishop.[65]

For men, avoiding war work was also closely connected to the issue of conscription. Draft board members might question the consistency of men who requested conscientious-objector status if they had already worked producing war material.[66] When a BIC man working for the Pennsylvania Railroad heard that the railroad might be classified as a defense industry, he sought advice, offering to resign immediately if his work would jeopardize his draft status. In response, Orie Miller of Mennonite Central Committee suggested that only workplaces in which the entire product went directly to the war effort posed problems with draft boards.[67] The far-reaching impact of mobilization certainly must have influenced Miller's interpretation, as more and more of the economy became part of the war effort. The 1943 General Conference ruling on war work ignored many areas that government leaders themselves undoubtedly saw as key to war mobilization. Most prominent among the occupations ignored was the "essential service" of agriculture, in favor of which many draft boards deferred conscientious objectors.[67]

Certainly, the BIC church's uncertain voice regarding the military connections of agriculture influenced the decisions of community members who participated in other jobs connected to mobilization. Church records and announcements in church school periodicals show that many BIC people chose work connected to the war effort. For example, Pennsylvania's Grantham district reported that some members violated the church standards on war work.[69] As noted in the previous chapter, BIC leaders in the Wainfleet, Ontario, district took the unusual step of blaming themselves for the lapses of those in their district who participated in war work.[70] In 1943, Benjamin G. Lenhert left his job as Beulah College business manager when his draft board authorized as war related his work as a chemical engineer in the Kaiser Company.[71] Several Messiah Bible College alumni, both women and men, worked in a nearby naval supply depot.[72] Not all of these individuals were official BIC church members. But their mention in these sources makes it clear that individuals within the BIC community were working openly in war-related businesses.

Retrospective accounts reveal similar instances of such participation. One questionnaire respondent described his work as packing "ration bars" in the Hershey chocolate factory for the military.[73] E. Morris Sider remembers one member from his BIC congregation working in an air force facility. Sider describes the individual as a "fringe" member; he was disfellowshiped for his war work but later made a public confession and was reinstated.[74] In Dayton, Ohio, Paul S. Boyer's parents rented rooms to eight young Mennonite women who had moved to that city to work as secretaries at Wright-Patterson Air Force Base. Thus even his parents benefited economically, if indirectly, from the war.[75] People also remember that these job choices sometimes caused confusion in the minds of both BIC people and their neighbors. One woman wrote that her neighbors "could not understand . . . nor could I reconcile those who worked in defense related jobs as civilians and criticized those who joined the military service."[76] Grace French remembers that two longtime members of her Michigan BIC congregation moved during the war to work in "an airplane factory" and returned after the war ended to "raised eyebrows and skepticism, but . . . no especial fuss."[77]

But although some in the BIC community accommodated themselves to the war economy, others would brook no compromise. Michigan factories provided some of the most dramatic examples of industrial workers expressing nonresistant stands on the shop floor. A "Brother Montgomery" struggled with his foreman and superintendent, first over the issue of working on Sundays and then over war bonds. Montgomery offered to buy civilian bonds. When, however, his superiors checked with a city official connected to the War Department, they were informed that no such bonds existed. Montgomery, not easily defeated, brought a copy of the *Visitor* to prove that civilian bonds were indeed available.

> They tried to defeat me in my stand for God and right. They asked me the following question: "What do you believe is the cause of this? and also these wicked conditions?" . . . I just pointed him to the little write-up in the *Visitor*. So for several days they studied my case. They wrote to Chicago and to Philadelphia and New York, to different departments of the government. And this is what they said. "We have a fellow here who is a conscientious objector. He won't work Sundays, he won't buy Bonds. But he said he would buy Civilian Bonds. If you can help us, let us know."

Montgomery won his case, only to have the plant turn to "full war production." He promptly quit the job and took one that paid twenty-five cents less per hour. "I can't see how any one can work in a war plant and claim to be a non-resistant Christian. I trust not one member of the Brethren in Christ Church will drift with the world, being deceived to believe it is alright to make war material." Rather than do that, Montgomery would "live in the rocks eating grass in the summer and dry leaves in the winter." Family responsibilities or tenure on a job should not take priority, since *"the just shall live by faith."*[78]

Another example involved BIC community member George Bundy of Leonard, Michigan. Bundy had received an agricultural deferment during World War II. In 1948, however, Local Board 25 in Flint, Michigan, refused his request for conscientious-objector status. For the next three years Bundy made repeated appeals to have that decision changed, aided by BIC leader Harry Hock, "a big guy with a big voice." Meanwhile, Bundy got a job at Plymouth Motor Company placing "a chrome piece on front fenders." When the Korean War began, military vehicles occasionally came through the production line. Bundy simply ignored those vehicles. "They came looking for the person who wasn't doing his job. And they found me." Taking him by the arm, someone marched him to the office "and gave me a piece of paper and said that I refused to work related to war. And I was out of a job."[79]

That piece of paper played a key role in Bundy's extended struggle to receive selective service classification as a conscientious objector. In his final appeal, Bundy showed the Plymouth termination notice to an army colonel in East Lansing. The colonel made one call to the Flint draft board, instructing its members that "these are the kind of people that should be deferred because they believe or practice what they believe."[80]

George Bundy's younger brothers benefited from his struggle; the Flint draft board subsequently classified them as conscientious objectors without debate. Bundy remembers that other people in his hometown of Leonard saw his family as peculiar, as did the Federal Bureau of Investigation in a report on the family, mentioning an "odd" mother. Ethel Heisey Bundy notes that her husband's family was accustomed to ridicule that she, being from the BIC community's Pennsylvania heartland, would have found hard to endure. George simply says, "Once you make up your mind, it doesn't matter what people say."[81]

Nonresistance and Organized Labor

In the workplace, nonresistant stands against war production and military service sometimes converged with refusal to participate in organized labor. At midcentury, nonresistant groups used several rationales for their objections to organized labor. In part, they objected because unions used coercion in disputes with management, which, their argument contended, often led to violence. In addition, the argument went, nonconformity required separation from worldly organizations.[82]

George Bundy's experiences as a wage laborer in a laundry illustrate how the BIC community handled the problem. BIC leader Harry Hock once again helped Bundy, this time by negotiating an agreement with the Laundry and Linen Drivers' Union, which was affiliated with the Teamsters Union. The agreement exempted Bundy from attending union meetings and from participating in picket duty on the grounds of his membership in "the religious sect of Brethren in Christ."[83] The "Brother Montgomery" mentioned earlier, who quit his factory job when the plant converted to war production, faced the issue of union participation in his new job. A "Brother and Sister Lewis" worked out a way for him to be excused from union membership. Two BIC community women who worked in a meat plant were similarly excused. In the 1940s, the Brethren in Christ joined with the Mennonites in testimony at a Senate hearing and in extensive negotiations with labor leaders to exempt nonresistant people from participation in union activity.[84] These negotiations parallel those between peace church leaders and government officials regarding conscientious objection to military service.[85] In both cases, nonresistant leaders attempted to convey their beliefs to other groups in society and then to negotiate alternative structures agreeable to all parties.

Clarence W. Boyer, secretary of the BIC Industrial Relations Committee from its inception in 1939 through 1954, worked closely with Guy F. Hershberger, a key Mennonite scholar and administrator who articulated a nonresistant position on labor unions.[86] Bishop O. B. Ulery, another member of the BIC Industrial Relations Committee, also addressed labor issues in Ohio-Kentucky Joint Council meetings.[87] In 1940, Ulery and a Mennonite bishop testified at a Senate hearing on the Wagner Act. They argued for an amendment that would recognize workers trying to apply "non-resistance in the industrial strife of today."[88] Five years later, Hershberger renewed the push for such legislative recognition.[89] It was never attained.

Concessions to nonresistant wage laborers found more success in extended, careful negotiations with local and national labor leaders. Between 1939 and 1954, Hershberger, Boyer, and others carried on negotiations with Teamsters locals, the carpenters and joiners union, the United Packinghouse Workers, the United Auto Workers, the Amalgamated Clothing Workers of America, the American Federation of Hosiery Workers, the International Molders and Foundry Workers Union, the Bakery and Confectioner's International Union, and the Laundry Workers, as well as with national leaders of the American Federation of Labor and the Congress of Industrial Workers.[90] In a number of cases, Boyer suggested extending the services of these Mennonite and BIC efforts to smaller groups associated with the Brethren in Christ; he raised the possibility that others, such as Seventh-Day Adventists, might also be interested in participation.[91]

Correspondence between Boyer and Hershberger concerning their contacts with organized labor document the factory employment of BIC women and men across the United States. The correspondence mentions a BIC man working in an Elkhart, Indiana, packing company; a Buffalo, New York, man involved with the Teamsters in his bakery job; women in garment factories in Shippensburg and Chambersburg, Pennsylvania; an unidentified individual in Detroit; and a number of Brethren in Christ working in Hershey, Pennsylvania, food industries. At one point Hershberger asked Boyer to check out the claim of a Bakery and Confectioner's International Union official that three hundred Mennonites and Brethren in Christ were union members, some even officials.[92]

Overall, these frank letters also show that both men were often struck by the respectful treatment they received, especially from national labor leaders. Sending a copy of his 1946 General Conference report to Hershberger, Boyer worried, "I have been a bit uneasy lest I may have given the impression of being too militantly 'pro-labor,'" a very unlikely danger in a group that, although abjuring force, always allowed much more leeway to the state than to any other sector of society.[93] But both Boyer and Hershberger apparently recognized the validity of one union official's request that nonresistant parties "go on record somewhere saying that we believe in social justice, etc."[94]

Most union agreements exempted nonresistant workers from membership meetings and other organized activities but required them to donate an amount comparable to union dues to a mutually agreed-upon charitable organization.[95] The agreements also required nonresistant workers to stay off the job during strikes.[96] Between 1943 and 1945, the Industrial Relations Committee reported to General Conference that it had dealt with fewer labor cases, either because labor shortages had lessened union pressure or, more often, church members had left jobs associated with war work. In 1943, the committee recorded its refusal to help individuals "who were engaged in war work" and "had already compromised their position." In another case in that same year, a woman employed in a business that took on war-related contracts voiced her opposition to both those contracts and to union membership. Her job security was in question, but at the time of the General Conference report she still had the job and had been transferred into a part of the business that handled only civilian production.[97]

NONRESISTANCE AND CHILDREN

If General Conference and district-level committees concerned themselves with factory workers, nurses, and conscripted men, they paid much less attention to the children of the BIC community. Yet war mobilization and growing militarism invaded children's dreams, play, and especially their world in the public schools. Like many other American children, those in nonresistant families re-member fearing Adolf Hitler and air raid drills.[98] Gerald N. Wingert, ten years old when Hitler conquered Poland, remembers being "truly frightened by the rapid conquest." He wondered "if the war would reach our country. There were times I could not sleep but I did not discuss this with my parents. The kids in school talked a lot about the war and I remember . . . telling a boy to quit talking about it." Newscaster Lowell Thomas's radio voice "did little to comfort me," says Wingert; that of Gabriel Heaters was so frightening that Wingert refused to lis-ten to him. Yet Wingert once tried to impress other schoolchildren by bragging that Ray I. Witter, a BIC evangelist preaching in Wingert's home congregation, was Dwight Eisenhower's first cousin.[99]

Other men remember childhood fear tinged with excitement, often over military hardware.[100] Canadian Lester Fretz, age seven when Canada joined the war, "developed a fascination for geography" as he watched military fronts move across school maps. In Sunday school, he traded cards with pictures of warplanes and ships. When a hired man whom he "adored" appeared in uni-form, Fretz was thrilled. E. Morris Sider, four years older than Fretz, also found the war exciting, especially the aerobatics of planes at a base near his home in Cheapside, Ontario. He and friends carved wooden guns to play war games. Excelling in schoolwork sometimes led him to daydream, "If I was in the army, I would be a general." However, Sider pressed his father for stories about being a World War I conscientious objector. Similarly Fretz, the same boy who ad-mired men in uniform, also found conscientious objectors heroic. One of his heroes was Ross Nigh, a conscientious objector who left home for the Alterna-tive Service Work program in British Columbia.[101]

As boys, both Sider and Fretz got into schoolyard fights in connection with their religious affiliation. One older boy, knowing Sider was not supposed to fight back, would repeatedly "throw me down and punch and pummel me." One day when Sider's older sister was no longer at school and therefore unable to report to their parents, Sider fought back. That ended the bullying. Fretz remembers fighting two peers who later became his friends. Both Sider and Fretz reported these stories as failures of childhood nonresistance. Neverthe-less, they saw their families' strong nonresistant stands as shaping and eventu-ally enveloping their own normal childhood aggression.[102] Other BIC commu-nity members also recall parental prohibitions on fighting or playing with guns.[103] Several writers during the war years worried about the effect of toys associated with violence.[104]

Public school provided a focal point of concern about the general glorifica-tion of the military. Walter Winger, despite his family's nonresistance, never accepted it himself. He later pointed to an experience in a one-room Ontario schoolhouse, an experience that contested the biblical rationale of nonresistance. The fiancé of a well-loved teacher came to the school in his military uniform and, to the delight of the students, embraced the teacher in farewell. That event and the man's subsequent death while in the military became an important image in Winger's mind, although other factors also influenced his rejection of nonresistance.[105]

Government-sponsored drives to enlist the American public in the war effort were pervasive. Even in elementary school, children felt pressure to contribute to war-materiel drives or to buy war bonds.[106] Myron Mann, who grew up in a small town near Dayton, Ohio, remembers being castigated for his lack of interest in a war-bond prize at school. J. Norman Hostetter, a child during the war in a BIC mission church in Clarence Center, New York, vividly remembers his promilitary Roman Catholic neighbors and his own embarrassment that his BIC family did not buy war bonds. Lester Fretz remembers buying war stamps, geared to children, on the sly. Paul S. Boyer once contributed a pencil stub to a material drive. Overwhelmed by guilt, he tried to retrieve it and thereby earned the epithet "Indian giver" from his teacher. Benjamin W. Myers also secretly gave to material drives in Mechanicsburg, Pennsylvania, but later confessed the infraction to his mother. His parents did allow him to contribute milkweed pods, which were supposedly used in the production of parachutes. His parents described these as life saving—"probably a rationalization to help me feel a part of my peers," says Myers.[107]

Gerald N. Wingert kept one of his school experiences secret from his parents. Wingert was in sixth grade in 1940 and 1941, years when an increasing number of men faced the draft. He remembers,

> There was a sizable group of Mennonites and Brethren in Christ in our school district. We were being excused one day for the afternoon recess and as we congregated around the door, to rush out the moment the teacher opened it, some gentle pushing started behind me. To keep from being over balanced in close quarters, I reached out and put my hand on the student ahead of me. In that moment the teacher told me to leave the group and go to my seat. I immediately responded by respectfully saying, (so I thought) "I wasn't pushing, Dick was pushing me." Before I had time [to] "blink [an] eye" she reached through several students standing in front of me and soundly slapped me on the mouth. Needless to say I was greatly humiliated as I took my seat. After the rest of the group went out to play, the teacher came to me and gave me a brief lecture. I wish I could recall the full text but all I can remember [is] that she spoke about me belonging to a group of people who will not defend their country. Sometime later I came to realize

that she did not slap me for what I said but it was an opportunity to express her displeasure regarding the peace group to which I belonged. Also her boyfriend had been drafted.[108]

The proselytizing fervor of other BIC children sometimes matched that of their parents. Paul Boyer, seven years old in 1942, tried to persuade a friend on biblical grounds that war was wrong and that Hitler should be loved. His friend responded with an angry shove. Boyer went back to his mother for additional biblical authority. Boyer recalls a compromise—although Hitler's soul should be loved, his body could be hated.[109] A didactic report in the records of the Ohio-Kentucky 1943 Joint Council annual meeting, the jurisdiction in which Boyer's family lived, described childhood fervor: "A boy of our faith when asked by his teacher if he hated the Japs said, 'No.' He was ridiculed by his class mates. The teacher said, 'What would you do if Hitler came over?' He replied, 'I'd leave him to Jesus to handle.' How good for this Elementary Youth."[110]

Nonresistance and Youth

In the late nineteenth century, the BIC community had begun to devote increasing attention to programs and literature geared specifically to children and youth.[111] But the attention of BIC leaders from 1939 to 1958 focused mostly on older youth. The report on the elementary child just quoted concluded with the assertion, "In High School according to many the need is even greater for Christian witness."[112] Responses to the leadership survey, however, still pointed to the BIC community's failure to understand and support youth adequately.[113] Interwar correspondence among members of the Board for Young People's Work also shows concern over how to present BIC beliefs to youth. One letter, for example, urged a curriculum writer to present youth topics "in a suggestive thought provoking manner rather than [as] a simple statement of facts." Others worried that BIC literature would not appeal to youth, because it was dull and overly serious.[114] By 1939, the *Sunday School Herald* had a special page devoted to youth, with many articles written by BIC young people themselves. Those articles included descriptions of youth gatherings across the country. Youth programs were also part of larger annual gatherings. Some of these programs included nonresistant teaching and opportunities to contribute to relief efforts.[115]

C. N. Hostetter argued that young people should see themselves not as members of a distinct sector of the BIC community but as contributors to the whole. But some sources suggest that youth were less sure that a commonality of effort existed.[116] At both the beginning and end of the 1940s, students at Messiah Bible College started newspapers for "students alone."[117] Adult calls for discipline, responsibility, and growth perhaps reflected concerns about the younger generation. For example, a 1942 message to the Young People's Societies urged them to raise funds for medical work in India and more generally to "bear responsibility."[118] A youth group curriculum entitled "Achieving Success" described that goal in terms of gradual development, diligence, persistence "year after year," and faithfulness that negated the need for "outward recognition."[119] These emphases in contemporary records support Ruth Herr Pawelski's recollection that BIC community life urged young people "toward maturity," as well as Ray M. Zercher's retrospective view that on the farm and in the church, "childhood was regarded as a stage to be shed in favor of practical utility."[120]

On the other hand, BIC leaders could accommodate waywardness, at least by young men. Joel Climenhaga was the son of a BIC minister but not a participating church member himself. He described being cared for by the family of a BIC bishop after he was assaulted while hitchhiking through Kansas in 1949; Anna Engle nursed him, and the family provided medical and financial aid. Despite the church's strong opposition to all tobacco use, the bishop bought cigarettes that Climenhaga requested.[121]

During the war years, the BIC community blended this concern for youth with an expectation that BIC young people would accept the burden of being different in a society seemingly intent on becoming homogenized.[122] For those in public high school the difficulties were obvious, but even those attending the BIC schools were not isolated from the intrusions of the larger society.

Two experiences of Lela Swalm Hostetler illustrate the impossibility of maintaining complete separation from the larger society. As a daughter of one of the church's leading peace advocates, Hostetler was completely immersed in the BIC subculture in Ontario. When she saw a bumper sticker for sale that read "There'll always be an England," however, its wartime implications escaped her. She bought it and put it on the family car. "Well, my dad had a fit about that. He took it off right away." Hostetler also briefly dated a student who attended one of the BIC schools, Ontario Bible School. He was not part of the Brethren in Christ, and he joined the army soon after war began. She remembers once discussing the issue of nonresistance, "because he knew our stand." He told her, "'You know that I believe in doing unto others as they'd do unto me.'" She was aware of his position but says, "It didn't seem to bother me much then because I liked him a lot."[123] Hostetler apparently formulated her nonresistance while engaging in experiences common to many adolescents.

Public high schools often exerted direct pressure to join war mobilization efforts. The 1943 establishment of a High School Victory Corps worried the BIC community, but this worry apparently did not lead to concrete action. Although it was a voluntary organization, the corps introduced military themes into the

general curriculum and displaced standard classes in favor of mobilization activities.[124] Howard L. Landis attended high school in Souderton, Pennsylvania, an
area with numerically and economically strong nonresistant populations. Yet he
remembers that often school authorities replaced classes with agricultural work
to support the war effort.[125] Ironically, war mobilization benefited Beulah Heisey's
family when classmates came to help harvest potatoes on the family farm.[126]

For Alice Grace Hostetter Zercher, the conundrums of nonconformity and
nonresistance crystallized after the bombing of Pearl Harbor—"Current events
came crashing into my consciousness." As she remembers it, on the evening
after the bombing Zercher sat in a church service listening to a conscripted BIC
man who was leaving for Civilian Public Service. He spoke "of an uncertain
future, of an unpopular stand, and of being willing to die for conscience sake."
The next morning she sat in a "Problems of Democracy" class with one of her
favorite teachers:

> [He] taught government with the zeal of a fire-and-brimstone preacher. He
> paced back and forth across the room; [his] voice carried beyond his class-
> room. . . . Democracy and freedom were gravely threatened; this was not a
> time for selfishness and cowardice; every worthy citizen needed to rise in
> defense of the United States government. It was a noble cause that would
> demand the very best, maybe even the lives, of each of us. How could any
> one dare think differently[?]
>
> I sat there feeling inspired and proud of my country—yes, I was a citizen
> who enjoyed all these benefits, and I wanted to do something, yet how could
> I? I thought of Earl and the conscientious objectors, how they were misun-
> derstood and disliked, because, for conscience-sake, their ultimate allegiance
> was to God. I wished for a way to help my teacher and classmates under-
> stand that citizens could have differing convictions and yet be worthy citi-
> zens. I had no solutions, and I certainly didn't want to be ridiculed, so inter-
> nalizing my feelings of despair, I listened quietly.[127]

As mobilization proceeded, the nonresistant position became more visible.
Esther Tyson Boyer remembers, "I was not very popular." Because she would
not buy war bonds, her high school homeroom could never win the school
competition. She was greatly relieved when her mother intervened, sending a
note to the school principal to request that "because of our Peace values," Tyson
be excluded from the total figures determining the outcome.[128] Lois Raser
summed up her war years in an Iowa public high school as "rationing, pressure to buy war bonds, unpopularity of being nonresistant[,] . . . gloom."[129]
Critics of nonresistance sometimes focused on the benefits received by consci-

entious objectors. Beulah Heisey remembers excitedly telling a school friend about the impending visit of her brother, on furlough from his CPS assignment. The friend challenged the right of conscientious objectors to come home while other young men were risking their lives overseas. "After that I was always very cautious about my comments," she remembers.[130]

In contrast, Earl Hensel felt a sense of satisfaction when a classmate recognized him as a conscientious objector. He remembers a high school friend discussing the draft questionnaire he had just received.

> His very words remain vivid in my mind: "and then there was this question, 'are you a Religious Objector?'—I didn't sign it" then, after a pause, he looked straight at me and said "Earl, you'll sign that." I don't remember ever talking about this; I just credit the daily living as a nonaggressive, separatist life style. I was pleased that I had made such an impact on my peers. There were about 30–35 boys in my class—non[e] ever spoke disrespectfully to me.[131]

BIC youth formed their own supportive networks in their schools and congregations—and also in the larger grouping of Historic Peace Churches. Paul Hostetler of North Lawrence, Ohio, often felt isolated. But he was a member of a young people's group that met weekly to discuss the war and BIC community nonresistance. "We often prayed for more courage to withstand the shame and constant pressures of war hysteria." Although he remembers the group being united in its peace witness, he also recalls praying "for the safety of our friends and relatives who were in the armed services."[132] E. Morris Sider recalls that in Ontario the annual meeting of the Conference of Historic Peace Churches was "the really big event." At that gathering, "we were in a big body[;] . . . we could see that our tiny little group wasn't alone in what we thought."[133]

In a 1946 article, Wendell E. Harmon argued that alternative-service programs for conscientious objectors and volunteer-service work would allow the BIC youth program to "grow out of the immediate project and the need."[134] He saw young people as the central players in that program. "Without doubt the most encouraging aspect of our move into the relief and service field is the fact that much of the moving has been done by the young people of the church. This is *their* program!"[135]

While the nonresistant mobilization required contributions from the entire BIC community, Harmon rightly noted its special call and appeal to youth.

The war brought dramatic changes to the workplace and to the schools. It took away family members and neighbors. Despite their ideal of separation from the world and its wars, the Brethren in Christ could not help being part of the American home front. Individual members tried to draw a variety of lines to maintain their identity, but increasingly those lines seemed either arbitrary or inconsistent. In the end, it proved impossible for the Brethren in Christ to detach themselves entirely from the larger society, even as their nonresistant position prevented them from fitting in with classmates, coworkers, and neighbors.

For some, the complex and uncomfortable dilemmas of the home front would be resolved only when the nonresistant community itself mobilized—for peace.

CHAPTER FOUR

Nonresistant Mobilization

✐

Very little is ever said in public relative to sewing.

In the 1940s, North American society was mobilizing for war—and pressuring every citizen to join the effort. In response, a substantial number of nonresistant people mounted their own mobilization, a mobilization for peace and service. In doing so, these nonresistant people cemented the connection, already expressed in World War I, between humanitarian service and nonparticipation in the military. They extended the idea of peaceful living to include neighbors beyond local communities and national boundaries.

During World War II, the Brethren in Christ (BIC) participated in various programs instituted by the Historic Peace Churches to express the peace witness. Some wrote letters and visited alternative service camps for conscientious objectors. BIC districts and General Conference devised quota systems to fund Civilian Public Service (CPS) camps in the United States. Married women joined their husbands in CPS work, particularly in state hospitals. Young men and women volunteered for a variety of newly emerging volunteer service programs at home and overseas. Farm families contributed food and live animals for relief efforts in war areas. Sewing circles produced and gathered clothing and quilts.

In many of these activities, the Brethren in Christ were one small constituent group of the Mennonite Central Committee (MCC), which cooperated with the other Historic Peace Churches and with the larger pacifist movement. The war influenced many of the programs of the Mennonite Central Committee. But the organization had been founded well before that, in 1920, to aid Mennonites suffering in the Soviet Union. Old Anabaptist ideas of mutual aid informed the people shaping the Mennonite Central Committee and those who worked in it. Other influences were experiences of alternative work in war periods, including work with Quakers after World War I.[1]

The Brethren in Christ joined the Mennonite Central Committee in 1940 and participated in Church of the Brethren programs. At the same time, nonresistant mobilization by the Brethren in Christ drew on their own community traditions and put them to new purposes. Calls for food donations activated BIC farmers, already accustomed to sharing their agricultural production in various aspects of church life. Calls for donations of clothing and processed food provided avenues for BIC women to use their traditional skills in the peace witness. Young people too were already familiar with calls to raise funds and volunteer time. This mobilization had great influence on individual lives. Many Brethren in Christ—as evidenced by district minutes, diaries, and correspondence of the period—thought this peace work was integral to the religious beliefs of their community.

Nevertheless, retrospective accounts reveal that much of this substantial group effort has now been forgotten, and for a number of reasons. For one thing, although much of the nonresistant mobilization was powered by the work and willingness of women, both women and men in the BIC community continued to associate peace issues primarily with men. The contributions of women, although essential and acknowledged as such during the war years, had the flavor of auxiliary work. This was a common position for women in organizations headed by men.[2] But the lack of formal recognition of women's work parallels the loss from collective memory of women's stories of nonresistant practice.

For another thing, conflict over definitions of nonresistance, as well as reluctance in some parts of the BIC community to fund men in Civilian Public Service, gave many of the men affected the impression of a general lack of support from the home community. Memory of conflict overshadowed recollections of efforts by many people to support the program. In addition, the Brethren in Christ's sense of their small size within the larger Mennonite world encouraged a conviction that others were doing more, a perception that downplayed contributions that BIC people did make. Furthermore, the desire, especially among BIC leaders, to maintain a distinct identity in that larger grouping and to strengthen simultaneously older BIC institutions made even the strongest BIC peace leaders cautious in promoting the new peace programs for volunteers.

Taken together, these sentiments make memories of what the Brethren in Christ accomplished in the war years less fruitful as a historical source than the contemporary record, which documents the efforts of many ordinary BIC members. At the same time, the loss of memory in itself is important to an understanding of the BIC peace witness.

MOBILIZING FOR ALTERNATIVE SERVICE PROGRAMS

During World War II, both Canada and the United States set up alternative service programs for men who met certain legal definitions of conscientious objection. In 1952, the United States set up a new conscription system and also a new alternative service program. BIC leaders called for congregational support of all these programs. U.S. Civilian Public Service ended up costing participating organizations seven million dollars. The majority of this money came from the Historic Peace Churches; the BIC portion of that amount totaled about $142,000.[3] An early Peace, Relief, and Service (PRS) Committee appeal for funds for Civilian Public Service listed three rationales for BIC support: first, that sacrificial giving is always important for its own sake; second, that this funding would keep churches, rather than governments, in control of the program; and finally, that peace church funding of the program would prove the national loyalty of conscientious objectors.[4]

Both contemporary and retrospective appraisals by CPS participants insist that the BIC community remained largely uninvolved in the program. But actual documentation contradicts these impressions. The BIC church, through its PRS Committee and other General Conference boards, provided small monetary gifts to CPS men, allowances for their dependents, and postwar benefits, particularly college tuitions.[5] District BIC leaders set up systems to raise money for local CPS men and sometimes their dependents. BIC farmers, particularly women, produced food and clothing for Civilian Public Service. In addition to financial and material support, many members of the BIC community, particularly families of alternative service participants, stayed in touch through letters and visits with conscientious objectors scattered across North America.

In 1941, the PRS Committee began a dollar-per-member-per-year quota to fund the CPS program, adding that figure to an equal amount established the year before for Mennonite relief work in England, France, and Poland.[6] At its highest level in 1944 and 1945, the quota was ten dollars per member.[7] From 1941 on, district council minutes show a variety of methods implemented to collect the funds and, after 1943, for additional direct funding of many districts' own CPS men.[8] The Rapho district in Pennsylvania, often noted for its conservatism, tied its funding system to a visitation system designed "to keep in close enough touch with our boys to ascertain their Spiritual c[h]aracter, being worthy of the Church and Her support."[9] Three years into the program, district councils began noting the need for additional funding for married men with family members, because men in the program did not receive wages.[10] The annual deacons' report of visits to each home in the Pennsylvania's Dauphin and Lebanon district noted that "several members" had raised concerns

E. J. and Maggie Swalm family, ca. 1936, Ontario. L to R: Lela Swalm, Pearl Swalm (E. J.'s sister), Mildred, E. J., Ray, Maggie, Jean. E. J. Swalm was a BIC conscientious objector in World War I and a leading BIC peace leader in the World War II era. Lela helped her mother run the family farm during the war, sewed for nonresistant relief programs, and dated a man who would join the military. *(Courtesy of the Brethren in Christ Historical Library and Archives)*

about family support of men in alternative service.[11] The PRS Committee and various districts repeatedly roused members to continue giving for Civilian Public Service, especially after the war ended. (The CPS program continued into 1947.) The BIC community, like the larger American society, was apparently growing weary of calls for sacrifice.[12]

A number of BIC leaders—E. J. Swalm, C. N. Hostetter Jr. and Jesse W. Hoover—were deeply involved in the alternative service programs. Less apparent in official records is the extent to which family and community support made the work of these men possible. For example, E. J. Swalm's daughter Lela stayed out of school during the war years to help her mother run the family farm. She also regularly drove her father, who disliked driving, himself, from the farm to meetings with government officials in Ottawa or with other leaders of the Conference of Historic Peace Churches in Kitchener and Waterloo, Ontario. In another capacity, Lela Swalm used her shorthand skills to record a speech given by Hostetter at one of that conference's annual meetings, thereafter providing Mennonite Central Committee with a transcript.[13] When Swalm traveled to visit Canadian or U.S. camps, another preacher from the BIC community covered his ministerial duties in the district.[14]

Perhaps even more than Swalm, Hostetter spent time away from his home and his college presidency during the war years. Anna Lane Hostetter's 1945 diary reflects his frequent trips, his exhausting schedule, and her own work on CPS and college matters.[15] Other pastors, particularly from Pennsylvania and California, also made visits to camps or smaller units, sometimes accompanied by women in the family.[16]

Other members of the BIC community also traveled to alternative service units for visits. For example, women's music groups from Messiah Bible College and Beulah College traveled to CPS camps to sing.[17] Grace Herr Holland remembers her family traveling north to sing in an Alternative Service Work camp where conscientious objectors were helping to build the Trans-Canada Highway.[18] The *Visitor* ran a report by two sisters from Palmyra, Pennsylvania, of a trip to visit a man in the CPS camp at Marietta, Ohio, adding the editorial comment, "We miss these boys from our group and pray they may soon return to us."[19]

Messiah Bible College Ladies Quartet with BIC minister, April 1941. L to R: Lois Smith, Henry Hostetter, Avis Saltzman, Arlene Miller, Dorothy Pfautz. Women's music groups from BIC church schools traveled to CPS camps to sing. As representatives of Messiah Bible College, the women pictured wore cape dresses and head coverings that met the clothing definitions legislated in 1937. *(Courtesy of the Brethren in Christ Historical Library and Archives)*

BIC districts and sometimes state councils not only provided funding to men in Civilian Public Service but also set up committees to stay in touch with them by sending personal items, letters, and church periodicals. Often they sent the same literature to men in the military.[20] Vera Clouse Beachy suggested that Sunday school members should take turns writing at least monthly letters and sending periodicals.[21] Some individuals remember corresponding with men in alternative service and sending packages.[22] Mildred Charles, with other young women in her Kansas district, took turns writing letters and sending cookies and candy to men in camps. When one man mentioned going without socks because he had no money to replace his worn-out pairs, Charles bought him new socks and had him send her the ones with holes to darn.[23]

In the spring of 1943, Mennonite Central Committee began calling on constituent groups to produce and process fruits and vegetables for CPS camps. Government controls of food consumption sometimes made it difficult for those camps to provide certain foods in quantities sufficient for the large numbers of conscientious objectors living there. By December of that year, Mennonite Central Committee estimated that approximately 169,000 quarts of food had been contributed, not including items given directly from congregations to camps in their own locales. One MCC article on the canning project described food arriving with names of "parents, relatives, neighbors or friends" on the labels. Mennonite Central Committee described the program as "a means of uniting all of us in the Cause of Christ and His Way of Peace."[24]

BIC involvement in this program built on a well-established practice of producing food for church gatherings, BIC schools, benevolent institutions, and urban missions.[25] Pennsylvania's Donegal district council reported in 1946 a comparable amount of food canned for the Messiah Bible College and for Civilian Public Service—over three hundred quarts of fruits and vegetables for each, along with cases of peas and three gallons of fruit cocktail.[26] Another Pennsylvania district, Cumberland, assigned deacons to oversee congregational canning for Civilian Public Service.[27] In fact, the response to MCC's call for help was overwhelming; by 1945 almost sixty thousand quarts of food sat in storage in Pennsylvania and Indiana.[28]

Mobilizing Relief Contributions

The collection of food for the CPS program quickly merged with its collection for relief shipments to Europe. In 1945, Mennonite Central Committee shipped to Europe its first ton of canned food—excess items produced for Civilian Public Service. The organization reported that three more tons shipped to Puerto Rico had arrived in good shape.[29] In the same year, the *Visitor* began advertising requests for dried fruit, dry beans, and canned fruits, vegetables, and meats for shipment to the Netherlands and France.[30] In 1946, the Rapho district contributed two tons of food to the Philadelphia BIC mission and 1,232 quarts of fruit to Civilian Public Service. In response to reports of starvation in Central and Eastern Europe, the district also contributed more than $1,500 in cash to be used to purchase meat, along with three live beef cattle, three live hogs, sixty bushels of wheat, three hundred pounds of flour, and five dozen hand cultivators.[31] The neighboring Manor-Pequea district processed food for Messiah Bible College, Mennonite Central Committee, and the BIC mission in Stowe, Pennsylvania. To the west, Cumberland district resolved to raise in-kind contributions of food and clothing in each congregation through committees comprising officials and lay "brethren and sisters."[32]

Throughout the rest of the 1940s and 1950s, the BIC community continued to emphasize contributions of relief food.[33] A 1947 newspaper photo shows Brethren in Christ from the Manor-Pequea district preparing fourteen bushels of apples from Hostetter's orchard for drying and shipment by Mennonite Central Committee to Europe.[34] PRS Committee correspondence noted that raising money to purchase baby food for postwar Europe especially appealed to the BIC community.[35] Seven years later, Marjorie H. Haines reported that seventy-five people from two Ohio congregations had canned meat for two days.[36] Farmers also contributed live animals, usually heifers, to the Brethren Service Committee's "Heifer Project," which shipped farm animals to Europe.[37]

Women were particularly involved in food processing and even more so in sewing and collecting clothing for relief.[38] Mary Olive Lady remembers that BIC women contributed to relief goods "in a big way." Lady's mother "always insisted [that clothing or bedding] had to be clean and nice, or well mended, before anything could be given to relief. . . . I remember that point being made that we don't want to send anything shoddy to these people. And the quilts. My mother was a beautiful quilter. . . . I know that some of her quilts went to relief[;] . . . they sent things that were nice."[39] Lela Swalm Hostetler remembers being the only young person among the women of her Ontario district who "sewed and sewed" in daylong sessions.[40]

In 1954, the Dorcas Sewing Circle of the South Dickinson, Kansas, district reported seven meetings, with an average attendance of twelve women, in the previous year. The list of goods it had processed included 130 pounds of used clothing and twenty-three items of new clothing, which had been sent to the MCC center in Newton. The group had also sewed for a "Leper colony" on Formosa, probably also in connection with relief work; for the Salvation Army; for a neighbor whose home had been destroyed by fire; and for the BIC community's Mount Carmel, Illinois, home for orphans. The report concluded,

"As we laboured together through out the year making new articles and mending used clothing, we have done it as unto the Lord."[41]

"Sewing circle reports" in BIC district, state, and provincial council minutes document that this aspect of women's work was specifically connected to nonresistant beliefs.[42] A 1944 committee report from the Rapho district made that point explicitly.[43] The committee recommended setting up an association of Pennsylvania sewing circles, to be headed by Anna Lane Hostetter. As the committee envisioned events, BIC sewing circles would produce clothing and bedding for the Mennonite Central Committee, missions, local hospitals, and poor neighborhood families. The preface to the recommendations provided a biblical rationale for the proposal: "Very little is ever said in public relative to sewing, and yet very special mention is made in the New Testament about a seamstress, Acts 9:36–39. It must therefore be remembered that sewing is a part of the church's program as much as any other phase of church work." The preface further notes that "we are a group of C.O.['s] opposed to war, but [who] definitely believe in helping humanity instead."[44] The district council adopted the recommendations and passed them on to the Pennsylvania state council, where they were discussed in 1945 but tabled.[45] Apparently, BIC leaders had difficulty in recognizing women's contributions to the nonresistant mobilization. Anna Lane Hostetter's 1945 diary records that she wrote a newsletter for the sewing circles, though that newsletter is not in the BIC archives.[46]

Mobilizing Volunteers

Mobilization to produce funds, food, and clothing for Civilian Public Service and for relief paralleled the growth of volunteer programs. Volunteers, often BIC youth and young adults, distributed those goods and worked in a variety of other service settings as well. The determination of the Historic Peace Churches to maintain control of the CPS program brought a financial burden, but it also spurred volunteer programs. The fifteen years from 1939 to 1954 powered a variety of interconnected and sometimes competing service experiments.

Partly because of the magnitude and diversity of these experimental programs, records from the period are often fragmentary and sometimes inaccurate. Yet even these records document substantial BIC interest and participation in the new volunteer programs. Soon after the Brethren in Christ became a constituent group of the Mennonite Central Committee in 1940, the organization began tapping its new member not only for material goods but also for personnel to administer Civilian Public Service and relief programs. Contemporary and retrospective evaluations of BIC participation in Mennonite Central Committee often fault lay BIC members for lack of enthusiasm for relief and service work, but a closer examination of the records reveals that in fact a substantial number of Brethren in Christ participated.[47]

The same records document the BIC community's fears that such exposure would affect their religious and social identity. Some members feared that their small community would be absorbed into the larger Mennonite world. A 1947 PRS Committee report, while noting appreciatively the Mennonite Central Committee's help during the war, described the Brethren in Christ "as a non-Mennonite minority group" in the organization.[48] Others feared that relief work might supplant mission work or dull BIC doctrinal stands. Leah Dohner, speaking at the 1947 Ohio-Kentucky Joint Council meeting, listed relief work among six "dangers that threaten the church." The focus of relief on "the unspiritual," she contends, might compete with mission work and required mixing with others who did not fervently teach holiness doctrines.[49] Dohner was right in noting that the new, institutionalized peace programs necessitated additional contributions from a group that already underwrote numerous institutions.[50]

Nevertheless, the earliest call for a relief volunteer elicited a prompt and positive response from the BIC community. In September 1940, the PRS Committee ran notices in the *Visitor* recruiting a male volunteer to work in MCC's relief program in Europe. The person, "preferably a layman" who would bring "prestige" to the job, would serve at least a six-month term, possibly for "the duration of the need."[51] The two final candidates, however—Alvin C. Burkholder and Jesse W. Hoover—were both ordained ministers. Hoover was chosen and served in France from March until late 1941.[52]

Three men in addition to Burkholder and Hoover, representing different constituencies in the church, presented themselves to the PRS Committee. None was ordained. One of the three was a farmer from Hamlin, Kansas, who wrote to PRS Committee member Henry G. Brubaker:

> Dear Brother,
>   I am writing to you instead of to R. I. Witter [another committee member] because of family ties. I feel like offering to go as a relief worker to France.
>   Verland could take my place on the farm until I returned.
>   My family are healthy and could be supported. If any accident occurred to me the family would have protection by a $5000 life insurance policy. If you need me for this place I am at your service.
>   Yours truly, Glen D. Byer

Byer writes simply, drawing on old images of sacrifice to the point of death, but he suggests an intriguing new response—reliance on a life insurance policy, a symbol of modern self-sufficiency and a point of contention in the community,

Jesse W. Hoover with a child from a home for displaced
children in France, 1941. Hoover worked under Mennonite
Central Committee to distribute food and begin the work of
establishing homes in southwestern France for Jewish and
Spanish children. *(Courtesy of the Brethren in Christ Historical
Library and Archives)*

to help cover of the cost of such a sacrifice. The response of committee members to Byer and the other two men who expressed interest was hesitant; there
is no record that any of them served as BIC volunteers.[53]

Although the committee was apparently not prepared to consider them seriously as candidates, women were also eager to volunteer for relief work. Just
after the call for a volunteer, Clara E. Stoner wrote to the PRS Committee that
"work in Europe interests me very much." Stoner was not the only woman to
express deep interest in European relief work. Reporting on a 1942 interview
with Jesse W. Hoover, just returned from relief work in France, Miriam Nolt
wrote, "My interest was keen, because I felt it is one of the many things we as
Christians can render in the present situation."[54] Yet no BIC women served as
international relief workers until 1945.[55]

The committee's initial preoccupation with "prestige" may have blinded its
members to some important insights being offered by women. For example,

Stoner had noted that financial constraints might limit many interested people. She proposed that the BIC church fund the entire family of a volunteer. Thus the home community could participate with those who served and would thereby understand that relief work was a "task in which such large numbers of fathers and mothers, young men, wives, sisters, and sweethearts in the church are vitally involved."[56] Stoner's perception that relief workers must be well integrated with the home community was an important but not always realized goal. Without that connection, relief work sometimes moved individuals away from BIC community life.

In 1944, responding to a push from Mennonite women for more active ways to express their own nonresistance, as well as to the example of the American Friends Service Committee, the Mennonites began setting up Women's Service Units in state mental hospitals that already had CPS units. Women worked in these units in summer programs between 1944 and 1946.[57] Four BIC women served in a state mental hospital in Howard, Rhode Island: Elsie C. Bechtel, Elizabeth Heisey, Ruth Heisey, and Esther Mann. Irene L. Bishop, a Mennonite woman attending Messiah Bible College, also served there.[58] That unit included a group of BIC men in alternative service, as well as a number of women working for wages alongside their husbands.[59] An undated and unsigned letter—the last page is lost—to Anna Lane Hostetter from one of the women working at Howard graphically describes her work there. She was given no training, and when she led residents through hospital buildings, she did not know where she was going. In the evenings, the women in the unit, "who portray every shape and angle of Mennonitism," attended classes on mental health, relief work in Europe, and one "showing differences in our or[i]gin and background."[60]

Two unsigned evaluations from volunteers at a state mental hospital in Ypsilanti, Michigan, gave more positive appraisals of the experience. One of these evaluations is probably that of a BIC woman who worked there in 1945. Both insisted that the summer had yielded no disappointments, except for being too short. The evaluations appraised highly what they had learned that summer: to control one's temper, to assume responsibility, and to be "more broadminded and thoughtful." Above all, one participant stated, the summer had helped her overcome her "erroneous notion that they [the residents] were all savage-like persons."[61]

The experiences of these women in state hospitals parallel those of CPS participants and of high school and college-age BIC men and women who later worked in MCC summer programs in state hospitals. Those summer programs evolved out of the Women's Service Units after the war.[62] Clara Meyer Eberly worked at the Howard, Rhode Island, state hospital in 1946 as a "medical assistant in the acute hospital" in an MCC program. She says the experience convinced her to become a nurse and led to her marriage to a Mennonite. Above all, it enlarged her understanding of the world. As an example, she describes being introduced to overt American racism. "A Negro girl from Heston College came & no one eagerly volunteered to be her roommate. So I did and we spent the summer developing a Wonderful relationship & it was an eye-opener for me. Made real to me what race discrimination was in the 1940's in [the] U.S.A. I could not believe such existed. Also challenged feelings on how broad the 'Peace' & 'Justice' attitudes *Really* were even in a volunteer group. I lost some friends? over rooming with her."[63]

In a 1976 letter, Ruth Brubaker Davis described the year, from 1948 to 1949, in which she and her husband Harold volunteered in an MCC project in Gulfport, Mississippi.[64] As a conscripted man, Harold Davis had earlier served in three different assignments until his discharge at the end of 1945.[65] Ruth described her motivation for voluntary service as "a continuing idea" coming from her husband's experience. She had initially undertaken service because of her interest in him. The two of them helped to build and install electrical wiring in homes and an African American church. They ran recreation programs in segregated African American schools, tutored students, and sewed clothing from feed sacks for an African American teacher.[66]

Articles in the early 1950s give details on the actual work and the meanings participants gave to that work. In 1950, Ruth E. Pye reflected on her previous year at a children's summer program at Camp Bennett, near Washington, D.C. She described episodes of children running away from the camp and epidemics of "pink eye" and lice. After being gone from the camp for a few days, she missed the children.[67]

In 1951, Esther G. Book served in a unit providing religious education to migrant workers in the Santa Clara Valley, near San Jose, California. She thought her three years as a relief worker in India helped to prepare her for this summer volunteer work. "One cannot work with the migrant people without learning to know a bit of their hardships. . . . In a land of abundance and prosperity, it is hard to realize the fact that large families live in small, musty tents without running water or proper sanitary facilities, being almost entirely at the mercy of heartless growers." What she could bring, she concluded, was "the most lasting and satisfying thing in life—the knowledge of Christ as a personal Savior."[68]

After the war, many new volunteer opportunities emerged outside the United States and Canada. Numerous BIC students from Messiah Bible College and Beulah College participated in student tours, sponsored by the Council of Mennonite and Affiliated Colleges. After the initial 1947 tour, the program included not only travel and Anabaptist history but also a few weeks of participation in MCC work camps. In the camps, American students worked alongside European Mennonites and other young people from a variety of backgrounds.[69] Probably the largest number of BIC students was involved in the 1950 tour. C. N. Hostetter Jr. led one of the groups, which included four BIC students. John Engle, a faculty member at Messiah Bible College, led a second group, which included two BIC students.[70] Esther Tyson Boyer, part of the first group, describes helping to build homes for refugees in Donaueschingen, West Germany. "There were young people in our group from Germany, Holland, Austria and the U.S. We also worked with the families that planned to move into the houses. After years of terrible suffering it was very healing for all of us to be working together in this way."[71]

John Engle remembers his trip as a difficult one. He struggled with his inadequate foreign-language skills and felt uncertainty about his leadership abilities. More than once he was mistaken for a communist spy. But he also remembers lifting a little girl onto his shoulders to see the pope, then hearing the words *Merci beaucoup* behind him; he turned around to see the girl's father, who had no arms, smiling at him. Engle struggled over whether he should wear his plain coat and how he should respond to the unfamiliar "Russian" Mennonites. Logistical problems sometimes landed the students in the wrong town at the wrong time. But one of those errors led the group to a tiny church in northern Italy where they sang hymns with people with whom they could not converse—they knew the same tunes.[72]

In attempts to document the level of interest in relief work, it is difficult to determine when particular individuals wanted to participate but were discouraged by leaders and when individuals disqualified themselves. Furthermore, BIC leaders struggled with budgetary concerns, since the Brethren in Christ paid for the support of each BIC volunteer in the Mennonite Central Committee—fifty dollars per month in 1949.[73] But delays in processing applicants undoubtedly occurred at many junctures in the new bureaucracies. Lela Fern Williams Gwinner, for example, remembers hearing about the need for volunteers when she was at Messiah Bible College in 1943 and 1944. She filled out an application, returned home to Buffalo, New York, and began work in a hospital. "After several months, perhaps even a year, I was accepted by MCC." Since she was by then established in a job, she decided to remain in Buffalo.[74] In 1944, MCC's C. L. Graber wrote Hoover asking if any BIC nurses were interested in foreign relief work. Hoover responded with only one name, that of Martha L. Rosenberger, who "had volunteered for service over a year ago."[75]

A letter from J. N. Byler, of the Mennonite Central Committee, to Jesse W. Hoover stated that eight CPS men from the BIC community had been notified of needs in the Philippines. Below those names, nineteen more were listed who had "at some time [had] expressed an interest in Relief." Please "check over this list" Byler urged.[76] Yet none of these men served in MCC volunteer programs;

other names as well show up and then disappear. From 1946 to 1951, six BIC community members did, however, serve in what was planned as a BIC-led MCC relief unit in the Philippines. The goal, which did not materialize, was to turn the relief project into an ongoing BIC mission center.[77]

With a pool of only six thousand official church members from which to draw, the BIC church's ambitious institutional program sometimes competed with the new peace programs for personnel. Several retrospective sources record cases in which BIC members' interest in relief work was likely diverted by leaders into other BIC work. Doyle Book and Thelma Heisey Book, interested in working with European displaced people, already knew their departure date when the Foreign Mission Board "re-routed" them to a new mission in Japan.[78] Miriam Knepper Stern recalled in her 1980s account of her life in missions being determined to use her nursing vocation "maybe even by doing relief work in Europe following the war's devastation." Instead, she and her husband went in 1952 to a BIC mission in Southern Rhodesia.[79] Dorothy Sherk, who considered relief work, remembers being advised to choose the less glamorous task of teaching in a BIC school.[80]

Volunteers who were starting families worried about finances, despite denominational promises that dependents would be provided for by financial aid allotments.[81] Duane Engle remembers that in 1951 he and his wife, Eileen, planned to go to Germany for relief work but that when Eileen became pregnant, they changed their minds.[82]

Those who did choose to volunteer describe the lifelong impact of that decision. Lester C. Fretz's experiences between November 1951 and February 1952 bring together several strands of the nonresistant mobilization. They also link the production of food for relief on the home front with the experience of overseas relief work. During the war years, this Ontario farm boy had admired, as we have seen, both a hired man in military uniform and a conscientious objector Sunday school teacher serving in an Alternative Service Work camp. At age nineteen, he combined the romance of both as he left home in a pacifist relief program that took livestock to war-torn farms in Europe. As an attendant on a cattle boat, Fretz helped care for the animals, which had been donated through the Heifer Project. Although some volunteers made the round trip quite quickly, Fretz's parents had encouraged him to spend time traveling in Europe. When the ship docked in Bremerhaven, Fretz traveled by train in West Germany, looking up families who had received donated cattle. He observed rubble from the bombings, which had killed thousands of people. He listened to German war stories and visited the Dachau concentration camp. He was sometimes homesick, sometimes frightened by "remnants of war I didn't expect to see."[83]

Looking back now, Fretz realizes that his experiences made him different from other people. When he would resole his shoes, church members found his frugality odd. When he later left a job as a school principal to teach in Rhodesia, the school board found his decision difficult to understand. As a child, Fretz had secretly contributed to war material drives. After the war, to his parents' dismay, he had worn army surplus clothes. But his parents allowed him to make his own decisions, and his nonresistant roots channeled him into a life of service and peace advocacy in the BIC community.[84]

For those in the BIC community who personally linked service to nonresistance, the peace witness often retained a central position in their religious expression. Their commitments were often passed on to their children. John Engle lists one of "the long range benefits" of his difficult trip as a tour leader—"Of our six children, five of them, after they were married, went into some type of voluntary service work." Now in his eighties, Engle wonders how members of the upcoming BIC generation will put nonresistance into practice. Reflecting on his experiences and those of the conscientious objectors during the war years, he asks, "Are our young men (and women) prepared to take a similar stance if and when universal conscription is enacted?"[85]

Universal conscription may not be the issue facing peace advocates of the future, but Engle's question implies not just the events of one period but the importance of memory in sustaining the peace witness over generations. During the World War II era, the Brethren in Christ struggled hard to translate their nonresistance into service in the larger world. That effort financed Civilian Public Service, encouraged volunteers, and contributed to relief efforts in areas of the world devastated by total war. The wide-ranging nonresistant mobilization drew on often-overlooked segments of the BIC community— farmers, women, and youth. But for the most part, memories of that collective effort remain dim in the community.

In the postwar world, many elements of the BIC nonresistant mobilization would be challenged. The traditional work of women, the family farm, even the BIC bond with smallness would undergo fundamental changes. Furthermore, the intractable problem of diversity within the BIC community, particularly in regard to the military service of men, would soon overshadow the efforts of the nonresistant home front.

CHAPTER FIVE

Conscientious Objection, Civilian Public Service, and Community Life

✑

Learning to be democratic.

There is no blue star in our window
We hang no emblems of hate;
There is no glib talk of heroes
Or of victories soon or late.

But our boy is gone this evening,
Gone like a million more;
But not to train for destruction
Nor attack on foreign shore.

He will drop no bombs on the helpless,
There is no red stain on his hand;
No mother will wait for a boy
That he killed in a foreign land.

But our blessings overflow this evening,
A blessing that comes from above;
While others are trained for hatred,
Our boy is trained for love.[1]

For members of the Brethren in Christ (BIC) community, conscientious objection to military service was only one expression of nonresistance. But the issue of conscientious objection during World War II provides a particularly good lens for considering community life.[2] Faced with compulsory military conscription during World War II, conscientious objectors in the United States had three options. They could refuse to cooperate at all and be sent to prison; they could request a noncombatant classification within the military; or they could request alternative service. Civilian Public Service (CPS), the U.S. vehicle for alternative service, was the result of negotiations between a coalition of pacifist groups, including the Historic Peace Churches, and various branches of the federal government. The program reflected the compromises of the negotiators. All of them hoped to avoid the conflicts and chaos engendered by conscientious objection in the last war. The government and military officials, however, hoped to keep the program out of the spotlight and to require conscientious objectors to shoulder an equal burden as citizens. Pacifist groups wanted a system that would recognize various conscientious stands against war. Mennonites wanted a program that they could administer. Civilian Public Service itself soon became a complicated bureaucracy with unclear lines of authority. In the end, the program drew criticism from all parties. The Selective Service System, various federal departments, and the National Service Board for Religious Objectors administered the program. The Historic Peace Churches provided most of the funding. In the earliest years of the program, participants were housed in Civilian Conservation Corps camps and worked on soil conservation or forestry projects. Even after work opportunities diversified, all men spent an initial period in such camps. Then they could transfer into other work settings, such as state mental hospitals, dairy farms, forest fire fighting units, medical guinea-pig experiments, and public health projects. Almost twelve thousand men were officially a part of the program. They received only small stipends provided by the Historic Peace Churches for the "over eight million mandays of work" contributed from 1941 through 1947. Some humanistic and political conscientious objectors and individuals who objected to working under selective service administration spent time in prison.[3]

Of the men who participated in Civilian Public Service, Mennonites were the largest contingent; they were often noted for their cooperation with and lack of protest against the program. The BIC men, usually counted as Mennonites, took a similar stance, one categorized as being "the good boys" of the program or as "going the second mile."[4] Reflecting their evangelical bent, the major complaint of BIC men was a lack of spirituality in the institutional setup of the program and in the lives of the other participants.[5] By and large, correspondence between

Brethren in Christ and Mennonite administrators seems to suggest that BIC men got along quite well with the Mennonites and with the other denominations and persuasions. Only one letter noted tensions caused by a "cliquish ... self-righteousness" among certain men. The camp administrator asked that a BIC leader visit and "speak to your own men rather definitely."[6] No other explicit comments refer to conflict between BIC members and other groups in Civilian Public Service.

Like many Mennonites, the Brethren in Christ tended to see their alternative service as a religious expression more than as a civic challenge or as social pioneering. Many were from farm or other laboring backgrounds, some of them just out of high school or college. Yet they did not hesitate to make discerning evaluations of Civilian Public Service. Referring to the BIC cooperation in enforcing selective service rules, one man wrote, "The church is helping administer punishment to men for a principal [sic] which the church itself has taught." Another hoped the next alternative service program would more directly oppose "participating in war evil." A third worried about the lasting impact of the program's compromises on the peace witness.[7]

Wendell E. Harmon was one of the more highly educated participants. His writings also include thoughtful analysis of problems and complexities of the CPS program. An introductory section of *They Also Serve,* probably written by Harmon, described Civilian Public Service as "the long, long trail . . . which during the war years, seemed to wind interminably through the forest of uncertainty, compromise, and criticism toward a goal which was never quite clear in the minds of most of those who sought it." Earlier, he summarized tensions in the program. Critics found Civilian Public Service "too liberal or too strict, too religious or too secular. The work was too hard or too easy, too insignificant or too closely connected with war activities. The men were too zealous for their cause or too apathetic and lethargic. The work bosses were too particular or too slipshod. The bosses thought the men were the same."[8]

In 1945, a twenty-six-year-old farmer and student wrote an extended response, signed but confidential, to a questionnaire on his experiences. Not only had his two years in Civilian Public Service not been wasted, he claimed, but they had been the most profitable in his life.

> It is here that I have learned more about working with common, ordinary people than I ever learned at any other time in my life. In spite of the fact that CPS men are supposed to be a pretty good sort of group, the fact remains that to live in a place like this is harder than living in any other situation that one might name. Men crowded together in a place like this where it is generally felt that we are going no place and making no contribution

are unhappy and difficult to understand. But from this experience I have learned a little bit about folk; how they really feel inside them selves, how they react to difficult situations, and the fact that people are better than one gives them credit for being. I am learning to be democratic, less critical of folks, and more ready to believe that there are many truths in life that I have not discovered, and that there are many men who differ with me radically who perhaps know many of the truths that I have never found. ... But most valuable of all is the fact that here I have been led to rethink my religion and my beliefs; to decide actually what constitutes Christianity and what is dogma, prejudice, and [valueless]. And from this experience I conclude that in reality, there are only a few great and unalterable principles. Those principles are "musts" for a world of peace and right relationships with God and our fellow men. Each man's own experience leads him to his own way of life and interpretation of these principles, but the principles remain. To me these are expressed simply and clearly in Christ's teaching . . . "In as much as ye have done it unto the least of these, you have done it unto Me."[9]

This respondent's positive appraisal of Civilian Public Service mirrors other evaluations expressed in response to the questionnaire. Asked if they considered time in the program wasted, 83 percent answered a strong negative, and only 4 percent stated an emphatic "yes." Respondents most often listed spiritual growth as the greatest benefit of the program, with a growing tolerance of diversity a close second.[10] Taken together, these responses reflect religious devotion, to which the peace witness was integral, and social change that accompanied exposure to new people, places, and ideas.

DIVERSITY AMONG CONSCRIPTED BIC MEN

Civilian Public Service was experimental. Bureaucratic intransigence and shifting political winds created a tangle of rules, structures, and goals.[11] Administrators and dreamers made up programs as they went along. But the men who landed in alternative service brought with them their own tangles and tensions, as well. Part of the difficulty in the BIC community arose from young men's taking the measure of each other's responses to conscription.

As in World War I, many BIC men in World War II gained occupational deferments for agricultural work, for ministerial work, or for theological studies.[12] Shortly before the first CPS camp was opened in 1941, however, an announcement in the *Visitor* warned against appealing for occupational deferments unless absolutely necessary, and then only after consulting with the Peace, Relief, and Service Committee (PRS). Antagonism aroused by such deferments during

Messiah Bible College male chorus, 1941–1942. L to R (front row): Mahlon Engle, William Boyer, Warren Sherman, Vernon Martin, Professor Earl Miller, Eugene Wenger, Ira Hoover, Lyle Myers, Gerald Wenger; (second row): Ira Stern, Gordon Engle, C. Nelson Hostetter, Robert Elthrington, Seth Ford, Daniel B. W. Engle; (third row): Wilmer Heisey, William Herr, Simon Lehman Jr., Joe Lehman, William Wenger, John Niesly, Robert Smith, Wilmer Haas, Jesse Dourte, Paul Book, Eldon Bert; (fourth row): Musser Martin, Donald Engle, Jay Sisco, Orville Bert, Willard Stump, John Hoffman Jr., Ezra Hoover; (back row): Robert Martin, Earl Martin Jr., Vernon Brandt, William Georgeadis, Elbert Smith. Nine of these men would serve in Civilian Public Service; some would serve as noncombatants in the military; some would receive occupational deferments; and a few would choose combatant military service. *(Courtesy of the Brethren in Christ Historical Library and Archives)*

World War I must have informed the announcement; it also advised circumspection in "any discussions or expressions that might incite resentment."[13] By 1944, occupational deferments for ministers received a more ambiguous evaluation. Jesse W. Hoover argued that biblical passages permitted ministerial deferments, although he also acknowledged the inconsistency of such a stand in a nonconformist church that theoretically rejected distinctions between the clergy and laity.[14] In the same year, the Peace, Relief, and Service Committee recommended that deferred men give a special monthly contribution to help finance

Civilian Public Service. Such contributions by deferred men would acknowledge that their wartime income contrasted sharply with that of the unpaid men in alternative service. Ideally, such giving would foster "equality of sharing as brethren." General Conference approved this recommendation with a comment that indicated how sensitive the prevailing feelings were: "A request came from a C.P.S. man for General Conference to rise and thereby show how many of the delegates are backing the C.O. stand. This request was granted, and the Conference arose almost to the man. In this way the Conference body testified that they too would take the C.O. stand if they were inducted into national service."[15]

Paul Hostetler, a strong peace advocate in the BIC community, remembers some of the difficulties of his agricultural deferment. Men working on farms sometimes had to answer more questions than the men in isolated camps. "A common question often hurled at me at home and on the streets of [the] nearby city of Massillon, Ohio, was 'Why aren't you in a uniform?' When I explained my situation, I usually was either branded a coward or was treated to meaningful looks and silence." Sometimes he wishes he would have served in alternative service, which he now thinks might have seemed "more legitimate." But he notes that both dairy farming and Civilian Public Service helped the war effort, so going to prison might have been the best symbol of nonparticipation.[16]

In a nation mobilizing civilians as well as military personnel, individuals sometimes had little control over their classifications. Ray M. Zercher's parents, who were farmers, requested an agricultural deferment for their son. The local draft board denied the request, and Zercher entered Civilian Public Service. Abe Yoder Jr., part of the Amish community during the war, received an agricultural deferment after his employer at a feed mill put economic pressure on a member of the local draft board.[17] Yet conscientious objectors who ended up with farm deferments received little commendation from any quarter.[18] Compared to their CPS counterparts, deferred men had less prestige in the BIC community, even if they did have more money.[19]

Initially strong statements against military service—combatant or noncombatant—reinforced cautions against requests for occupational deferments. Taken together, these sentiments point to substantial backing for Civilian Public Service as the BIC expression of conscientious objection.[20] But though BIC prescriptive literature largely rejected noncombatant service, some BIC families and districts, particularly in Oklahoma and California, accepted it as a legitimate expression of conscientious objection.[21] Elsewhere, some men chose to do noncombatant military service because they had never been taught or had never considered the possibility of doing anything else. Others felt that medical or other noncombatant service expressed their conscientious objection to killing. A. James Alderfer, who served in the military medical corps, remembers a sense of following the example of World War I noncombatants.[22] Arthur M. Climenhaga, who changed his own draft classification from alternative service to noncombatant military service, advocated both as options for conscientious objection. He reports that Dwight and Orville Bert of the Upland, California, BIC congregation also chose noncombatant service. In the military, Climenhaga describes the Berts' refusing orders to carry arms, simply standing at attention and repeating, "Sir, we are conscientious objectors." Their superiors offered to advance the men into officer training if they would renounce their position, to which they continued to reply, "Sir . . . we are conscientious objectors."[23]

A variety of contemporary and retrospective sources list many others who accepted military service without specifying noncombatant duty.[24] In 1941, Dan Thuma visited Messiah Bible College. The report of his visit in the *Clarion* noted, "He is the same old Dan"—but now had the pride and gait of a sailor.[25] Paul Winger, who served in the navy in the South Pacific, spoke to several classes at the school on his experiences.[26] Some retrospective accounts mention military service that the BIC community did not challenge. One person remembers an uncle in military service who during the war lived with the family and attended a BIC church. The family displayed in a window a blue service star (denoting that a member was in the armed forces), about which other church members never commented.[27] BIC members in Ontario's Bertie district remember the deaths of two sons of BIC families: Joe Nigh, a paratrooper, and James Sherk, who died in an accident in his last training run as a radio operator in the Royal Canadian Air Force.[28] To the south in 1945, the Charles Winger family chose to "make public mention" of the death of their son Verle, two years after the fact. Verle, who joined the BIC church at age fourteen, had died "on a mission over Germany."[29]

One set of statistics on conscripted men in World War II suggests that the percentage of Brethren in Christ in combatant military service ranked lower than that for the three largest Mennonite groups. But the percentage of BIC men in noncombatant military service ranked higher than two of those same three Mennonite groups.[30] By the early 1950s, however, most conscripted BIC men avoided noncombatant service, choosing instead either combatant duty or alternative service.[31]

The BIC community's response to those who chose military service changed over time. General Conference passed legislation in 1942, 1943, 1948, and 1958 that spelled out varying definitions and discipline. In addition, the imposition of discipline varied from district to district. In its strictest formulation, discipline for noncombatant or combatant military service led to disfellowshiping. But even the meaning of disfellowshiping varied throughout the BIC community. The term was often used interchangeably with *excommunication*, but disfellowshiping usually suggested a milder discipline. Most often, it entailed a public announcement of the fact that a member of the BIC community was not in good standing. In visible terms, the disfellowshiped member could not take Communion or hold a church office. Also, other members might not greet that member with the holy kiss until a confession brought the member back into full fellowship.[32]

Numerous people recall BIC members being disciplined for their military service. Gerald N. Wingert remembers that "during the morning worship service, my uncle Bish. Laban Wingert, in a broken voice, announced to the congregation that Abram Hostetter and Keith Kipe were officially excommunicated from the body. It was an emotionally charged event since it was a deep wound shared by the congregation. The bishop called the congregation to remember these young men in prayer."[33]

Kenneth B. Hoover, a BIC member with a ministerial deferment, remembers that a good friend, John Zercher, and Zercher's brother joined the military during the war. Though Hoover and the Zerchers had different perspectives on military service, they remained good friends. Hoover visited Zercher in a military camp on his way to a new job at Messiah Bible College. Hoover relates that C. N. Hostetter Jr., bishop of the Grantham district, placed Zercher on probation rather than disfellowshiping him. Hoover argues that Hostetter thereby violated the letter but not the spirit of the church's legislation. Furthermore, Hoover believes that Hostetter's approach led to John Zercher's return to the church and eventual "ardent" advocacy of the peace witness.[34]

The Zercher brothers had to make a confession before their probations were ended. Harold Zercher's confession appeared in Grantham district minutes.

Whereas my entry into the army as a 1-A ["available for induction"] forfeited my church membership, and whereby such action was in full discord with the principles of the Brethren in Christ Church, I sincerely ask forgiveness of the Church for so doing and say that I'm sorry for offending the brethren and the Church. I am not proud to admit to the Church my actions as a participant in war and as I now look back over the situation I do not feel that I should have entered the service as a 1-A. I don't believe that war is right or has ever in our present age righted a wrong. I feel that it is definitely contrary to the teachings of Christ to take human life. I hereby desire that the Brethren in Christ Church will see fit to again grant me membership.

The request was granted, and Zercher returned to full membership.[35] In the Manor-Pequea district, Carl Hunt likewise acknowledged his error in joining the military. The BIC community "warmly" extended forgiveness with a show of hands, followed by prayer and the singing of the hymn "Bless Be the Tie That Binds."[36]

Others in the BIC community saw church discipline as a violation of individual conscience or as self-righteousness. Paul J. Winger remembers being "publicly read out of the B.I.C. church when [he] joined the Navy December 1942." He describes nonresistance as "part of my early faith" as having little influence on him, since "I think for myself."[37] Similarly, Gordon H. Schneider describes his brother-in-law returning from military service as a baker during the Korean War. Congregational leaders urged the man to make a public confession. "Feeling that it was not their call[,] . . . he never again darkened that church door except to attend the funerals of his parents."[38] Clara Gibboney Kritzberger had a brother in Civilian Public Service and two brothers-in-law who served in the military. She remembers "as if it happened only yesterday" the tone and words of a man in Civilian Public Service who asked her two brothers-in-law to leave the BIC church building when they attended a service in uniform; none of them returned to a BIC church.[39]

Numerous other BIC members, including strong advocates of the peace position, retrospectively fault disfellowshiping. Isaiah B. Harley was a member of the Peace, Relief, and Service Committee in 1958 when General Conference replaced disfellowshiping with peace education. He describes committee members as "very eager" for an end to disfellowshiping. To support his objection to disfellowshiping, Harley cites the example of Hostetter's lenience toward John E. Zercher.[40] But Zercher illustrates more than one point. His case showed flexibility but also individual submission to group discipline, including public confession.[41] During the 1940s, Ray M. Zercher worried about the decline of the peace witness and strongly supported disfellowshiping as a sign of BIC support for Civilian Public Service. But now he too describes such a procedure as intolerant.[42]

These evaluations of the procedure for maintaining a corporate peace witness address not only the power accorded the group but also the content of the nonresistant stance. They reflect the changing relationship between the individual and the community. Peter Brock, a historian of pacifism, describes a very similar procedure of disfellowshiping, public confession, and reinstatement used by other nonresistant communities during the Civil War. Brock describes the "time-honored practice" as a relatively lenient way for the older generation to maintain the corporate body while allowing for the lapses and dilemmas of young men.[43] During World War II—and even more so in retrospect—people registered discomfort with public confession in particular. Many deemed this approach an intolerable infringement on the individual.

By the late twentieth century, the BIC understanding of peacefulness had changed from a corporate position to interpersonal reconciliation. Frances and

Wendell E. Harmon were part of the Upland BIC congregation, one of the most divided on military service. Although this congregation did not discipline members for military service, divisions, in Frances's evaluation, remained. Relationships "never were really very deeply healed." She remembers "emotions were pretty high then[,] . . . so you didn't do anything that would make it more hurtful to yourself. You tried to keep your nose clean and do the best you could."[44] The BIC community there proved unable to use its peace ideology to address conflict within the group.[45] Mennonite congregations struggled through these divisions in similar ways. Mennonite men who went into the military often quietly left their home churches. Perhaps relative size alone helps to explain why memory of the World War II peace witness remains strong among Mennonites but conflict plagues that of the Brethren in Christ.[46]

BIC MEN IN CIVILIAN PUBLIC SERVICE

As the foregoing makes clear, men who elected alternative service had close peers who made different decisions. Once in Civilian Public Service, their experiences also varied widely, depending on their assignment. Participants might work in a camp with large numbers of other conscientious objectors or in small but tightly knit units in state hospitals. They might work in lonely individual assignments, in dramatic firefighting teams, or as guinea pigs in experiments.[47]

John M. Wolgemuth came from the largest BIC constituency, Pennsylvania's Donegal district. Wolgemuth's departure for CPS camp in May 1941, soon after the institution of conscription, warranted a front-page story in the city of Lancaster's *Intelligencer Journal.* Wolgemuth was "the first conscientious objector in Lancaster county to be called to camp." Twenty-three-year-old Wolgemuth was quoted as saying, "I am ready. . . . If I can serve my country in this way I am willing to do it." In the accompanying photograph, Wolgemuth appears poised and determined in a dark suit coat and a white shirt, a high collar held upright not with a tie but with a bar pin.[48]

Unlike many other men in alternative service, Wolgemuth spent nearly his entire four-and-one-half years of service in the same assignment, a Soil and Conservation Service project in Virginia.[49] In *They Also Serve,* he described his work as simply that of a "clerk."[50] Another BIC man, however, remembers Wolgemuth as a key manager, helping to oversee work details.[51] In an issue of the camp's newsletter, Wolgemuth described with satisfaction how CPS crews helped alter the path of the North River to prevent the flooding of twenty-five farms.[52]

Ray M. Zercher, also from Donegal district, worked with the National Park Service in Luray, Virginia, and later at a state hospital in Howard, Rhode Island.[53] In this second location, Zercher labored part of the time in the ward for people

John M. Wolgemuth, BIC conscientious objector in World War II. Wolgemuth was the first conscripted conscientious objector from Lancaster County, Pennsylvania. He served for more than four years, most of that time at CPS Camp 4, Grottoes, Virginia. (*Lancaster Intelligencer Journal*, May 8, 1941)

BIC Ruth Landis Hess (far right) and Mennonite Winifred Gerber (far left) worked with their CPS husbands in Delaware State Hospital. Here Hess and Gerber received Christmas gifts from Dr. M. Tarumianz, superintendent of the hospital. Hess worked for the superintendent as a secretary; Gerber worked in his department as a stenographer. Olive Truitt, second from left, was the doctor's private secretary. *(Courtesy of Ruth Hess)*

classified as "criminally insane." After two years at Howard, Zercher transferred for health reasons to Camp 5 at Colorado Springs, where he spent his last year in CPS working in a Soil and Conservation Service project. Zercher, who would become an English and fine arts professor at Messiah College, now sees his experiences "as valuable as equal time spent in formal education," even though they "ranged from the tedious to the hazardous, and so were not welcomed at the time."[54]

Ruth Niesley married Zercher in 1944 and joined him at the Howard hospital, working as a paid employee in the occupational therapy department. In *Nonresistance under Test*, she wrote about the experiences of women like herself who were connected to the CPS program.[55] She focused on women who worked in state hospitals, but she also spoke of others who found jobs near CPS camps, who worked as nurses or dieticians in CPS camps, or worked beside their husbands in agricultural or public-health settings. She also included women who remained at home, living on minimal incomes while their husbands were away in alternative service. She concluded, "In spite of these difficulties each one of us, with few exceptions, was glad to make these sacrifices for the cause of Service and Peace."[56]

CPS experiences varied in part because of financial considerations. The Historic Peace Churches, largely responsible for food, clothing, and stipends for twelve thousand conscientious objectors in Civilian Public Service, called for contributions from their constituencies.[57] Many levels of the institutionalized BIC church, as well as the CPS program itself, responded to the straitened financial situation of CPS men and families with funds. But the results produced only modest stipends, not living wages. In an evaluation written soon after his more than three years in alternative service, Eber Dourte wrote, "One of the most difficult camp experiences was the sense of constant material dependency upon families and friends."[58] Perhaps remembering letters from his own three sons in Civilian Public Service, C. N. Hostetter Jr. noted those financial strains in a speech in 1946: "CPS boys served three or four years without even enough to buy clothes. I admire boys who have taken that difficult period with poise."[59]

The heaviest burden in covering costs fell on the men themselves and on their families. Official and private sources document that a BIC man in Civilian Public Service was expected to support his dependents. If his resources proved inadequate, he was to turn first to his family and only after that to the local BIC district. Peace, Relief, and Service Committee and the Mennonite Central Committee (MCC) dependency funds were to be the last resort.[60] A number of sources suggest that participants followed that sequence closely. In 1946, a PRS letter to demobilized men commended the cooperation of "each parent, sweetheart, wife, and child," noting especially "the loyalty and sacrifice" of wives "in bearing the peace testimony."[61] The personal financial record of J. Wilmer Heisey, unmarried throughout his three years in alternative service, shows that family and friends constituted his largest single source of cash income—31 percent of the total. Money arrived from his widowed mother, his two sisters, aunts, uncles, and both maternal and paternal grandparents. Not included in the 31 percent is a loan from his mother. With it he bought a car, important for his travels from farm to farm as a dairy tester.[62] Apparently, the first tier of the financial-aid system met the basic needs of most men and their families, but the cases that required additional resources are the most revealing.

Not surprisingly, the decentralized polity of the BIC community struggled under the budgetary and administrative burdens of the nonresistant mobilization. The relatively new Peace, Relief, and Service Committee sometimes fell short in its response to the needs of those in Civilian Public Service. At other times, poor communication or recalcitrant districts confounded the committee's best efforts.[63] In 1944, an official MCC statement on dependency aid unequivocally stated that the funding of dependents represented mutual aid, not charity. A 1944 General Conference statement agreed, though a little less strongly. But BIC emphasis on self-help and family funding suggested that appeals to the Mennonite Central Committee or the Peace, Relief, and Service Committee should be a last resort.[64]

Two months after the Mennonites set up their dependency system, Jesse W. Hoover informed an MCC administrator that the Brethren in Christ had decided to handle their own dependency cases. Hoover also recorded the "reluctance" of some PRS members to accept all dependency requests. Some on the committee "seem inclined rather to fall back on the emergency charity idea which was exactly the thing we tried to get away from."[65] A little more than a year later, however, Hoover wrote to Hostetter about the birth of yet another baby in one CPS family. Hoover suggested the policy on dependents should be discussed, particularly "whether there is any limitation to these dependency payments."[66]

During these same years, others were commenting on the reluctance of participants and family members to ask for aid of any sort. In 1945, the Dependency Trust Fund Committee of Pennsylvania's Dauphin-Lebanon district recorded the following observation: "We have found that dependents are hesitant to accept help from the committee as long as they have any resources of their own. We would like to urge our dependents not to wait until they are in embarrassing circumstances before they avail themselves of this provision."[67]

Hostetter's correspondence describes two cases of atypical family costs. Dorothy Meyer Baldwin worked with her husband at a state hospital in Greystone Park, New Jersey. Apparently, she had not requested aid despite the fact that in addition to supporting her husband with her wages, she made quarterly payments to support her father in the BIC retirement home.[68] Elsewhere, CPS man Jacob Glick had been hospitalized after being hit by a car. "It would be a distinct hardship for this boy or his parents to pay a large hospital bill. They would 'work their fingers off' to do so, but should not be required to do so."[69] Hostetter urged financial assistance in both these cases. Later, during demobilization, the PRS correspondence again expressed concern that participants in Civilian Public Service were not telling their home districts about their financial needs, much less availing themselves of other benefits, such as loans. Hoover also worried about the disparity in aid offered by the different denominations and even by various BIC districts.[70]

Despite all the evidence that CPS participants requested aid only as a last resort, the few petitions that did arrive on administrators' desks were rarely treated as emergencies. The clearest example comes from Pennsylvania's Granville congregation, a BIC mission church. One of its members, Betty Grove, ran her husband's coal and ice delivery business and received dependency payments for their three children while he was in Civilian Public Service. Recalling those years,

Betty remembers enjoying her work in the business and credits it with funding the family's nonresistant stand. In contrast, she explains, her husband's brother Lloyd chose military service in order to support his wife and child.[71] Although other factors may have been involved, correspondence soon after the induction of the two Grove brothers shows that Lloyd had first chosen Civilian Public Service. His pastor had written a letter to MCC headquarters asking for immediate financial aid for both of the Grove men but designating Lloyd's need as the more urgent. Because the letter should have gone to the Peace, Relief, and Service Committee first, for the next month the two institutions discussed procedure.[72] Eventually, Lloyd's wife received dependency payments, but perhaps not soon enough.[73] The sequence of events is unclear, but a list dated April 1945 indicates that Lloyd Grove had left Civilian Public Service to enter military service.[74]

In June 1946, the Peace, Relief, and Service Committee reported that $17,500 in dependency payments had been made to date. It listed twenty-seven women who had received payments ranging from fifteen dollars to $1,800. The listed recipients include a mix of ethnic and nonethnic surnames, and heartland and outlying church districts.[75] Their requests appear straightforward and diffident. One woman in 1945 wrote the following:

> Dear Sirs,
>   Could you please drop us a few lines to answer . . . my question.
>   We would like to know if the church helps pay for Dr and Hospital bills at a time like ours will be? It is quite a while yet till that time but in case the Church don't help in those bills, than we would like to know it. So that we would save a little every month of the $25.00 which you send me for every month now for my living. . . . [I]f not then we don't entend to ask it of the Church. . . . I don't have a bank account at home and the Dr don't see other way but for me to go to the hospital. . . . We thank you for the answer.

"Dear Sister in the Lord," the response began, but then it advised her that she must follow procedures—she was to send her request first to her bishop. (The committee treasurer sent a copy of the letter to the woman's bishop as well.)[76]

Problems in the system of financial aid led John S. Kohler and Anna Mae Rohrer Kohler to look for help elsewhere. John, from Mansfield, Ohio, spent his first twenty months of alternative service in Maryland. During that time Anna Mae lived with her parents, had a child, and developed kidney problems that required surgery. Lacking money for this, the Kohlers turned to a BIC nurse and doctor, who donated their time during the surgery to help cover the costs. A 1945 letter written by the PRS treasurer noted that the Kohler's home district was quite upset that the Kohlers had not received the full dependency amount that the district had requested. Contributions from Ohio went down after that incident.[77]

John Kohler spent the remainder of this CPS service as a dairy tester in Michigan. Most nights he stayed in the homes of farmers for whom he tested. Once, having no place to stay on a day off, he asked for a bed in the county jail. He picked up day jobs beyond his CPS work to pay off his wife's medical bills. One farmer, a Methodist with a son in military service, offered a tenant house so the couple could live together. Anna Mae's life there remained difficult, especially while John was gone and food ran low or when she was ill. A neighbor and a woman from a sister denomination helped provide child care and warm winter clothing.[78] These experiences undoubtedly informed John Kohler's 1947 article on Civilian Public Service and the BIC church: "It would be impossible to find in books the things which I learned from Henry Miller (Amish), Gordon Alderfer (General Conference Mennonite), Mose Brenneman (Old Mennonite), Atlee Miller (Old Order Amish Mennonite), or Ira Lehman (Brethren in Christ). Let me tell you one or two of these lessons from the Amish who have many excellent principles which I sometimes wish more Brethren in Christ people had." The lessons from the Amish were all examples of mutual aid— loans that could be repaid slowly, without interest, and quick aid in emergencies. How good, he contended, the Amish system would have been for participants in Civilian Public Service.[79]

Kohler was not alone in measuring BIC support for alternative service in financial terms. Certainly finances provided one key connection to the home community. Two surveys of CPS men reveal their strong concern about money. In a 1944 MCC survey focusing on postwar needs, 63 percent of the BIC respondents indicated that they hoped to return to their home communities, but another 15 percent chose the answer, "Any Mennonite community where there is opportunity to earn a living." BIC interest in financial aid, for farming and for funding education, was ten points higher than in the general Mennonite constituency: 56 percent of BIC respondents indicated that they needed some sort of financial aid.[80]

A 1945 BIC survey sponsored by the Pennsylvania state council also addressed financial issues. Eighty-one responses, all signed, offered not only statistics but often frank criticism of the BIC community.[81] Of these, 43 percent indicated that they had had to go into debt or draw on reserves to fund themselves in Civilian Public Service. Another 9 percent had not—but only because they had relied on income provided by a working wife or on help from parents and friends. On the other end of the need spectrum, 26 percent noted that they had managed to save a little money while in alternative service.[82] These figures suggest that a substantial number of participants felt financially pinched in the program. Any hesitation, therefore, on the part of the home community to support them financially must have been perceived as lack of support for conscientious objectors.

Another survey provides more general evaluations of the home community by BIC men in Civilian Public Service. In 1944, Wendell E. Harmon compiled confidential responses of sixty-six BIC men and presented the results in a series of articles in the *Sunday School Herald*.[83] This survey and the 1945 BIC survey cited earlier reveal similarly high percentages of men who thought their loyalty to the BIC community increased in alternative service—73 percent and 76 percent, respectively. At the same time, both surveys also show a high value placed on the role of the program in increasing tolerance and appreciation of religious expressions different from those learned in the home community. This new receptivity led one respondent to express love for the BIC community and interest in its "progress," even as he stated his disagreement with some BIC doctrines. Another noted, "I never had any great amount of loyalty for any church group." But, he continued, Civilian Public Service had increased his interest in all religious groups, especially in the Brethren in Christ.[84]

Both surveys also reveal substantial reservoirs of disappointment in the home community. Some of that dissatisfaction pointed directly to the lack of a unified BIC stance on conscientious objection. Why, wrote one, did the BIC church disfellowship combatant military men while choosing noncombatant military men as missionaries? Another called on the BIC community to take a clear stand on the issue of military service, though acknowledging that conflict existed throughout "the Major Peace Churches." Looking back, one participant describes the lasting imprint of the unresolved issue:

> I attended the B in C Church in Upland [California] where I had relatives to visit. I sat in disbelief on Sunday morning when a man wearing an army uniform stood up with his wife and sang a special song before the sermon and was adored for being "in the service" and "witnessing" for God, etc. I felt shame and disbelief that I was in a "PEACE" church congregation. My final six months were as an attendant in a mental hospital. While there a fellow attendant turned violent one night and tried to kill me for being a C.O. In a fit of anger, he threw a heavy bench against the office glass wall, the wall was sturdy and I was able to get into another room and escape his anger. As I went home after my release I wondered *what* had I done? *Why* had I done it? The western B in C church didn't seem to appreciate what I had done; the Harrisburg [Pennsylvania] church was mostly very elderly people who didn't involve themselves with "worldly" happenings—they did not know or seem to

care what I had done or gone through. I, like Mary in the Bible, "pondered these things in my heart." The General Church Board did offer me month-for-month tuition at a church school which I chose to accept and I went to Beulah (Upland) College where I tried to piece everything together. My final conclusion: what I did, I did for myself—*my own* conscience.[85]

Disappointment in the home BIC community also focused on a perceived lack of support, especially in comparisons with Mennonites. One man compared the five dollars he received each month to the twenty-five dollars his Mennonite coworkers got. One suggested his bishop had been slow to fill out forms requesting dependency aid, presumably from PRS funds. Some complained about church leaders who seemed uninterested in the program. Few BIC ministers visited the camps. One participant noted that few BIC women were involved as CPS staff nurses or dieticians, compared to the Mennonites. "Don't we have anyone qualified? Or aren't they willing to sacrifice as so many Mennonite nurses and [dieticians] have?" One wondered how the "old brethren back home" would get along if they were put in camp. Although BIC men might not have been aware of it, some Mennonite men made the same criticisms of their own home communities.[86]

On the other hand, many BIC men in alternative service expressed appreciation for the support offered by the home community. In an article for the *Sunday School Herald,* Jesse Heise noted particularly the sincerity of BIC leaders; he "most cherished . . . [the BIC church's] staunch testimony against war."[87] Of course, positive comments were the most likely to be published in church periodicals; sometimes these public comments came from individuals who spoke more negatively in private. Similarly, members of the Board for Young People's Work sometimes complained among themselves that men in Civilian Public Service rarely acknowledged the more than eight thousand dollars raised for them by church youth groups.[88] Publicly, however, the board carefully shared letters of appreciation it received or comments, such as the following: "It is so easy for us fellows here in camp to start running down the home church."[89] Private letters also revealed a sense of camaraderie with the home church. One CPS participant wrote to Hostetter, "I really appreciate the sacrifice our Church is making in providing for our C.P.S. camps." In a questionnaire this same individual noted that "our Kansas churches have done very well in helping us every month."[90]

After the CPS demobilization began in October 1945, concern grew about relations between the returning participants and the home BIC community.[91] In urging C. N. Hostetter Jr. to write an article on the needs of returning BIC men, Jesse W. Hoover noted that the home community and the men would need to make adjustments.[92] About the same time, Hoover wrote to the Peace,

Relief, and Service Committee: "I cannot feel at all certain that all these men are being cared for properly in a financial way as they go back to their home communities." Hoover always passed along to "home officials" any papers indicating a need for financial assistance, but no system had been set up to monitor what those officials did with the information. Hoover noted Mennonite Central Committee's willingness for the Brethren in Christ to participate in that organization's Mutual Aid Committee. Hoover urged immediate action on financial support, or "we will have lost to a greater or less degree some of our young brethren."[93]

During the CPS years, the small BIC community did worry about members of the group moving outside its well-established boundaries. Gerald N. Wingert remembers his older brother leaving for camp:

> Early on the morning of his departure, bags were packed, conversation at the breakfast table was somewhat forced. Our practice was to have family worship following breakfast. Father led in Bible reading and then we knelt for prayer. The only conversation I remember took place after the prayer and we were standing in a circle. It was time to leave, goodbyes were spoken and father said, "Remember what you have learned at home." I am sure he heard reports drifting back from CPS camps of the very few boys who went spiritually and morally "berserk" when they got out of the home environment.[94]

The "world" did pose a danger, one that the BIC community had faced since its beginnings. Early in the CPS program, Hostetter suggested moving the men out of the camps into more challenging service work: "It appears to me we can over do the matter of sheltering and protecting these youth."[95] But the smaller world of Civilian Public Service also posed its own threat to the cohesiveness of the small BIC community. In this new setting, the Brethren in Christ could not help but compare themselves with other similar groups on the small details of daily practice. The details and rationales of their own habits, so self-evident at home, here sometimes seemed difficult to explain or justify.

Conscientious Objectors in Canada and in the 1950s

The experiences of BIC conscientious objectors in Canada's Alternative Service Work program and in the U.S. I-W program (the alternative service program for conscientious objectors from 1952 to 1974) differed somewhat from the CPS experience. Neither of these programs required substantial financial outlays by the BIC community. The Canadian program initially placed conscientious objectors in Ontario, Manitoba, Saskatchewan, Alberta, and British Columbia

Ross and Rose Bearss and son Mervyn with E. J. Swalm (right), Port Alberni, British Columbia, World War II. Ross Bearss was a BIC conscientious objector who served in Canada's Alternative Service Work program. *(Courtesy of the Brethren in Christ Historical Library and Archives)*

camps. These were similar to those in the United States but were funded by the government, which paid participants a small daily wage. The civilian Department of Mines and Resources administered the camps. By 1943, most of the Canadian camps had closed, and conscientious objectors were working on farms or in industries in their home neighborhoods, donating some of their income to the Red Cross.[96]

Alternative Service Work (ASW) participant Louis Heise, who spent the war years working on his father's farm, remembers being aware of the U.S. program. Looking back, he suggests that CPS participants did more "meaningful service." His suggestion that many ASW men believed "they were wasting their time, by and large," however, sounds very close to the contemporary comments of many men south of the border.[97] In 1944, the executive secretary of the U.S. National

Service Board for Religious Objectors described Alternative Service Work "as more satisfactory to individuals" than Civilian Public Service but as less of a "total pacifist witness."[98] This sentiment stands in contrast to E. J. Swalm's article on Canada's program in *They Also Serve* soon after the war; he entitled his article, "Canadian CO's Served under a Plan the U.S. Might Well Have Copied."[99]

As the United States plunged into the Cold War and then the Korean War, the Canadian context for pacifists distinguished itself further from that to the south. After the demobilization of its World War II military forces, Canada discontinued conscription. The 1953 Ontario Joint Council committee working on peace issues reported little activity but warned against complacency and urged consistent living in a world beset by evil powers.[100] In 1954, the peace committee noted, "We thank God, that even though other countries are engaged in war, both cold and hot, we in Canada enjoy relative peace. How long this will continue, none of us knows."[101]

Meanwhile, in the United States, conscientious objectors in the 1-w program could choose paid work in approved institutions, most often hospitals, or give voluntary service. Both alternatives were under civilian oversight. BIC leaders urged the latter option, but it remained the minority choice.[102] Those conscientious objectors who volunteered for overseas relief work in the Mennonite program, called PAX, joined the larger volunteer movement in war-ravaged areas, often with life-changing impact.[103] A leading American historian, Paul S. Boyer, who was a PAX volunteer in Bielefeld, West Germany, and then in Paris between 1955 and 1957, argues that the "cosmopolitan experience changed the direction of my life." Clarence Sakimura, a PAX volunteer in Austria in the same years, describes the very personal approach taken in the distribution of relief goods, the "many cultural opportunities," and the flow of refugees out of Hungary in 1956. Such experiences, Sakimura asserts, shaped "a period of growth and social awareness for me that no doubt has colored my interpretation of the world ever since."[104]

Paul Carlson did less dramatic 1-w service between 1954 and 1956 at Messiah College. His experiences connect several themes of the BIC experience: community life in the World War II years, continuing discord over conscientious objection, and emphasis on an individual rather than corporate position.[105] As a BIC child in Chicago during the 1930s and 1940s, Carlson was embarrassed by his mother's plain dress and by a sign at the local BIC mission building proclaiming, "After death the judgement" and "The wages of sin is death." He remembers BIC missionaries as unable to answer adequately his questions about cultural relativity. He despaired of explaining his people's outward appearances but nevertheless felt that his world "in reality . . . was motivated by the highest ideals."[106]

Paul S. Boyer, Bielefeld, West Germany, 1955. Boyer, a BIC conscientious objector, served first in West Germany and then in Paris under Mennonite Central Committee's PAX program. In Bielefeld, he helped to build homes for postwar refugees. (*Courtesy of Paul Boyer*)

Carlson's mother encouraged his love of music, and he attended the Chicago Conservatory of Music. The world of music teaching and performance eventually took him on visits to the Hanoi (North Vietnam) National Conservatory of Music and the Shanghai Conservatory of Music. In those settings, he contrasted his own experiences as an I-W participant to those of musicians caught in the bombing of Hanoi or China's Cultural Revolution:

> I was very fortunate, and didn't actually realize how privileged I had been until later. I served my [I-W] period of two years teaching in the Music Department of Messiah College. . . . One summer I worked for George Lenhart in making repairs on the Messiah campus. Dr. C. N. Hostetter was concerned that as a violinist I might hurt my hands doing manual labor. He made the contacts for me to serve the second summer as a normal control patient at the National Institutes of Health in Bethesda MD. These privileged experiences still hold many positive memories.[107]

Carlson remembers no disagreements over nonresistant practice in the Chicago BIC mission where his family worshiped during World War II. "Young people who served in the military were given acceptance and respect." While at

Messiah College, however, he remembers a music professor referring back to the fifteen-year conflict over a corporate peace witness. The professor dreamed of writing a pamphlet that he would entitle, "When I Needed You Most, You Rejected Me," an apparent allusion to the disfellowshiping of members who served in the military. Carlson describes his own position today as one of "a deep inner loathing of war" and suggests that his BIC roots made him empathize with the "noble and innocent civilians" who lived through the American bombing of Hanoi. He accepts, however, some wars as just.[108]

Carlson, like many other participants in programs for conscientious objectors, values the BIC community as having fostered nonresistant beliefs and built concrete programs to express them. At the same time, he defines nonresistant beliefs individually. In this sense, Carlson is like many others in the BIC community. Prompted first by World War I conscription, the Brethren in Christ began formulating their own individual and diverse definitions of nonresistance. The old method for dealing with that diversity—disfellowshiping—no longer appeared to work. Within the BIC community, the debate over this diversity often led to discord, fear of decline, and uncertainty about how to perpetuate the peace witness.

In the face of such perplexing problems, the Brethren in Christ largely abandoned the attempt to agree on a corporate understanding of nonresistance, instead skirting the issue whenever possible. Some families continued to pass the peace witness from one generation to the next. Perhaps they had always been the primary conduits.

CHAPTER SIX

The Private Life of Nonresistance

〰

It's a wonderful but terrible thing to deal with actualities.

During World War II and the following decade, the Brethren in Christ (BIC) debated definitions of nonresistance and means of perpetuating the peace witness. Diversity on nonresistant issues within the BIC community challenged a unified, corporate expression. Individual members were too deeply enmeshed in American society to maintain nonresistance simply as nonparticipation. How, then, would their nonresistance and nonconformity persist?

The private writings of two BIC members provide perhaps the clearest picture of this persistence. The letters and diaries of C. Nelson Hostetter and Elsie C. Bechtel make clear that nonresistance was central to them both. However, the larger society, their families, their genders, and their individual aspirations influenced its expression. Within the context of these interactions, Hostetter and Bechtel each had to accommodate the ambiguities of daily life. Both observed the world in settings far from their home communities. Hostetter served in four Civilian Public Service (CPS) assignments and then continued as a volunteer in Puerto Rico between 1943 and 1946. Bechtel volunteered as a relief worker in France from 1945 to 1948.[1] While away from home, they wrote frank, critical, and affectionate letters to their families about their experiences in new settings—the South, a state mental hospital, and France. Their curiosity, openness, and enjoyment in these new settings suggest individuals who had been prepared by their families and by the BIC community to respond positively to the larger world. Here we see nonresistance passing successfully from one generation to the next, accommodating new ideas and new forms.

The differences between Hostetter's and Bechtel's experiences illustrate the ways in which gender shaped nonresistant practice. Hostetter's continuing reflections on definitions of nonresistance in his letters demonstrate the way in which male gender roles, particularly the expectation that they would perform military duty, forced nonresistant men to reflect on their peace witness. While in orientation for relief training, Bechtel also articulated a sophisticated analysis of nonresistance. But her private writings demonstrate nonresistance not so much proclaimed as expressed in the massive work of nurturing those under her care—again reflecting old and ongoing gender expectations.

Neither Bechtel nor Hostetter were typical BIC members. Bechtel loved opera, and Hostetter once admitted his disinclination to articulate his religious beliefs to strangers.[2] However, both encountered issues common to many BIC people. They represent the diversity within the small BIC community. Furthermore, both made lifelong commitments to BIC causes, including volunteer work and support of and participation in inter-Mennonite service bodies. Thus, both represent important strands of the religiously motivated humanitarian service that powered BIC community life and corporate nonresistance in the first half of the twentieth century.

C. Nelson Hostetter

Hostetter was born in Lancaster, Pennsylvania, on October 16, 1923. His family was one of the most prominent in the BIC community. Its paternal ancestry included BIC deacons, ministers, bishops, educators, and denominational administrators. His grandfather and father provided prominent leadership during both world wars. Nelson would continue that tradition, working for part of his adult life as an executive coordinator of Mennonite Disaster Service, an affiliate of Mennonite Central Committee (MCC).[3]

If the men in the family illustrated typical leadership patterns among the Brethren in Christ, several women of the family epitomized the typical blending of Brethren in Christ with other churches through marriage. Nelson's paternal grandmother grew up Mennonite. His mother, Anna Lane Hostetter, joined the United Zion Church as a young woman. She attended and then taught at Messiah Bible College, where she met her husband. Nelson himself married a Mennonite. At the age of thirty, he changed his church membership from the Brethren in Christ to the Mennonite Church.[4]

Less than a year after finishing high school at Messiah Bible College's academy, Hostetter was drafted. He served in four assignments in Civilian Public Service. He began his alternative service in February 1943 at Grottoes, Virginia; transferred in November 1943 to a public health project in Mulberry, Florida;

L to R: Nelson Hostetter, Wilmer Heisey, Lyle Myers, three
BIC conscientious objectors at CPS Camp 4, Grottoes,
Virginia. The three sang together at the Grottoes camp,
devoted to soil conservation projects and agricultural work.
(Courtesy of J. Wilmer Heisey)

and then, in 1945, began working in a state hospital in Ypsilanti, Michigan. In
1946, he transferred to Puerto Rico, where he continued as a volunteer public
health worker.[5]

Hostetter had three younger brothers, two of whom also served in Civilian
Public Service.[6] The three in alternative service—Nelson, Lane, and Ray—wrote
often to their parents between 1943 and 1946.[7] In ways similar to Elsie Bechtel,
the Hostetter brothers' letters to their parents were frank, especially about nonresistance and the BIC community. Unlike Bechtel, they moved in a network of
Brethren in Christ in each CPS setting. Nonetheless, Nelson's experiences often
evoked reflections on pacifist expressions beyond those nurtured by the BIC
church. Furthermore, his ongoing reflections on the peace witness reflect the
influence of the larger pacifist movement.

In May 1942, less than a year before he was drafted and as he considered life after high school, Hostetter wrote an article for the *Clarion,* the Messiah Bible College periodical. With its sense of foreboding, its expression of patriotic sentiments, and its explicit admiration for humanitarian and national service, the article demonstrates the weight of the war on the BIC community's young men. "We Seniors," he began, "undoubtedly have the darkest and most discouraging promises of an existence for life, [that] any previous graduating class has had." Instead of despairing, he continued, "we are determined to make this world a better place to live and undertake this task with utmost courage." The means, he said, would be service to "our fellowmen . . . our country . . . and . . . for Christ." Combining loyalty to "the heavenly kingdom" and love of nation, Hostetter pointed to the alternative of Civilian Public Service and a desire to "do all that we conscientiously are able to preserve the democratic policies of the country we cherish." His understanding of what he "conscientiously" could do would change in the next four years, as he moved into the larger pacifist movement.[8]

In CPS camp at Grottoes, his work, leisure, and social relationships followed the routines of many other conscripted conscientious objectors. His letters described manual and clerical labor—office work, hauling coal, husking corn.[9] But much more of his attention focused on the growing BIC group in the camp as well as on visitors from the home church. Starting in Grottoes and continuing throughout his CPS years, music served as both a marker of BIC identity and as an introduction to other communities. In June 1943, for example, he noted that it had become possible for a BIC trio to form, due to the arrival in the camp of another BIC man who could sing. Later the trio grew to a quartet, which sang in churches on weekends and furloughs. The people Hostetter mentioned in his letters were most often from his BIC community.[10]

Hostetter seemed pleased when selective service approved his requested transfer to a unit in Mulberry, Florida. Work, leisure, and personal relationships in a CPS unit far from concentrations of BIC or Mennonite conscientious objectors provided new experiences for Hostetter. The Mulberry unit in central Florida addressed public health issues. Approximately thirty CPS men and staff there worked to install privies, septic tanks, and wells. Florida state officials praised their efforts to improve sanitation as the best in the country. The Mulberry unit also served as one of CPS's training schools for men hoping to do overseas relief work. Hostetter, therefore, installed privies by day and in the evenings took classes in first aid, sanitation, geography, sociology, and bookkeeping.[11]

Like his earlier correspondence, Hostetter's letters from Mulberry described his work, leisure, and contacts with other Brethren in Christ. But now his letters also detailed his thoughts on nonresistance and the larger pacifist movement, the connections between the peace witness and relief work, and evaluations of Civilian Public Service and the involvement of the Brethren in Christ in administering the program. When he transferred to a state hospital in Ypsilanti, his reflections on nonresistance continued, but within the context of the violence that sometimes attended his work there.

Starting with the letters from Mulberry, Hostetter increasingly advocated relief work as an avenue of service and, therefore, an active expression of nonresistance. He coupled his advocacy of relief work with criticism of the pervasive militarism in American society. In his high school graduation article, notwithstanding his patriotic statements, he warned against "the great suction of sentiment in which such slogans as 'Remember Pearl Harbor,' or 'V for Victory' thwart our ideals" and engender hate for national enemies.[12] Events in 1943 strengthened his criticism. Congress passed an army appropriations bill with an amendment forbidding CPS work outside the United States.[13] This ended Hostetter's dream of doing relief work in a war zone. Despite the 1943 bill, he continued to hope for relief work, while acknowledging that the prospects were not good as long as the war continued.

At this time, new questions appeared in his letters. After the war, he wondered whether relief work in areas under Allied occupation would be tainted by connections to the military.[14] In one letter he directly stated that Civilian Public Service had made him an "anti-militarist." In any case, despite his impatience to get on to his dream of relief work, Hostetter acknowledged that his current work met his criteria for service. The sanitation work in Mulberry "might be our greatest service as COs during the War," he wrote one Thursday evening, after complaining about a "very militaristic religious person" who had discussed the fate of Japan on the radio. At the Ypsilanti state hospital, he wrote to his parents, perhaps to encourage himself, that he would continue trying to do a good job as a ward attendant while awaiting release for relief work. It was from the hospital that he wrote one of his clearest statements on the connection between nonresistance and service: "A progressive non-resistant (I don't like that word, I prefer) Christian pacifism program of active aid to others is our only testimony in this crisis."

Hostetter's letters provide a picture of the many points at which BIC conscientious objectors drew dividing lines regarding their peace witness. Disappointed with one BIC man whose draft board had granted what was apparently his request for an agricultural deferment, Hostetter wrote, "I'm not prejudiced, but its a shame the way the Brethren in Christ boys go running to the farm." He hoped his brothers would not make that choice, which seemed "more 'yellow' than going to CPS." Yet he also once criticized some CPS camps as "havens for conchies" (a slang for conscientious objectors) rather than communities of peacemakers. Such camps were unworthy of the CPS name, and he would refuse to work there.

In another letter, he acknowledged that Civilian Public Service itself aided the system of conscription, a key criticism of conscientious objectors who opposed the program.[15] Hostetter, however, targeted only specific projects in Civilian Public Service. For example, he once wrote to his parents that he would not participate in the guinea-pig project in which CPS men served as live subjects in scientific experiments. Presumably, he thought these experiments might benefit the military, although he had earlier applied to serve as a subject in experiments on atypical pneumonia.

Even within the Hostetter family, the brothers apparently discussed where conscientious objectors should draw lines. At one point Nelson counseled his brother Lane against the noncombatant military position—"Please remember that if you take the oath of allegiance to militarism or slip on the uniform, you are a definite part of a gigantic machine of destruction, so [no matter] how I-AO [Selective Service classification for noncombatants in the military] you are, or how non-combattant [*sic*] your job is, you might as well be out front bayonetting your fellow-man. So please think it over. I have had many service-men tell me that I did the right thing."[16] Aware of the lure of military glory, Nelson also worried about his brother Ray. From Ypsilanti, he wrote to his parents, "Military propaganda vs. a good home-training of non-resistance and pacifism really puts a teen-age kid on a fence." In another letter from Ypsilanti in late 1945 or early 1946, he told his parents that he had written Ray a "strong letter." Nelson wondered if the local draft board might approve work for Ray on boats transporting cattle to Europe. This might seem more exciting than most CPS projects and therefore meet "military propaganda" that made "army life look inviting for adventure."[17]

Nelson Hostetter, older than his brothers and apparently more content with his nonresistant position and his alternative service assignments, reflected on peace issues beyond his own struggles as a drafted conscientious objector. He worried about a war bond given to him by his grandparents but considered civilian bonds "a farce" given the interconnections of financial institutions, corruption, and war. He pronounced World War III "inevitable" in fifteen years. He chided his parents for their fear of German prisoners of war held in the United States. He wrote twice about the dangers of registered nurses being drafted with no provision for conscientious objection. He described a female friend as "becoming more of a CO than ever before" as she visited CPS camps. At another point, he expressed disappointment that "more girls from Grantham" had not volunteered for relief work. These comments on women facing nonresistant issues differ from his pre-CPS sentiments. Earlier he had noted the possibility of alternative service for conscientious objector men and had appeared to assign a neutral role to women. Women from his school class, he

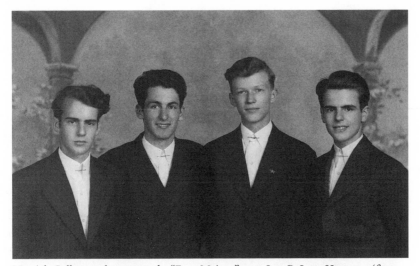

Messiah College male quartet, the "Four Majors," 1945. L to R: Lane Hostetter (first tenor), Eugene Haas (second tenor), Royce Saltzman (baritone), Ray Hostetter (bass). Haas and Nelson Hostetter's two younger brothers served in Civilian Public Service. Saltzman served as a livestock attendant on a ship to Poland in 1946. As representatives of Messiah Bible College, the men pictured did not wear neckties in accordance with the dress codes legislated by the Brethren in Christ in 1937. *(Courtesy of the Brethren in Christ Historical Library and Archives)*

had written, would be asked to fill agricultural and industrial jobs "where the men have stepped out to help protect our country."[18]

Although Hostetter easily connected nonresistance to his daily life during his CPS years, its practice was not without ambiguities. Particularly in the state mental hospital at Ypsilanti, he had to make decisions about using force. Reminiscing about that work in a 1977 interview, Hostetter remembered a kind of excitement in the work and even a sense that sometimes the risks were similar to those of men in the armed services.[19] His first letter home from Ypsilanti gave particulars. He had been attacked with a broom, intervened in fights, caught a resident attempting to leave the building, and helped to foil a suicide attempt. As an afterthought, he urged his parents not to worry about him, adding, "When a fellow gets to a mental hospital he loses a certain degree of his non-resistance and pacifism." At another point he described to his mother a confrontation with a resident in which the resident needed to be taught "the hard way." The resident later accused Hostetter of giving him a black eye. Apparently, his mother worried as much about his nonresistant practice as about his safety.[20] Responding to her concern, he argued that she could not understand the weight of responsibility for so many people with so few staff. If she could visit the ward,

Nelson Hostetter, Ypsilanti, Michigan, state mental hospital.
Hostetter joined more than 2,000 other conscientious objectors
in CPS who helped both to relieve the labor shortage in mental
institutions and to challenge the dehumanizing conditions in
them. *(Courtesy of C. Nelson Hostetter)*

she would change her mind, as "all of us have." Actually, however, CPS men and
women in state hospitals during the war worked to decrease the use of force in
the care of residents and to improve living conditions in general.[21]

Although he pondered the implications of the peace witness, numerous personal relationships tied Hostetter to people serving in the military. He once described the men fighting the war as "buddies and friends." At Mulberry, he tem-
porarily had a job on Saturdays working for a discharged Marine. He once
recorded a visit and "long chat" with Dick Minter, a friend from home and an
official member of the same BIC congregation—who had, however, chosen military service.[22] None of his references to Minter express any discomfort with his
military position. In fact, Hostetter said he felt part of the Minter family. Minter
would be disciplined by the home congregation that Hostetter's father pastored.[23]

Nevertheless, Hostetter's letters never raise with his parents the disjunction between different choices made by sons from the same BIC congregation.

Personal relationships in Civilian Public Service raised other issues about nonconformist practice. During Nelson Hostetter's time in Mulberry, he dated a Methodist woman who had a brother in the military. For people in their twenties and early thirties, courting must have seemed as pressing an issue as the practice of nonresistance. Hostetter was particularly caught up in questions of whom he might marry. So were BIC leaders, who voiced concerns that men in Civilian Public Service might meet and marry women from outside the BIC community. "Mixed marriages" not only posed problems for the extensive BIC kinship networks but also threatened the very existence of a small group that maintained its member base, both by conversions and by generational continuity. Even marriages within the Historic Peace Churches were sometimes seen as problematic.[24] In the 1940s, the Brethren in Christ and Mennonite Church still excluded each other from Communion—even while functioning as one group within Civilian Public Service.[25] This complicated mix led to multiple and shifting boundaries in daily life.

Dick Minter's father sounded the alarm to Hostetter's father after visiting Nelson. The relationship between Nelson and "the Methodist girl" was becoming serious, he wrote in a letter. The woman and her family were wonderful people, making the relationship "more 'dangerous.'"[26] Hostetter had probably met the woman at a Methodist church in Lakeland, near Mulberry.[27] The pastor there warmly welcomed CPS men to his church. The relationship raised conflicting emotions for Hostetter. At one point, he told his father not to worry; distance from home had taught him that his "best bet on a girl will be to find one from my own background," with ideals "as [eccentric] as mine." But at another point, he wrote about marrying the woman and thanked his parents for assuring him that his choice of a marriage partner would also be theirs. He wanted to give the woman a diamond ring, though traditional BIC nonconformity rejected most jewelry, including wedding bands.[28] But the wider issue of marrying outside the BIC church troubled him. "I'm sorry for your sake that I went outside the church, but I don't think I could be happy with a conservative girl." Perhaps to reassure them of his commitments, he noted that the woman wanted him to go into relief work, because of his convictions. The engagement did not proceed. Hostetter left Mulberry for Ypsilanti and then transferred to Puerto Rico. By the end of 1946 he had married Esther Miller, a Mennonite Church volunteer serving in the Puerto Rico unit. Seven years later, he became a member of Miller's denomination.

Although Hostetter's letters often criticized the BIC community, he seems to have been relaxed in this network of relationships that sustained and sup-

ported him. All the members of the Hostetter family communicated frankly
and expressed affection for each other. Spurred by an upcoming Mother's Day,
Hostetter conveyed his appreciation while offering an explanation for his critical evaluations of the BIC community.

> For the large and small things; for loving me, for praying for me, for sac-
> rificing for me, for punishing me, for helping me, for all your kindness and
> favors I want to thank you from the bottom my heart.
>
> Being reared in a good Christian home is what is most significant to me.
> For high standards, for sound doctrines, for simple life, for a deep faith, it
> has all been implanted in my life because of you, but due to the progress of
> time each generation is compelled to some minor changes.[29]

His father's deep involvement in the CPS program undoubtedly encouraged Hostetter, but it was his mother's work overseeing the collection of clothing for men in the program that he emphasized in one letter: "When I think of
the time you put in the project it makes me know you are behind me in relief
work and I want to do it all the more."

For Hostetter, the "family" often blended into the BIC community. His extended family found itself at the center of several key institutions within a community reinforced by kinship. In one letter, Hostetter was interested in what
"our other boys think of the [CPS] setup," especially their responses to a questionnaire sent out by his uncle Henry N. Hostetter, secretary of the Board for
Young People's Work.[30] During the period of these letters, a number of women
lived with the Hostetter family to help Anna Lane Hostetter with domestic chores.
Hostetter's salutations often included these women as integral members of the
family, and he sometimes addressed comments directly to them.

Beyond this extended family, Hostetter consistently noted the many contacts he made with other BIC people. While in the Mulberry unit, he mentioned writing to other BIC men in alternative service.[31] At one point, Hostetter
considered transferring to a Rhode Island state hospital to "be with all the B. in
C. boys up there."

In his letters from Mulberry, Hostetter complimented both Harold S. Martin, the BIC director of the unit, and his wife, Grace Martin, who served as unit
matron.[32] Harold Martin's message in an Easter service impressed Hostetter,
eliciting the comment that the home church often marginalized talented people.
"Sometimes I think it is too bad that his [Martin's] local district is so narrow-
minded that they will not let him be of service to the church. After this War
someone is going to have to give in on the code of the church and its rules and
regulation." Although reiterating his commitment to "the fundamental prin-

ciples which I learned at home," Nelson Hostetter felt his separation from home and church had changed his religious sensibility from one of "emotional force of outward appearances and high flying banners of good deeds" to one of "letting my light shine in a quiet way." Yet deeds continued to be important criteria for him in defining what being Brethren in Christ should mean. On receipt of an MCC newsletter at Ypsilanti, Hostetter was disappointed that no one from his BIC community appeared among the lists of new relief workers. All three of the Hostetter brothers traveled to BIC churches and missions in the areas of their assignments. They attended weddings of Brethren in Christ. Perhaps most telling, since they had other options, in Civilian Public Service they often socialized with BIC peers. In addition, Nelson Hostetter frequently noted that news about the BIC church and school had made him homesick.

Although all three Hostetters moved easily in the BIC community, they also had much in common with the larger CPS population. Music provides an example of this blending. Music appreciation and performance played a key role in the life of young people at Messiah Bible College and was also an important part of CPS life.[33] All three brothers appreciated music, and two participated in quartet performances while in alternative service.[34] Music not only connected Nelson Hostetter to his BIC community but took him into many other settings. His letters from Mulberry are filled with news about music. He enjoyed hearing choral music, an opera singer, and masses on the radio. He noted with pleasure that the men in this unit "have an appreciation for high calibre music." In his relief class on health and sanitation, he liked two films on tuberculosis, "especially the music" provided by a Tuskegee Institute choir. He allowed himself to be persuaded by his girlfriend's mother to sing in the Methodist church choir when he was not busy with quartet performances. The Mulberry quartet sang in a county revival, in Assembly of God and Baptist churches, at the Quaker-administered Orlando CPS camp, in a county prison, at a Halloween party, and—the setting he described most extensively—in the songfest of a number of African American churches.[35] He believed his quartet was the first white musical group to participate there and thought the audience enjoyed the music; several people "remarked how different our singing was and how they liked it so well." Hostetter supposed his group would be invited to other "Negro congregations." They were, and this activity even led to a meal in an African American home.

Hostetter's observations on the songfest are one of his many observations on the world beyond his home community. As in his musical life, he moved back and forth between his small group and other larger communities rather easily. Observations on Mennonites, the larger pacifist community, the local Mulberry community, and racial and economic structures provide a focus for considering his understanding of his own place in the larger world. Hostetter wrote from the Mulberry unit that he and a Lutheran man joked about the Mennonite attempt to convert them as they participated in the unit's Mennonite Faith and Heritage class. Most of the time, however, Nelson Hostetter seemed quite at home with Mennonite colleagues. He pronounced the Mennonites at Grottoes mostly "Goshen boys," "a swell group." He threatened that if Messiah Bible College balked in any way at accepting for school credit the courses he was taking at Mulberry, he would simply go to Goshen College, a Mennonite school in Indiana. Perhaps comparing his own community to his assumptions about the larger Mennonite group, he found Eastern Mennonite School in Harrisonburg, Virginia, disappointing. He had thought the school "would be more than what it is."[36]

Nelson Hostetter's one strong criticism of the Mennonites in relationship to the Brethren in Christ, the only time Hostetter made sharp distinctions between himself and the Mennonite men in his unit, may have been an expression of his general frustration at the lack of relief work. Mennonites perhaps provided a convenient target. He began by noting that the possibility of relief work during the war seemed remote; after the war, the United Nations Relief and Rehabilitation Agency would probably require three years of college education from its workers, ruling out men like Hostetter. To top off the dismal picture, Hostetter wrote to his parents, Mennonite Central Committee would prefer its own Mennonite people as it chose relief workers. "Honestly, I think our church will get a raw deal from the MCC after the War." He added that another BIC man in Civilian Public Service had already told him that he would not go into relief work because he did not "cherish" working under Mennonites. Hostetter went on to propose establishing BIC relief projects under the auspices of several cooperating boards. Hostetter's willingness to work in Mennonite programs represents that of BIC participants generally. In addition, Hostetter's complaints about the lack of meaningful service opportunities is representative of similar complaints by many Mennonite CPS men.[37]

The broader pacifist population in the Mulberry unit seemed to invigorate Hostetter. His contentment in this larger group was probably atypical of the Brethren in Christ, but he never articulated any sense of that. Instead, his letters home assumed his family would share his interest in the variety of conscientious objectors around him. Mennonite Central Committee administered the Mulberry unit; Quakers and Church of the Brethren administered two other CPS units, in Orlando and Tallahassee, respectively. Hostetter wrote of "camaraderie" between the units. He described men in the Friends unit repairing radios in their spare time, selling them at low cost to others in Civilian Public Service. At another point, sixteen men from the two other camps attended a conference at Mulberry on the public health program. In the Sunday morning service, about thirteen denominations were represented. "In spite of all our different ethical codes and customs, today the world does not think so much of that, but the thing that really counts when you are Christians is to live according to Christ's way of life." There were apparently work exchanges between the units; Hostetter worked for a few weeks in the two other camps.

Hostetter also wrote about Fellowship of Reconciliation literature and speakers; about the case of a public school teacher fired for registering as a conscientious objector; and about the inspiring pacifist stands of a number of women, including an elderly Presbyterian missionary. He found very interesting a Christian anarchist who was also a vegetarian. He noted the influence of new ideas, while reconfirming his roots in his own tradition. "When I don't get anywhere on religion with a fellow, then I turn to social and political reasons. Although the last two are secondary to me, they should occupy a big place in any pacifist's life."

Although Hostetter found ways to connect with a variety of new ideas, particularly on issues of pacifism, he noted differences within his unit on dancing and alcohol consumption. But even here he expressed a measure of tolerance, noting simply that some of the CPS men danced but that his female partner at a party did not seem to mind that he did not. He recorded an argument over drinking alcohol but then reminded his parents that this information about drinking was confidential. "If they [Hostetter's coworkers] can do it," he asserted, "that is up to them." This personalized approach to corporate prohibitions paralleled a comment on Bible study. At Mulberry, Hostetter reported that he enjoyed a Bible class on the teachings of Jesus because the teacher did not instruct so much as elicit viewpoints. Each person, after considering multiple interpretations, formed a personal one. In all these interactions, Hostetter seemed to blend traditional BIC church stands with a new toleration of differences.

Intolerance, however, was also part of the CPS experience. CPS units in the American South were forced to address racial segregation. But their responses varied, producing tension with the Historic Peace Church coalition. Mennonites accepted racially segregated units in the South, whereas units administered by Quakers and the Church of the Brethren more directly challenged racial segregation.[38] Although Hostetter's unit did not directly challenge racial discrimination, it did provide services in African American neighborhoods. Hostetter described installing privies in a "Negro fish market" and at an African American Baptist church. His experiences raised his awareness of racial injustice. In one letter, he indicated that race tension increased problems for the unit: "Although most of us will not go out of our way to cause jealousy of the whites, yet none of us will [let] Southern tradition bind us up." He mentioned that in response to the tension a camp newsletter addressed racial issues strongly, and he himself spoke to the Methodist League on the "Independence of the Negro." He wrote to his parents, "It was the hardest thing I ever did. I prayed and studied plenty." He thought the audience had responded positively; he attributed its response to the fact that its members were young and therefore less racist than their parents' generation. At another point, he attributed "a small race riot" in Mulberry to a drunken white man "disturbing" a "colored girl." Reflecting on that, he wrote, "I really do pity the colored people here, the Health Service keeps reminding us boys to treat them as Niggers, but we don't listen to them too closely. But the colored people seem happy." Like many Americans, Hostetter mixed an awareness of injustice with his own accommodation of racism. He described in stereotypical language "an Old Negro Mammy," and he wrote with no apparent concern about "pickaninnies" and a place called "Nigger Ridge."

Hostetter was to follow the same pattern in his years in Puerto Rico when describing economic exploitation of the people there. In two articles, he would explicitly note inequities and offer an explanation that acknowledged structural poverty and American complicity. "When arriving on the mystic isle of Puerto Rico one is puzzled by its great extremes of living conditions." He went on to describe urban opulence next to shacks, the smallness of the middle class, political corruption, grasping landowners, and an American government unwilling to consider local opinions. In summary, he wrote, "The rich live in extravagant luxury, the middle class ride along carelessly, and the poor struggle for an existence."[39] In an earlier article, he attributed the high rate of anemia to the extremely inequitable distribution of wealth and to a health system that catered to the wealthy.[40] But while noting the structures that confined poor people, he also attributed their problems to individual failings such as laziness, irresponsibility, and "spiritual weakness." He pointed to vices easily recognizable to a Brethren in Christ or Mennonite—too much alcohol and gambling. Although Hostetter expressed wariness of political solutions, he also recorded the desires of poor, rural Puerto Ricans—independence from the United States and redistribution of land to small farmers.[41]

After his years in Civilian Public Service and in additional volunteer work, Nelson Hostetter continued his strong advocacy of pacifism, his questioning of the church he had grown up in, his condemnation of American militarism, and his devotion to voluntary programs. In 1971, he became the national director of MCC's Mennonite Disaster Service. He urged that all Mennonites participate in some volunteer work and share their material wealth with others less fortunate. In a 1977 interview about Civilian Public Service, he said he had moved away from the Brethren in Christ not only because he married a Mennonite but also because he increasingly saw "the Brethren in Christ going middle-of-the-road evangelical Americana." Some Mennonites might also be moving in that direction, he acknowledged, but in general he saw the Mennonites as more successful at transforming their traditional nonresistance into service and at critiquing the society in which they lived. To a question about whether he had ever considered refusing to register for the draft altogether, Hostetter replied that although he did not consider such action in World War II, he might have if he had been facing the decision during the Vietnam War years. His rationale was that growing militarism drew alternative service into its web. Like many other BIC people, Hostetter seemed to have forgotten the passion and activism of the earlier era, when he had raised the very same questions about conscientious objectors caught in the larger social web of a world at war.[42]

Nelson Hostetter's story shows us a BIC member defining nonresistance both theoretically and in daily practice. Doing this required him to reformulate many of his understandings of community life and of the larger society. His nonresistant expressions suggest openness to and tolerance of ideas different from those of his home community. They suggest personal desires that did not always conform to that community's corporate life. His reformulations entailed accommodation to the larger world and to the ambiguities daily life posed for him. Yet Hostetter's Anabaptist identity remained his preeminent guide.

Hostetter's memories of his CPS years do not gloss over the tensions and compromises of a young BIC man in alternative service, but his stronger images are embedded in stories in which all the pieces seemed to fit together. Occasionally, even as events unfolded, Hostetter noted success in holding belief and practice together—always, however, with a hint of the complexities of daily life. On Christmas night, probably in 1944, Hostetter wrote to his parents about an incident that had occurred one day while he was hitchhiking back to the unit. The man who picked him up offered him first a beer and then a cigarette. Both of these Hostetter declined, to the driver's surprise. The conversation then turned to the war and finally to the fact that Hostetter was a conscientious objector.

> We got to talking and I told him all about my Christian philosophy of life. When we parted he told me that he wanted to come out to camp and meet 35 more fellows like me. This made me feel good. I've learned that if you stick by your convictions when people get down to the point they have much respect for you, and wonder how they can get rid of their bad habits etc. also.
>
> Mother and Dad, again I want to thank you for you being faithful and always challenging your boys with the best. I hope that none of us let you down again.

Elsie C. Bechtel

As a conscripted conscientious objector from a prominent BIC family, Hostetter was expected to address the issues of nonresistance in the 1940s. Elsie Catherine Bechtel, in contrast, did not face conscription, her family was much less prominent than Hostetter's, and her Ohio district was a tiny BIC community. But she too joined the voluntary movement to express nonresistance in relief service. To a considerable extent, the content of such service—food production, clothing distribution, caring for those in need—had long been an integral part of women's work. In many ways Bechtel's service drew on those traditional roles as much as on any new thinking about nonresistance. At the same time, her personal, less traditional interests influenced her response to the larger world.[43]

Elsie Bechtel was born October 26, 1913, to a BIC farm family near Canton, Ohio. This was one of two areas in Ohio where Brethren in Christ had settled by the 1880s. Bechtel's father homesteaded in the area and continued farming those original family lands until he died, a week before Bechtel turned sixteen. Bechtel's mother, Laura Myers, had met her future husband when she came to work on the Bechtel farm. Laura described for her children how she drove home after the wedding, changed into old clothes, and went to work in the fields.[44]

The small Valley Chapel BIC congregation near Canton provided a focus for the Bechtel family. Like many other Brethren in Christ with memories going back to before World War II, Bechtel describes the "great occasion" of the love feast as a high point of the year. The two-day celebration drew BIC people from five other Ohio districts. This gathering of a larger church community was important to congregations like Valley Chapel, which had about twenty-five members in the 1930s.[45] Another family focus was the BIC school at Grantham, Pennsylvania. Bechtel's parents somehow found the money to send their three children to the academy at Messiah Bible College, in part to avoid public high school. The school's faculty members inspired Bechtel with their dedication and acceptance of wages lower than their training might command elsewhere. When she dreamed of doing service, she emulated these people. After finishing high school in 1931, Bechtel worked for three years doing domestic work, earning enough to pay for two years at Messiah Bible College. Then came two more years of domestic work to fund her final two years of study, which earned her a teaching certificate at Goshen College.[46]

After four years of teaching, Bechtel's desire to serve—and world events—led her to volunteer for an MCC Women's Service Unit in 1944, working at a state hospital in Howard, Rhode Island. The next summer, the Mennonite Central Committee appointed Bechtel to relief work in France.[47] The following month Bechtel presented a rousing speech to other relief work candidates at training sessions at Goshen College. Her speech made the connection between nonresistance and relief work explicit. Her strongest image, however, described nonresistance as a kind of recklessness:

> I like the lowly geranium. The winter snows can be piled high on the window sill; frost may obscure the view, yet it blooms with a certain recklessness and abandon that all the ice, sleet, and cold winds can not bother.
>
> Curing hate by love may seem like a wintry task, but we can pour on love as recklessly and with as great abandon as the geranium pours out color and brightness, for our God is the God of love and there is no limit to His supply.[48]

Bechtel's speech at Goshen College is the only source directly addressing her understanding of nonresistance. That belief, she contended, grew from group interpretation of Scripture. But nonresistant people were not the only people with a corporate task. In fact, the collective work of war provided meaning in many people's lives precisely because it transcended individual experience. Because of war's appeal, she said, nonresistant people had to find a positive way to make their stand visible. Relief work provided that positive channel for the nonresistant stand against war. Nonresistant people had also to acknowledge that those who were fighting were in fact protecting "our political freedoms." American strength, superiority, and material wealth also mandated relief work. Finally, Bechtel thought that relief work made it possible to practice nonresistance rather than experience it only as a theory.[49]

Ironically, the practice of nonresistance for relief workers often included one of the most common experiences of all people in the war years: waiting.[50] For more than a month after the Goshen orientation, Bechtel waited to leave for France. Bechtel described these weeks as some of the worst of her life. Delays in leaving for France, a sense that Mennonite Central Committee might be mishandling matters, and the lack of work discouraged her. Keeping the people she would be serving in mind, however, she wrote in her diary, "Imagine feeling like this plus having no source of income, no food, no clothes no shelter and all this added to the . . . [loss of] a family." A month later, Bechtel sailed to Le Havre, France. Finally, Bechtel could begin her real relief work.[51]

Her sense of mission seldom wavered. But tensions, frustrations, and complex settings, which she sketched concisely and evocatively in her diary, often shadowed her determination and high purpose. Arriving in France, Bechtel discovered she had lost a piece of luggage. "I felt quite bad but considering that I

Elsie Bechtel, Chateau de Lavercantière, France. Bechtel served as an MCC volunteer in France from 1945 to 1947. For most of that time she worked under Secours Mennonite Américain aux Enfants (American Mennonite Aid to Children) in a home for displaced children in the Lot River Valley of south-central France. Here Bechtel visits with a neighbor and her goats outside the chateau. *(Courtesy of Elsie C. Bechtel)*

came to France ready to give my life complaining about a suitcase would be . . . inconsistent."[52]

On October 20, 1945, Bechtel reached her work assignment, a home for children at Lavercantière, in south-central France.[53] Bechtel worked with orphans, with children whose homes had been destroyed, and with children who had been living in poverty or in troubled families. This relief work in France went under the name *Secours Mennonite* (Mennonite Aid). Several of her coworkers were Spanish, including Coma, a man with administrative responsibilities, who was perhaps her closest friend during these years.[54]

Bechtel was now free to work, sometimes to the point of exhaustion. This daily regimen became her chief expression of nonresistance, because she almost never wrote directly about nonresistance in her diary. On the day she arrived at Lavercantière, she decided that a major part of her work would be to overturn the Mennonite Central Committee's plan to close the home because of the high cost of making it more habitable. In her diary, Bechtel sketched her first impressions of the home and her determination to keep it open. The entry includes common themes in her private writing: a love of the natural world;

the importance of cleanliness; quick, emotional responses; and a determination to do what she thought best.

> Our walk from the station to [Lavercantière] seemed like a last reprieve. The scenery was so immense and the day so perfect that I hated to suddenly go into a dirty place with dirty people and children.
>
> To my utmost pleasure I found the spirit of the place as great as all nature. The seventy-nine children rushed out to greet Coma kissing him on both cheeks and going into a very frenzy at his return.
>
> The house while needing repairs and equipment was *"clean"* gloriously clean and all the children were polite and dressed neatly. I fell in love with the place right away . . . and prayed for some way to keep it from closing by December.[55]

In 1947, Bechtel became the full director of Lavercantière, performing a multitude of tasks. She once described her work as "doing little things that don't amount to much but take up a lot of time." This included unpacking and distributing relief clothing; sewing and ironing; gathering, scavenging, and shopping for food; cleaning; bathing the small children and caring for sick ones; planning programs and dramas for the children to present to villagers; building fires and sawing wood; purchasing goods; writing reports; overseeing staff and construction projects and vehicles; meeting with government officials; writing promotional materials for Mennonite Central Committee; teaching religious sessions; corresponding with administrators; attending MCC unit meetings; dealing with villagers angry at the children; and, last but not least, battling with American and French coworkers. Although repairs made the home—a chateau reportedly built in the thirteenth century—more habitable over time, for part of Bechtel's term all water needed to be hauled by oxcart, and cooking was done over a fireplace.[56]

Although she took delightful vacations, loved solitary walks, and enjoyed the opera, much of her passion was invested in work. Describing the distribution of clothing to fifteen children, she wrote, "Oh it's wonderful to be really doing relief work." When she experienced conflict with coworkers, she resorted to sweeping the floor—proving to herself, at least, that she could work.[57] For Bechtel, work provided meaning to her days. The children, always at the center of her work, affirmed her by their greetings when she returned from trips—with hugs and kisses, with shining eyes, once even with a surprise birthday party for her. This display of affection was important in a job in which Bechtel gave and received much criticism.[58] Daily life as a relief worker apparently was fraught with disagreements.

Bechtel responded sensitively, if sometimes defensively, when others directed criticism at her. Her diary leaves unclear whether she confided her responses only to the diary or whether that record reflected what she had actually said to coworkers. But to Charles Cocanower, the MCC administrator overseeing her from Chalon, she once wrote spirited point-by-point responses to questions about her actions. She noted that overseeing the purchases of the ex-director was not always possible and that wine purchases were necessary when local people were hired by the colony. She asked if Cocanower realized the extent of her workload. Responding to a question about excessive use of vehicles, she gave a detailed description of the purpose of each trip. Bechtel had complaints of her own: MCC administrators from Chalon seldom came to observe the work; when they did, their visits were brief; and they could not speak French. Furthermore, when she asked Cocanower and others for suggestions, "all [she] could ever get was, 'Keep up the good work.'"[59]

Bechtel sometimes exhausted herself. Once, after announcing the home's imminent closing to the staff, Bechtel made a trip by herself to Lyon. She stayed in a small hotel, talked to no one, and went for walks in the countryside. Her recovery came quickly. "What ever ailed me is over," she wrote after waking up one morning with "a longing" for Lavercantière. When the children and staff welcomed her back, she concluded, "It's being tired that makes one discouraged—No one should get as tired as I have been. I love my place with a wildness tonight."[60]

If work was at the center of Bechtel's sense of mission, the war-ravaged French setting shaped both her actions and her understanding of their meanings. Nonresistance did not provide her with ready responses to the horror. Her diary recorded observations and questions instead. She often wrote about the lasting marks of the war on people, buildings, and landscape. Like other BIC observers in Europe, Bechtel mentioned seeing bombed cities and almost always connected them to American actions. A town burned by Germans "sickened" her. She heard numerous stories about the German occupation—the looting of homes, the roasting alive of a baker who had supplied bread to members of the Resistance, torture during interrogations, the head of a German carried in a basket. When her friend Coma described his desire to kill police during the war, Bechtel wrote, "I was horrified but question my own feelings in a similar case." Almost thirty years later, she would still remember the suffering humans had inflicted on each other "with seeming relish." For her, this was the most difficult aspect of her contacts with war. But she coupled her incomprehension of inhumanity with "marvel at the courage and endurance of men's spirits."[61]

In her earliest months in France, she commented on the lack of food, especially fruits and vegetables. Once when she received two oranges, she ate both the fruit and the skins. Throughout her diary, she recorded comments on food shortages, even starvation, in England, France, and the occupation zones in Germany. She described new children arriving at the home "thin and desolate."

Although she had grown up feeling different from many of her American neighbors, in France she sometimes assumed or was assigned by others a generalized American identity. She noted several things: that the French did not seem to appreciate Americans; that the American embassy, a Singer sewing machine, or *Time* magazine made her homesick; and that wearing a housecoat and eating toasted cheese sandwiches made her feel like an American. She wrote to friends that she dressed like an Indian for Mardi Gras, so the other revelers could experience the "wild and wooly west." A man in a home she visited asked her "about the negro question—a blot on America."[62]

Bechtel, like Hostetter, addressed sexuality both in her evaluations of men she met and in her comments on the sexual mores of another culture. Like many Americans, Bechtel commented unfavorably on French sexual mores. But she also recorded her French neighbors' points of view, usually without a rebuttal. She was particularly scandalized by a promiscuous woman who had once used "a good Mennonite blanket to lie in some barn." Bechtel was interested enough in the woman's response to criticism to record it. Her sexual life, the woman argued, was kept out of sight of the Lavercantière children, and her behavior was common among French women. Bechtel also recorded that another coworker, for whom she expressed affection and admiration, contended that unhappy marriages should be dissolved, that humans like animals needed sex, and that the man she had had sexual relations with for six years never once said *bonjour*. The woman added, "We are Christian *'autant' que vous*" (as much as you are). When another woman described being sexually assaulted by a doctor, she feared that Bechtel would not believe her. Bechtel wrote, however, "I believe anything now of Frenchmen."[63]

Both Roman Catholicism and antireligious attitudes troubled Bechtel. On several occasions, the director who had preceded Bechtel reprimanded her for introducing religion in the classroom. As she remembers it, he also objected to her asking the children to "bow" in prayer; the French, he said, bow to no one. At another point, he told her, French law prohibited prayer in the classroom. Because of her infraction, the school could be closed. This confrontation occasioned one of the few prayers Bechtel recorded: "Remember me oh God who am so alone and fearful!"

Bechtel joined discussions on God's existence, glad that she could say she believed in a God. Although she wrote to her family that she was trapped between unbelievers and Roman Catholics, her tolerance for the latter seems to have been lower. She pronounced mass "a poor affair" one time and "a roaring good time" another. She described a nun who asked for relief aid for orphans as "begging," even though Bechtel herself pushed the Mennonite Central Committee to share such goods. She wrote home about a priest who preached against Mennonites. The Catholicism of her beloved French children was another matter. Seeing the girls cross themselves shocked Bechtel—she had forgotten about their religion. She once advised a young woman who wanted to leave the Roman Catholic church to move slowly.[64]

Despite her criticism of religious aspects of French culture, Bechtel's love for France dominates her diary. "If I were to choose the life of a vagabond I would choose it in France this time of year with all the nuts, grapes and apples," she wrote.[65] Near the end of her assignment, she wrote a reflective piece on the closing of Lavercantière for the MCC *European Relief Notes*.[66] Loose sheets still lodged in her diary appear to be a draft of the article; several parts of the draft do not appear in the published version. Describing her battle to keep the doors of the chateau closed in cold weather and the building warm, Bechtel described her defeat and her becoming a little "French" herself. "I gave up trying to educate the 'French' about closing doors and learned to live with them open. Now I feel stuffy in a house with central heating and wish I could open the doors."[67] Throughout her diary, Bechtel described with rich imagery the landscape, the old villages, and the rhythms of peasant agriculture. She was proud of her ability to work as hard as a peasant and of her growing proficiency in the French language.[68] Although at first she often commented on the dirtiness of homes, she was later irritated by new workers' comments on the dirtiness of the children. She was "ashamed" when other relief workers described the French as foreigners.[69] This new world would leave a lasting imprint on her. When Lavercantière closed, she wrote in the unpublished draft, "There is a little corner of my heart that is [dead]. . . . When I have an autopsy the doctors will be surprised at the strange scar [that] will appear on my [heart]."[70]

In her diary and letters, Bechtel never referred to herself as Brethren in Christ. Instead, she described herself as Mennonite.[71] Yet she sometimes measured her new experiences against the yardstick of the BIC community. In France, she wrote, "The church at home would have been horrified to see us" in certain settings: sitting in a cafe with a coworker who drank enough wine to fall asleep at the table, or walking through the "back allies" of Toulouse.[72] She herself probably never went beyond tasting alcohol, despite her French and Spanish friends' incomprehension.[73] But she described, for her family at least, feeling "strange" wearing pants on her three-week trip to Italy.[74] Beyond that she commented little on dress. One of her strongest statements concerned her understanding of the Sabbath. She wrote to her family that she refused to sell jars to village women on a Sunday: "I can adjust to a lot of things but there are some that I just can't give in to."[75]

She held to some practices while ignoring other prohibitions that might have lessened her appreciation of dance and opera, although she described one performance as "very interesting but not very 'Mennonitish.'"[76] She raised questions about basic aspects of her religious background, such as evangelism. One new worker at Lavercantière created tension by attempts to convert others. "Never did I think I could have too much religion," Bechtel wrote in response.[77] A Sunday school class reminded Bechtel of "all the dull sessions I had sat through . . . and the many more to come—Oh save me some one!"[78] In one of her most extended comments on her own background, she wrote:

> I find it so silly that the church should fight about neck-ties and covering strings when there are things so much more real to think about. How much of a Christian am I? What do I really have to offer these people? What can I give them that will change their lives? Do I really believe the things I think and say I do? Or do I believe them because some one told me to believe them. Its a wonderful but terrible thing to deal with actualities. God help me to never live superficially again.[79]

At the same time, Bechtel valued the warmth and sincerity of French Mennonites, who reminded her of "the folks at home."[80]

Bechtel's letters home suggest family support for a lively, sometimes iconoclastic, beauty-loving member. She expressed deep affection for her family as well as frank criticisms of her home BIC community. She occasionally noted that her devotional life or the prayers of others strengthened her. Despite tensions in the relief unit, she found deep satisfaction in the worship services, especially the music. "Singing eased out all the bumps—and ah it was wonderful to sing again."[81]

Bechtel apparently placed the importance of service above even devotional aspects of religious life. She seemed most content with religious life when she had her sleeves rolled up. On the day a car of relief clothing arrived at Lavercantière, she wrote sideways in the margin of her diary: "Was proud of being a Mennonite for the first time in my life. That true religion."[82] That sentiment was reiterated in 1974 when she wrote, "I still remember the feeling of spiritual gratitude I had of belonging to a Christian group who had service as a strong tenet."[83]

Art and the beauty of the natural world were also part of her religious life. Once in a letter to her family she made the connection explicit. After describing a meal in a French home, she complained, "We rush and tear so that half the fun of life is passed by. These people are more spiritually minded than we there is no doubt about it. They love and know music and art in a way that only experts know it at home."[84] In Bechtel's eyes, appreciation of art covered a multitude of sins, from lack of cleanliness to administrative ineptitude.[85]

Bechtel often described the natural world as the place where she found solace. There she felt most herself. The diary is filled with lyrical descriptions of the beauty surrounding her. Watching a man broadcast wheat seed, she noted his "definite rhythm which could be worked up into a beautiful dance for school children."[86] With the onset of fall, she mused, "The weather is perfect—It's purple with fall flowers—odiferous with grapes—bronze with nuts and leaves— White with fog in the mornings—white with heat at noon and white with frost & moon light at night—I'm coming aware of myself again."[87]

Bechtel seemed enchanted by what was hidden and fleeting. She found spring in the countryside "startling for the grayness—even the fields looked gray. The houses and village rose out of the hills and every thing seemed so clear and enchanting in a finished way—The world seems done and closed with the secrets embedded inside."[88] Searching for food in the countryside around Lavercantière, she described "broken down stone walls and half houses, round buildings which plainly showed that we are just a passing phase in this world."[89] As the children left Lavercantière, she wrote, would the "ghosts of the children" be "free to mingle" with older ghosts of the house, or would the older ones see the children as outsiders?[90]

Perhaps Bechtel was wondering about the lasting presence of her own ghost. She returned to the United States in 1948. There she tried to convey her relief work experience to the BIC community. She remembers speaking in several churches in Ohio and Canada. She talked about the distribution of clothing and food. But her personal understanding of nonresistance remained carefully out of sight, between the covers of her diary.[91]

However, that commitment to nonresistance continued to shape Bechtel's life. In 1959, after some years of teaching school, she again volunteered as a relief worker. She worked in an MCC building project in West Germany and then in an agricultural project in Greece. Relationships and living conditions were often difficult. But for Bechtel, the beautiful Greek countryside made up for any hardships. Later she returned to teaching and to attending Valley Chapel, the BIC congregation of her childhood. She continued extensive volunteer work throughout her working years and on into retirement.[92]

To both Bechtel and Hostetter, service grew from their nonresistant beliefs and, in turn, strengthened their ability to connect peace to people beyond their

BIC community. Hostetter wrote explicitly about that connection, Bechtel much less so. The institutionalization of volunteer relief work, however, convinced both of them to see service as a way women and men could practice the peace witness. Furthermore, both individuals assumed that other members of their families would appreciate their experiences and accept their new ideas. Once again family life appears as the setting most conducive to reshaping and transmitting nonresistance. Nonresistant culture, like other belief systems, survived best as "daily practice rather than an indelible guide to uniform behavior."[93] In the experiences of these two Brethren in Christ, daily practice might appear incoherent. But in fact, this very confusion fostered the flexibility an old belief needed to accommodate individual desires and the changing world. At the same time, that flexibility led to diversity within families and within the community. In the decades after World War II, the community remained uncertain whether to welcome diversity and, if so, how and where to bound it.

CHAPTER SEVEN

Legacy and Conclusion

∽

We're still conscientious objectors—our lives are lived with that sense.

A number of individuals who value the lasting influence of nonresistance in their lives explain that legacy in terms of intergenerational families. "The early experiences of [Brethren in Christ] nonresistance influenced me greatly," Esther Tyson Boyer writes. "I still subscribe to these values. We raised our daughter and three sons to value Peace and nonresistance and they are passing it on to their families."[1] Anna Mae Rohrer Kohler bequeathed the legacy to her daughter and son-in-law, who taught for nine years as Mennonite Central Committee (MCC) volunteers in Indonesia. She also points to a nephew, who "does not have any church affiliation but told the government he is a C.O. like his uncle when they wanted to draft him."[2]

Others point to the persistence of nonresistance within families in which different members made different choices regarding military service. Civilian Public Service (CPS) participant Donald Engle describes how the peace witness has passed through four generations of his family:

> In my own family, 2 boys, one a C.O. And the other in Navy. . . . I asked no one for Advi[c]e. Not Even my father, he told me just before I Boarded Bus for C.P.S. Camp that were he in my shoes today, would have done what I chose to do. . . .
>
> My Son Stan, on his own Accord without Consulting with me, took A 4E [conscientious objection requiring civilian work] classification during the Vietnam War. He is not BIC, Raising family Catholic, his oldest son wants to

go to Air Force [Academy] to Learn to fly. Stan has pointed out he may have to kill. Interesting 3rd & 4th generation.[3]

In another family mosaic, Clarence Byer, who accepted noncombatant work as a World War I conscientious objector, urged his sons to do the same. Two of his sons took that route during World War II and served in the medical corps. A third son, Curtis, was conscripted in 1952. Curtis chose the conscientious objection classification requiring civilian work. "My father was very disappointed in my co position & so declared himself," Curtis remembers. In 1956, however, his father wrote that though he wished Curtis had chosen noncombatant military service, he "wholeheartedly" supported his son's choice. Clarence hoped that all his sons would "adhere consistently to . . . principle whether in time of war or peace."[4]

Of course, some from the Brethren in Christ (BIC) community have come to believe that the nonresistant teachings of their youth proved inadequate guidance in later life. CPS participant Daniel L. Hoover today describes nonresistance as a belief without a biblical base. He also argues that in the World War II years the BIC church presented its definition of nonresistance as nonnegotiable and regarded those who disagreed with it as "heretics."[5] Gordon H. Schneider describes his current affiliation with the Southern Baptist Convention as one that has taught him "tolerance and . . . acceptance of others as they are." Furthermore, his sister, still a member of the Brethren in Christ, had told him that "she didn't think there was a [nickel's] worth of difference" between his church and hers.[6] Thus, those who reject their childhood upbringing often point as reasons to the corporate nature of the belief and perhaps the power behind corporate definitions. The BIC church, writes Eugene H. Feather, "tried to do your thinking for you."[7]

On the other hand, those who value their nonresistant heritage have seemingly crafted it into individual stances that reflect diverse influences and values. One woman wrote, "Nonresistance and the peace position are simply practices with which I have grown up, they seemed right according to Scripture and I made them my own."[8] Paul S. Boyer says nonresistance gave him his suspicion of militarism and "super-patriotic appeals," a suspiciousness reflected in a college text he helped to edit, which stresses the suffering and costs of war. His continuing support of peace and social-action organizations and his alienation from modern mass culture also reflect his upbringing, even though he has left the Brethren in Christ. "Brethren in Christ folk," he notes, "and even those of the historic peace churches more generally, hardly have an exclusive claim on finding war abhorrent! Indeed, some of the strongest 'peace activism' of recent decades has come from Catholics, Jews, liberal Protestants, and persons of wholly secular background."[9] Grace Herr Holland, Boyer's cousin, sees the influence of nonresistance on her willingness to take unpopular positions. She advocates tolerance among Christians on the issue of adherence to pacifism but questions that looseness in other connections. "I am disappointed now to see some peace promoters using the nonresistant stand to promote pluralism, refusing to confront any other religious system on the ground that this is non-Christian. When Christianity ceases to be exclusive in the good sense of the word, it is no longer Christian."[10]

Both Boyer and Holland see their nonresistant pasts as important. Both evaluate nonresistance in terms of relationships beyond the small BIC community in which they grew up. The difference in their evaluations of where boundaries might be drawn represents a challenge to a corporate peace stance.

We often find the legacy of nonresistance portrayed not in analytical terms but in intricate stories, sometimes only half-remembered. In these stories, we see the BIC community caught up in international events and influenced by unlikely neighbors. Small kindnesses and acts of neighborliness—traditional personal virtues in the BIC community—carry weight in this shadowy world of memory. We even hear echoes of the 1939 doctrinal statement that urged "an open and approachable spirit toward humanity."[11]

Ray M. Zercher vaguely remembers a story he was once told about a BIC member named Menno Richer. During World War I, Richer and several other conscientious objectors refused to participate in any way with the U.S. military. Military officers hoisted them off the ground by the shackles on their wrists, hoping that would thin out the conscientious objectors' ranks. But the attempt failed—the shackles repeatedly and miraculously clicked open.[12]

During the next world war, Clarence H. Sakimura's family was allowed to leave an Arizona internment camp for Japanese Americans when his parents found a farm family in southeastern Michigan willing to sponsor them.[13] One Christmas an evangelical Quaker minister brought the Sakimura family a fruit basket. Clarence describes this as an "appropriate moment, a small act of kindness, a small word of encouragement" that had "such a tremendous impact." The Quaker minister worked with a local BIC minister—Menno Richer. Through this unlikely labyrinth, Clarence Sakimura's family made its way to Messiah Bible College, where his father was hired as the landscaper and gardener.

Even in the college town of Grantham, Sakimura's family find no reprieve from hostility directed at Japanese Americans. There were unfriendly gestures, and attempts at arson in their home.[14] Clarence Sakimura remembers the emotional difficulty of carrying "the burden of being [an] exemplary Japanese American and then coming into a Brethren in Christ environment where there was another set of uniquenesses associated with that group that set them apart from the rest of the world," a uniqueness that sometimes resulted in "isolation and intolerance." After World War II Sakimura joined the BIC church, from which, as he put it, conscientious objection "almost automatically" flowed. From 1955 to 1957, he did his alternative service work with the Mennonite Central Committee in Austria. As he recalls: "The Material Aid unit was responsible for distributing food and clothing to the needy in the area. At Christmastime we were responsible for distributing Christmas parcels packed by Mennonite children in towel-wrapped parcels earmarked for children. . . . In a desire to be as personal as possible in this distribution, . . . I participated often in personally handing out these items."[15]

There he met Herta Aschenbrenner, an Austrian woman, whom he would marry. A young secretary, she was spending her vacation with an international work group, helping Eastern European refugees. As a child in World War II, she herself had been a refugee, and she later remembered relief aid from the "Mennonite or Brethren in Christ or other denominations" as being "greatly appreciated."[16]

Writers of doctrinal statements may have been unaware of these stories. But in just such ways, the "open and approachable spirit" makes its way—by small acts of kindness and unlikely neighbors, past wars and community conflict—from generation to generation.

THE PEACE WITNESS AFTER 1958

In 1958, the BIC church stopped disciplining members for military service. This step followed the church's repeal of legislation prescribing personal appearance and prohibiting life insurance for its officials. The succeeding decades saw further loosening of rules and mores concerning all manner of religious expression and daily practices. These events recast the corporate nature of BIC community life and dramatically changed the look of individuals and even of church buildings.[17]

The Brethren in Christ were changing in other ways as well. In a 1989 survey, only 6 percent of members remained in farming. In the 1970s and 1980s, BIC men tended to move from farming into professions and small businesses; BIC women remained housewives or moved into professions, sales, or clerical work. Meanwhile, the Brethren in Christ sustained their relative prosperity, with incomes and rates of home ownership above those of the American population in general. Many continued to live in rural areas or small towns. In a 1972 survey, the education levels of a BIC sample were almost identical to those recorded for the general American population in the U.S. census of 1970.[18]

In the years since 1958, many people in the BIC community continued to see nonresistance as a central part of their community's religious expression. The peace witness, having embraced service work, now began to include broader social justice issues. A 1978 BIC pamphlet entitled *Peacemakers* urged conscientious objection to military service, advocated voluntary service, and promoted the changing of life patterns to respond to "the unjust distribution of . . . resources."[19] By 1998, MCC's voluntary-service program had placed 230 BIC volunteers in relief, social service, and development programs, domestically and internationally.[20]

But the issue of conscientious objection to military service continued to divide the BIC community. A 1980 report of the BIC Peace and Social Concerns Commission decried the huge U.S. military budget and "the ravages of unjust economic and social systems." It described "peace and justice . . . as [collectively] a 'central facet' of biblical faith." The commission also urged draft-age men to note their conscientious objection on the forms to be provided in the new draft-registration plan set up by the U.S. government. The report also briefly noted that an individual might instead choose some other way to express a personal conviction on conscription, a cryptic reference that reflected disagreement over the purpose and meaning of the community's peace witness. According to Arthur M. Climenhaga, at least some commission members wanted young men to break the law and resist registration entirely, a proposal that elicited "warm" debate.[21] The decades had changed, but the disputes had not.

Conclusions

All self-conscious religious communities see themselves as unique, and the Brethren in Christ are no exception. They point to transcendent power and commitment—or their members' lack of it—to explain the persistence or loss of a peace witness. Although these self-perceptions must be taken into account, analysis of the BIC community allows for many other explanations as well.

This study has argued that to be adequate, all explanations must account for the daily lives of ordinary members of the BIC community. When we consider these people and observe their daily lives, we find a more complex picture than that portrayed in official statements and doctrine. In this picture, ordinary days were marked by a looseness that allowed a flexibility that offset sectarian doctrinal formulations. As we have seen, daily life also involved the influences of many neighbors; these influences, in turn, helped to shape the BIC community. Nonresistance required responding to neighbors, not only in passive attempts to avoid conflict but also in active attempts to build amicable relations. During the world wars, this dual approach meant nonparticipation in war mobilization but at the same time participation in humanitarian efforts to alleviate human suffering. Furthermore, BIC community members attempted to explain nonresistance in terms understandable to farm neighbors, factory coworkers, labor leaders, and military and government officials.

A portion of the BIC community, however, thought membership in the Brethren in Christ should not preclude participation in the war efforts. They participated in a variety of ways, including service in the armed forces. Even BIC conscientious objectors to military service were divided, beginning in World War I. Some defined their stands as simply refusal to kill; others went farther and refused to participate in the military; a few hoped to challenge militarism itself. These differences became open conflicts in the World War II and early Cold War periods. These conflicts challenged the belief that nonresistance emerged from and produced unity within the community.

Although people within the BIC community often explain the differences in terms of biblical interpretation, in fact a variety of daily experiences influenced the thinking of the community. With respect to the daily requirements of nonresistance, it mattered whether one was a man or a woman, a draft-aged male or middle-aged farmer, a child in public school or a young adult at Messiah Bible College. The conscripted conscientious objector was the primary symbol of nonresistance in these years. He sometimes faced challenges in isolation, particularly in World War I; however, most denominational and ecumenical aid to nonresistant members focused on these men. In contrast, BIC children practiced nonresistance during a period of life in which nonconformity was most excruciating. Like that of their fathers, uncles, and older brothers, their practice was often lonely, but their hardships received much less notice from the BIC church. Similarly, women—the majority in both BIC membership and missions—played a crucial role in nonresistance, as expressed in service and material aid. But many Brethren in Christ continued to think of nonresistance as a male issue. BIC leaders encouraged that thinking by failing to recognize women's contributions (in the production of food and clothing) as integral to nonresistance. In addition, they failed to draw women into leadership, particularly in the BIC schools and in volunteer settings clearly tied to the peace witness. Finally, because the BIC community still had a large contingent in agriculture, the centrality of farm production to prosecuting total war made official definitions of nonparticipation in the war mobilization seem arbitrary to many.

In addition to internal divisions, influences from the larger society differed in the various locales of the scattered Brethren in Christ. One's neighbors were important but not necessarily in obvious ways. Living in regions with other strong Anabaptist groups often strengthened nonresistance; BIC leaders in

Ontario and Pennsylvania, for instance, worked closely with Mennonites in both world wars. But close association with Mennonites sometimes fostered a desire to assert differences from the larger groups in order to maintain the distinctness of the BIC community. Outlying BIC communities—and even individuals on the edge of the BIC community—sometimes advocated nonresistance most strongly. BIC people in Michigan, without German ethnic roots, demonstrated abiding commitment to the peace witness. So too did young men wearing ties, such as Nelson Hostetter.

Not only geographical settings but also intellectual currents influenced the BIC community. Some in the BIC community mention theological influences, such as fundamentalism and evangelical Protestantism. Certainly, the nationalism and militarism that had helped to shape those religious expressions undermined the peace witness. But many Brethren in Christ drew on the emotional warmth of revivalism and devotional practices to build their own nonresistant countercultures. Furthermore, a broad survey of BIC literature shows that ecumenical leanings, reformist thinking, and radical social critiques influenced the Brethren in Christ even as they situated themselves in conservative settings. Sometimes intergenerational tensions as much as ideological differences influenced the course of events. Increased levels of education required some members to face the issues of nonresistance in medical school or graduate school. Leaders, who were often farmers chosen to lead by their BIC fellows, now oversaw younger members with graduate degrees and seminary training. Leaders in the 1940s and 1950s drew on the skills of these younger members. But in several cases the voices of younger advocates of nonresistance disappeared from official church organs.

At the most basic level, the larger society challenged the Brethren in Christ in the same way it challenged all smaller communities that aimed at alternative ways of living. Like many others in those years, the BIC community wrestled with concerns about localism, smallness, individualism, and economic livelihood. Regarding nonresistant beliefs in particular, the Brethren in Christ asked themselves: What belongs to the individual and what to the community? When should the community maintain its standards, and when should it entertain new ideas? Which new ideas? How could a small community, woven together by faith, by kinship, by the farm economy, by mutual aid—all expressions of personal exchange—survive in a world run by bureaucracies and church growth programs?

Between 1914 and 1958, the U.S. government required that conscientious objectors prove their individual religious convictions. At the same time, the government acknowledged the power of corporate tradition in the Historic

Peace Churches. Ironically, the Brethren in Christ, although representative of the corporate tradition, increasingly emphasized individual religious convictions. Sometimes they even denigrated nonresistance that was tied to historical traditions rather than to personal religious experience. That individualism produced some very strong nonresistant stances, but it left unanswered the question of how individual convictions could be mediated by a group that promoted corporate life as central to religious life. Therefore, individualism ended up threatening community life and intergenerational pacifism.

In another conundrum of the World War II years, the growing emphasis on increasing tolerance and democracy left undefined the object of the new openness. Should nonreligious pacifists be tolerated? What about nonpacifist coreligionists? Specifically, should tolerance be extended to BIC community members who had joined the military? Should an end to community standards on distinctive plain dress and life insurance also mean an end to community rules about killing? Did conceiving of the peace witness merely as reconciliation mean losing "the steely character of nonresistance?"[22] Did replacing coercive rules with persuasion spell the end of a two-hundred-year-old peace witness?[23]

Finally, though the BIC church doubled its membership between 1910 and 1958, it seems to have tripled its sensitivity about its small size. Some BIC members say that the goal of growth overshadowed the church's tradition of faithfulness to unpopular and corporate beliefs. But during the war years, the Brethren in Christ had felt overshadowed by the larger Historic Peace Churches, particularly the Mennonites. In Civilian Public Service and the Mennonite Central Committee, the Brethren in Christ had missed their small, tightly knit congregations and their own style of religious expression.

That the Brethren in Christ did not adequately answer any of these questions either before or after 1958 is not surprising. More surprising is that the BIC community mounted an impressive intergenerational peace witness while seriously entertaining these questions. More baffling still: Why did a peace witness that required such sacrifice, discipline, and hard work fade so quickly from community memory?

In contrast to those of the Brethren in Christ, Mennonite roots reach back to Europe.[24] It is in their "historylessness" that perhaps the Brethren in Christ best show their American roots; they share the larger society's general amnesia.[25] Many Mennonite homes have copies of *The Martyr's Mirror*, a large work devoted especially to the martyrdom of sixteenth-century Anabaptist ancestors. But a mere twenty years after World War I, the Brethren in Christ had largely forgotten the experiences of their own members in that tumult. Similarly, the corporate community now recalls few stories of nonresistance during the World War II years. Even those who do retell stories of nonresistance in families remember little of the extent of their community's peace witness. As the Brethren in Christ enter the twenty-first century, their collective memory of nonresistance is in disrepair.

In 1944, a young BIC woman named Esther Mann heard the call to peace service. She volunteered, first at MCC headquarters in Pennsylvania and then in the Women's Service Unit at Howard, Rhode Island. The next summer she worked in another women's unit, this one at Hudson River State Hospital in Poughkeepsie, New York.

In 1995, people who had been her fellow volunteers at the state hospital wanted to have a "grand reunion." While most of the rest of America celebrated the fiftieth anniversaries of various World War II battles, these former coworkers wanted to reunite their own small band of conscientious objectors. But no one could locate Mann.

Finally, they received word: Esther Mann had succumbed to tuberculosis, which she had contracted during her voluntary service at the hospital. None of her coworkers had realized it, but Esther had been dead for nearly fifty years.[26]

On a lovely green hill, a short walk from the BIC archives at Messiah College, lies the grave of Esther Mann. For one small religious community, born along the banks of a river not far from this hill, the meaning of the peace witness persists not only in what can be named but also in what is unstated; not only in what is passed on but in what has been lost.

Questionnaire on Brethren in Christ Nonresistance: World War I through the Early 1950s

ↄ∕ↄ

Date of birth _____ Female _____ Male _____

Part I. Nonresistance and War, 1914–1953

1. What are your most vivid memories of the World War II years?
2. What was being Brethren in Christ like in those years?
3. Describe any ways you remember nonresistance or the peace position being taught and practiced in congregational or district church life as you were growing up.
4. Describe any ways you remember peace concerns being a part of family life as you were growing up.
5. During the war years, were there disagreements in your congregation and district or in your family about nonresistance? If there were, please describe them.
6. What did your neighbors (for example, in the local community, in school, in camp, or at work) think of the peace witness as the Brethren in Christ practiced it?
7. Did you participate in the Civilian Public Service, i-w, the military, voluntary service, or relief programs during the war or in the decade after the war? For example, were you a drafted man, a volunteer, a staff member, a contributor of food or clothes for cps or relief, active in a Young People's Society raising funds for cps? Or did you support or encourage a relative or friend involved in any of these programs? Please describe.
8. Do you remember stories about World War I or nonresistance in that earlier war? If so, please describe.
9. How have the experiences of Brethren in Christ nonresistance in the first half of the century affected your life?
10. Additional stories or comments

Part II. Personal Information

1. Place of birth and important places you have lived since then:
2. Nature of your life's work:
3. Educational experiences that have been important to you:
4. Expressions of faith that are important to you:
5. Important influences on you in addition to the Brethren in Christ Church:
6. Occupations of your parents and of any children:
7. Do you have any diaries or letters from the period between 1914 and 1953 that you would be willing to let me use for research? If so, please describe:
8. Other Brethren in Christ people I should contact:
9. Would you be willing to answer follow-up questions? Yes_____ No_____

Optional: Name (include maiden name) (please print) _____

Signature _____

(My signature means I am willing for my name to be used in your writing.)

Conscripted Men Related to the
BIC Community in World War I

This list has been compiled from a variety of sources, as cited for each man. See the Selected Bibliography for more information on sources. The information has been used directly, without attempt to verify its accuracy against other sources. co=conscientious objector

Bohen, Jacob T.,

Hope, Kans. (parents); response to conscription unknown; probably military service; U.S. forces [Herbert Englebert Bohen, Obituary, *Evangelical Visitor* (*EV*), May 19, 1919, 11].

Book, Jake, Jr.

home location unknown; response to conscription unknown; probably military service, U.S. forces [C. N. Hostetter Jr., diary, Sept. 16, 1917, Hostetter Papers, 7-23.1, Archives of the Brethren in Christ Church and Messiah College (BICA)].

Book, Maynard C.'s uncles

home locations unknown; probably CO [Maynard C. Book, questionnaire].

Brown, Robert Clyde

Smiley, Sask.; military service, Canadian forces; died in Hastings Hospital, Suffolk, England, after contracting tuberculosis in trenches; memorial service led by BIC minister Joram Nigh [Obituary, *EV*, Mar. 5, 1917, 21].

Brubaker

home location unknown; agricultural exemption [Ruth Brubaker Davis, questionnaire].

Brubaker, Harry L.

Mount Joy, Penn.; co refused military uniform and noncombatant work; Camp Meade, Md., 154 Depot Brigade; furloughed to work on Phares Martin farm near Maugansville, Md.; received no pay except when discharged; dishonorable discharge [Brubaker to Kreider, July 4, 12, 21; Dec. 26, 1918; GC GEB I-7-1.1; Harry L. Brubaker and Benjamin J. Herr, "A Word from Camp," *EV*, Feb. 25, 1918, 24–25; Brubaker to Wittlinger, Feb. 23, 1974, Wittlinger Papers, Quest 1, 35-1.22, "Peace and Service, 1910–50" file; Bert, "BIC Peacemakers," BICA; Harry L. Brubaker, interview by Allan Teichroew].

Burkholder
>Ohio; CO treated badly and put in prison [Judson Hill, questionnaire].

Byer, Clarence
>Brown County, Kans.; CO noncombatant; inducted in Medical Officer Training Camp, Fort Riley, Kans.; later refused all work that might require bearing arms; subsequently placed with other COs in camp; performed custodial duties; refused pay until required to accept for discharge; discharge document states Byer refused to wear uniform [Byer to Harley, attached copy of Byer's discharge papers, Jan. 24, Feb. 2, 1956, GC PRS Reports, I-21-1.4, "Testimonials, 1956" folder, BICA].

Carver, Frank
>Canada; CO refused uniform and signing of willingness to die for "King & Country"; received fourteen days detention [Carver to Wittlinger, July 29, 1974, Wittlinger Papers, Quest 1, 35-1.22 "Peace and Service, 1910–50" folder, BICA].

Charlton, William
>Wainfleet Twp., Ont.; CO refused military uniform; reported to Exhibition Grounds, Toronto, Ont.; placed in detention; appeared before military body; D. W. Heise testified on his behalf, presenting a certificate of church membership; exempted and granted leave of absence [Charlton to Harley, Feb. 4, 1956, GC PRS Reports, I-21-1.4, "Testimonials, 1956" folder; Bert, "BIC Peacemakers," BICA].

Dixon, Howard R.
>Dysart, Iowa (location of wife's funeral); military service, U.S. forces, France [Fern Gagny Dixon, Obituary, EV, Nov. 18, 1918, 21–22].

Dourte, Monroe
>Manheim, Penn.; agricultural exemption [Allon B. Dourte, questionnaire; Esther Dourte Snyder, "Their Legacy in Our Hearts: Reflections on the Lives of Monroe and Susie Dourte," Brethren in Christ History and Life (BICHL) 13 (Dec. 1990): 346].

Eavey, Charles Benton
>Grantham, Penn.; CO refused noncombatant work; Camp Lee, Va.; furloughed to do relief work under AFSC in France [Questionnaire, Mar. 8, 1946, MCC Report Files 1, IX-12-1, "Mennonite Relief Work in World War I, Questionnaires Answered, E–G" folder, Archives of the Mennonite Church (AMC); Bert, "BIC Peacemakers," BICA].

Eberly, Abram
>Home location unknown; CO noncombatant [Bert, "BIC Peacemakers," BICA].

Elliot, Clyde Fisher
>Nottawa, Ont., and Western Canada; military service, Canadian forces; killed in action in France, about Sept. 19, 1916; BIC member at one time [Obituary, EV, Jan. 8, 1917, 20].

Engle, Benjamin Howard
>Home location unknown; military service, U.S. forces, Hancock, Ga.; sergeant [Viola Ruth Engle, Obituary, EV, Jan. 13, 1919, 9].

Engle, Charles E.
>Dickinson County, Kans.; CO refused to bear arms; wore military uniform, performed noncombatant work; Fort Riley, Kans.; clerical work in medical corps general medical ward, venereal diseases ward, wounded rehabilitation war, general surgical section [Engle to Wittlinger, Aug. 2, 1974, Wittlinger Papers, Quest 1, 35-1.22, "Peace 1910–50" folder, BICA; Engle, My Story, My Song (MSMS), 118; Viola Ruth Engle, Obituary, EV, Jan. 13, 1919, 9].

Engle, Leonard (J. Lenhart?)

Home location unknown; response to conscription unknown; Camp Upton, Long Island, N.Y. [C. N. Hostetter Jr. diary, Jan. 18, 1918, Hostetter Papers, 7-23.1, BICA; J. Lenhart Engle, son of S. G. Engle, served as a military surgeon, "A Saskatchewan Prayer at U.N. Session," *EV*, Dec. 8, 1947, 5].

Engle, Paul E.

Claremont, Calif.; military service, U.S. forces; Student Army Training Corps [Engle to Wittlinger, Jan. 5, Jun. 25, 1974, Wittlinger Papers, Quest 1, 35-1.22, "Peace 1910–50" folder, BICA; Viola Ruth Engle, Obituary, *EV*, Jan. 13, 1919, 9].

Eyer, W. B.

Calif. BIC church; probably CO noncombatant [Engle to Wittlinger, Jan. 5, 1974, Wittlinger Papers, Quest 1, 35-1.22, "Peace 1910–50" folder, BICA].

Fishburn, Harry J.

Hummelstown, Penn.; CO noncombatant work; Camp Lee, Va.; worked in base hospital, food preparation in nurses mess hall [Fishburn to H. Kreider, Nov. 7, 1918, GC GEB I-7-1.1, BICA; Fishburn to E. Kreider, Nov. 19, 1918, Misc., 5-1.6, "Ethan Kreider" folder; Bert, "BIC Peacemakers," BICA].

Gish, Aaron Kuhns

Elizabethtown, Penn. (birthplace); military service, U.S. forces; died of pneumonia in France [Obituary, *EV*, Dec. 2, 1918, 21].

Hahn, George

Kindersley, Sask. (parents); military service, Canadian forces; France [Susanna Baker Hahn, Obituary, *EV*, Dec. 3, 1917, 21].

Heise, Edgar C.

Brown County, Kans.; CO refused military uniform; Camp Funston; Fort Riley, Kans.; placed in detention for two weeks; contracted flu, which developed into fluid on chest, in military hospital for six months before release [E. Heise to Wittlinger, July 29, 1974, Wittlinger Papers, Quest 1, 35-1.22, "Peace 1910–50" folder, BICA; J. Heise to author, June 28, 1996].

Heise, John Henry

Richmond Hill, Ont.; CO refused military uniform; reported to Exhibition Grounds, Toronto, Ont.; 3235130 Second Battalion, Canadian Garrison Regiment; court-martialed; D. W. Heise spoke on his behalf; sentenced to two years hard labor; served six weeks in Don Jail, Toronto, Ont., then Burwash prison farm, south of Sudbury, Ont.; released because of wording error on his registration; granted leave of absence without pay [Heise, "First World War Experiences of John Henry Heise, May 1918–January 1919, "Certificate of Leave of Absence" for Heise, copies in possession of author; Bert, "BIC Peacemakers," BICA].

Heisey, David

Union, Ohio; military service, U.S. forces, France; did not see action [Book, "In Pursuit of Great Spoil" 13, 20].

Herr

Home location unknown; ministerial exemption [Millard Herr, questionnaire].

Herr, Benjamin J.

Home location unknown; CO Camp Meade, Md.; furloughed probably to farm [Herr to Kreider, July 4, Dec. 27, 1918; GC GEB I-7-1.1, BICA; Harry L. Brubaker and Benjamin J. Herr, "A World from Camp," *EV*, Feb. 25, 1918, 24–25].

Hershey, Paul E.

Abilene, Kans.; military service; U.S. forces, Guipavas, France; naval air service; died Jan. 29, 1919 of pneumonia in naval hospital, Brooklyn, N.Y. [Obituary, *EV*, Apr. 21, 1919, 9].

Hess, Abram M.

Mount Joy, Penn.; agricultural exemption [Kenneth E. Hess, questionnaire; "A. Z. Hess Family Festival Notes," 12, pamphlet in possession of author].

Knepper, May Pyke's uncle

Home location unknown; military service, U.S. forces; wagon driver taking goods to front lines [Mae Pyke Knepper, questionnaire].

Landis, Henry L.

Home location unknown; CO; noncombatant work in quartermaster corps; served in Europe [Isaiah Harley and Doris Brehm Harley, interview by author].

Leaman, J. B.'s oldest son

Upland, Calif.(parents); military service, U.S. forces, stationed Columbia, S.C.[J. B. Leaman, "Home Again," *EV*, Feb. 11, 1918, 21–25].

Leaman, J. B.'s son

Upland, Calif. (parents); military service, U.S. forces, Camp Beauregard, La. [Leaman, "Home Again," 21–25].

Lenhert, Samuel

home location unknown; military service, U.S. forces; 3658329, Sanitary Squad No. 15, 1st Depot Division A.O.P. 727 A.E.F., France; wounded [Samuel Lenhert, "A Testimony from France," *EV*, Apr. 7, 1917, 7; Harriet Trautwien Byer, questionnaire].

McNeal, Abrim Jay

Guilford Township, Franklin County, Penn.; response to conscription unknown; stationed Camp Dix, N.J.; died in camp of bronchial pneumonia [Obituary, *EV*, Dec. 2, 1918, 22].

McNeal, Azel W.

home location unknown; military service; U.S. forces; Fort Sill, Okla.; major [Abrim Jay McNeal, Obituary, *EV*, Dec. 2, 1918, 22].

Miller, Henry S.

home location unknown; CO; noncombatant work; Fort Jackson, Charleston, S.C.; custodial, hospital unit [Martha Long, Anne Verle Miller, questionnaires].

Murry, Lewis Wood

Ashland County, Ohio; military service, U.S. forces; killed in action, Argonne, Verdun, France, Sept. 7, 1918 [Obituary, *EV*, Jan. 13, 1919, 11].

Myers, Clarence A.

Franklin County, Penn.; response to conscription unknown; Camp Lee, Va. ["Bible School Department," *EV*, Nov. 18, 1918, 6].

Oldham, Loni

Pigeon Hills, Penn.; military service, U.S. forces [A. Ruth Lehman, "Earthen Vessels: Jesse S. Oldham and the Springhope Congregation," *BICHL* 15 (Aug. 1992): 198].

Richer, Menno

Mich.; CO [Ray M. Zercher, questionnaire].

Saylor, Gordon

Stevensville, Ont.; military service, Canadian forces; wounded in Europe [Harold K. Sider, "Willing to Serve: The Story of Christian and Cora Sider," *BICHL* 15 (Aug. 1992): 258].

Sider, Earl M.
Wainfleet, Ontario; CO refused military uniform; reported to Exhibition Grounds, Toronto, Ont.; appeared before military body; D. W. Heise spoke on his behalf; granted leave of absence but required to remain in military camp for additional two weeks ["My Experiences as a C.O. in World War I, 1918," attached to Sider to Harley, Mar. 3, 1956, GC PRS Reports, I-21-1.4, "Testimonials, 1956" folder; Sider to Wittlinger, Feb. 6, 1976, Wittlinger Papers, Quest 1, 35-1.22, "Peace 1910–50" folder; Bert, "BIC Peacemakers," BICA].

Sollenberger, Margaret's uncle
Chambersburg, Penn. (brother); military service, U.S. forces, France [Margaret Elizabeth Sollenberger, Obituary, *EV*, Mar. 24, 1919, 12].

Swalm, Ernest J.
Collingwood, Ont.; CO refused military uniform; D-3109171; reported to first Depot Battalion, Second C.O.R. Hamilton, Ont.; court-martialed; D. W. Heise spoke on his behalf at court-martial; leave of absence without pay [Swalm, *Nonresistance under Test*, 1949, and *My Beloved Brethren*, 23–33; Bert, "BIC Peacemakers," BICA].

Taylor, Walter
Lapeer County, Mich.; CO questioned before official body, perhaps local draft board at point of registration; target of vigilante violence [M. Taylor, "Our War-Time Experiences," 11–12; Swalm, videotaped interview by Pauline Cornell].

Trautwein, Herman C.
Calif. congregation; CO noncombatant work; wore uniform; refused to bear arms; Camp Kearney, San Diego, Calif.; worked in kitchen; after armistice helped with military discharges [Engle to Wittlinger, Jan. 5, 1974, Wittlinger Papers, Quest 1, 35-1.22, "Peace 1910–50" folder, BICA; Harriet Trautwein Byer, questionnaire].

Walters, Jesse
Mansfield, Ohio; response to conscription unknown; contracted measles in camp, died of pneumonia, Jan. 18, 1918 [Obituary, *EV*, May 6, 1918, 22].

Wenger, Rolla Leroy
Englewood, Ohio (born); CO ignored summer 1917 conscription because he was not certain how to proceed as a CO; reported for conscription spring 1918; initially refused military uniform and noncombatant work; in camp, officers forcibly dressed him in military uniform; performed work as hospital orderly; refused overseas service; court-martialed; sentenced to fifteen years; served nine months at Fort Leavenworth, Kans.; dishonorable discharge [Bert, "BIC Peacemakers," BICA].

Wenger, Samuel S.
Fairview, Ohio; CO refused military uniform; placed in barracks with other COs; furloughed to county home in Ohio [Samuel Wenger, "From One of Our Boys," *EV*, Apr. 7, 1919, 7–8; Myron Mann, questionnaire; Bert, "BIC Peacemakers," BICA].

Williams, Russell
Toronto, Ont.; CO sought help to establish CO position [Williams to Kreider, Dec. 29, 1917, GC GEB I-7-1.1, BICA].

Wolgemuth, Graybill
Mount Joy, Penn.; agricultural exemption [Wolgemuth to Wittlinger, Jan. 3, 1974, Wittlinger Papers, Quest 1, 35-1.22, "Peace 1910–50" folder, BICA].

Wright, Charles H.
Willandport, Ont.; CO refused military uniform; performed custodial work; court-martialed; sentenced to hard labor; sent to Don Jail, Toronto, Ont., then Burwash

prison farm, south of Sudbury, Ont.; released with John Henry Heise because of incorrect information on registration [Wright to Wittlinger, Jan. 22, 1976, Wittlinger Papers, Quest 1, 35-1.22, "Peace 1910–50" folder, BICA].

Zook, Samuel Andrew

Morrison, Ill.; military service, U.S. forces; killed in action in Argonne Woods, France, Nov. 1, 1918 [Editorial notes, *EV*, Dec. 16 and 30, 1918; Obituary, *EV*, May 19, 1919, 11].

Brethren in Christ Men in Canadian Alternative Service Work

cⱭ

Baker, Bruce, Kindersley, Sask.
Baker, Calvin, Kindersley, Ont.
Baker, Marshall, Stayner, Ont.
Baker, Orville, Stayner, Ont.
Baker, Robert, Kindersley, Sask.
Bartlett, Vernice, Nanticoke, Ont.
Bearss, Leo, Ridgeway, Ont.
Bearss, Ross, Ridgeway, Ont.
Bennett, Frank, Gormley, Ont.
Bossert, John, Fenwick, Ont.
Cassel, Harvey, Preston, Ont.
Chapman, Vernon, Glen Meyer, Ont.
Charlton, Hubert, Stevensville, Ont.
Climenhaga, Clarence, Kindersley, Sask.
Cover, Harold, Gormley, Ont.
Cronk, Hazen, Nanticoke, Ont.
Cullen, Roy, Gormley, Ont.
Ebersole, Stanley, Stevensville, Ont.
Ellis, Charles, Unionville, Ont.
Gilmore, James, Lowbanks, Ont.
Grant, John, Aylmer, Ont.
Hall, John, Hagersville, Ont.
Heise, Arthur, Gormley, Ont.
Heise, Carl, Gormley, Ont.
Heise, Clarence, Stevensville, Ont.
Heise, Edgar, Gormley, Ont.
Heise, Harold, Gormley, Ont.
Heise, [Louis] [name correction],
    Gormley, Ont. [Louis Heise,
    interview by author]

Heise, Paul, Gormley, Ont.
Henderson, Melvin, Gormley, Ont.
Hyde, Lorne, Stevensville, Ont.
Jarvis, Norman, Markham, Ont.
Main, Osborne, Welland, Ont.
Marr, Glen, Wainfleet, Ont.
Marr, Merlin, Wainfleet, Ont.
Marr, Sheldon, Wainfleet, Ont.
McCombs, Norman, Hagersville, Ont.
McNiven, Andrew, Fenwick, Ont.
Moore, Clare, Wainfleet, Ont.
Moore, Clifford, Wainfleet, Ont.
Morphet, Donald, Stayner, Ont.
Nigh, Edgar, Stevensville, Ont.
Nigh, Harold, Hagersville, Ont.
Nigh, Ross, Stevensville, Ont.
Nix, Bruce, Stevensville, Ont.
Osburn, Robert, Stayner, Ont.
Pollard, Howard, Fenwick, Ont.
Putman, Alvin, Wainfleet, Ont.
Pye, Arthur, Wainfleet, Ont.
Reaman, Norman, Stouffville, Ont.
Reaman, Peter, Stevensville, Ont.
Riegle, Chester, Ridgeway, Ont.
Sherk, Bert, Fisherville, Ont.
Sherk, Joseph, Fisherville, Ont.
Sider, Claude, Sherkston, Ont.
Sider, Edwin, Stevensville, Ont.
Sider, Elmer, Wainfleet, Ont.
Sider, George, Perry Station, Ont.

Sider, Harold, Perry Station, Ont.

Sider, James, Stevensville, Ont.

Sider, Lorne, Sherkston, Ont.

Sider, Murray, Wainfleet, Ont.

Sider, Ray, Stevensville, Ont.

Sider, Ross, Wainfleet, Ont.

Stickley, [Gordon] [name correction], Gormley, Ont. [Gordon Stickley, questionnaire]

Stickley, Harvey, Gormley, Ont.

Stickley, Orval, Gormley, Ont.

Traver, Howard, Wellandport, Ont.

Tyrell, Grant, Nanticoke, Ont.

Wideman, Clarence, Unionville, Ont.

Wideman, Harold, Gormley, Ont.

Wideman, Mervin, Unionville, Ont.

Wideman, Murray, Richmond Hill, Ont.

Wilson, Sheldon, Fort Erie, N. Ont.

Winger, Bennie, Wainfleet, Ont.

Winger, Bert, Fenwick, Ont.

Winger, Earl, Stevensville, Ont.

Winger, Freeman, Stevensville, Ont.

Winger, Harold, Stevensville, Ont.

Winger, Kenneth, Jarvis, Ont.

Winger, Murray, Wainfleet, Ont.

Winger, Ross, Stevensville, Ont.

Winger, Roy, Stevensville, Ont.

Winger, Vincent, Stevensville, Ont.

Source: Harmon, *They Also Serve,* 47.

Brethren in Christ Men in U.S. Civilian Public Service

ॐ

This list is compiled from information in Harmon, *They Also Serve*, 56–60; DCPS, 1947; DCPS, 1994; DCPS, 1996. Only the number of CPS units is listed under "CPS Assignment." For the camp name, see DCPS, 1996, xxii–xvii. Occupations are recorded as listed in DCPS, 1947. Information from the three sources sometimes conflicts. This appendix records dates of induction and release from DCPS, 1994, unless another source is obviously more accurate. If different sources included conflicting CPS assignments, I listed all of them.

The list order is as follows: NAME; DOB; HOME LOCATION; OCCUPATION; CPS ASSIGN.; CPS ENTER; CPS DISCHARGE.

Alleman, Melvin I.; 1922; Newburg, Pa.; Farmer; 4 63; Jan. 26, 1943; Mar. 26, 1946
Baldwin, Martin E.; 1922; Harrisburg, Pa.; Student; 8 77; Dec. 22, 1942; Apr. 12, 1946
Ballard, Delbert R.; 1921; Garlin, Ky.; Farmer; 39 64 110; Nov. 17, 1942; Apr. 10, 1946
Benner, George T.; 1927; Souderton, Pa.; Dairy worker; 18; June 20, 1945; Nov. 2, 1945
Book, Maynard C.; 1920; Upland, Calif.; Fruit processor; 35 107 18; June 21. 1944; July 14, 1946
Book, Orland Wayne; 1922; Upland, Calif.; Photographer; 35 107; June 15, 1943; May 17, 1946
Bosler, Harvey James; 1917; Lousiville, Ohio; Farm, shopworker; 20 85; Feb. 5, 1942; Jan. 21, 1946
Bricker, Amos A., Jr.; 1923; Florin, Pa.; Truck driver; 52; Dec. 18, 1944; Sept. 19, 1946
Brosey, John S. ; 1920; Elizabethtown, Pa.; Shoe repairman; 20 40 20 4 52; Aug. 17, 1942; Mar. 2, 1946
Brown, Nevin; 1919; Centre Hall, Pa.; Laborer; 4 111 128; Jan. 13, 1943; May 23, 1946
Brubaker, Abram Hess1924; Lewistown, Pa.; Farmer; 45 100; Sept. 13, 1944; Aug. 21, 1946
Brubaker, James M.; 1919; Mount Joy, Pa.; Teacher; 4 77 63; Jan. 29, 1942; Jan. 10, 1946
Brubaker, Matthew G.; 1907; Grantham, Pa.; Cold storage clerk; 4 142; May 28, 1943; Oct. 28, 1945
Brumbaugh, Ralph V.; 1920; Dayton, Ohio; Stockkeeper; 20 77 4; Jan. 21, 1942; May 1, 1945
Buckwalter, Erlis R.; 1926; Canton, Ohio; Student; 31 150 107; Mar. 19, 1945; May 7, 1946

Burkholder, Asa D.; 1924; Chambersburg, Pa.; Farmer; 45; Jan. 3, 1945; ————
Burkholder, John D.; 1919; Schellsburg, Pa.; Teacher; 45 52; July 4, 1944; Aug. 13, 1946
Burrel, Wilbert O.; 1925; Greencastle, Pa.; Farmer; 45 52; Dec. 11, 1945; Sept. 24, 1946
Byer, Verland M.; 1918; Hamlin, Kans.; Farmworker; 25 64; May 15, 1942; Feb. 17, 1946
Charles, Kenneth H. ; 1921; Hamlin, Kans.; Student, farmer; 35 64; Sept. 25, 1942; Mar. 19, 1946
Charles, Landon H. ; 1924; Hamlin, Kans.; Farmer, student; 33 34; Mar. 21, 1946; Dec. 3, 1946
Charles, Paul D.; 1924; Hamlin, Kans.; Farming, student ; 35 93; Sept. 5, 1944; Aug. 12, 1946
Cott, Winfred T.; 1922; Hope, Kans.; ————; 67 97; Oct. 22, 1944; Aug. 26, 1946
Crider, Paul D.; 1920; Chambersburg, Pa.; Construction worker; 45 85; Sept. 3, 1942; Mar. 26, 1946
Davis, Harold T.; 1921; Clarence Center, N.Y.; Farmer; 45 147 28 27; Sept. 20, 1944; Aug. 13, 1946
Dourte, Allon B.; 1918; Manheim, Pa.; Farmer; 24 77; June 8, 1942; Mar. 1, 1946
Dourte, Eber B.; 1921; Manheim, Pa.; Student; 39 107 24; Dec. 2, 1942; May 6, 1946
Ebersole, Alvin F.; 1922; Palmyra, Pa.; Grocery clerk; 8 35 31; Dec. 22, 1942; May 18, 1946
Engle, Daniel B. W.; 1922; Mifflintown, Pa.; Student, laborer; 48 92 36 60 107; Apr. 26, 1943; May 18, 1946;
Engle, Donald D. ; 1921; Detroit, Kans.; Farmer; 5 60 66; Sept. 3, 1942; Mar. 28, 1946
Engle, Gordon D.; 1920; Abilene, Kans.; Farmworker; 5 101 5 93; Sept.3, 1942; Mar. 28, 1946
Engle, Hiram Eldon; 1923; Detroit, Kans.; Farmer; 5 55; Mar. 28, 1944; July 14, 1946
Engle, Mahlon V.; 1927; Abilene, Kans.; Student; 31 151; Oct. 5, 1945; Dec. 10, 1946
Engle, Ralph L. ; 1922; Detroit, Kans.; Farmer; 31 85; Apr. 28, 1943; May 16, 1946
Engle, Royce A.; 1918; Archbold, Ohio; Farmer, student; 64 147 28; Feb. 20, 1943; Mar. 12, 1946
Engle, Virgil R.; 1924; West Milton, Ohio; Farmer; 28 55 34; Jan. 24, 1946; Mar. 29, 1947
Ensminger, Samuel F.; 1905; Palmyra, Pa.; Shoe last sorter; 20 85 18 31; July 9, 1942; Oct. 25, 1945
Fetters, Robert L.; 1918; Merrill, Mich.; Farm laborer; 18 97 57; Aug. 28, 1941; Jan. 31, 1944
Fisher, Donald R.; 1925; Mattawana, Pa.; Farmer; 4 97; June 8, 1944; July 25, 1946
Fohringer, Ray D.; 1920; Centre Hall, Pa.; Carpenter; 39 107; Jan. 5, 1943; June 1, 1946
Forry, Henry M. ; 1923; Manheim, Pa.; Farmhand; 45 52 27; Sept. 5, 1945; Dec. 10, 1946
Franklin, Glenn E.; 1922; Cucamonga, Calif.; Farmer; 35 97 31; July 28, 1943; May 21, 1946
Freed, Marvin F.; 1911; Souderton, Pa.; Farmer; 24 100; May 27, 1942; Mar. 7, 1946
Funderburg, Virgil L.; 1926; Grantham, Pa.; Student; 45; July 25, 1944; Oct. 24, 1944
Gade, Ray M. ; 1924; Upland, Calif.; Farmworker; 67 107 31; Nov. 7, 1944; Sept. 17, 1946
Gibboney, William A.; 1925; Pleasant Hill, Ohio; Student; 45 85 43; Feb. 7, 1946; Mar. 29, 1947
Glick, Jacob; 1925; North Lawrence, Ohio; Carpentry, Farmer; 28 52; Jan. 10, 1946; June 25, 1946
Glick, Owen A.; 1923; North Lawrence, Ohio; Farmer; 24 45 55 103 125; Mar. 3, 1943; May 20, 1946
Goins, Mabrie L. ; 1912; Ontario, Calif.; Shoe salesman; 35 31; Oct. 14, 1942; Apr. 15, 1946
Goodling, Reuben J.; 1918; Florin, Pa.; Factory laborer; 4 34; Aug. 22, 1941; Nov. 16, 1945
Grabill, E. David; 1921; Massillon, Ohio; Laborer; 45 100; Sept. 3, 1942; Mar. 1, 1946
Gramm, James R.; 1918; Claremont, Calif.; Boarding school worker; 31; May 11, 1943; Nov. 24, 1943

Grove, Bruce; 1921; Lewistown, Pa.; Ice and coal dealer; 4 143; July 4, 1944; Jan. 31, 1946

Grove, Lloyd C.; 1924; Lewistown, Pa.; Truck operator; 4 143; July 4, 1944; Apr. 13, 1945

Guengerich, Leslie L.; 1927; ————; ————; 31 52; Sept. 12, 1946; Mar. 29, 1947

Haas, J. Eugene; 1926; Dryden, Mich.; Student; 4 35 142 52; Mar. 7, 1945; Sept. 27, 1946

Haines, Lester L.; 1918; Springfield, Ohio; Bookkeeper, Acct.; 4 28 24; Mar. 10, 1944; June 10, 1946

Hammaker, Alvin E.; 1925; Mechanicsburg, Pa.; Sales clerk; 45; Feb. 22, 1944; July 4, 1946

Harmon, Wendell E.; 1920; Upland, Calif.; Student, teacher, journalist; 21 31 127 107; Dec. 5, 1941; Dec. 26, 1945

Heffley, Melvin S.; 1925; Chambersburg, Pa.; Farmer; 4 85; Oct. 4, 1944; Aug. 20, 1946

Heise, Alvin L.; 1924; Upland, Calif.; Student; 18 63; Dec. 20, 1944; Sept. 23, 1946

Heise, Jesse; 1921; Hamlin, Kans.; Student; 25 63; Sept. 25, 1942; Mar. 27, 1946

Heisey, Aaron F.; 1917; Spring Mills, Pa.; Truck driver; 4 64 100; Jan. 7, 1942; Jan. 23, 1946

Heisey, D. Earl ; 1912; Landisville, Pa.; Salesman; 20 85 34; June 17, 1942; Feb. 28, 1946

Heisey, Ezra D.; 1919; Millersville, Pa.; Farmer; 4 97; May 15, 1942; Mar. 1, 1946

Heisey, J. Wilmer; 1923; Mount Joy, Pa.; Student; 4 100; June 15, 1943; July 1, 1946

Heisey, Martin W.; 1912; Washington Boro, Pa.; Farm laborer; 4; June 16, 1941; Aug. 15, 1941

Helfrick, Isaac W.; 1919; Columbiana, Ohio; Farmer; 45 55 63; Aug. 21, 1942; Mar. 27, 1946

Hensel, Earl G.; 1926; Linglestown, Pa.; Clerk; 45 107 66; July 11, 1944; Aug. 9, 1946

Hensel, Glenn A.; 1922; Upland, Calif.; Student; 4 24 107; Jan. 14, 1943; May 28, 1946

Hensel, John S.; 1914; Harrisburg, Pa.; ————; 45 44; Nov. 9, 1943; June 26, 1946

Herr, William M.; 1924; Upland, Calif.; Mortician student, musician; 35 93 34; May 25, 1945; Nov. 12, 1946

Hess, E. Glenn; 1919; Waynesboro, Pa.; Office clerk; 45 97; Aug. 10, 1944; Jan. 31, 1946

Hess, Kenneth E.; 1921; Mount Joy, Pa.; Factory worker; 20 35 52; Aug. 17, 1942; Mar. 29, 1946

Hess, Raymond E.; 1920; Souderton, Pa.; Carpenter; 20 58; June 5 1942; Feb. 11, 1946

Hill, Judson W.; 1918; Alma, Mich.; Tank wagon truck driver; 13 57 66; June 26, 1941; Dec. 28, 1945

Hoffer, Abram S.; 1922; Manheim, Pa.; Asbestos worker; 45; Oct. 17, 1942; Feb. 11, 1944

Hoffer, Emanuel S.; 1920; Manheim, Pa.; Factory worker; 45; Sept. 25, 1942; Jan. 28, 1946

Hoffman, Clair H.; 1918; Mount Joy, Pa.; Business mgr. church pubs.; 4 85; Feb. 11, 1944; Feb. 26, 1946

Hoffman, John H., Jr.; 1922; Maytown, Pa.; Farmer; 45 85; Oct. 17, 1942; Nov. 30, 1945

Hoke, Daniel D.; 1919; Clayton, Ohio; Carpenter; 45 77; Oct. 8, 1942; Apr. 9, 1946

Holt, Norman D.; 1922; Abilene, Kans.; Farmer; 57 58; Jan. 5, 1945; Oct. 22, 1946

Hoover, Daniel L.; 1924; Ludlow Falls, Ohio; Farmer; 52 34; June 25, 1946; Mar. 29, 1947

Hoover, David R.; 1921; Ludlow Falls, Ohio; Farmer; 4 93 4 34; Dec. 22, 1943; July 17, 1946

Hostetter, C. Nelson; 1923; Grantham, Pa.; Student; 4 27 90 43; Feb. 25, 1943; May 13, 1946

Hostetter, D. Ray; 1927; Grantham, Pa.; Manufacturer; 45 69 141; Dec. 5, 1945; Dec. 10, 1946

Hostetter, S. Lane; 1926; Grantham, Pa.; Student; 45 147 28; Feb. 6, 1945; Apr. 9, 1946

Kipe, D. Franklin; 1920; Waynesboro, Pa.; Shipping clerk; 39; Jan. 5, 1943; Apr. 5, 1943

Knutti, David F.; 1919; North Lawrence, Ohio; Factory worker; 45 77; Sept. 2, 1942; Mar. 16, 1946

Kohler, John S.; 1918; Ashland, Ohio; Farmer; 24 100; May 15, 1942; Mar. 13, 1946

Landis, Paul W.; 1925; Des Moines, Iowa; Laborer; 5 55 93; Mar. 28, 1944; July 13, 1946

Lehman, Clarence S.; 1925; Mount Joy, Pa.; Farmer; 4 55 4; Feb. 11, 1944; July 1, 1946

Lehman, Ira R.; 1912; York, Pa.; Farm laborer; 24 71; May 27, 1942; Feb. 21, 1946

Lehman, J. Robert; 1927; Mount Joy, Pa.; Electrician; 4 52; Dec. 30, 1945; Dec. 10, 1946

Lehman, Jacob A.; 1913; York, Pa.; Laborer; 4; Mar. 21, 1944; Mar. 7, 1946

Lehman, Melvin A.; 1914; Carlisle, Pa.; Mail carrier; 39 109 100; Jan. 16, 1943; May 22, 1946

Lyons, Clare J.; 1926; Wheeler, Mich.; Farmer; 33 126; Apr. 5, 1945; Oct. 24, 1946

Mann, Leroy K.; 1923; Manheim, Pa.; Secretary-Stenographer; 35 34 43; June 8, 1943; July 2, 1946

Martin, Carl S.; 1922; Chambersburg, Pa.; Farmer; 121 134; Nov. 21, 1944; June 1, 1946

Martin, Harold S.; 1912; Elizabethtown, Pa.; Men's clothing store; 4 126 101 27 141; May 15, 1942; Feb. 25, 1946

Martin, Vernon M.; 1923; Marietta, Pa.; Student, dairy inseminator; 45 115 44; Sept. 10, 1943; Apr. 18, 1946

McCulloh, W. Paul; 1898; Dillsburg, Pa.; Farmer; 45; Aug. 21, 1942; June 30, 1943

Myers, Daniel O.; 1921; Iron Springs, Pa.; Farmer; 20 107; July 21, 1942; Apr. 1, 1946

Myers, Ernest L.; 1923; Harrisburg, Pa.; Engine block test operator; 4 111 128; June 8, 1943; June 25, 1946

Myers, Lyle K.; 1918; Greencastle, Pa.; Student; 4 58; Feb. 25, 1943; May 11, 1946

Myers, Roy L.; 1918; Chamberburg, Pa.; Farmer; 4 97; May 22, 1941; Dec. 6, 1945

Redcay, Paul A.; 1919; Ephrata, Pa.; Hospital attendant; 20 4 52 77; Nov. 25, 1941; Dec. 18, 1945

Rohrer, Donald E.; 1921; Clayton, Ohio; Grain elevator; 45 77 24; Oct. 18, 1942; Apr. 8, 1946

Rohrer, Eugene D.; 1915; Louisville, Ohio; Farmer; 28 55 31; July 20, 1945; Dec. 10, 1946

Rohrer, Paul M.; 1914; Troy, Ohio; Milkman; 4 28 24; May 4, 1945; Aug. 15, 1946

Rosenberger, Norman; 1905; Upland, Calif.; Laborer; 35 77 4 57; July 28, 1942; Oct. 20, 1945

Sherk, G. Millard; 1923; Mount Joy, Pa.; Student; 4 63; Feb. 25, 1943; May 15, 1946

Sherk, Morris N.; 1926; Mount Joy, Pa.; Student; 4 35 117 85; Jan. 5, 1945; Oct. 15, 1946

Shetter, Leroy C.; 1919; Abilene, Kans.; Farmer; 5 97 5; Jan. 26, 1943; Mar. 30, 1946

Slabaugh, Jerry; 1919; North Lawrence, Ohio; Farmer; 8 55 97 28 31; June 2, 1941; Dec. 17, 1945

Slabaugh, Roman J.; 1921; North Lawrence, Ohio; Farmer; 39 64 90; Nov. 5, 1942; Apr. 10, 1946

Smith, Robert; 1924; Grantham, Pa.; Student; 45 18 26; June 15, 1943; July 20, 1946

Stoner, Jesse B.; 1921; Mifflintown, Pa.; Mechanic; 45 55 100; Oct. 17, 1942; Apr. 18, 1946

Stoops, Edwin L.; 1926; Waynesboro, Pa.; ———; 45 52; Dec. 5, 1945; Dec. 10, 1946

Stubbs, Elmer L.; 1915; Des Moines, Iowa; Salesman; 33; June 8, 1944; Jan. 29, 1946

Ulery, Dale W.; 1911; Springfield, Ohio; Florist; 4 72; May 11, 1944; Jan. 28, 1946

Unruh, Lawrence W.; 1916; Upland, Calif.; Farmer; 21 31 58; Dec. 5, 1941; Dec. 18, 1945

Weller, Kenneth G.; 1917; Shippensburg, Pa.; Mill operator; 52; June 20, 1945; Aug. 13, 1946

Wenger, Byron L. ; 1920; Clayton, Ohio; Railroad clerk; 4 45; June 11, 1943; June 8, 1946

Wenger, Gerald; 1923; Mechanicsburg, Pa.; Railroad clerk; 39 107 77; Feb. 16, 1943; Mar. 20, 1946

Whitesel, Alfred U. ; 1919; Salona, Pa.; ———; 20 4 52; Oct. 8, 1941; June 28, 1946

Winger, Stanley H. ; 1916; Millersburg, Pa.; Poultry farmer; 45; Mar. 10, 1943; Mar. 16, 1946

Wingerd, Paul E.; 1925; Ramona, Kans.; Farmer; 35 93 138–3; Feb. 6, 1945; Oct. 20, 1946

Wingert, Avery M.; 1920; Chambersburg, Pa.; Farmer; 52 34; Jan. 19, 1945; Oct. 9, 1946

Wingert, Norman E.; 1916; Chambersburg, Pa.; Laborer; 8; Dec. 22, 1942; May 4, 1943

Wingert, Solomon L.; 1926; Fayetteville, Pa.; Farmer; 45 52; Jan. 19, 1945; Oct. 2, 1946

Witter, Paul E.; 1922; Navarre, Kans.; Student; 35 31; June 15, 1943; June 17, 1946

Wolgemuth, C. Arthur 1921; Mount Joy, Pa.; Farmer; 45 58; Oct. 20, 1942; Apr. 20, 1946

Wolgemuth, John M.; 1918; Mount Joy, Pa.; Poultry farmer; 4 39 4; May 22, 1941; Dec. 7, 1945

Zercher, Ray M.; 1921; Mount Joy, Pa.; Farmer; 45 85 5; Nov. 13, 1942; Apr. 12, 1946

Zook, A. Leroy; 1921; Wheeler, Mich.; Teacher; 39 107 100; Jan. 5, 1943; June 25, 1946

Civilian Public Service and Mennonite Central Committee–Related Participants

∽

The list below details sources within brackets:

[1] Questionnaires.
[2] Heisey, "They Also Served."
[3] Swalm, *Nonresistance under Test*, 156–58.
[4] Gingerich, *Service for Peace*, app. 16.
[5] Harmon, *They Also Serve*, 26, 30, 32, 36.
[6] J. W. Heisey to author, July 15, 1998.
[7] C. Nelson Hostetter letters, Hostetter Papers, Correspondence, Family, 7-22.8, BI Calif.

WOMEN EMPLOYED IN STATE HOSPITALS WITH CIVILIAN PUBLIC SERVICE UNITS

Baldwin, Dorothy Meyer, No. 77, Greystone Park, N.J. [1, 5]
Dourte, Jeannette Frey, No. 77, Greystone Park, N.J. [2, 5]
Harmon, Frances Logan, No. 127, American Fork, Utah [2, 5]
Heisey, Bertha Sollenberger Crider, No. 85, Howard, R.I. [2]
Hefley, Lorraine, No. 85, Howard, R.I. [5, 6]
Helfrick, Laura Blosser, No. 63, Marlboro, N.J. [1],
Hess, Ruth Landis, No. 58, Farnhurst, Del. [2]
Hoffman, Betty Collins, No. 85, Howard, R.I. [2]
Hoffman, Laura, No. 85, Howard, R.I. [2]
Wenger, Anna Mae Lehman, No. 77, Greystone Park, N.J. [2]
Wolgemuth, Amanda Kraybill, No. 58, Farnhurst, Del. [5, 6]
Zercher, Ruth Niesley, No. 85, Howard, R.I. [3]

Civilian Public Service Staff

Book, Eilene Frey, Dietician, No. 107, Three Rivers, Calif. [4]
Books, Titus, Eastern Area Pastor [4]
Brubaker, Grace Book, Matron, No. 31, Camino, Calif. [4]
Brubaker, Henry H., Director, No. 31, Camino, Calif. [4]
Heisey, Clara Lyons, Matron/secretary, No. 97(M), Bolton, Mass. [5]
Helfrick, Laura Blosser, Volunteer dietician, No. 45, Luray, Va. [1]
Martin, Grace, Matron, No. 27(2), Mulberry, Fla. [4, 7]

Some conscripted CPS men served in staff positions, including James A. Brubaker, Leroy Mann, D. Earl Heisey, Clair H. Hoffman, Harold S. Martin, Maynard C. Book, O. Wayne Book, and Avery Wingert. See Gingerich, *Service for Peace,* app. 16.

Mennonite Central Committee–Related Members

Books, Titus, Brook Lane Farm Advisory Committee [4]
Dourte, Eber B., Mennonite Aid Section member [4]
Engle, Paul, Peace Section member; West Coast Advisory Committee [4]
Witter, R. I., Central Area Advisory Committee [4]

Brethren in Christ Service Workers in Mennonite Central Committee and Related Programs, 1944–1955

ↀↀↀ

This list was compiled from a variety of sources. Those from the MSS Collection, in particular, may be inaccurate. MCC personnel listings were verified against corroborating sources whenever possible. The list below details sources within brackets:

[1] MCC Collection: CPS and Central Correspondence, Personnel Files, IX-6–4.1, 4.2; Report Files, Set 1, IX-12–1, "Voluntary Service Personnel to 1953" folder; Report Files, 5, Personnel Listings, X-12–5; Personnel Files, IX-30, AMC.

[2] Unruh, *In the Name of Christ,* apps.

[3] "Brethren in Christ Personnel in MCC, 1941–1970," produced for Nancy R. Heisey by MCC.

[4] Isaiah B. Harley, comp., "Brethren in Christ People in Alternate Service," Dec. 7, 1956, MCC Report Files 1, IX-12–1, "BIC Men in CPS" folder, AMC.

[5] *BICMissions,* 42–76.

[6] Questionnaires.

[7] Interview by author.

[8] Personal communications with author.

Key: PAX (Overseas I-W voluntary service); SS (Short-term Summer Service); VS (Voluntary Service); WSU (Women's Service Units)

Aker, Gladys Lehman, WSU Howard, R.I., 1946 [1]

Bechtel, Elsie C., WSU Howard, R.I., 1944; relief service France, 1945–48 [1; 2]

Bert, Harry D., PAX Peru, 1954–56 [3; 5]

Blackketter, Ruth Heisey, WSU Howard, R.I., 1944; VS Matron, St. Elizabeth Hospital, Washington, D.C., 1948 [1; *Clarion,* Oct. 6, 1944, 1]

Boese, David, unknown Germany, 1952 [3]

Book, Doyle, VS, 1949; BIC (I-W/VS) Japan, 1955–57 [1; 4]

Book, Lila Fae, SS migrant unit, Madison, N.Y., 1953 [1]

Book, Thelma Heisey, vs Japan, 1955–57 [4; MSMS, 25]

Bowers, Miriam, relief service Germany, 1947–51 [2]

Boyer, Ernest, ship livestock attendant, 1946 [8—P. Boyer, W. Boyer, S. Herr]

Boyer, Esther Tyson, European student tour/work camp, 1950 [1; 6]

Boyer, Paul S., PAX France, 1955–57 [5]

Boyer, William, European student tour/work camp, 1950 [1]

Brubaker, Mary M., SS, 1949; European student tour/work camp, 1950 [1; PRS News, EV, May 23, 1949, 16]

Brubaker, Norma, SS state school, Vineland, N.J., 1949 [1]

Burkholder, Asa D., ship livestock attendant [1]

Byer, Donald, train livestock attendant, 1948 [8—J. Byer Wolgemuth]

Byer, Everett, ship livestock attendant, 1946 [8—J. Byer Wolgemuth]

Byer, Harriet Trautwein, vs Mexico, 1948, 1951 [1; 3; 6; GC Minutes, 1949, art. 18]

Byers, Elizabeth Heisey, WSU Howard, R.I., 1944; WSU Ypsilanti, Mich., 1945 [1; *Clarion*, Oct. 6, 1944, 1]

Charles, Landon, relief service Philippines, 1947–48 [2; 5]

Davis, Harold K., vs Gulfport, Miss., 1948–49 [1; 6]

Davis, Ruth Brubaker, vs Gulfport, Miss., 1948–49 [1; 6]

Eberly, Carl, vs New Mexico, 1952–54 [GC Minutes, 1953, art. 22; 1954, art. 24]

Eberly, Clara Meyer, WSU Howard, R.I., 1946 [1; 6]

Engle, Daniel B. N., ship livestock attendant [1]

Engle, Harold, relief service Formosa, 1950–52 [1; 5; 6; 7]

Engle, John, European student tour/work camp, leader, 1950 [1; 6; 7]

Engle, June Hostetter, SS Vineland, N.J., 1949 [1; G. Wingert to author, June 17, 1996]

Engle, Mary Elizabeth, relief service Formosa, 1950–52 [1; 5; 7]

Eyer, John R., PAX Germany, 1953–55 [5; GC Minutes, 1954, art. 25]

Fadenrecht, Ruth Zook, WSU Ypsilanti, Mich., 1944; SS, 1952 [1; 6; *Clarion*, Apr. 1944, 9]

French, Grace, European student tour, 1947 [1; *Clarion*, Mar. 28, 1947, 1]

Fretz, Lester, ship livestock attendant, 1951–52 [7]

Fretz, Norman A., SS London, Ont., 1949, 1951 [1]

Frey, Beth L. Winger, SS? Vineland, N.J. [1; MSMS, 155]

Frey, Glenn C., European student tour/work camp, 1949 [PRS News, EV, May 23, 1949, 16]

Frey, John K., PAX Germany, 1954–56 [5; GC Minutes, 1954, art. 24]

Frey, Paul S., vs Heifer Project, Modesto, Calif., 1955–57 [3; 4]

Frey, Pauline E., European student tour/work camp, 1950 [1; 7—John Engle]

Garis, Vera, European student tour/work camp, 1948 [1; 7—John Engle]

Gibboney, William, vs P.R., 1947–48 [1; 2]

Ginder, Joseph G., BIC (1-w/vs) Southern Rhodesia, 1954–56 [5; MSMS, 161]

Glick, Paul, ship livestock attendant, 1947 [*Clarion*, Mar. 28, 1947, 1; Obituary, EV, Apr. 7, 1947, 11]

Gordon, Richard, vs N.M., 1951; vs Topeka, Kans., 1952 [1; GC Minutes, 1951, art. 25]

Heise, Alvin, European student tour/work camp, 1948 [1; *Echo*, June 1948, 2]

Heise, Arthur, ship livestock attendant, 1948 [8—J. Byer Wolgemuth]

Heise, Austin, ship livestock attendant, 1948 [8—J. Byer Wolgemuth]

Heise, Howard, SS? National Institute of Health, Bethesda, Md., 1955 [1; J. Heise to author, Jan. 26, 1998]

Heise, Jesse, SS, 1948 [1]

Heisey, Beulah, ss Boy's Village, Ohio, 1953 [1; 6]

Heisey, Chester, PAX Germany, Greece, 1953–55 [1]

Heisey, J. Wilmer, relief service Philippines, 1946–50 [1; 2; 5]

Heisey, Marion, vs Brethren in Christ Navajo Mission, Bloomfield, N.M., 1956 [4]

Heisey, Velma Climenhaga, relief service Philippines, 1947–50 [1; 12]

Hennigh, Esther Elizabeth, ss migrant workers unit, Hamilton, N.Y., 1955 [1]

Hennigh, Lois, ss Camp Bennett, Washington, D.C., 1949 [1]

Hensel, Earl G., ss Camp Paivka, Crestline, Calif., 1949 [1; 6]

Herr, Samuel L., ship livestock attendant, 1946 [8—S. Herr]

Hoffman, Glenn, relief service Indonesia, 1955–58 [3; 4; 5]

Hoover, Albert, PAX Indonesia, 1956 [6]

Hoover, David R., relief service Philippines, 1946–49 [1; 2; 5]

Hoover, Edgar, PAX Indonesia, 1956 [6]

Hoover, Jesse W., relief service France, 1941; Special Commissioner Far East, 1947–48;
     Peace Section, Assistant Secretary [2]

Hoover, Ruth Hilsher, relief service Philippines, 1946–49 [1; 2; 5]

Hostetler, Lloyd, ship livestock attendant, 1947 [*Clarion,* Mar. 28, 1947, 1; P. Hostetler to
     author, Dec. 3, 1996]

Hostetter, C. Nelson, vs P.R., 1946–47 [2; 5]

Hostetter, Glenn, vs Gulfport, Miss., 1948–49 [1]

Hostetter, James G., PAX Germany, 1953–55 [5; GC Minutes, 1954, art. 24]

Johnson, Ruth Frey, relief service Netherlands, Germany, 1948–51 [1; 2; 5]

Kanode, Avery O., vs N.M., 1952–54 [7; GC Minutes, 1953, art. 22]

Kanode, Ruth E., European student tour/work camp, 1951 [1]

Kern, Edith, relief service Germany, 1951–53 [5; GC Minutes, art. 25]

Kreider, Ethel Wolgemuth, relief service Jordan, 1952–54 [1; 5]

Lady, Charles Spurgeon, vs Maine General Hospital, Portland, Maine, 1955–57 [4; 5]

Landis, Howard L., European Builders Unit/PAX Germany, Greece, 1951–53 [6; GC Min-
     utes, 1951, art. 25]

Landis, Pauline Alderfer, European student tour/work camp, 1948; MCC headquarters,
     1952; ss Kings View Home Reedley, Calif., 1953. [1; *Echo,* June 1948, 2; *UC Bulletin,*
     July 1952, unpaginated]

Lehman, Anna Marie, ss Boy's Village, Ohio, 1953 [1]

Lehman, Bruce, ship livestock attendant, 1946 [8—S. Herr]

Lehman, Clarence, ship livestock attendant [7—Lester Fretz]

Light, Earl, vs Wiltwyck, N.Y., 1954–56 [3; 5]

Light, Faithe, European student tour/work camp, 1949 [7; PRS News, *EV,* May 23, 1949, 16]

Mann, Esther, MCC headquarters, Akron, Penn., 1944; WSU Howard, R.I., 1944; WSU
     Poughkeepsie, N.Y., 1945 [1; 2; Leroy K. Mann, telephone conversation with author,
     Oct. 10, 1996]

Mann, Leroy K., vs P.R., 1946–47 [1; 2; 5]

Melhorn, Charles I., European student tour/work camp, 1951 [1]

Mellinger, Gladys, ss Skillman, N.J., 1948; ss London, Ontario, 1953 [1]

Minter, Donald, ship livestock attendant, 1946 [8—S. Herr]

Mumma, Ruth E., European student tour/work camp, 1949 [PRS News, *EV,* May 23,
     1949, 16]

Musser, Irvin, vs Md., 1948–49 [1]

Peters, James F., PAX Peru, 1956–58 [3; 4; 5]

Poe, M. Evelyn, European student tour/work camp, 1949; ss Topeka, Kans., 1950 [1; PRS News, *EV*, May 23, 1949, 16]

Pye, Ruth E., ss Camp Bennett, Washington, D.C., 1949 [1; *EV*, Feb. 6, 1950]

Raser, John R., PAX Germany, France, 1955–57 [3; 4; 5]

Rittgers, Philip, PAX Europe or Jordan, 1952–54 [3; GC Minutes, 1952, art. 25; 1954, art. 24]

Reesor, John C., ship livestock attendant, 1946 [6]

Ruegg, Lorne, vs United States, 1949–50 [Martin to Heisey, Jan. 14, 1998]

Sakimura, Clarence, relief service Austria, 1955–57 [3, 4, 5]

Saltzman, Royce, ship livestock attendant, 1946? [*SSH*, Sept. 29, 1946, 7–8]

Schrag, Dorothy Witter, European student tour/work camp, 1950; relief service Germany, 1950–51 [1; 2; 5]

Sherman, Warren, European student tour, 1947 [1; BC *Echo*, Oct. 1947, 1]

Sider, C. Neale, vs Gulfport, Miss., 1949–50; ship livestock attendant, c. 1951 [1; Fretz to author, Feb. 2, 1998]

Sider, Dorothy Myers, European student tour, 1947 [1; *Clarion*, Mar. 28, 1947, 1; 7]

Sider, Harold K., ss Brandon, Manit., 1953; Livestock ship attendant [Harold K. Sider, "I Spent Last Summer Working in a Mental Hospital," *SSH*, Jan. 31, 1954; 6]

Slabaugh, Ella, WSU Ypsilanti, Mich., c. 1945 [N. Hostetter to mother, Hostetter Papers, Correspondence, Family, 7–22.8, BICA]

Smith, Frances, WSU Howard, R.I., unit leader, 1946 [1; Ediger to Hostetter, May 28, 1946, Hostetter Papers, CPS, 1944–47, 7–5.1, BICA]

Smith, Robert H., relief service Philippines, 1946–48, Okinawa, 1948–50 [1; 3; 5]

Stickley, Gordon, ship livestock attendant, [6]

Stiefel, Viola, European student tour/work camp, 1950; ss Gulfport, Miss., 1954 [1; 7— John Engle]

Ulery, Esther G. Book, relief service, India, 1946–49; ss migrant workers unit, San Jose, Calif., 1951 [1; 2]

Ulery, Keith, BIC (1-w/vs) Southern Rhodesia, 1955–57 [4; 5; GC Minutes, 1955, art. 23]

Wilson, Ellis E., ship livestock attendant [1]

Wingerd, Eldon, PAX Germany, 1953–55 [5; GC Minutes, 1954, art. 24]

Wingert, Eunice Lady, relief service Germany, 1948–49, Austria, 1950–52, Japan, 1953–57 [2; 5]

Wingert, Gerald N., ss Cleveland, Ohio, 1947, 1948 [1; Wingert, diary, in possession of its author]

Wingert, Laban, ship livestock attendant [G. Wingert, diary, Feb. 27, 1947]

Wingert, Norman A., relief service Germany, 1948–49, Austria, 1950–52, Japan, 1953–57 [2; 5]

Wolgemuth, Earl, vs Brethren in Christ Navajo Mission, Bloomfield, N.M., 1956 [4]

Wolgemuth, J. Carl, ss North Topeka, Kans., 1953; vs migrant workers unit, Coalinga, Calif.,1955–57 [1; 5]

Wolgemuth, Marilyn, vs migrant workers unit, Coalinga, Calif., 1955–57 [5]

Zook, Donald R., BIC (1-w/vs) Southern Rhodesia, 1955–57 [5]

Zook, Miriam Frey, European student tour/work camp, 1950 [1; 6]

Brethren in Christ Men in U.S. I-W Service

൚

Unless otherwise noted, these lists are compiled from two sources: "List of Brethren in Christ I-W Men," Aug. 14, 1953, Hostetter Papers, Mennonite Related Papers, 7-6.1, "NSBRO" folder, BICalif.; Isaiah B. Harley, comp., "Brethren in Christ People in Alternate Service," Dec. 7, 1956, MCC Report Files 1, IX-12-1, "BIC Men in CPS" folder, AMC. This list excludes men working in the PAX or domestic voluntary service positions, since they are listed in app. 6. City names are included if they are explicitly stated. The lists are typed directly from the documentation. No attempt was made to verify the lists in other sources.

1953 LIST

Base, Wesley H., State Hospital, Larned, Kans.

Bohland, Wilbur E., TB Hospital Center, State University, Columbus, Ohio

Brauen, James F., General Hospital, West Rochester, N.Y.

Eyer, Frederick S., Department of Charities, Los Angeles, Calif.

Georgiades, Stergos, Goodwill Industries, Los Angeles, Calif.

Glick, Daniel, Hawthornden State Hosptial, Macedonia, Ohio

Glick, Earl, Messiah Rescue and Benevolent Home, Harrisburg, Pa.

Glick, James S., Hawthornden State Hosptial, Macedonia, Ohio

Goins, Dwight L., Department of Charities, Los Angeles, Calif.

McGuire, Robert, Department of Public Welfare, Manteno, Ill.

Negley, William G., State Hospital, Norristown, Pa.

Rohrer, Donald E., Department of Charities, Los Angeles, Calif.

Trost, John L., General Hospital, Rochester, N.Y.

1956 LIST

Asper, Dale, Goodwill Industries, Los Angeles, Calif.

Bert, Robert, Lankanau Hospital, Pa.

Carlson, David, Upland College, Upland, Calif.

Egolf, Amos, Norristown State Hospital, Norristown, Pa.

Engle, Delbert, Norristown State Hospital, Norristown, Pa.

Ginder, Roy, Philadelphia State Hospital, Philadelphia, Pa.

Gish, David, Patton State Hospital, Calif.

Gramm, Donald, Evanston General Hospital, Ill.

Hade, Donald C., Philadelphia State Hospital, Philadelphia, Pa.

Heidler, Eugene, Philadelphia State Hospital, Philadelphia, Pa.

Heisey, Orville, Messiah College, Grantham, Pa.

Hershey, Dale, Philhaven Hospital, Lebanon, Pa.

Hilsher, Clair, T.B. Sanatorium, South Mountain, Pa.

Holsinger, Joe, Philadelphia State Hospital, Philadelphia, Pa.

Kelchner, Robert L., Messiah Home, Harrisburg, Pa.

Kennedy, Charles Ray, DHIA

Lehman, Carl Henry, [D.]ayton State Hospital, Ohio

McBeth, Joseph, Dayton State Hospital, Ohio

Mann, Myron, Niagra Christian College, Fort Erie, Ont.

Martin, Emory, Blanchard Valley Hospital, Ohio

Martin, Tennyson, Lancaster General Hospital, Lancaster, Pa.

Musser, Harold, DHIA, Montgomery County, Pa.

Musser, Ray, Dayton State Hospital, Ohio

Myers, Benjamin, Norristown State Hospital, Norristown, Pa.

Myers, Joseph, Norristown State Hospital, Norristown, Pa.

Myers, Levi, Norristown State Hospital, Norristown, Pa.

Myers, Thomas, Philadelphia State Hospital, Philadelphia, Pa.

Nealy, Charles Richard, Norristown State Hospital, Norristown, Pa.

Newmyer, Edward R., Norristown State Hospital, Norristown, Pa.

Sides, Paul, Brooklane Fram, Hagerstown, Pa.

Slick, John, Philadelphia State Hospital, Philadelphia, Pa.

Smith, Ralph, The Dicksmont Hospital, Pa.

Tyson, Paul, T.B. Sanatorium, South Mountain, Pa.

Urey, Bruce, Lancaster General Hospital, Lancaster, Pa.

Weaver, Gerald, Lancaster General Hospital, Lancaster, Pa.

Wengert, Paul, Lancaster General Hospital, Lancaster, Pa.

Wingerd, Roy, Millersville State Teachers College, Millersville, Pa.

OTHER SOURCES

Beaver, Percy, Mount Carmel Home, Morrison, Ill., 1953 [GC *Minutes,* 1953, art. 22.]

Bender, Richard, Denied 1-0 classification, refused induction, convicted in federal court, given two-year sentence, case appealed, out on bail, 1953 [GC *Minutes,* 1953, art. 22.]

Bulgrein, Kenneth, Messiah College, Grantham, Pa., 1953 [GC *Minutes,* 1953, art. 22.]

Carlson, Paul, Messiah College, Grantham, 1954–56 [Paul B. Carlson, questionnaire.]

Heise, Howard, Mennonite administered school, before 1955 [J. Heise to author, Jan. 26, 1998.]

Heise, Loren, Patton State Hospital, Patton, Calif., 1954–56 [J. Heise to author, Jan. 26, 1998; *Upland College Bulletin,* June 1954, unpaginated.]

Hershey, Dale, Denied 1-0 classification, case pending, 1953 [GC *Minutes,* 1953, art. 22.]

Holt, Rosen Lee, Denied 1-0 classification, refused induction, tried, convicted, paroled to Mennonite Central Committee service, 1953 [GC *Minutes,* 1953, art. 22.]

Myers, Lloyd S., Norristown State Hospital, Norristown, Pa., 1954–56 [Lloyd S. Myers, questionnaire.]

Notes

❧

Preface

1. Natalie Zemon Davis, "Who Owns History? History in the Profession," *Perspectives* 34 (Nov. 1996): 4.

2. Ibid.

3. The following archives were used in this study: Archives of the Brethren in Christ Church and Messiah College, Grantham, Penn. 17027 [hereafter BICA]; Archives of the Mennonite Church, Goshen, Ind. 46526 [hereafter AMC]; Mennonite Library and Archives, Bethel College, North Newton, Kans. 67117 [hereafter MLA].

4. For a copy of the questionnaire prepared for this study, see app. 1.

Introduction

1. Qtd. in Donald B. Kraybill and Carl F. Bowman, *On the Backroad to Heaven: Old Order Hutterites, Mennonites, Amish, and Brethren* (Baltimore: Johns Hopkins Univ. Press, 2001), 179.

2. Carlton O. Wittlinger, *Quest for Piety and Obedience: The Story of the Brethren in Christ* (Nappanee, Ind.: Evangel Press, 1978), 343–56.

3. Martin E. Marty, *Pilgrims in Their Own Land: Five Hundred Years of Religion in America* (Boston: Little, Brown, 1984), 476.

4. Wittlinger, *Quest for Piety*, chaps. 1–2, 6, 15–16.

5. *Questions and Answers in Bible Instruction: Children's Edition* (Nappanee, Ind.: E. V. Publishing House, 1931), 45; *Manual for Christian Youth: Doctrines and Practices Based upon the Holy Scriptures as Taught by the Brethren in Christ* (Nappanee, Ind.: E. V. Publishing House, 1945), 131; *Constitution: Doctrine, By-Laws, and Rituals* (Nappanee, Ind.: E. V. Publishing House, 1939), art. 7.

6. Charles DeBenedetti, *The Peace Reform in American History* (Bloomington: Indiana Univ. Press, 1980), xi, 198–99.

7. Wittlinger, *Quest for Piety*, chap. 16. The BIC language change reflected that of Mennonite churches. In their study of changing Mennonite peace positions, Leo Driedger and Donald B. Kraybill note a shift from use of the term *nonresistance* to terms that included *peace*, beginning in World War I. Many Mennonites and BIC, how-

ever, continued to employ the term *nonresistance* and emphasized its prohibitions much longer. See Leo Driedger and Donald B. Kraybill, *Mennonite Peacemaking: From Quietism to Activism* (Scottdale, Penn.: Herald Press, 1994), 65–67.

8. Throughout the study, I will use *community* to refer to the larger, looser grouping and *official church members* to indicate the smaller grouping.

9. Studs Terkel notes even "the disrememberance" of World War II. See his *"The Good War": An Oral History of World War Two* (New York: Ballantine Books, 1984), 1.

10. Martin Luther King Jr., "Pilgrimage to Nonviolence," in *Nonviolence in America: A Documentary History*, ed. Staughton Lynd and Alice Lynd (Maryknoll, N.Y.: Orbis Books, 1995), 219.

11. On Brethren in Christ history and theology, see Owen H. Alderfer, "The Mind of the Brethren in Christ: A Synthesis of Revivalism and the Church Conceived as Total Community" (Ph.D. diss., Claremont Graduate School, 1963); Martin H. Schrag, "The Brethren in Christ Attitude toward the 'World': A Historical Study of the Movement from Separation to an Increasing Acceptance of American Society" (Ph.D. diss., Temple University, 1967); E. Morris Sider, *The Brethren in Christ in Canada: Two Hundred Years of Tradition and Change* (Nappanee, Ind.: Evangel Press, 1988); Wittlinger, *Quest for Piety*. An earlier denominational history is A. W. Climenhaga, *History of the Brethren in Christ Church* (Nappanee, Ind.: E. V. Publishing House, 1942).

12. Luke L. Keefer Jr., "Three Streams in Our Heritage: Separate or Parts of a Whole," in *Reflections on a Heritage: Defining the Brethren in Christ*, ed. E. Morris Sider (Grantham, Penn.: Brethren in Christ Historical Society, 1999), 45; John R. Yeatts and Ronald J. Burwell, "Tradition and Mission: The Brethren in Christ at the End of the Millennium," *Brethren in Christ History and Life* [hereafter BICHL] 19 (Apr. 1996): 108.

13. Ida Wenger, <bic@messiah.edu>, July 11, 2001, personal e-mail; Wittlinger, *Quest for Piety*, app. C. Between 1916 and 1972, Mennonites grew from about seventy-nine thousand in the United States to approximately 250,000 official members in the United States and Canada. Gerlof D. Homan, *American Mennonites and the Great War, 1914–1918* (Scottdale, Penn.: Herald Press, 1994), 31; J. Howard Kauffman and Leland Harder, *Anabaptists Four Centuries Later: A Profile of Five Mennonite and Brethren in Christ Denominations* (Scottdale, Penn.: Herald Press, 1975), table 1–1. In 2000, there were about 444,000 baptized members in thirty-four organized Mennonite bodies, including the BIC, in the United States and Canada. Elisabeth Baecher, ed., *Mennonite and Brethren in Christ World Directory* (Strasbourg, France: Mennonite World Conference, 2000).

14. Wittlinger, *Quest for Piety*, app. C, 88–90, 145–55, 178–92, 202, 207–13, 261, 284–86.

15. I will be using the common name, the *Visitor*, throughout the text. "Constitution of the Church of the Brethren in Christ (Formerly Known as River Brethren)," 1904, arts. 24, 27, 29, in *Minutes of General Conference* [hereafter GC *Minutes*]; *Constitution and By-Laws of the Brethren in Christ Church* (n.p., 1924), 85–94. In the World War I period, love feasts were usually semiannual, several-day gatherings, which included testimony periods; preaching on church doctrines; the practice of the ordinances of feet washing, the holy kiss, and communion; and community meals. A district that hosted a love feast provided hospitality for many attendees from other districts. Pennsylvania harvest-praise services were community gatherings often hosted by one family in its barn and focused on a service of thanksgiving. They too included testimony meetings, preaching, and a community meal. All of these traditional practices are prominent in the *Visitor*, 1914–19. Wittlinger, *Quest for Piety*, 77–97, 84–85, 489–90, 492–93; Sider, *BIC in Canada*, 96–102.

16. Wittlinger, *Quest for Piety,* 347–56. Lawrence M. Yoder interprets this legislation as an attempt to "guard the borders" as the organic unity of the community declined. See his "Why Changes in Brethren in Christ Hermeneutics? A Sociological and Anthropological Analysis," BICHL 9 (Dec. 1986): 253–56.

17. Wittlinger, *Quest for Piety,* 91–96.

18. Alderfer, "Mind of the Brethren," 5, 15, 78–80; Schrag, "BIC Attitude," chap. 2, part 2; Martin H. Schrag, "The Life and Times of Christian Lesher," BICHL 18 (Apr. 1995): 42–44; Sider, BIC *in Canada,* chap. 2; E. Morris Sider, "The Anabaptist Vision and the Brethren in Christ Church," BICHL 17 (Dec. 1994): 283–96; Wittlinger, *Quest for Piety,* 9–11, 15. On the use of surnames that connect the BIC to other Anabaptist groups, see Paul Boyer, "The Ironies of Separateness and Assimilation: A New Look at the Mennonite Experience in America: A Review Essay," BICHL 14 (Dec. 1991): 417. Richard K. MacMaster's history of colonial Mennonites portrays the first members of the new group less as unique than as spawned by Mennonites, also influenced by the religious ferment of the period. See his *Land, Piety, Peoplehood: The Establishment of Mennonite Communities in America, 1683–1790* (Scottdale, Penn.: Herald Press, 1985), 222–25. An 1848 description of the River Brethren notes that they were also sometimes called River *Mennonites.* See Schrag, "BIC Attitude," 14. In a social and cultural consideration, Yoder too argues that while the BIC established "a particular blend of forms and practices," their social structures replicated those of rural Anabaptist neighbors. See his "Why Changes in BIC," 240. On colonial Mennonites and pietism, see MacMaster, *Land, Piety, Peoplehood,* chaps. 6, 8, esp. 206–24. On pietism, see Dale W. Brown, *Understanding Pietism,* rev. ed. (Nappanee, Ind.: Evangel Publishing House, 1996); Stephen L. Longenecker, "*Wachet Auf:* Awakening, Diversity, and Tolerance among Early Pennsylvania Germans," in *Nonviolent America: History through the Eyes of Peace,* ed. Louise Hawkley and James C. Juhnke (North Newton, Kans.: Bethel College, 1993), 227–43.

19. On Anabaptist and Mennonite history and in North America in particular, see Cornelius J. Dyck, *An Introduction to Mennonite History: A Popular History of the Anabaptists and the Mennonites,* 3d ed. (Scottdale, Penn.: Herald Press, 1993); Frank H. Epp, *Mennonites in Canada, 1786–1920: History of a Separate People* (Toronto: Macmillan of Canada, 1974), and *Mennonites in Canada, 1920–1940: A People's Struggle for Survival* (Scottdale, Penn.: Herald Press, 1982); T. D. Regehr, *Mennonites in Canada, 1939–1970* (Toronto: Univ. of Toronto Press, 1996); Calvin Redekop, *Mennonite Society* (Baltimore: Johns Hopkins Univ. Press, 1989); Theron Schlabach, ed., *The Mennonite Experience in America,* vols. 1–4 (Scottdale, Penn.: Herald Press, 1985–96); James M. Stayer, Werner O. Packull, and Klaus Deppermann, "From Monogenesis to Polygenesis: The Historical Discussion of Anabaptist Origins," *Mennonite Quarterly Review* [hereafter MQR] 40 (1975): 83–121. On Amish history, see Steven M. Nolt, *A History of the Amish* (Intercourse, Penn.: Good Books, 1992). On Brethren history, see Carl F. Bowman, *Brethren Society: The Cultural Transformation of a "Peculiar People"* (Baltimore: Johns Hopkins Univ. Press, 1995). Important examinations of the social content of Anabaptism include John A. Hostetler, *Amish Society,* 3d ed. (Baltimore: Johns Hopkins Univ. Press, 1993); Kraybill and Bowman, *On the Backroad to Heaven;* Redekop, *Mennonite Society.*

20. Alderfer, "Mind of the Brethren"; Terry L. Brensinger, ed., *Focusing Our Faith: Brethren in Christ Core Values* (Nappanee, Ind.: Evangel Publishing House, 2000), 8–9; Keefer, "Three Streams"; Rodney J. Sawatsky, "Translating Brethren in Christ Identity," BICHL 22 (Aug. 1999): 213–20; Donald Shafer, "The Pastor and Church Loyalty," in *We*

Have This Ministry: Pastoral Theory and Practice in the Brethren in Christ Church, ed. E. Morris Sider (Nappanee, Ind.: Evangel Press, 1991), 322; E. Morris Sider, ed., *Reflections on a Heritage: Defining the Brethren in Christ* (Grantham, Penn.: Brethren in Christ Historical Society, 1999); Wittlinger, *Quest for Piety;* David L. Zercher, "Is There a 'Brethren Mindset'? Reflections on the Alderfer Thesis," BICHL 19 (Apr. 1996): 161–78.

21. Redekop, *Mennonite Society,* 47–56; Dyck, *Mennonite History,* 133–38; A. G. Roeber, "The Origin of Whatever Is Not English among Us: The Dutch-speaking and the German-speaking Peoples of Colonial British America," in *Strangers within the Realm: Cultural Margins of the First British Empire,* ed. Bernard Bailyn and Philip D. Morgan (Chapel Hill: Univ. of North Carolina Press, 1991), 220–83, n. 16.

22. These quotations come from a River Brethren statement written sometime before 1788. For a discussion and full text of the confession see Wittlinger, *Quest for Piety,* 16–17, n. 13, 14, app. A. For discussions of alternate versions, see Schrag, "BIC Attitude," 24–25, app. A. Also see Wittlinger, *Quest for Piety,* part 1.

23. "Brief History of Brethren in Christ (River Brethren)," in *Minutes of the General Conferences of the Brethren in Christ (River Brethren), 1871–1904* (Harrisburg, Penn.: n.p., 1904), 314. Schrag discusses historical evidence that exists for River Brethren communication with federal government officials during the Civil War. See his "BIC Attitude," 110–12, app. C. Also see Wittlinger, *Quest for Piety,* 133–40.

24. Wittlinger, *Quest for Piety,* 1, 16–17, 129–33, 145–55; Sider, BIC in Canada, chaps. 2, 8; Richard Hofstadter, *The Age of Reform: From Bryan to F.D.R.* (New York: Random House, 1955), 23–59.

25. Paul Boyer, *Mission on Taylor Street: The Founding and Early Years of the Dayton Brethren in Christ Mission* (Grantham, Penn.: Brethren in Christ Historical Society, 1987); Wittlinger, *Quest for Piety,* 88–91, 145, 343–47, chap. 13; Omer King, "From Pennsylvania Dutch to English in the Brethren in Christ Church," BICHL 8 (Apr. 1985): 37–46; Wilma I. Musser, "Rhoda E. Lee," BICHL 2 (June 1979): 3–20; Schrag, "BIC Attitude," chaps. 8–10; 158–212; E. Morris Sider, *Messiah College: A History* (Nappanee, Ind.: Evangel Press, 1984), and *Nine Portraits: Brethren in Christ Biographical Sketches* (Nappanee, Ind.: Evangel Press, 1978), 16–45, 158–212; Ray M. Zercher, *To Have a Home: The Centennial History of Messiah Village* (Mechanicsburg, Penn.: Messiah Village, 1995), 3–4.

26. Myron S. Augsburger, "Perspectives on the Brethren in Christ Experience," BICHL 16 (Dec. 1993): 347; Boyer, *Mission on Taylor Street,* 79–82; Darrel Brubaker, "The Pastoral Call in the Brethren in Christ Church," BICHL 7 (Dec. 1984): 135–48; Robert T. Handy, *A History of the Churches in the United States and Canada* (Oxford, U.K.: Oxford Univ. Press, 1976), 294–99; James C. Juhnke, *Vision, Doctrine, War: Mennonite Identity and Organization in America, 1890–1930* (Scottdale, Penn.: Herald Press, 1989), 27–30, 163–77, 257–71, chap. 11; Keefer, "Three Streams," 37–40; Schrag, "BIC Attitude," 54, chap. 1; E. Morris Sider, "A Question of Identity: The Brethren in Christ in the Interwar Years," MQR 60 (Jan. 1986): 31–33; Wittlinger, *Quest for Piety,* 60, 258–62, chaps. 11, 14.

27. Sider, *Messiah College,* 189; Wittlinger, *Quest for Piety,* 299–312, 348, chaps. 18–19.

28. On changes among Mennonites, see Juhnke, *Vision, Doctrine, War,* chaps. 9–11; Paul Toews, *Mennonites in American Society, 1930–1970: Modernity and the Persistence of Religious Community* (Scottdale, Penn.: Herald Press, 1996), chaps. 1–10. On changes among Brethren, see Bowman, *Brethren Society,* chaps. 10–12.

29. In the River Brethren's first hundred years, only glimpses remain of nonresistant practice in periods of war. How established the new group was during the American

Revolution remains unclear. But it is clear that no River Brethren who appear in historical documents joined militias or openly supported the revolutionary movement. One of the earliest recorded migrations, soon after the community emerged, took families to Upper Canada, where they assumed the name "Tunker," perhaps a reference to their baptism ritual of immersion or "dipping" (the German *tunken* means "to dip"). In Upper Canada the first Brethren families did not claim loyalist status, a status that would have made free Crown land available to them. To gain that benefit, they would have had to join a local military body. So although the movement of some of the Brethren from Pennsylvania to Upper Canada appears to have been motivated primarily by the desire for land or the preservation of German culture, the war in their homeland must have influenced the nonresistant emigrants. A 1793 Militia Act in Upper Canada exempted the Tunkers, along with Mennonites and Quakers, from militia service. See MacMaster, *Land, Piety, Peoplehood*, 223–24, chap. 10; Sider, *BIC in Canada*, 5–7, 50–51, 219–20. For documentation of one individual connected to the early River Brethren, see Martin H. Schrag, "Henry Lesher, Jr., and the American Revolution," *BICHL* 18 (Dec. 1995): 382–95. During the U.S. Civil War, records of BIC men facing conscription show varied responses: exemption as conscientious objectors, payment of commutation fees, hiring of substitutes, noncombatant military service and enlistment. See "Brief History of Brethren in Christ (River Brethren)," 314; Wittlinger, *Quest for Piety*, 133–40. Schrag discusses historical evidence that exists for River Brethren communication with federal government officials during the Civil War. See his "BIC Attitude," 110–12, app. C.

30. Ray D. Bert, "Brethren in Christ 'Peacemakers' and World War I," Oct. 2, 1970, Academic Documents, IX-1–1.17, BICA; Climenhaga, *History of the BIC*, 304; John A. Fries Jr., "A History and Philosophy of Nonresistance in the Brethren in Christ Church" (M.Div. thesis, Western Evangelical Seminary, 1972); Homan, *American Mennonites and the Great War*, chaps. 5–6; Juhnke, *Vision, Doctrine, War*, chap. 8; Albert N. Keim and Grant M. Stoltzfus, *The Politics of Conscience: The Historic Peace Churches and America at War, 1917–1955* (Scottdale, Penn.: Herald Press, 1981), chaps. 1–2; Sider, *BIC in Canada*, 217, 224–30; Wittlinger, *Quest for Piety*, 366–74.

31. Wittlinger, *Quest for Piety*, 376–77; E. J. Swalm, *Nonresistance under Test: The Experiences of a Conscientious Objector, as Encountered in the Late World War* (Nappanee, Ind.: E. V. Publishing House, 1938), 5–6; Morris N. Sherk, questionnaire.

32. Mary Jane Heisey, "They Also Served: Brethren in Christ Women and Civilian Public Service," *BICHL* 18 (Aug. 1995): 228–71; Nancy R. Heisey, "Brethren in Christ Participation in Mennonite Central Committee: Integral Part or Burden?" *BICHL* 18 (Aug. 1995): 187, 195; Sider, *BIC in Canada*, 231–39; Wittlinger, *Quest for Piety*, 376–404.

33. Mark Charlton, "Trends in Political Participation among Brethren in Christ Ministers," *BICHL* 4 (Dec. 1981): 142–60; David L. Hall, "A Critical Analysis of the Hermeneutical Presuppositions in the Brethren in Christ Church on the Peace Position" (D.Min. diss., Eastern Baptist Theological Seminary, 1988), 10–11; Heisey, "BIC Participation," 201, 218–20; Kauffman and Harder, *Anabaptists Four*, chap. 9, esp. 169; Lucille Marr, "Peace Activities of the Canadian Conference of the Brethren in Christ Church, 1945–1982," *BICHL* 8 (Apr. 1985): 13–36; Martin H. Schrag and E. Morris Sider, "The Heritage of the Brethren in Christ Attitudes toward Involvement in Public Policy," *BICHL* 12 (Dec. 1989): 204–208; Toews, *Mennonites*, 242–43; Wittlinger, *Quest for Piety*, 391–93, 528–29.

34. Schrag and Sider, "Heritage of the BIC," 206–208; Wittlinger, *Quest for Piety*, 404–406, 476–95; David Zercher, "Opting for the Mainstream: The Brethren in Christ Join

the National Association of Evangelicals," BICHL 10 (Apr. 1987): 55–56, 58–61. Toews argues that BIC shifts in the 1950s, although they were more deliberate, were similar to those in the Mennonite Church; *Mennonites*, 226.

35. Owen Alderfer, "Anabaptism as a 'Burden' for the Brethren in Christ," in *Within the Perfection of Christ: Essays on Peace and the Nature of the Church*, ed. Terry L. Brensinger and E. Morris Sider (Nappanee, Ind.: Evangel Press, 1990), 250–64; Heisey, "BIC Participation," 201, 218–20; Kauffman and Harder, *Anabaptists Four*, 42–45, 330–32; Wittlinger, *Quest for Piety*, 495–98, 522–23, 544–49, app. C; Zercher, "Opting for the Mainstream," 51–53, 65–67.

36. "Articles of Faith and Doctrine of the Brethren in Christ—North America," sec. 5, *Manual of Doctrine and Government of the Brethren in Christ Church* (Nappanee, Ind.: Evangel Publishing House, 1998), 17–18; Harriet Sider Bicksler, "Pursuing Peace," in *Focusing Our Faith: Brethren in Christ Core Values*, ed. Terry L. Brensinger (Nappanee, Ind.: Evangel Publishing House, 2000), 129–41; Brensinger, *Focusing Our Faith*, 9–10; "Exploring the Brethren in Christ Identity," BICHL 19 (Apr. 1996); Sider, *Reflections on a Heritage*, 3, 7; Gwen White, "An Unlikely Journey," *Evangelical Visitor* [hereafter EV], Jan. 1991, 9–10; Zercher, "Is There a Mindset?" 174–78. Bicksler edits a BIC publication focused on peace and social concerns, *Shalom! A Journal for the Practice of Reconciliation*; Brensinger, *Focusing Our Faith*, 6.

37. Schrag uses the term "historylessness" in "BIC Attitude," 54; Sider, "A Question of Identity," 31–33. On the activism of "consent" or converted members, see Jan Shipps, "Making Saints: In the Early Days and the Latter Days" in *Contemporary Mormonism: Social Science Perspectives*, ed. Marie Cornwall, Tim B. Heaton, and Lawrence A. Young (Urbana: Univ. of Illinois Press, 1994), 64–83.

38. The BIC appear briefly in many works on Mennonites, including the synthetic histories *Mennonite Experience in America*, vols. 1–4, and *Mennonites in Canada*, vols. 1–3. A number sociological and anthropological studies of Mennonites and Mennonite-based organizations in the United States and Canada include the BIC as a constituent group. Kauffman and Harder, *Anabaptists Four*; J. Howard Kauffman and Leo Driedger, *The Mennonite Mosaic: Identity and Modernization* (Scottdale, Penn.: Herald Press, 1991).

39. The word *mosaic* has become a common signifier of this complexity. For a recent and lyrical reflection on this diversity, see Marlene Epp, " Purple Clematis and Yellow Pine: On Cemeteries, Irony and Difference," MQR 74 (2000): 183–89.

40. Leo Driedger, *Mennonites in the Global Village* (Toronto: Univ. of Toronto Press, 2000), 15–19; Juhnke, *Vision, Doctrine, War*, chap. 1; James C. Juhnke, *A People of Two Kingdoms: The Political Acculturation of the Mennonites* (Newton, Kans.: Faith and Life Press, 1975), 153–57, chaps. 3–4; Redekop, *Mennonite Society*, chap. 3; Schlabach, *Peace, Faith, Nation*, chaps. 8, 11.

41. Homan, *Mennonites and the Great War*, esp. chaps. 2, 5; Juhnke, *People of Two Kingdoms*, chap. 7, and Juhnke; *Vision, Doctrine, War*, chap. 8.

42. Ellis W. Hawley, *The Great War and the Search for a Modern Order* (New York: St. Martin's Press, 1979); Homan, *Mennonites and the Great War*, 169–75; Juhnke, *Vision, Doctrine, War*, 294–99; Keim and Stoltzfus, *Politics and Conscience*, 54–55, 61–65.

43. Perry Bush, *Two Kingdoms, Two Loyalties: Mennonite Pacifism in Modern America* (Baltimore: Johns Hopkins Univ. Press, 1998); Driedger and Kraybill, *Mennonite Peacemaking*; Keith Graber Miller, *Wise as Serpents, Innocent as Doves: American Mennonites Engage on Washington* (Knoxville: Univ. of Tennessee Press, 1996), 1–7, 33; Albert N.

Keim, *Harold S. Bender, 1897–1962* (Scottdale, Penn.: Herald Press, 1998), chaps. 6–17, esp. 317–18; Toews, *Mennonites*, chaps. 4–8, 10.

44. Keim, *Bender*, 525.

45. Cornelius J. Dyck, ed., *Witness and Service in North America*, vol. 3 of *The Mennonite Central Committee Story* (Scottdale, Penn.: Herald Press, 1980), 9.

46. E. Morris Sider, *Messenger of Grace: A Biography of C. N. Hostetter, Jr.* (Nappanee, Ind.: Evangel Press, 1982), 60, 128–29, chaps. 9–10; Wittlinger, *Quest for Piety*, 378, 499.

47. Hostetter's most important role in the NAE was his participation and leadership in the organization's World Relief Commission from 1953 to 1967. See Sider, *Messenger of Grace*, 217–18.

48. Perry Bush, "Anabaptism Born Again: Mennonites, New Evangelicals, and the Search for a Usable Past, 1950–1980," *Fides et Historia* 25 (Winter/Spring 1993): 27–28, 33–35; Zercher, "Opting for the Mainstream," 61–65.

49. Redekop, *Mennonite Society*, 286–91, also see 86–89. The impact of American revivalism—pietistic, holiness, neo-evangelical—as well as fundamentalist and premillenial thought on Mennonites is evident in historical and sociological studies. See Bush, *Two Kingdoms*, 158–60; Schlabach, *Mennonite Experience in America*, vols. 1–4; Kauffman and Driedger, *Mennonite Mosaic*, chap. 10; Kauffman and Harder, *Anabaptists Four*, part 2; Calvin W. Redekop, *Leaving Anabaptism: From Evangelical Mennonite Brethren to Fellowship of Evangelical Bible Churches* (Teleford, Penn.: Pandora Press, 1998); Theron F. Schlabach, *Gospel versus Gospel: Mission and the Mennonite Church, 1863–1944* (Scottdale, Penn.: Herald Press, 1980), chap. 4. Histories of evangelicalism sometimes include Anabaptists or Mennonites within their fold as well. See James Davison Hunter, *American Evangelicalism: Conservative Religion and the Quandary of Modernity* (New Brunswick, N.J.: Rutgers Univ. Press, 1983), 39; George Marsden, ed., *Evangelicalism and Modern America* (Grand Rapids, Mich.: William B. Eerdmans Publishing, 1984), viii, 13, 94. For a BIC counter to Redekop's explanation of evangelical impact in *Leaving Anabaptism*, see Luke Keefer, Jr., review of *Leaving Anabaptism*, by Redekop, BICHL 23 (Aug. 2000): 369–71.

50. Qtd. in Driedger and Kraybill, *Mennonite Peacemaking*, 76. On the centrality of daily practice and "mundane existence," see Juhnke, *Vision, Doctrine, War*, 32; Keim, *Bender*, 271, 275; Redekop, *Mennonite Society*, 326.

51. Driedger and Kraybill, *Mennonite Peacemaking*, 33. In the last thirty years of the twentieth century, disjunctures between institutional positions and rank-and-file members on peace issues also suggested lack of knowledge of the presence, let alone the nature, of peace practice in daily life. See Bush, *Two Kingdoms*, 259–68; Kenneth L. Eshleman, "Thirty Years of MCC-Washington Office: A Unique or Similar Way?" *MQR* 75 (2001): 293–313.

52. Elise Boulding, *Cultures of Peace: The Hidden Side of History* (Syracuse, N.Y.: Syracuse Univ. Press, 2000), 15.

53. On American social history, see the 1960s and 1970s overview by Peter N. Stearns, "The New Social History: An Overview," in *Ordinary People and Everyday Life: Perspectives on the New Social History*, ed. James B. Gardner and George Rollie Adams (Nashville, Tenn.: American Association for State and Local History, 1983), 4–10. Also see introductory discussions in Thomas R. Frazier, ed., *The Private Side of American History: Readings in Everyday Life* (San Diego, Calif.: Harcourt Brace Jovanovich, 1987);

Philippe Ariès and Georges Duby, eds., *A History of Private Life*, vols. 3–5, trans. Arthur Goldhammer (Cambridge: Harvard Univ. Press, 1989, 1990, 1991); Henri Lefebvre, *Everyday Life in the Modern World*, trans. Sacha Rabinovitch (New Brunswick, N.J.: Transaction, 1984). On theoretical moorings for attention to daily and ordinary activities, see cultural theorists Pierre Bourdieu, *Outline of a Theory of Practice* (Cambridge, U.K.: Cambridge Univ. Press, 1977); Michel de Certeau, *The Practice of Everyday Life* (Berkeley: Univ. of California Press, 1984).

54. Drew Gilpin Faust, *Mothers of Invention: Women of the Slaveholding South in the American Civil War* (Chapel Hill: Univ. of North Carolina Press, 1996), 53–54; Herbert G. Gutman, *Work, Culture, and Society in Industrializing America* (New York: Random House, 1966), 3–78; Eugene Genovese, *Roll, Jordan, Roll: The World the Slaves Made* (New York: Pantheon, 1972), xv.

55. DeBenedetti, *Peace Reform*, xi, 197–200.

56. Theodore Glenn Grimsrud, "An Ethical Analysis of Conscientious Objection to World War II" (Ph.D. diss., Graduate Theological Union, 1988), 176, 240–47.

57. Ibid., 200–201.

58. Ibid., 173, 203–204, 244–45.

59. Kraybill and Bowman, *Backroad to Heaven*, 15–16, 237, 243–57.

60. Donald B. Kraybill, introduction to *The Amish Struggle with Modernity*, ed. Donald B. Kraybill and Marc A. Olshan (Hanover, N.H.: Univ. Press of New England, 1994), 4. Also see Kraybill and Bowman, *Backroad to Heaven*, 4.

61. Redekop, *Mennonite Society*, chap. 10, esp. 157–58, 161–65; Kraybill and Bowman, *Back Road to Heaven*, 46–47. Redekop argues that as soon as the persecution of early Anabaptists eased, the family "became the basic element in the congregation and thus also the means for the preservation of Mennonite society." He describes Mennonite families as "conventional and Western" even as the church congregation provided "beliefs, norms, and values" for the family. He does describe the exceptions of Hutterite families subordinate to the communal society and the "quasi-extended" families of Old Order and Old Colony groups.

62. Elizabeth Jameson, "Rachel Bella Calof's Life as Collective History," in *Rachel Calof's Story*, ed. J. Sanford Rikoon (Bloomington: Indiana Univ. Press, 1995), 146–47.

63. Clarence E. Heise, "Signs of the Times," *EV*, May 15, 1916, 10–11.

64. Elise Boulding, *One Small Plot of Heaven: Reflections on Family Life by a Quaker Sociologist* (Wallingford, Penn.: Pendle Hill Publications, 1989), 7–8, 83–84, 94–95, 96, 114–16. On Boulding's extended attention to the family as a place for the construction of peace cultures, see *Cultures of Peace*, 5–7; Elise Hansen Boulding, interview, in Judith Porter Adams, *Peacework: Oral Histories of Women Peace Activists* (Boston: Twayne Publishers, 1991), 188–90; Elise Boulding, "Who Are These Women? A Progress Report on a Study of the 'Women Strike for Peace,'" in *Behavioral Science and Human Survival*, ed. Milton Schwebel (Palo Alto, Calif.: Science and Behavior Books), 196–99. On Mennonite families, see J. Howard Kauffman and Thomas J. Meyers, "Mennonite Families: Characteristics and Trends," *MQR* 75 (2001): 199–209; Lucille Marr, "Ontario's Conference of Historic Peace Church Families and the 'Joy of Service,'" *MQR* 75 (2001): 257–72; Redekop, *Mennonite Society*, 167–68. Drawing on a number of sociological studies on Mennonites and BIC, Kauffman and Meyers report coercion and violence in the home, albeit at lower levels in most cases than in the general public. Marc A. Olshan and Kimberley D. Schmidt suggest

that community nonviolent beliefs limit male aggression in Amish homes. They acknowledge, however, that no studies of domestic violence among the Amish have been done. See "Amish Women and the Feminist Conundrum," in *Amish Struggle*, ed. Kraybill and Olshan, 225, 227–28.

65. Barbara Ehrenreich, *Blood Rites: Origins and History of the Passions of War* (New York: Henry Holt, 1997), 125; see chap. 7's discussion of war and masculinity.

66. For contrasting overviews of the historical literature on American women's experiences and its significance, see "Introduction: Gender and the New Women's History," in *Women's America: Refocusing the Past*, 5th ed., ed. Linda K. Kerber and Jane Sherron De Hart (New York: Oxford Univ. Press, 2000), 3–24; Nancy A. Hewitt, "Beyond the Search of Sisterhood: American Women's History in the 1980s," in *Unequal Sisters: A Multicultural Reader in U.S. Women's History*, ed. Ellen Carol DuBois and Vicki L. Ruiz (New York: Routledge, 1990), 1–14. On contrasting evaluations of gender roles in Anabaptist settings, see Joel Hartman, "Power under the Cover of Tradition: A Case Study of a 'Plain Community,'" in *Power, Authority, and the Anabaptist Tradition*, ed. Benjamin W. Redekop and Calvin W. Redekop (Baltimore: Johns Hopkins Univ. Press, 2001), 115–35; Karen Johnson-Weiner, "The Role of Women in Old Order Amish, Beachy Amish and Fellowship Churches," *MQR* 75 (2001): 231–56; Kauffman and Meyers, "Mennonite Families," 202–205; Kraybill and Bowman, *Backroad to Heaven;* Dorothy Yoder Nyce and Lynda Nyce, "Power and Authority in Mennonite Ecclesiology," in *Power*, ed. Redekop and Redekop, 155–73; Redekop, *Mennonite Society*, 158; Olshan and Schmidt, "Amish Women," 216.

67. Rachel Waltner Goossen, *Women against the Good War: Conscientious Objection and Gender on the American Home Front, 1941–1947* (Chapel Hill: Univ. of North Carolina Press, 1997); Leila J. Rupp, review of *Women against the Good War*, by Rachel Waltner Goossen, *American Historical Review* 104 (1999): 586–97.

68. Wittlinger, *Quest for Piety*, 522–25. On the complicated interplay of gender and war, see Jean Bethke Elshtain, *Women and War* (New York: Basic Books, 1987), 3–10, part 2. On gender roles among pacifists in World War I, see Frances H. Early, *A World without War: How U.S. Feminists and Pacifists Resisted World War I* (Syracuse, N.Y.: Syracuse Univ. Press, 1997), chap. 4, esp. 102–108.

69. Calvin Redekop, "Power in the Anabaptist Community," in *Power*, ed. Redekop and Redekop, 189–92. Also see Redekop, *Mennonite Society*, 69–70.

70. Attention to settlement patterns focuses on immigrant populations, the Swiss and south German Mennonites in colonial America, and the Dutch/North German/ Russian Mennonites after the 1870s. See MacMaster, *Land, Piety, Peoplehood*, chaps. 3, 4; Schlabach, *Peace, Faith, Nation*, chap. 10; Juhnke, *People of Two Kingdoms*, chap. 2, and *Vision, Doctrine, War*, chap. 3. For mobility and some information on more general settlement patterns before World War I, see Juhnke, *Vision, Doctrine, War*, chap. 7.

71. Kraybill and Bowman, *Backroad to Heaven*, 33, 79 n. 27, 190–92. In one small study of twenty-one family heads in a newly established Old Order Mennonite settlement in Ontario, 76 percent indicated that they had "good" friendships outside the Mennonite faith.

72. See Kraybill and Bowman, *Backroad to Heaven*, ix–xi; Juhnke, *Vision, Doctrine, War*, 30; Schlabach, *Peace, Faith, Nation*, 32, 60.

73. Perry R. Duis, "No Time for Privacy: World War II and Chicago Families," in *The War in American Culture: Society and Consciousness during World War II*, ed. Lewis A. Erenberg and Susan E. Hirsch (Chicago: Univ. of Chicago Press, 1996); Terkel, *"The*

Good War," 1–14. Paul Fussell notes that even among conscripted men there was a camaraderie between those experiencing "chickenshit" in military camps and those encountering it in conscientious-objector camps. See his *Wartime: Understanding and Behavior in the Second World War* (New York: Oxford Univ. Press, 1989), 116.

74. John M. Blum, *V Was for Victory: Politics and American Culture during World War II* (New York: Harcourt Brace Jovanovich, 1976), chaps. 5–6; Herbert Gutman, "Historical Consciousness in Contemporary America," in *Power and Culture: Essays on the American Working Class,* ed. Ira Berlin (New York: Pantheon Books, 1987), 395–412; Jerre Mangione, *Mount Allegro: A Memoir of Italian American Life* (Syracuse, N.Y.: Syracuse Univ. Press, 1998), 11–12, 207–27; Jane Marie Pederson, *Between Memory and Reality: Family and Community in Rural Wisconsin, 1870–1970* (Madison: Univ. of Wisconsin Press, 1992).

75. BIC historian E. Morris Sider analyzes indiscriminate borrowing from such theological streams as evidence of identity confusion, growing from a lack of historical consciousness of Anabaptist roots and slipshod biblical interpretation. See his "Question of Identity," 31–37.

76. Paul Boyer, *When Time Shall Be No More: Prophecy Belief in Modern American Culture* (Cambridge: Harvard Univ. Press, 1992), ix–xii, chap. 3; Robert Wuthnow, *The Restructuring of American Religion: Society and Faith since World War II* (Princeton, N.J.: Princeton Univ. Press, 1988), chaps. 7–8. The quote is Martin E. Marty's, *The Noise of Conflict, 1919–1941* (Chicago: Univ. of Chicago Press, 1991), 346. On conservative Mennonite political leanings in the late twentieth century, see Kauffman and Driedger, *Mennonite Mosaic,* 56–57.

77. Paul S. Boyer, foreword to *America's Communal Utopias,* ed. Donald E. Pitzer (Chapel Hill: Univ. of North Carolina Press, 1997), ix–xiii; Wendy E. Chmielewski, Louis J. Kern, and Marilyn Klee-Hartzell, eds., *Women in Spiritual and Communitarian Societies in the United States* (Syracuse, N.Y.: Syracuse Univ. Press), 3; Redekop, *Mennonite Society,* xii, 48–55, 309–22.

78. On the appeal of being a "peculiar people," see Armand L. Mauss, quoting R. Laurence Moore in *The Angel and the Beehive: The Mormon Struggle with Assimilation* (Urbana: Univ. of Illinois Press, 1994), 60. Roger Finke and Rodney Stark's work is a statistical study of the attraction of what they label demanding "upstart sects" in America. The Southern Baptists are their model "upstart sect"; the demands include traditional doctrines, "vivid otherworldliness," stigma, and sacrifice. They are explicit on the definition of stigma, much less so on that of sacrifice. See their *The Churching of America, 1776–1990: Winners and Losers in Our Religious Economy* (New Brunswick, N.J.: Rutgers Univ. Press, 1992), 237–38, 250–55, 266, 274–75.

79. Choosing non-Anabaptist groups as a point of comparison allows for explanations different from those that combine apostasy and acculturation. In his study of the Church of the Brethren's shifts toward mainstream American culture, Carl Bowman concludes with a powerful quotation that illustrates classic Anabaptist analysis, an explanation that is also a jeremiad: "Only a dead fish floats with the current" (A Brethren elder speaking, in *Brethren Society,* 417). For example, writing on American communal experiments, Donald E. Pitzer suggests that analysis of such groups should focus on the dynamic process of development rather than on one period that supposedly expresses the essence of the group. Furthermore, judgments of success or failure should include the goals and perspectives of participants rather than simply the evaluations of outsiders. See his introduction to *America's Communal Utopias,* 3–6.

80. Handy, *History of the Churches in the United States,* 225–27; Mauss, *Angel and the Beehive,* ix–xiii, 14–15, chaps. 2–5, esp. 5–86. Dean L. May argues for the ongoing importance of communal values in Mormon culture in his "One Heart and Mind: Communal Life and Values among the Mormons," in *America's Communal Utopias,* ed. Pitzer, 135–55.

81. The draft resistance and antiwar activity of some Mennonites, of course, mirrored that of the larger society. Bush shows, however, that the Mennonite counterculture often claimed the authority of their Anabaptist heritage. See his *Two Kingdoms,* chap. 8, esp. 246–48.

82. Maren Lockwood Carden, *Oneida: Utopian Community to Modern Corporation* (Syracuse, N.Y.: Syracuse Univ. Press, 1998), xiii–xix, 22, 49, 71–77, 80–84. Marilyn Klee-Hartzell suggests that the rearrangement of domestic relationships may attract women. At the same time, she argues, rearranged domesticity may reinforce or even reinstitute a patriarchal setup. See her introduction to *Women in Spiritual and Communitarian Societies,* ed. Chmielewski, Kern, and Klee-Hartzel, 3–14.

83. Carden, *Oneida,* 84; Mauss, *Angel and the Beehive,* 62, 112.

84. DeBenedetti, *Peace Reform,* xi–xii, 2, 34–39, 62, 95, 331; Peter Brock, *Pacifism in the United States: From the Colonial Era to the First World War* (Princeton, N.J.: Princeton Univ. Press, 1968), 943–48, and *Freedom from Violence: A History of Sectarian Nonresistance from the Middle Ages to the Great War* (Toronto: Univ. of Toronto Press, 1991); Charles Chatfield, *The American Peace Movement: Ideals and Activism* (New York: Twayne Publishers, 1992), and *For Peace and Justice: Pacifism in America, 1914–1941* (Knoxville: Univ. of Tennessee Press, 1971), 6–7; Charles Chatfield and Peter van den Dungen, eds., *Peace Movements and Political Cultures* (Knoxville: Univ. of Tennessee Press, 1988), xvi; Lawrence Wittner, *Rebels against War: The American Peace Movement, 1941–1960* (New York: Columbia Univ. Press, 1969), 95–96; Schrag and Sider, "Heritage of the BIC," 204–208; Toews, *Mennonites,* 84–96; Kauffman and Harder, *Anabaptists Four,* 292.

85. Chatfield, *American Peace Movement,* ix–x; Charles Howlett, *The American Peace Movement: References and Resources* (Boston: G. K. Hall, 1991); Mitchell Lee Robinson, "Civilian Public Service and World War II" (Ph.D. diss., Cornell Univ., 1990), 4.

86. Harriet Alonso, *Peace as a Women's Issue: A History of the U.S. Movement for World Peace and Women's Rights* (Knoxville: Univ. of Tennessee Press, 1989), 261–65; Boulding, *Cultures of Peace;* Early, *World without War,* chap. 7; Amy Swerdlow, *Women Strike for Peace: Traditional Motherhood and Radical Politics in the 1960s* (Chicago: Univ. of Chicago Press, 1993), 234–37.

87. Chatfield, *American Peace Movement,* ix–x; Robinson, "Civilian Pubic Service and World War II," 4; Schrag and Sider, "Heritage of the BIC," 207.

88. T. D. Regehr, "Lost Sons: The Canadian Mennonite Soldiers of World War II," *MQR* 46 (1992): 461–80; Keith L. Sprunger and John D. Thiesen, "Mennonite Military Service in World War II: An Oral History Approach," *MQR* 46 (1992): 481–91.

89. Shirley Hershey Showalter, introduction to *Proclaim Peace: Christian Pacifism from Unexpected Corners,* ed. Theron F. Schlabach and Richard T. Hughes (Urbana: Univ. of Illinois Press, 1997), 5–9. Hughes in his preface makes similar points about pacifist tradition and narrative, xi–xii. Studies in *Proclaim Peace* of the loss of pacifism that point to loss of memory include the Church of God, Church of God in Christ, Assemblies of God, and Churches of Christ. On "History and Memory," see "AHR Forum," *American Historical Review* 102 (Dec. 1997): 1371–412. On the importance of this

historiographic trend to the BIC, see E. Morris Sider, "Community, Memory, and the Brethren in Christ," *BICHL* 18 (Dec. 1995): 396–407.

90. Thomas D. Hamm, *The Transformation of American Quakerism: Orthodox Friends, 1800–1907* (Bloomington: Indiana Univ. Press, 1988); Marsden, introduction to *Evangelicalism,* vii–xix.

CHAPTER 1: NONRESISTANCE IN WORLD WAR I

1. Editorial notes, *EV,* Aug. 10, 1914, 4; Sider, *Nine Portraits,* 215; Boyer, *When Time Shall Be No More,* ix–xi, 1, 100; Schlabach, *Peace, Faith, Nation,* 95–105. All quotations in this study will be recorded verbatim, unless a spelling or grammatical correction is necessary to make the meaning clear. Any corrections (aside from the first letter) will be placed in brackets. The authors of contributions in the *EV* are not always clear. George Detweiler was the editor during the period from 1914 to 1918. V. L. Stump became the new editor in January 1919. See *EV* mastheads.

2. C. N. Hostetter Jr., diary, C. N. Hostetter Jr. Papers [hereafter Hostetter Papers], Diaries, Hist. MSS 7–23.1, BICA; Sider, *Messenger of Grace,* 18.

3. Histories of the Brethren in Christ have drawn on war-related denominational legislation, writings by leaders in the *EV,* and retrospective accounts of the experiences of conscripted conscientious objectors. For this study additional archival sources, although limited, proved useful. The most important archival sources are the General Executive Board records, the papers of E. J. Swalm, C. N. Hostetter Sr., and C. N. Hostetter Jr., as well as a number of other diaries from the period, all in BICA. The *EV,* not yet systematized or controlled by church leaders in World War I, serves as an important source, because it provided a platform for many BIC women and men who chose to write letters, articles, or obituaries. Gerlof D. Homan's study of Mennonites during World War I describes BIC cooperation with Mennonites during the war. See his *Mennonites and the Great War,* 31, 33, 53.

4. Bert, "BIC Peacemakers"; Climenhaga, *History of the BIC,* 302–306; Sider, *BIC in Canada,* chap. 10, 224–25; Wittlinger, *Quest for Piety,* chap. 16; Swalm, *Nonresistance under Test,* 5–6; GC *Minutes,* 1917, arts. 25, 60; editorial notes, *EV,* June 4, 1917, 4. A military service bill came late in Canadian participation in the war, because conscription had provoked conflict between Quebec and the other provinces, threats to coalition governments, and reservoirs of sentiment against the war. See Robert Bothwell, Ian Drummond, and John English, *Canada, 1900–1945* (Toronto: Univ. of Toronto Press, 1987), chap. 7, 146–47; W. L. Morton, *The Kingdom of Canada* (Toronto: McClelland and Stewart, 1963), 420–28; David Kennedy, *Over Here: The First World War and American Society* (New York: Oxford Univ. Press, 1980), chap. 3, especially 163–66; Homan, *Mennonites and the Great War,* 45–55; DeBenedetti, *Peace Reform,* 99–103.

5. Homan, *Mennonites and the Great War,* 41, 48–49, chap. 5; Juhnke, *Vision, Doctrine, War,* chap. 8; Keim and Stoltzfus, *Politics of Conscience,* chap. 2; Kennedy, *Over Here,* 163–66; E. J. Swalm, *Nonresistance under Test: A Compilation of Experience of Conscientious Objectors as Encountered in Two World Wars* (Nappanee, Ind.: E. V. Publishing House, 1949), 27–28. See app. 2.

6. The literature on World War I continues to debate how to weigh the persistent idealism throughout and after World War I, and how the war is to be assessed as a psychic and economic watershed. On World War I as a key event in a long-term economic

transformation, see Hawley, *The Great War and the Search for a Modern Order*. Kennedy describes older ideals powering mobilization in *Over Here*, 88, 143, 224–30. For a study of the war as a psychic watershed, see Paul Fussell, *The Great War and Modern Memory* (New York: Oxford Univ. Press, 1975), ix, 66, chap. 9, esp. 315–25. For challenges to Fussell, see Mark Meigs, *Optimism at Armageddon: Voices of American Participants in the First World War* (New York: New York Univ. Press, 1997) and, with analysis of Canadian sources, Jonathan F. Vance, *Death So Noble: Memory, Meaning, and the First World War* (Vancouver, B.C.: Univ. of Vancouver Press, 1997).

7. Climenhaga, *History of the* BIC, 302–306; Wittlinger, *Quest for Piety*, 102–109, 401; Sider, *BIC in Canada*, 71–74.

8. GC *Minutes*, 1889, art. 7; editorial notes, *EV*, June 14, 1915, 3–4. Also see Wittlinger, *Quest for Piety*, 107, 220; *Minutes*, ON Joint Council [hereafter JC], Sept. 10, 1914, art. 9; C. N. Hostetter Jr., diary, Jan. 7, 1916, Hostetter Papers, 7–23.1.

9. GC *Minutes*, 1903, art. 29; 1904, art. 7; C. N. Hostetter Jr., diary, Feb. 4, 1919, Hostetter Papers, 7–23.1.

10. GC *Minutes*, 1913, art. 56. While the extent of such sentiments is unclear, *EV* statements on labor combined condemnations of unions with concern for the living and working conditions of workers. See C. C. Cook, "The Social Regeneration Fad," selected, *EV*, Mar. 9, 1914, 21–22; J. I. Long, "Violation of God's Law of a Weekly Rest Day," *EV*, Oct. 16, 1916, 14–15; A. Sims, "Labor Unions and Suffering Saints," *EV*, May 6, 1918, 12–13; B. M. Books, "Initiative and Obedience," *Orthos* (Grantham, Penn.: Alumni Association of the Messiah Bible School and Missionary Training Home, 1922), 16–17, BICA. In 1942, even as the church officially once again condemned labor union participation, a curriculum for church youth groups asked, "An investigation of what labor unions have done for the working class in an economic way may demand that we give them a great deal of credit. If your employment has been bettered by their existence, what defence have we for not supporting them?" See "Biblical Standards of Industrial Relations," Aug. 30, 1942, Board for Young People's Work [hereafter BYPW], VIII-2–2.1, BICA. This statement was in a curriculum for a youth program for Labor Day.

11. "The Way to World Peace," n.d., Eli M. Engle Papers [hereafter Engle Papers], Hist. MSS 3–1.1, folder 4, BICA. The typewritten manuscript is undated; the text describes the League of Nations as six years old.

12. During World War I, however, Elliot and Baker favored their countries of birth, England and Prussia, later Germany, respectively. Elliot published a poem attacking the kaiser in a local paper, and in the *Visitor* worried about friendship between "our Empire and your Republic" after Canada was drawn into the war and while the United States remained aloof. Baker, on the other hand, outspokenly defended Germany during the war. According to E. J. Swalm, only Baker's old age and neighborhood respect for him prevented repercussions for such disloyal sentiments during the war. See Sider, *Nine Portraits*, 90–92, 101, 112–13, n. 87, 271–73; Fred Elliot, "Here and There," *EV*, Feb. 22, 1915, 14.

13. Sider, *BIC in Canada*, 224, and *Nine Portraits*, 114.

14. Wittlinger, *Quest for Piety*, 27, n. 63; Sider, *Nine Portraits*, 312; Curtis O. Byer letter to author, July 3, 1996; Isaiah B. Harley, questionnaire.

15. Obituaries, *EV*, Oct. 16, 1916, 20; Mar. 5, 1917, 21; Feb. 11, 1918, 21. For the experiences of Mennonites in the Civil War, see Schlabach, *Peace, Faith, Nation*, chap. 7.

16. Kennedy, *Over Here*, 24–29, 45–84, 105–106, 143, 151; Homan, *Mennonites and the Great War*, 58; Bothwell, Drummond, and English, *Canada*, 155–68; Desmond Morton

and J. L. Granatstein, *Marching to Armageddon* (Toronto: Lester and Orpen Dennys, 1989), 23–26, 86.

17. Detweiler's editorials and selected articles from other magazines articulated the cardinal tenets of nonresistance in the *EV*, as did General Conference's 1917 statement on "nonresistant principles." See George Detweiler, "Where Civilization Fails," *EV*, Sept. 7, 1914, 2–4, and "If All Were Christians Who Would Fight?" *EV*, July 24, 1916, 2–5; Charles E. Orr, "Christianity Separates from the World," selected by S. H. Bert, *EV*, Mar. 22, 1915, 29–30; *GC Minutes*, 1917, art. 60.

18. Eli Engle, "The Principles of a Non-resistant," attached to letter of D. E. Engle to C. N. Hostetter Jr., Feb. 12, 1950, Engle Papers, 3–1.1.

19. The following provide a sampling of the many articles, all in the *EV*: "Near the End of the Chapter," from the *Mail and Breeze*, selected by S. H. Bert, May 18, 1914, 26; Norman E. Church, "Armageddon," Nov. 16, 1914, 12–13; L. F. Sheetz, "The Budding Fig Tree," July 30, 1917, 5–7; C. C. Burkholder, "Revelation 12:1–6," Feb. 11, 1918, 6–12. Even Detweiler discussed the possibility that the war might be the final battle. He concluded that it was not but that it might lead to Armageddon. In his eclectic approach, however, he ran an article by a Quaker who argued that peace must be practiced in the present to encourage "the advent of that millennium wherein carnal warfare will be a woe unknown." See Detweiler, "What May It All Mean," *EV*, Nov. 16, 1914, 2–5; Josiah Leeds, "'Not Peace But a Sword,'" from *The Christian*, *EV*, Oct. 8, 1917, 28–29. From the late nineteenth century through the interwar years, the Brethren in Christ drew on fundamentalist, dispensational, and premillenial ideas. As noted earlier, E. Morris Sider analyzes such borrowing as evidence of identity confusion. Mennonite historians also document the impact of fundamentalism on their communities. Toews argues that some Mennonites used it to slow cultural change. For example, both the Mennonite Church and the Brethren in Christ drew up detailed dress codes in the 1930s, shortly after fundamentalist coalitions challenged new orthodoxies. Marty's study of the modernist-fundamentalist conflict in the interwar years uses Mennonite battles in educational institutions as an example. Similarly, Boyer's study of belief in biblical prediction of the future, important in premillenial and dispensational thinking, demonstrates the malleable nature of the system and the changing groups drawing on it. World crises and political revolutions between 1914 and 1945 strengthened apocalyptic thinking, in both its literal and figurative forms, across the theological spectrum. See Wittlinger, *Quest for Piety*, 9–12, 155–58, 178, 227–57, 476–81; MacMaster, *Land, Piety, Peoplehood*, chaps. 5–6; Schlabach, *Peace, Faith, Nation*, 22, chap. 4; Juhnke, *Vision, Doctrine, War*, 257–73; Toews, *Mennonites*, chap. 3; Sider, "Question of Identity," 31–37; Paul A. Carter, "The Fundamentalist Defense of Faith," in *Change and Continuity in Twentieth-Century America: The 1920s*, ed. John Braeman, Robert H. Bremner, and David Brody (Columbus: Ohio State Univ. Press, 1968), 179–214; Marty, *The Noise of Conflict*, 212–13; Boyer, *When Time Shall Be No More*, ix–xii, chap. 3.

20. All in the *EV*: Detweiler, "The Close of the Year," Dec. 28, 1914, 3. Editorial notes, Sept. 20, 1915, 4–5; Mar. 25, 1918, 3–4; Apr. 8, 1918, 3–4; Dec. 2, 1918, 3–4. "War," selected by William S. Hinkle, Nov. 2, 1914, 29; Ira Kanode, "Testimony," Sept. 24, 1917, 29–30; A. C. Rosenberger, "The Law of Retribution," Feb. 8, 1915, 16, 31. In 1913, ten thousand miners struck against the Colorado Fuel and Iron Company in Ludlow, Colorado. Entire mining families joined the work of the strike and became targets of management attempts to break the strike with home evictions and eventually the state militia. When the militia fired into the tents of evicted families on Easter 1914, fourteen people died, eleven of

them children. See Joshua Freeman et al., *Who Built America?* (New York: Pantheon Books, 1992), 196–98.

21. A. C. Rosenberger, "War What For?" *EV*, Sept. 7, 1914, 11–13.

22. John Garman, "Put Up Thy Sword," *EV*, Dec. 13, 1915, 13. Also see "A Soldier in War," from *The Common People*, *EV*, Sept. 21, 1914, 32; George Detweiler, editorial notes, *EV*, June 14, 1915, 5–7, 23–24. Also see editorial notes, *EV*, Nov. 27, 1916, 1, 4.

23. One full article by Leida M. Wise did directly address pacifism. See her "Jesus Was No Slacker," *EV*, Mar. 11, 1918, 12, 29. Other women commenting briefly on the war connected it to an increase in sexual immorality or encouraged "the saints" to prepare themselves for unknown sufferings ahead. "Fiendish Devices of White Slavers: A Warning to All Women," from the *Gospel Messenger*, selected by Clara Cober, *EV*, Feb. 9, 1914, 25–26; Amanda Snyder, "A Letter," *EV*, Aug. 13, 1917, 30–31; Sarah McTaggart, "A Letter of Encouragement," *EV*, Sept. 24, 1917, 9.

24. Mary Allison, letter, *EV*, Apr. 30, 1917, 27–28.

25. Wittlinger, *Quest for Piety*, 46–50, 348–56; Sider, *BIC in Canada*, 77–82, 242–45.

26. A sample of many writings on dress by women all in the *EV* include: Edith Haldeman, "Redeeming the Time," May 17, 1915, 6–7; Ida Caufman, "Extravagance," May 17, 1915; R. J. Landis, "A Sister's Concern," Mar. 6, 1916, 31; Cora Albright, "Experience," Mar. 25, 1918, 28–29.

27. Rozella Boyer, "A Young Sister's Letter," *EV*, Sept. 18, 1916, 28–29; P. Boyer, *Mission on Taylor Street*, 32, 83, n. 21; Grace Herr Holland, questionnaire. Both her nephew Paul Boyer and her daughter Grace Herr Holland had heard Rozella Boyer Herr's account of her refusal to salute the flag. On a Mennonite community struggling with the issue of flag veneration during the war, see David L. Zercher, "Between Two Kingdoms: Virginia Mennonites and the American Flag," *MQR 70* (April 1996): 165–90.

28. Mrs. Girven Sider, "Experience," *EV*, Jan. 26, 1914, 18. Church statistics between 1937 and 1954 show that 57 percent of official members were women. A listing of missionaries between 1871 and 1978 show 56 percent of the personnel were women. See "Church and Sunday School Statistical and Financial Reports," *GC Minutes* [hereafter "Church Statistics"], inside back cover; *Brethren in Christ Missions, 1871–1978* (Elizabethtown, Penn.: Brethren in Christ Missions, 1978), 42–76. For a discussion of the impact of women's majority in most American churches, see Ann Braude, "Women's History *Is* American Religious History," in *Retelling U. S. Religious History*, ed. Thomas A. Tweed (Berkeley: Univ. of California Press, 1997), 87–107.

29. Qtd. in Driedger and Kraybill, *Mennonite Peacemaking*, 76.

30. "A Timely Warning to Our Young People," *EV*, Oct. 4, 1915, 12.

31. Heise, "Signs of the Times," *EV*, May 15, 1916, 10–11.

32. A. Sims, "They Fought from Heaven," *EV*, 17, Dec. 31, 1917, 13–15.

33. "Nevers—for Boys," selected, *EV*, Mar. 22, 1915, 30.

34. Sider, *Nine Portraits*, 271.

35. J. H. Myers, "A Visit to Philadelphia," *EV*, Nov. 2, 1914, 15.

36. *GC Minutes*, 1923, art. 12. The records of the General Executive Board, though restricted, would provide an important source for considering the nature of group conflict, General Conference, General Executive Board [hereafter GC, GEB], I-7–1.1, 1.2, BICA.

37. D. W. Heise, "Undue Officiousness," *EV*, Sept. 22, 1919, 12–13.

38. Editorial notes, *EV*, Nov. 27, 1916, 5; J. R. Zook, "Brotherly Love," *EV*, Feb. 19, 1917, 7–8.

39. "Special Personal Interview Sheets," Ernest J. Swalm and Alvin L. Winger on BIC ministers, Misc., Hist. MSS 5–1.6, BICA.

40. Solomon Solenberger, "Chambersburg, Penn.," EV, Dec. 14, 1914, 17–18; H. G. Brubaker, "Report of the Ninth Annual Bible Term," EV, Dec. 25, 1918, 25–26.

41. Lillian C. Baker, "For He Is Our Peace," EV, Jan. 13, 1919, 6.

42. Lydia Williams, "From a Canada Sister," EV, Sept. 18, 1916, 29–30.

43. Fred Kniss titled his sociological study of conflict in Mennonite communities between 1870 and 1965 *Disquiet in the Land,* a play on the characterization of Mennonites as *die Stillen im Lande.* In fact, Kniss argues, Mennonites' "actual historical experience has abounded in internal disquiet and contention over religious values and cultural practice." Their conflicts reflect internal tensions over the distribution of power and the goals of community life as well as the influence of the larger society on the small one. See his *Disquiet in the Land: Cultural Conflict in American Mennonite Communities* (New Brunswick, N.J.: Rutgers Univ. Press, 1997), 1–11, 193.

44. George Detweiler, "General Conference Notes," EV, June 1, 1914, 2–3.

45. Editorial notes, EV, May 6, 1918, 4–5.

46. Some of the differences in nonresistant statements might reflect pressures of war mobilization. See Fred Elliot, "A Conference Advisement," EV, Apr. 17, 1916, 3–4. Homan contends that after mid-1918, Mennonites muted their nonresistant statements and increased expressions of loyalty in public writings. At about the same time, war legislation posed legal threats to some Mennonite leaders who advocated conscientious objection. See *Mennonites and the Great War,* 60–61, 74–76. There appears to be no direct connection between Detweiler's strong advocacy of nonresistance and his removal as editor of the *Visitor* by a General Conference decision in June 1918. Minutes recording that decision point only to the "younger shoulders" of the new editor. Sider's biographical article on Detweiler ties his removal to the growing power of one definition of Wesleyan holiness in the Brethren in Christ; Detweiler had consistently represented a variety of views in the magazine. In fact, Detweiler allowed a variety of opinions on many topics, including nonresistance. Publicly, he accepted his removal graciously. In his last editorial, he expressed appreciation for the 1918 "Vote of Thanks." But he added that it had come despite a statement at an unreported "previous session" that "the testimony of the *Visitor* was *not in harmony* with what the church stood for." Detweiler concluded, "We make no effort to harmonize the two actions: we [can't]." The man who was editor of the EV during most of World War II, another a strong advocate of nonresistance, would also be removed from the position under unhappy circumstances, again for reasons apparently not directly connected to peace issues. See GC *Minutes,* 1918, art. 41; Sider, *Nine Portraits,* 233–37; Wittlinger, *Quest for Piety,* 268–69.

47. Editorial notes, EV, June 14, 1915, 4–5.

48. George Detweiler, "As to Carnal Warfare," EV, April 16, 1917, 2–7.

49. Frances B. Heisey, diary, 1918, Hist. MSS 25–1.1; Abram Z. Hess, diary, 1918–19, Hist. MSS 10–1.1; C. N. Hostetter Jr., diaries, 1914–18, Hostetter Papers, 7–23.1; Ethan Kreider, diary, 1918, Misc., Hist. MSS 5–1.6, "Ethan Kreider" folder, BICA.

50. W. H. Boyer and Susie Boyer, "Dayton Mission," EV, Aug. 23, 1915, 9–10; C. E. Heise, "My Visits in Different Districts," EV, Aug. 12, 1918, 24–25. All of the following from the EV note wartime shortages: editorial notes, Jan. 28, 1918, 32; Feb. 11, 1918, 3; Aug. 26, 1918, 4; Nov. 4, 1918, 4–5; Jan. 13, 1919, 3; "Bible School Dept.," Sept. 9, 1918, 5; Bertha Boulter, "A Virginia Letter," Feb. 11, 1918, 25–26. Also see Kreider, diary, Feb. 5, 1918, Misc.,

5–1.6. All of the following from the EV note military presence: Wilbur and Elizabeth Snider, "Philadelphia Mission," Apr. 30, 1917, 13; Elizabeth G. Myers, obituary, Aug. 26, 1918, 21. For missionary delays: editorial notes, EV, Apr. 8, 1918, 3; Nellie M. Dick, *My Story, My Song* [hereafter MSMS], ed. E. Morris Sider (Happanee, Ind.: Brethren in Christ World Missions, 1989), 114.

51. Obituaries in the EV went from two in the Oct. 21, 1918, issue to twelve in the next, Nov. 4, issue, which had reports of quarantines and deaths from across the country. In obituaries, influenza was a common cause of death up through April 1919. The C. N. Hostetter Jr., Ethan Kreider, and Frances B. Heisey diaries discuss much illness and death, as do retrospective accounts. On the influenza epidemic, see Alfred W. Crosby, *America's Forgotten Pandemic: The Influenza of 1918* (Cambridge, U.K.: Cambridge Univ. Press, 1989).

52. All of the following references in the EV provide a sample of the many articles employing military analogies or expressing admiration of military discipline: George Detweiler "War—Against Sin," Nov. 30, 1914, 2–3; editorial notes, Oct. 8, 1917, 3; J. R. Zook, "A Good Soldier for Jesus," Aug. 3, 1917, 9–10; Carl J. Carlson, "Chicago Mission," Oct. 8, 1917, 16–17; C. N. Hostetter and J. R. Zook, "An Urgent Appeal," Jan. 13, 1919, 8; I. O. Lehman, "An Earnest Reminder," Jan. 27, 1919, 4; Omar G. Worman, "Souderton, Penn.," Aug. 25, 1919, 10–11. Also see the GC discussion of the "Flying Squadron," a group proposed to do "aggressive mission work," *GC Minutes,* 1919, art. 23.

53. Although many Brethren in Christ and Mennonites descended from eighteenth-century German-speaking emigrants, they were associated during World War I with the larger nineteenth-century German-American community, which had established "an assertive ethnic counter culture." During the war, long-term tensions between that ethnic culture and mainstream America developed into open hostility against German Americans. See Frederick C. Luebke, *Bonds of Loyalty: German Americans and World War I* (DeKalb: Northern Illinois Univ. Press, 1974), x–xv, 39–40.

54. S. R. Smith, "General Conference, 1916," EV, Apr. 3, 1916, 1, 32; Elliot, "A Conference Advisement," 3–4.

55. "General Conference," EV, May 1, 1916, 2. The GC record states that the Nottawa district requested that GC not be held in Canada; See *GC Minutes,* 1916, art. 32.

56. George Detweiler, "As to the Non-Resistant Attitude," EV, Apr. 30, 1917, 2–4. Detweiler's article included extensive quotations from an article in the Mennonite *Gospel Herald* entitled "Our Attitude."

57. Avner Offer argues that the reasons for both Great Britain's impetus for entering the war and Germany's eventual defeat lay in access to agricultural rather than industrial resources. See his *The First World War: An Agrarian Interpretation* (Oxford, U.K.: Clarendon Press, 1989), 1–5.

58. The exact details of how those pledges would be contributed to the church, Enos Hess wrote, would be left to the Holy Spirit. See his "The War and Our Attitude," EV, June 18, 1917, 6–7. Minutes from the conference do not record such a pledge. In the next issue of the EV, Detweiler noted Hess's call to address the issue of war profits; he ran an article from *The Montreal Witness* that made similar points. See July 2–16, 1917, 7. In the same year, another article illustrated a more compromising sentiment, noting with satisfaction that the demands of war had increased respect for farmers. See Howard Mann, "The Nobility of Agriculture," EV, Oct. 8, 1917, 6–7.

59. Hoover to Kreider, June 29, 1918, GC, GEB, I-7–1.1, BICA.

60. GC *Minutes,* 1919, art. 9.

61. Editorial notes, *EV,* June 18, 1917, 4–5.

62. Boyer, *Mission on Taylor Street,* 83; Paul Boyer, Grace Herr Holland, questionnaires.

63. Elizabeth Engle Heise, interview; unsigned questionnaire; Kenneth Bert Hoover, audiotaped response to questionnaire.

64. "Bible School Department," *EV,* Mar. 25, 1918, 4–5. For retrospective accounts of refusal to buy war bonds, see Melinda Taylor, "Our War-time Experiences," *EV,* Oct. 9, 1939, 11; Millard Herr, questionnaire; Sider, *Nine Portraits,* 112, 330.

65. Grace Herr Holland, questionnaire.

66. "Letter from I. J. Ransom," *EV,* Nov. 5, 1917, 24–25. In another contact outside the Historic Peace Church grouping, J. R. Eyster preached in a Congregational Church while visiting his brother in Idaho. He enjoyed the church but wrote of withholding his vocal consent, the "Amen," though the pastor spoke "finely" on the duty of citizens to participate in war. See his "Camp-Meeting in Oregon," *EV,* Aug. 13, 1917, 25–26.

67. Editorial notes, *EV,* Aug. 7, 1916, 6; "A Day of Prayer," *EV,* Sept. 4, 1916, 1; *EV,* Nov. 5, 1917, 30–31; Meshack P. Krikorian and S. C. Krikorian, "Watchman! What of the Night in Armenia?" *EV,* Jan. 28, 1918, 11–13; Mary A. Stoner, "Where Are They Now?" *Orthos,* 1922, 34, BICA.

68. Editorial notes, *EV,* Oct. 7, 1918, 4.

69. T. A. Long and Mary J. Long, "A Texas Letter," *EV,* Aug. 13, 1917, 28–30. Even before the United States entered the war, Detweiler had called for the BIC community to look for ways to give relief aid. See his "War's Doing," *EV,* May 3, 1915, 2–3, and "As to the Non-Resistant Attitude," 2–4.

70. "An Organized Effort For the Relief of Sufferers," July 15, 1918, Engle Papers, 3–1.1, folder 7; "An Organized Effort For the Relief of Sufferers in the War Stricken Countries," July 15, 1918, Public Domain, Misc., VIII-10–1.2, folder 4, BICA. Some months later, the GEB advertised the availability of the pamphlet and a receipt book to document contributions. See his editorial notes, *EV,* Oct. 7, 1918, 4.

71. Editorial notes, *EV,* Sept. 23, 1918, 4–5; "Work in France," *EV,* Feb. 24, 1919, 5; "American Friends Service Committee," *EV,* Dec. 1, 1919, 13. On American Friends Service Committee (AFSC) relief work and Mennonite participation in those efforts, see Homan, *Mennonites and the Great War,* 141, 169–76; Keim and Stoltzfus, *Politics of Conscience,* 29–31, 61.

72. Mary Zook, "A Worthy Appeal," *EV,* Sept. 23, 1918, 17. Her emphasis on the importance of photographs is significant, because in these years the community debated the acceptability of photographs. See Wittlinger, *Quest for Piety,* 344–45.

73. Mary Zook, "From Sr. Mary Zook," *EV,* Dec. 2, 1918, 16.

74. H. K. Kreider, "A Letter of Instructions to the Various Sewing Circles of the Brotherhood, as Well as to Individuals, Who Are Interested in War Relief Work," *EV,* Feb. 24, 1919, 5–6.

75. Editorial notes, *EV,* June 18, 1917, 5.

76. Seth Adams, "Testimony," *EV,* Oct. 7, 1918, 17.

77. In the earliest church statistics in 1933, the total official membership of four Michigan congregations was 108 people, with Sunday school enrollment 243. See "Church Statistics" inside back cover, GC *Minutes,* 1934; Wittlinger, *Quest for Piety,* 132, 167–69.

78. Determining which BIC men had been drafted, their relationship to the BIC community, and the positions they took in response to conscription is a difficult historical

task. Appendix 2 summarizes information available on individuals based on contemporary and retrospective sources. Sources for this composite portrait of conscripted men include the *Visitor;* the Peace, Relief, and Service Committee records; Carlton O. Wittlinger's papers [hereafter Wittlinger Papers]; Ray Bert's unpublished paper; and my own questionnaires and interviews. This documentation of conscientious objectors in military camps enlarges and buttresses the work already written by BIC and Mennonite historians. See Bert, "BIC Peacemakers"; Wittlinger, *Quest for Piety,* 366–76; Sider, *BIC in Canada,* 224–30; Juhnke, *Vision, Doctrine, War,* chap. 8; Homan, *Mennonites and the Great War,* chaps. 5–6.

79. Harry L. Brubaker, "Why I Could Not Fight," *EV,* Mar. 10, 1919, 5–6.

80. Homan lists three divisions: refusal to wear a military uniform, refusal to perform service in the military, and refusal to drill. See his *Mennonites and the Great War,* 104. In the 1920s and 1930s, H. S. Bender pushed the Mennonite Church to establish a clear and definitive conscientious-objection position. In World War I, he saw the noncombatant position as acceptable but later rejected that stance. See Keim, *Bender,* 276.

81. Probably most of those who chose active combatant service had not experienced the religious conversion that preceded the official joining of the BIC church. Also, young men needed official membership in one of the Historic Peace Churches in order to be recognized as conscientious objects by the U. S. selective service. See Homan, *Mennonites and the Great War,* 49–50; Kreider to Burkholder, July 6, 1917, GC, GEB, I-7–1.1, BICA. Examples, however, abound of people from the BIC community serving in the military. In his memoirs, H. H. Brubaker explained that when he registered in September 1918, he had had no religious conversion experience so would have accepted combatant duties, despite the fact that he had been reared in the BIC community and had been counseled on the issue by Mary Senseman, a beloved Sunday school teacher. See Brubaker, audiotape, BICA. Clyde Fisher Elliot, a BIC member for six years, died in action in France in September 1916. The author of his obituary described his enlistment as an expression of his being "[led] astray thru deceitfulness of the enemy." See his obituary, *EV,* Jan. 8, 1917, 20. Samuel Lenhert wrote from France that perhaps he would not be there if he had appreciated more the fellowship with the "Brethren in Philadelphia." See "A Testimony from France," *EV,* Apr. 7, 1919, 7. Looking back, BIC member Paul Engle remembered enlisting in the Student Army Training Corp because he "was illiterate" in nonresistance during World War I. Engle remembered that other members of his BIC congregation in California openly displayed service stars in their windows. See Engle to Wittlinger, Jan. 5, 1974, Engle handwritten notes on Wittlinger to Engle, June 25, 1974, Wittlinger Papers, "Quest for Piety and Obedience 1" folder [hereafter Quest 1], Hist. MSS 35–1.22, "Peace, 1910–50" folder, BICA. Despite the existence of nonresistant voices throughout the church, Engle's "illiteracy" issued from a decentralized, scattered, and often divided group. J. B. Leaman, one of the church's traveling ministers, came from Engle's congregation. In two *Visitor* articles, he described visits he made with his wife to their two sons in military camps in the South. Although many of his comments appear cryptic, tying together prophecy and perhaps community conflict over nonresistance, the emotions expressed suggest a man deeply touched by the possible future sacrifice of his sons but also by military pageantry and Civil War history. "Home Again," *EV,* Feb. 11, 1918, 21–25, and Heise, "The Signs of the Times," 6–10; GC *Minutes,* 1918, official directory. Such military connections were not confined to this California congregation. Detweiler's description of 1918 harvest praise services in Pennsylvania men-

tioned that many prayed for "sons called from the circle" in camps or already at the front. See editorial notes, *EV,* Aug. 26, 1918, 3–4. Cora Saylor Sider's brother Gordon was wounded in action. She related stories about him to her children, showing them a piece of his trench hardtack, which she carefully preserved. See Harold K. Sider, "Willing to Serve: The Story of Christian and Cora Sider," *BICHL* 15(Aug. 1992): 258. Chester Ray Heisey's older brother served with the U.S. Army in France. See Thelma Heisey Book, "In Pursuit of Great Spoil: A Biography of C. R. Heisey," *BICHL* 20 (Aug. 1997): 20, 22, 45, 49–52, 53. Jesse S. Oldham, a BIC bishop, also had an older brother who served in the army during World War I. See A. Ruth Lehman, "Earthen Vessels: Jesse S. Oldham and the Springhope Congregation," *BICHL* 15 (Aug. 1992): 198. Paul Boyer's mother kept her brother's helmet and uniform in her attic. See Paul Boyer, questionnaire.

82. Samuel Andrew Zook, Obituary, *EV,* May 19, 1919, 11. Overseas service, however, does not necessarily mean the absence of a conscientious-objector position, because noncombatant work, such as that of Henry L. Landis's in the quartermaster, sometimes took conscientious objectors overseas. Isaiah B. Harley, questionnaire, and interview by author. Another group of BIC men, also listed in appendix 2, received ministerial or agricultural deferments and in fact had been encouraged by government officials to request those exemptions before declaring religious objection to war. See Homan, *Mennonites and the Great War,* 51; C. N. Hostetter Sr., "Conscription Information," *EV,* Sept. 10, 1917, 6–7.

83. Bert, "BIC Peacemakers," part 2.

84. Byer to Harley, Jan. 24, 1956, GC, Peace, Relief and Service Reports [hereafter PRS], I–21–1.4, "Testimonials, 1956" folder; Engle to Wittlinger (see nn. 101, 103); Byer, handwritten notes on Wittlinger to Byer, June 25, 1974; Heise, handwritten notes on Wittlinger to Heise, July 29, 1974, Wittlinger Papers, Quest 1, 35–1.22, "Peace, 1910–50" folder.

85. Curtis O. Byer to author, July 3, 1996.

86. See app. 2.

87. Heise to Kreider [penciled in], Aug. 13–17, GC, GEB, I–7–1.1, BICA; Sider, *BIC in Canada,* 31–32.

88. Burkholder to O[b]erholser, June 21, 1917; Kreider to Burkholder, July 6, 1917; Kreider to Engle, July 6, 1917; Burkholder to Kreider, July 10, 1917; Stump to Kreider, July 19, 1917, GC, GEB, I–7–1.1, BICA. GC authorized the certificates and instructed the Publication Board to print them at once. Burkholder was not on that board. See *GC Minutes,* art. 1.

89. "Special Notice," in minute book after minutes, Nov. 11, 1917; *Minutes,* Dec. 28, 1917, GC, GEB, I–7–1.2, BICA.

90. "From the Boys at Camp Meade," parts 1, 2, 3, "Newsletter" of the Mennonite Historians of Eastern Pennsylvania, March, May, July, 1990, photocopy in possession of the author. The unnamed author of the account, detailed enough to be a diary, was probably a conscientious objector from the Franconia Conference of the Mennonite Church in eastern Pennsylvania. On October 6, 1917, he recorded a group of visitors from Lancaster County, Pennsylvania, in camp, including Michael Musser. A Michael B. Musser served as a BIC deacon from Mount Joy, the hometown of Harry L. Brubaker in Camp Meade. See *GC Minutes,* 1917, official directory. The same Mennonite account records a BIC minister visiting on November 24, 1917, and two River Brethren—perhaps BIC, since the older designation was still sometimes used during World War I—visitors from Lancaster County in February 1918. See Hostetter, diary, Sept. 28, 1918, Hostetter Papers, 7–23.1; Harry L. Brubaker, interview by Allan Teichroew.

91. Bert, "BIC Peacemakers," part 3. In his diary, C. N. Hostetter Jr. recorded his father's trip to Washington, D.C., with a delegation that worked on behalf of conscientious objectors. C. N. Hostetter Sr. also visited Leonard Engle in Camp Upton, Long Island, New York. Engle, however, may have been in combatant military service; Hostetter records that British and French officers in the camp trained men in trench warfare, including the use of bayonets and hand grenades. See Hostetter diary, Aug. 24, Sept. 28, 1917, Jan. 18, 1918, Hostetter Papers, 7–23.1.

92. *Minutes*, Penn. State Council [hereafter SC], Apr. 4, 1918, arts. 1, 3–7; Homan, *Mennonites and the Great War*, 129. Detweiler had earlier run an article, without attribution, arguing that nonresistant people could not conscientiously perform any noncombatant service. See "Non-Combatant Service," *EV*, Dec. 3, 1917, 23.

93. Homan, *Mennonites and the Great War*, 60.

94. Hostetter to Kreider, June 21, 1918, GC, GEB, I-7–1.1, BICA. Although the letter does not explicitly state that the certificates were for conscripted conscientious objectors, the wording seems to imply that they were. See Baum to Kreider, Feb. 3, 1918, GC, GEB, I-7–1.1, BICA. Mennonites also complained during the war and retrospectively about lack of teaching on nonresistance. See Homan, *Mennonites and the Great War*, 42–43.

95. Harry F. Fishburn, in Camp Lee, Virginia, wrote to H. K. Kreider and Kreider's children Ethan, Mary, and Grace thanking them for letters and religious tracts; Fishburn to Kreider, Nov. 19, 1918, Misc., 5–1.6, "Ethan Kreider" folder, BICA. Clarence Byer, although remembering little home-church support, did write that the church had held an all-day prayer meeting for him and for "another boy who had to go to the war." See Byer to Wittlinger, June 25, 1974, Wittlinger Papers, Quest 1, 35–1.22, "Peace 1910–50" folder. Family members also made visits to military camps. Theda Brubaker, who had married Harry L. Brubaker two days before he reported to the military, remembered traveling with "old Brother Engle" and C. N. Hostetter Sr. to Camp Meade. She had brought along a cake and other baked goods, but the group was refused entry because of a quarantine. She cried the entire trip home, perhaps knowing that food for the conscientious objectors was sometimes limited, as Harry confirmed years later. See Harry and Theda Brubaker, interview by author, April 21, 1977, in "History of Cross Roads Brethren in Christ Church, 1877–1977," prepared for the hundredth-anniversary celebration.

96. Harry L. Brubaker was eventually furloughed from Camp Meade to work on a farm near Maugansville, Maryland. Anticipating the furlough, Brubaker requested H. K. Kreider's help in finding a farm, "one among our faith[,] if you can[,] if not any place where they belong to plain people." Brubaker found himself at the farm of Phares Martin, a Mennonite. He admired both the man and the group. He attended a harvest service, probably with Mennonites and probably a service similar to those of the Brethren in Christ. But his comment was that no BIC churches were nearby. He wished he could come home for services, "for I Long to see the brethren and sisters." See Brubaker to Kreider, July 4, July 21, 1918, GC, GEB, I-7–1.1, BICA. Benjamin Herr, also in Camp Meade, described a sermon that made him think of home. See Herr to Kreider, July 4, Dec. 27, 1918; GC, GEB, I-7–1.1, BICA.

97. Fishburn to Kreider, Nov. 19, 1918, Misc., 5–1.6, "Ethan Kreider" folder, BICA.

98. Ernest J. Swalm, *"My Beloved Brethren": Personal Memoirs and Recollections of the Canadian Brethren in Christ Church* (Nappanee, Ind.: Evangel Press, 1969), 23–24; Earl M. Sider, "My Experiences as a C.O. in World War I, 1918," GC, PRS, I-21–1.4, "Testimonials, 1956" folder, BICA. On treatment of conscientious objectors in Canada, see

Desmond Morton, *When Your Number's Up: The Canadian Soldier in the First World War* (Toronto: Random House of Canada, 1993), 64–70.

99. Heise to Wittlinger, July 29, 1974, Wittlinger Papers, Quest 1, 35–1.22, "Peace, 1910–50" folder.

100. Samuel Wenger, "From One of Our Boys," *EV*, Apr. 7, 1919, 7.

101. Bert, "BIC Peacemakers," 17.

102. Ibid., 12–14; John Henry Heise, "First World War Experiences of John Henry Heise," photocopy in possession of author; Wright to Wittlinger, Jan. 22, 1976, Wittlinger Papers, Quest 1, 35–1.22, "Peace, 1910–50" folder.

103. Harvey and Naomi Lady, "A Letter," *EV*, Mar. 25, 1918, 27.

104. Harry L. Brubaker, interview by Allan Teichroew.

105. Lady, "A Letter," 27. Also see Harry L. Brubaker and Benjamin Herr, "A Word from Camp," *EV*, Feb. 25, 1918, 24–25.

106. Ulery quoted by Sider, *Nine Portraits*, 330.

107. Taylor, "Our War-time Experiences," 11.

108. Editorial notes, *EV*, Sept. 21, 1914, 4; Nov. 27, 1916, 3. D. V. Heise, "Preparedness," *EV*, Apr. 17, 1916, 14–15; Detweiler, "As to the Non-Resistant Attitude," 2–4.

109. Sider, *BIC in Canada*, 229–30; Wittlinger, *Quest for Piety*, 376; Ethan Kreider recorded in his diary, "Papa [H. K. Kreider] was at Mt. Joy to decide about having C. B. Eavey take up work with the American Friends Relief in France." See Sept. 19, 1918, Misc, 5–1.6, "Ethan Kreider" folder, BICA.

110. V. L. Stump, "Work in France," *EV*, Feb. 24, 1919, 5.

111. See note 89.

112. All in *EV*: C. Benton Eavey, "On the Way to France," Dec. 30, 1918, 14, and "From France," May 5, 1919, 15, and "Relief Work: From France," July 14, 1919, 10–11.

113. Charles Benton Eavey, questionnaire, Mennonite Central Committee Collection, Report Files [hereafter MCC Report Files], IX-12–1, "Mennonite Relief in World War I, Questionnaires—Answered, E–G" folder, AMC.

114. C. Benton Eavey, "Some Impressions on French Social Life," *Orthos*, July 1920, 29–30, Messiah College [hereafter MC], Student Affairs, Misc., XI-6–14.1, BICA.

115. Eavey, "Relief Work: From France," 10–11; Charles Benton Eavey, questionnaire, MCC Collection, Report Files, IX-12–1, "Mennonite Relief in World War I, Questionnaires—Answered, E–G" folder. On Wheaton College and the evangelical world, see George Marsden, introduction and "Evangelicals, Modernity, and History," in *Evangelicalism*, xv, 94–95.

116. Heisey, "They Also Served," 250.

117. Swalm, *Nonresistance under Test*, 41. Swalm also remembered Ohio bishop B. F. Hoover's "strong peace emphasis" when Hoover spoke at a love feast during World War I. See D. Ray Heisey, "The Force of Narrative: Portrait of Bishop B. F. Hoover," *BICHL* 11 (Dec. 1998): 271.

118. E. J. Swalm, videotaped interview by Pauline Cornell.

119. Swalm, *Nonresistance under Test*, 5–6.

120. E. J. Swalm referred to the story in an interview when he was ninety. See video-taped interview by Pauline Cornell. Both Wittlinger and Sider drew extensively on Swalm's memory, which reputedly was one of the best in the community. See Taylor, "War-time Experiences," 11–12.

121. Taylor, "War-time Experiences," 11–12. Swalm's account was the only retrospective

source used in this study noting without prompting the World War I experiences of Melinda and Walter Taylor. See videotaped interview by Pauline Cornell.

122. Taylor, "War-time Experiences," 11–12.

123. Ibid.

124. Swalm, interview; Taylor, "War-time Experiences," 11–12.

125. "In Camp!" *Clarion,* Jan. 1943, 10.

Chapter 2: Nonresistant Thought and Practice in the 1940s and 1950s

1. The quotation comes from *Minutes,* on JC, Sept. 3, 1949, art. 1.

2. Michael C. C. Adams, *The Best War Ever: America and World War II* (Baltimore: Johns Hopkins Univ. Press, 1994), 43–68; Bothwell, Drummond, and English, *Canada,* 315–16, 323–35; Morton, *Kingdom of Canada,* 475–77; Mulford Q. Sibley and Philip E. Jacob, *Conscription of Conscience: The American State and the Conscientious Objector, 1940–1947* (Ithaca, N.Y.: Cornell Univ. Press, 1952), chap. 3, part 3, app.

3. Harold K. Davis, Duane Engle, Joseph H. Ginder, Isaiah B. Harley, Rowena Winger Heise, Beulah Heisey, Judson Hill, Howard L. Landis, Benjamin W. Myers, Morris N. Sherk, Harvey Sider, Esther G. Book Ulery, and Gerald N. Wingert, questionnaires, and unsigned questionnaire; Gerald N. Wingert to author, June 17, 1996; Lester Fretz, Mary Olive Lady, E. Morris Sider, interviews by author; Lois Tidgewell, "Blooming Where Planted: The Brethren in Christ Experience," BICHL 16 (Dec. 1993): 318, 323; Lehman, "Earthen Vessels," 224.

4. Esther Tyson Boyer, questionnaire.

5. Harold Heise, questionnaire, and interview by author.

6. Daniel L. Hoover, Eugene H. Feather, Gordon H. Schneider, Paul Wingerd, questionnaires.

7. Paul S. Boyer, questionnaire; Sider, "Reflections on a Heritage," 326, 328. E. Morris Sider to author, July 2, 1998.

8. V. L. Stump, editorial, EV, Mar. 11, 1940, 3. In 1943, a general concern about inadequate teaching of church beliefs led General Conference to establish an Indoctrination Committee. This committee sent a survey to leaders across the BIC church to measure the state of church teachings. See Wittlinger, *Quest for Piety,* 428–32. The frank responses constitute important evidence of a perceived failure of "indoctrination." Doctrines, many argued, were taught only at love feast; emotional religious experience was emphasized, with no thought for instruction; teaching was timid; and teachings did not respond to the philosophical thinking of youth. See typed responses to questionnaire [hereafter Typed responses], Henry N. Hostetter Papers, Correspondence, Hist. MSS 13–2.1, "Indoctrination" folder, BICA. E. J. Swalm noted "under-indoctrination" as an error of all the Historic Peace Churches, which explained the high percentage of young men going into military service; "Indoctrination," EV, Mar. 26, 1945, 3.

9. "Brethren in Christ CPS Thinks," *Sunday School Herald* [hereafter SSH], Jan. 14, 1945, 4.

10. *Minutes,* Wainfleet District Council [hereafter DC], Dec. 4, 1945, art. 2.

11. *Minutes,* PRS committee, Jan. 3–4, 1947, GC, PRS, I-21–1.1, BICA; *Minutes,* Inter-College Peace Conference, Dec. 30, 1948, MCC Report Files, 2, "Inter-Collegiate Peace Fellowship" [hereafter ICPF] folder, AMC; *Beulah College Bulletin* [hereafter BC *Bulle-*

tin], Mar. 1949, 3; *Minutes,* Donegal DC, Feb. 1–2, 1950, art. 37; "Roxbury Peace Conference," *EV,* Aug. 21, 1950, 16; E. J. Swalm, "Annual Session of Conference of Historic Peace Churches," *EV,* Jan. 21, 1952, 16; "Peace Booklets," *SSH,* May 11, 1952, 5; "Peace Conference Held at Cross Roads Church, Donegal District," *EV,* Aug. 8, 1952, 10; "Program of the Brethren in Christ Church Peace Conference," July 3–5, 1953 and "Peace Conference: Roxbury Camp Grounds," July 1–3, 1955, Hostetter Papers, Lectures, Hist., MSS 7–17.5, "Non-Resistance" folder; *Minutes,* ON JC, Sept. 4–6, 1954, art. 5.

12. Terkel, *"The Good War,"* 1.

13. During the first half of the twentieth century, one Mennonite publishing house provided Sunday school material for the Brethren in Christ. By 1940, both Canadian and American leaders were meeting with Mennonite leaders to discuss peace issues. See Wittlinger, *Quest for Piety,* 209–10, 378–79. On formulations of Mennonite nonresistance in the first half of the twentieth century, see Bush, *Two Kingdoms,* 32–35; Driedger and Kraybill, *Mennonite Peacemaking,* 30–36; Juhnke, *Vision, Doctrine, War,* 215–16; Toews, *Mennonites,* 123–28.

14. *Constitution and By-Laws of the Brethren in Christ Church,* 1924, 92–94; *Constitution, Doctrine, By-Laws and Rituals,* 1939, art. 6; *Manual of Doctrine and Government* (Nappanee, Ind.: Evangel Press, 1961), art. 18.

15. Sider, "Question of Identity," 31–37; Bush, *Two Kingdoms,* 39–44.

16. *Manual,* 1961, art. 18.

17. "Memorial and Redeclaration of Non-Resistance," GC *Minutes,* 1939, art. 10, 1940, 139–44; "Nonresistance," Oct. 30, 1938, "The Christian at Peace," Nov. 5, 1939, "The Christian and Hist Government," July 2, 1944, Public Domain, Church Agencies, BYPW, VIII-2–2.1, BICA.

18. Arthur L. Musser, "Militarism, Pacifism, and Nonresistance," *Clarion,* Apr. 1943, 13; Myron Mann, "The Way of Love," *SSH,* July 6, 1952, 4, 6.

19. O. B. Ulery, *Can a Christian Fight?* (Nappanee, Ind.: EVPH, n.d.); and "The Bible Teaching on Non-Resistance," *Minutes,* OH-KY JC, Mar. 16, 1940, 48–49; and "The Doctrine of Non-Resistance," a sermon reported on by Beulah Lyons, *SSH,* Oct. 4, 1942, 7; and "Separation, Non-Conformity, and Nonresistance Are Closely Associated," *EV,* 12 April 1943, 3; *Minutes,* OH-KY JC, 9–Mar. 11, 1944, art. 4.

20. C. N. Hostetter Jr. "Spiritual Significance of Civilian Public Service," *EV,* Mar. 16, 1942, 14; and General Conference sermon, GC *Minutes,* 1943, 4; and "What to Pray For," sermon reported on in "Celebrating V-E Day," *Clarion,* May 25, 1945, 1; and "Non-Resistance: Is It Biblical?" sermon reported on in "Conference Echoes," *EV,* Aug. 26, 1946, 2; and "The Church and War," *EV,* June 12, 1950, 5–6; and "The Curse of War," *SSH,* Mar. 11, 1951, 4; and "Heralds of Love: A Christmas Message to I-W Men," *The I-W Mirror,* Dec. 16, 1953, 1, MCC Collection, Periodicals Assorted Titles, IX-40–2; and *The Christian and War* (n.p., n.d.), and *Rethinking Our Peace Position* (n.p., n.d.), Public Domain, Misc., VIII-10–1.2, BICA; and *War and the Word: A Study of the Problem of the Christian Conscience and War* (Nappanee, Ind.: E. V. Publishing House, n.d.), GC, PRS, Reports, I-21–1.4, BICA; and "The Application of Non-Resistance" handwritten sermon notes, Hostetter Papers, Lectures, 7–17.5, "Lectures, Nonresistance," folder; Nonresistance course outline, Hostetter Papers, MCC, Misc., Hist. MSS 7–4.2, BICA. Hostetter's language, probably not consciously, reflects some of the components of nonviolent formulations. See Peter Brock, *Twentieth-Century Pacifism* (New York: Van Nostrand Reinhold, 1970), 72–101.

21. E. J. Swalm, "Positive Christianity," *EV*, Jan. 30, 1939, 3; and "Evaluation and Challenge of Our Peace Activities," *EV*, Dec. 1, 1941, 2, 12; and "Peace Churches and the Post-War Period," *EV*, Nov. 20, 1944, 4; and "The War Has Taught Us," *EV*, Mar. 24, 1947, 3; and "Education for Peace," *EV*, Dec. 22, 1947, 4; and "Our Responsibility for the Peace Testimony," sermon reported on in *SSH*, Feb. 29, 1948, 7; and preface, *Nonresistance under Test*, 1949, 5; and "Beloved Brethren," 23, 25, 33; Swalm to BIC members, *EV*, Feb. 5, 1951, 12.

22. H. G. Brubaker, "When Is Conscience a Safe Guide?" *EV*, Nov. 20, 1939, 4; and "Relief and Service Committee Meets," *EV*, Dec. 1, 1941, 2; and introduction, in *Nonresistance under Test*, comp. Swalm, 7–10.

23. Harold S. Martin, "Forgive Them, for They Know Not What They Do," *EV*, Oct. 26, 1942, 2; P. J. Wiebe, "Nonresistance," *EV*, Mar. 6, 1950, 5; Eber B. Dourte, "The Foundation of Our Peace Testimony," *EV*, May 26, 1952, 5, 12; J. A. Toews, "Non-Resistance in the Old Testament," *EV*, Oct. 13, 1952, 5, 14–15, and Dec. 22, 1952, 4, 14–15; Ray L. Smee, "Living Peaceably with All Men," *EV*, Apr. 13, 1953, 3, 11–12; Ray I. Witter sermon notes, "The Peacemakers: Are You One?" Ray I. Witter Papers, Hist. MSS 28–1.2, BICA.

24. Wendell E. Harmon, "This World Is Not My Home," *SSH*, Jan. 27, 1946, 4; V. L. Stump, "Changing Attitudes," *EV*, Mar. 10, 1941, 3; Wendell E. Harmon, "I Am Not a Pacifist," *EV*, Mar. 1, 1943, 2; Jesse W. Hoover, "Quill Quirks," *SSH*, Sept. 10, 1944, 4; D. Earl Heisey, "In the Mental Hospital," in *Nonresistance under Test*, comp. Swalm, 117–18; "Sentence Sermons from Bible Conference," *Clarion*, Mar. 1942, 12; S E. Graybill, "An Interesting Old Letter," selected by E. J. Swalm, *EV* June 19, 1944, 13; *Minutes*, OH-KY JC, Mar. 11, 1944, Albert H. Engle, "Values of Separation in Dress," 55; "Sentence Sermons from Bible Conference," *Clarion*, Mar. 1942, 12; "Christmas Peace," *Clarion*, Dec. 22, 1944, 2; John A. Climenhaga, "Indoctrination," *EV*, Feb. 26, 1945, 3; Wendell E. Harmon, "Peace without the Prince," *SSH*, Nov. 18, 1945, 4; Ray Heisey, "Futility or the Way," *SSH*, Apr. 13, 1952, 5.

25. Edward Gilmore, "Five Fundamental Doctrines of the Brethren in Christ Church," *SSH*, Oct. 22, 1944, 7; Henry Ginder, "Knowing God's Will, *SSH*, Nov. 5, 1944, 7; McCulloh to Hostetter, Aug. 24, 1942, Hostetter Papers, CPS, Hist. MSS 7–5.2, "CPS Letters" folder. All GC and DC appeals to governmental bodies stressed community loyalty and patriotism: Orie D. Yoder, "Should We Pray to Be Kept Out of the War?" *EV*, Dec. 4, 1939, 11; V. L. Stump, "Circumstances and God," *SSH*, Jan. 11, 1942, 4; "Sentence Sermons from Bible Conference," *Clarion*, Mar. 1942, 12; Joel E. Carlson, "Do We Appreciate the Present Hour?" *EV*, Mar. 24, 1941, 4; Cecelia Wolgemuth, "An Autobiographical Account," *BICHL* 8 (Apr. 1985): 55. E. J. Swalm remembered C. N. Hostetter Jr. as having said that nonresistance would never die, that if it weakened among the BIC or other peace churches God would give it to some other church to carry; videotaped interview by Pauline Cornell. Also see articles by students: Arthur Musser, "We Dare Not Fail," *Clarion*, Nov. 1941, 6; "Why a Democracy," *Clarion*, Feb. 1942, 3; Royce Engle, "What Shall We Do?" *Clarion*, Oct. 1939, 5.

26. Brubaker, "Relief and Service Committee Meets," 2, and "Non-Resistance Is Not Too Expensive," *EV*, Jan. 27, 1941, 2. Mennonite leaders also viewed positively cooperation with government in running the World War II CPS camps. See Bush, *Two Kingdoms*, 75–80; Keim, *Bender*, 293.

27. Harmon, *They Also Serve*, 57; Hoover to Wittlinger, May 2, 1976, Wittlinger Papers, Quest 1, 35–1.22, "Peace and Service, 1910–50" folder; Sider, *Messenger of Grace*, 102; J. A. Huffman, "The Christian and War," *EV*, Jan. 18, 1943, 12–13; "Panel: Questions of Youth," *SSH*, Mar. 30, 1947, 7.

28. "Military Service Is Topic of Rally Discussion," *Beulah College Echo* [hereafter *Echo*], Dec. 1940, 5;

29. *Clarion*, Mar. 1940, 2.

30. Ray M. Zercher, questionnaire.

31. Harold S. Martin, "Why I Am a Conscientious Objector," *SSH*, Aug. 29, 1943, 7.

32. "What Is War?" *Clarion*, Jan 1942, 11.

33. Musser, "Militarism, Pacifism, and Nonresistance," 13, and *SSH*, Apr. 18, 1943, 4–5.

34. Walter H. Dyck, "What If They Say" from *The Mennonite*, *SSH*, July 18, July 25, Aug. 1, Aug. 8, Aug. 15, Aug. 22, 1943, 4; V. L. Stump, *EV*, Nov. 6, 1939, 3; "Current Events," *EV*, Jan. 1, 1940, Feb. 2, 26, 1940, 5; V. L. Stump, "The Constraining Power," *EV*, Aug. 12, 1940, 3.

35. Jesse W. Hoover, "Quill Quirks: Social Gospel—C.P.S. and A.S.W.?" *SSH*, Mar. 12, 1944, 4, and "Quill Quirks," *SSH*, Apr. 2, 1944, 4. On dispensationalism, see Boyer, *When Time Shall Be No More*, 86–87. O. B. Ulery also singled out the "Holiness church" in his criticism of ministers who supported the war. See "Can a Christian Fight?" in *Nonresistance under Test*, comp. Swalm, 257.

36. Wendell E. Harmon, "Seed Time and Harvest," *SSH*, Dec. 16, 1945, 4.

37. Stump, "Constraining Power," 3; V. L. Stump, "They Have Lost Their Souls," *EV*, Oct. 26, 1942, 3.

38. All by Wendell E. Harmon: "A Reproach to Any People," *SSH*, Dec. 2, 1945, 4; "The Scapegoat Still Lives," *SSH*, Dec. 30, 1945, 4; "The Flower of Ugly Street," *SSH*, Jan. 13, 1946, 4; "Lest We Forget," *SSH*, Mar. 17, 1946, 4; "One God for One World," *SSH*, Apr. 7, 1946, 4, 6; "The Thinking Reed," *SSH*, Apr. 28, 1946, 4; "The Fallacy of Realism," *SSH*, May 12, 1946, 4. Also see Jesse W. Hoover, "Abdication," *EV*, Jan. 28, 1946, 3. A postwar section in the *EV* addressed militarism, atomic weaponry, and anti-Semitism. See "Worldwide New Currents," Jan. 27, Feb. 10, June 30, July 14, 1947, 16.

39. Jesse W. Hoover, "Bibles or Bombs?" *EV*, Aug. 27, 1945, 3; also see "Veteran's Day," from the Upland College (previously Beulah College) student newspaper, *SSH*, Dec. 26, 1954, 5.

40. "News Gleanings," reprinted from *Between the Lines*, *EV*, Nov. 27, 1947, 19.

41. C. N. Hostetter Jr. "The Church and War," *EV*, June 12, 1950, 5.

42. Jesse W. Hoover, "Sentence Sermons from Bible Conference," *Clarion*, Mar. 1942, 12.

43. "Memorial Day Program," May 25, 1941, Public Domain, Church Agencies, BYPW, VIII-2–2.1, BICA. Other sentiments based on a general condemnation of war appear in a piece by MCC chair, P. C. Hiebert, "The Crime of War," in *Nonresistance under Test*, comp. Swalm, 221–54. Also see V. L. Stump, editorial, *EV*, Nov. 20, 1939, 3; R. A. Franklin, "After the War—What Will Our Church Do?" *EV*, Aug. 28, 1944; Jesse W. Hoover, editorial, *EV*, Sept. 25, 1944, 3; "War Begets War," *SSH*, Oct. 21, 1951, 4.

44. Shirley Lenehan, "Peace in 1943," *Clarion*, Jan. 1943, 6.

45. Henry L. Garber, "The Christian and His Neighbor," a sermon reported on by Paul L. Snyder, *SSH*, Sept. 27, 1942, 7.

46. Wendell E. Harmon, "The Look Ahead," *SSH*, Sept. 9, 1945, 4; Paul Crider, "Work and Testimony Cannot Be Separated," in *They Also Serve*, 28.

47. "Brethren in Christ CPS Thinks," *SSH*, Jan. 14, 1945, 5.

48. "Panel: Questions of Youth," *SSH*, Mar. 30, 1947, 7.

49. *Clarion*, Feb. 14, 1947, 1; *Minutes*, Dauphin-Lebanon DC, Feb. 22, 1945, art. 1; "Statement on Peace Time Conscription," Rapho DC, n.d., Misc., IV-2–1.1, BICA.

50. "What Would You Do If Called to Fight?" *Clarion*, Nov. 1940, 16. Among many other articles, see C. Nelson Hostetter, "A Senior Expresses the Challenge of the Unknown," *Clarion*, May 1942, 7.

51. *Minutes*, Dauphin-Lebanon DC, Feb. 22, 1941, art. 7.

52. Miriam Bowers, "Peace Unweaponed," *Echo*, Oct. 1947, 7–8.

53. Elsie C. Bechtel, "Why We Should Support Relief Work," *EV*, July 16, 1945, 5.

54. Wendell E. Harmon, "Education in C.P.S. Camps," *SSH*, May 7, 1944, 4.

55. Jesse W. Hoover, "Quill Quirks," *SSH*, Feb. 27, 1944, 4.

56. Swalm, "Glimpses from Civilian Public Service Tours," in *Nonresistance under Test*, comp. Swalm, 172.

57. Wendell E. Harmon, "Look Ahead," 4.

58. *Flash*, Feb. 17, 1940, 1.

59. Typed responses, Henry N. Hostetter Papers, Correspondence, 13–2.1, "Indoctrination" folder; Wittlinger, *Quest for Piety*, 431.

60. "PAX Men to Peru," *EV*, July 19, 1954, 14.

61. Ross Nigh, "A Shaper of Life: The Brethren in Christ Experience," *BICHL* 16 (Dec. 1993): 306.

62. "The Temptation to Retaliate," from *Youth's Comrade*, *SSH*, Apr. 12, 1942, 7.

63. "Students Discuss Everyday Nonresistance"—Evelyn Raser, "At Home"; Ruth Hunt, "At School"; David Musser, "In Business"; Elda Engle, "In Recreation"; Lynn Nicholson, "Toward Enemies," *Echo*, Mar. 1943, 8. Also see Eber B. Dourte, "Grounding the Church in the Doctrine of Non-Resistance," *EV*, May 31, 1948, 14.

64. Ira Lehman, "A Community Challenge to a Non-resistant People," *SSH*, Sept. 1, 1946, 4.

65. Dale Ulery, "You Must Have Patience to Work with Patients," in *They Also Serve*, 25–26; D. Earl Heisey, "In the Mental Hospital," 13–26, and Ruth Zercher, "Our Wives," in *Nonresistance under Test*, comp. Swalm, 156–58.

66. One unsigned questionnaire described being threatened twice by lawsuits but settling them amicably. Also see, Morris N. Sherk, questionnaire.

67. Allyne Friesen Isaac, "P. B. and Edna Friesen: Reminiscences of a Family," *BICHL* 17 (Apr. 1994): 24, 27. Ray Zercher remembers a case of his parents refusing to press charges against a neighbor boy whom a family member had caught "pilfering our house." See his questionnaire. Harold Heise remembers his father urging him to return money to a neighbor who had bought a horse from Heise, used it for a summer, and then returned it, demanding a refund. The neighbor had threatened to sue Heise if he did not return the money. See interview by author.

68. Erma Lehman Hoover, questionnaire; Lester C. Fretz, "The Legacy of E. J. Swalm: His Oratory and Humor," *BICHL* 16 (Apr. 1993): 68.

69. "Special Personal Interview Sheet," completed by Alvin L. Winger on Bert Sherk, Misc., 5–1.6, BICA; Ross Nigh, interview by author.

70. Lester Fretz, interview by author.

71. Mildred Byer Charles, audiotaped response to questionnaire.

72. Gordon H. Schneider, questionnaire.

73. Gerald N. Wingert recalls the farm he had grown up on as a prosperous one. His father was also a deacon, a Messiah Bible College trustee member, and one of the local bank's board of directors. Wingert's father often made financial loans to other family and church members. When another deacon told him to call in a loan on a church

member because the member was a poor risk, Wingert's father "rebuked his deacon brother and told him he would never do a thing like that. In time the brother made good on the loan." Gerald N. Wingert, questionnaire.

74. Marty, *Pilgrims in Their Own Land,* 365. Marty made the comment in the context of World War I.

75. Ruth Herr Pawelski, "Ohmer U. Herr: Quest for Obedience," BICHL 11 (Apr. 1988): 53.

76. C. N. Hostetter Jr.'s father and grandfather were both noted as such, as was O. B. Ulery's father. See Sider, *Messenger of Grace,* 13–14, 17; Carl Ulery, interview by E. Morris Sider.

77. Martha L. Lady and Mary Olive Lady, interview by author.

78. Typed responses, Henry N. Hostetter Papers, Correspondence,13–2.1, "Indoctrination" folder.

79. "Brethren in Christ CPS Thinks," SSH, Jan. 28, 1945, 4.

80. Jeanette Dourte, Ethel Wolgemuth Kreider, Maynard C. Book, questionnaires.

81. Mary Olive Lady attributed her mother's knowledge about the larger world and the military to her friendship and correspondence with a World War I soldier before her marriage. Martha L. Lady and Mary Olive Lady, interview by author.

82. E. Morris Sider, questionnaire, and interview by author.

83. Beth Ulery Saba, "Carl Ulery: Versatile Churchman," BICHL 11 (Apr. 1988): 46, 48.

84. E. Morris Sider, *Leaders among Brethren: Biographies of Henry A. Ginder and Charlie B. Byers* (Nappanee, Ind.: Evangel Press, 1987), 196; Bennie Fadenrecht, questionnaire.

85. Naomi Heise Marr, interview by author.

86. Heisey, "They Also Served," 243–44; James Brubaker, Harriet Trautwein Byer, S. Lane Hostetter, Dorothy Witter Schrag, Gordon H. Schneider, Winifred Hostetter Worman, questionnaires; Curtis O. Byer to author, July 3, 1996; Jesse Heise to author, June 28, 29, 1996; Paul Hosteler to author, Dec. 3, 1996, and *Preacher on Wheels: Traveling the Road to Sainthood with Happy Abandon* (Elgin, Ill.: Brethren Press, 1980), 108; Lester Fretz, Isaiah B. Harley, interviews by author.

87. E. Morris Sider and Leone Dearing Sider, interview by author.

88. John Hensel, Paul Carlson, unsigned questionnaires. On the centrality of families and mothers in the formation of individual conscientious-objection stands, see Cynthia Eller, "Moral and Religious Arguments in Support of Pacifism: Conscientious Objectors and the Second World War" (Ph.D. diss., University of Southern California, 1988), 40, 56.

89. Typed responses, Henry N. Hostetter Papers, Correspondence,13–2.1, "Indoctrination" folder.

90. Dorothy Meyer Baldwin, Mary Ellen Engle Thuma, Lucille Mann Wolgemuth, questionnaires; Naomi Heise Marr, interview by author.

91. Maurine Rosenberry, questionnaire; *Minutes,* Donegal DC, Aug. 12, 1944, art. 9; *Minutes,* OH-KY JC, Mar. 13, 1943, Young People's Meeting topic, "In the Storeroom."

92. *Minutes,* ON JC, 1940, art. 3. Also see *Minutes,* ON JC, 1939, art. 3; 1941, art. 3; 1942, art. 3 [emphasis added].

93. Dorothy Sherk, interview by author.

94. Dorothy Witter, "Fret Not," SSH, May 27, 1945, 7; Harriet Trautwein, "A Church to Be Proud Of," SSH, Sept. 17, 1944, 7. Witter volunteered in Europe, as did Bechtel and Bowers, qtd. earlier. Trautwein volunteered in Mexico. Harriet Trautwein Byer, Dorothy

Witter Schrag, questionnaires; Miriam Bowers, interview by author; Elsie C. Bechtel, audiotaped response to questionnaire.

95. Bowers, interview by author; Bechtel, audiotaped response, and "Why We Should Support Relief Work," 5.

96. Program, BIC Church Peace Conference, July 3–5, 1953, Hostetter Papers, Lectures, 7–17.5, "Nonresistance" folder.

97. Grace Herr was the daughter of Ohmer Herr and Rozella Boyer Herr, who left a job and school, respectively, in World War I to avoid participation in mobilization. Grace Herr, "This Is Non-Resistance," *SSH*, May 4, 1952, 5–6; Brock, *Twentieth-Century Pacifism*, 10–12.

98. Anna Verle Miller, "Our Nonconformist Witness," *SSH*, May 13, 1945, 7.

99. Anna Verle Miller, questionnaire. Other individuals described nonresistance as a father's stand. S. Lane Hostetter, Anna Heise Reesor, Dorothy Witter Schrag, questionnaires.

100. Ruth Pawelski, "A Stabilizing Influence: The Brethren in Christ Experience," *BICHL* 16 (Dec. 1993): 293–304.

101. Nigh, "Shaper of Life," 307.

102. See Linda K. Kerber's discussion of the impact of gendered military service, "'A Constitutional Right to Be Treated like American Ladies': Helen Feeney, Robert Goldberg, and Military Obligation in Contemporary America," in her *No Constitutional Right to Be Ladies: Women and the Obligations of Citizenship* (New York: Hill and Wang, 1998), 221–302.

103. The responses to the 1943 survey provide an important source on general conflicts among the Brethren in Christ. Typed responses, Henry N. Hostetter Papers, Correspondence, 13–2.1, "Indoctrination" folder.

104. E. Morris Sider, interview by author.

105. Millard Herr, questionnaire.

106. Dorothy Sherk, interview by author.

107. A. James Alderfer, questionnaire.

108. Clara Gibboney Kritzberger, questionnaire.

109. Book, "Pursuit of Great Spoil," 124, 126.

110. Frances Harmon, telephone interview by author.

111. Bush, *Two Kingdoms*, 121–25, 161; Redekop, *Mennonite Society*, 224–26; Toews, *Mennonites*, 173–80.

112. Jesse W. Hoover, "Democracy and Discipline," *EV*, July 29, 1946, 3, 13.

113. Articles from *Clarion* often noted visits and the exchange of speakers between Messiah Bible College and Mennonite schools or organizations: "Bishop Derstine Speaks at Evening Service," Apr. 1940, 3; "Young People and Tomorrow," Mar. 1943, 9; announcements, Apr. 1943, 5; Mar. 25, 1945, 15; Feb. 8, 1946, l. Numerous articles and correspondence noted BIC participation in the 1952 Mennonite World Conference: *EV*, Sept. 1, 1952, 4; Sept. 15, 1952, 4–5, 14–16; Hostetter Papers, Mennonite Related Papers, Hist. *MSS* 7–6.1, "Mennonite World Conference, 1948–1952" folder. BIC delegates participated in a variety of inter-Mennonite conferences. For example, four BIC delegates were listed on a statement issued from a Study Conference of Mennonite and BIC Churches of North America. See "A Declaration of Christian Faith and Commitment," Nov. 9–12, 1950, Public Domain, Misc., VIII-10–1.2, folder 9, BICA. Three BIC representatives, E. J. Swalm, C. N. Hostetter Jr.,. and youth representative Louis Cober, attended the "Meaning of

Love" peace conference at Bluffton College in 1954. See "MCC News Notes," *EV,* Sept. 13, 1954, 14–15. BIC delegates Daniel Hoover and Ray Stump were present at the founding of the Mennonite Inter-College Peace Conference in 1948. BIC George Bundy was elected president of the Intercollegiate Peace Fellowship and presided over the formulation of a constitution for the group in 1953; *Minutes,* Mennonite Inter-College Peace Conference, Dec. 30, 1948; *Minutes,* Intercollegiate Peace Fellowship, Dec. 7, 1953, MCC Report Files 2, IX-12–2, "ICPF" folder.

114. A 1941 *EV* editorial expressed surprise that the Church of the Brethren had joined the Federal Council of Churches and wondered how the sister group thought such a move would spread the gospel or maintain "that simplicity of faith . . . delivered unto the saints." See V. L. Stump, editorial, *EV,* July 14, 1941, 3, 8. Other articles drawing on the Church of the Brethren or Society of Friends sources include "Peace, vs. Defense in 1812," *EV,* Apr. 12, 1943, 3; "Intimate Introductions," *SSH,* Oct. 15, 1944, 4; Wendell E. Harmon, "With God in CPS," *SSH,* Feb. 11, 1945, 4; "Non-combatant? A Letter A.F.S.C.," *SSH,* Mar. 11, 1945, 4; William F. McDermott, "The Cattle Boats of God," *SSH,* Nov. 9, 1947, 1–2, 6; "PAX Men Tour Britain," *EV,* Aug. 29, 1954, 5.

115. PRS News, *EV,* Nov. 22, 1943, 2. Church periodicals also ran writings, often from earlier centuries, by members of the Society of Friends. See PRS News, *EV,* June 17, 1946, 2.

116. Swalm, *Beloved Brethren,* chap. 15; Ronald J. R. Mathies, "The Legacy of E. J. Swalm: As a Churchman in the Wider Christian Community in the Witness of Peace," *BICHL* 16 (Apr. 1993): 57.

117. Sider, *Messenger of Grace,* 164, 194. See especially his chap. 9 for a description of Hostetter's extensive contacts in the Mennonite world. See Lester Fretz, Lela Swalm Hostetler, E. Morris Sider, interviews by author. Also see *Minutes,* ON JC, Sept. 1, 1951, art. 4; Sept. 4–6, 1954, art. 5; GC *Minutes,* 1950, art. 20.

118. Horst to Hoover, Feb. 16, 1944, MCC Correspondence, IX-6–3, "Jesse W. Hoover, 1944" folder; C. N. Hostetter Jr. to J. N. Hostetter, May 26, 1950, Hostetter papers, Peace Conferences, Hist. MSS 7–8.1, "Church and War" folder; "Commission on Christian Conscience and War," Hostetter Papers, Peace Conferences, 7–8.2, "Church and War" folder; Muste to Hostetter, Sept. 20, 1951, Hostetter to Muste, Oct. 1, 1951, Hostetter Papers, XI-12–8.6, "1950–1951" folder.

119. "A Serious Problem," *EV,* Apr. 8, 1940, 9. Hoover to Miller, May 18, 1943; Miller to Hoover, May 20, 1943; Horst to Hoover, Jan. 3, 1944, MCC Correspondence, IX-6–3, "Jesse W. Hoover, 1943, 1944" folders. Jesse W. Hoover, "Quill Quirks," *SSH,* Sept. 10, 1944, 4; PRS News, *EV,* July 31, 1944, 2; "A Testimony from an Ex-C.P.S. Man: From the Methodist C.O.," *SSH,* Mar. 31, 1946, 4; Wiebe, "Nonresistance," 5.

120. Swalm, "Glimpses from Civilian Public Service Tours," 170.

121. V. L. Stump, "Changing Attitudes," 3; Mary Olive Lady to author, Sept. 22, 1996. This letter noted Henry A. Ginder's story about the conversion of a Nazarene professor to pacifism.

122. J. N. Hostetter, "Mohandas K. Gandhi," *EV,* Feb. 9, 1948, 35; C. N. Hostetter Jr., "The Church and War," 5; excerpts from a speech by Henry Wallace, "Christian Bases for New World Order," *SSH,* May 9, 1943, 4; "American Industry Hates War," *EV,* Feb. 26, 1940, 2; "The Testimony of Josephus against War," *SSH,* June 17, 1945, 7; "Wesley's Views on War," *EV,* May 19, 1941, 11; "Dwight L. Moody and War," *EV,* May 15, 1950, 7; Daniel Brenneman, "Moody's Idea of War," *EV,* Sept. 1, 1952, 15.

123. Editorial notes, *EV,* Feb. 12, 1940, 11.

124. Don Suits, "A Way without War: The Swedish People Were Resourceful," *SSH*, Jan. 11, 1948, 4.

125. Editorial notes, *EV*, June 22, 1942, 6; Hostetter, "Mohandas K. Gandhi," 35.

126. *Minutes*, OK SC, Mar. 13, 1942, art. 13. The question does not appear in the *GC Minutes*, 1942.

127. Noreen Trautwein, "Alma B. Cassel: The A.B.C. of Beulah (Upland) College," *BICHL* 16 (Apr. 1993): 31; "Military Service Is Topic of Rally Discussion," *Echo*, Dec. 1940, 5; Louise E. Mitchell, "This Happened in America: An Indian Trail That Led to Glory," *SSH*, Nov. 29, 1942; "Bible Ministry to the Negroes," *EV*, Jan. 2, 1939, 1; Velma Schlabach, "Working with the Waldensians," *EV*, Jan. 23, 1950, 15–16; Martin Niemöller, "Christianity or Nihilism," *EV*, Oct. 6, 1947, 13–14; W. O. Winger, "One Great Cause, One Great Power: Correspondence with Niemöller," *EV*, July 11, 1949, 4.

128. *Minutes*, Penn. SC, Apr. 3–4, 1946, art. 10. At least parts of the community in Ontario did not exclude Mennonites from Communion. See E. Morris Sider to author, July 2, 1998.

129. Irene Frey Hensel, diary, Jan. 14, 22, 28; Feb, 1, 10, 17, 22; Mar. 29; Apr. 4, 1940; May 3, 25, 30; June 2, 5, 9; July 17, 20; Oct. 25; Nov. 8; Dec. 2, 24, 28, 1941; Jan. 2; Feb. 2, 8, 19; Mar. 7, 23; Apr. 2; June 9; July 6, 19; Aug. 19, 23; Sept. 5; Nov. 10, 1942; Apr. 10; June 3; July 1, 6; Aug. 9; Oct. 24, 1943; Jan. 16; Mar. 29; Apr. 9; June 7; Nov. 15, 1944, Hist. *MSS* 79–1.2, BICA.

130. Catalog, 1933–34, Messiah College, Publications, 1924–35, XI-8–1.2, BICA.

131. Henry G. Brubaker, "Christian Citizenship," *EV*, Nov. 6, 1939, 4.

132. "The Church and the Community," July 18, 1945, BYPW, VIII-2–2.1, BICA.

133. "Christian Basis of Patriotism," Nov. 7, 1943, BYPW, VIII-2–2.1, BICA. In the same collection also see, "National Life," Feb. 16, 1941; "My Responsibility to My Community," Aug. 31, 1941; "A Christian Citizen," July 8, 1945; "Christian Patriotism," last half of 1947.

134. "Thank God for America," *EV*, Dec. 4, 1939, 11; "We Dare Not Fail," *Clarion*, Nov. 1941, 6; Hostetter, "A Senior Expresses the Challenge of the Unknown," 7; Edna Dean Procter, "Our Country," *SSH*, July 7, 1946, 7; Warren Sherman, "Back from Europe," *BC Bulletin*, Sept. 4, 1947, 4.

135. Wendell E. Harmon, "Educating Heaven's Citizens," *SSH*, June 9, 1946, 4, and "Learning by Doing," *SSH*, July 7, 1946, 4, 6.

136. "Statement on Peace Time Conscription," n.d., DC, Rapho District, Misc., IV-2–1.1, BICA.

137. Anna Lane Hostetter, diary, May 8, 1945, Anna Lane Hostetter, Hist. *MSS* 79–1.1, BICA.

138. Jesse W. Hoover, "Victory," and "'I Am an American' Day," *EV*, May 21, 1945, 3.

139. F. E. Mallott, "Can the Peace Churches Lead?" *SSH*, Dec. 3, 1944, 4–5.

140. J. H. Byer, "The Race Problem: From a Biblical Standpoint," *EV*, Sept. 24, 1945, 16. In 1940, Messiah Bible College academy juniors led a chapel service on "the American Negro," acknowledging their contributions in the fields of music, literature, education, science, and religion. See *Flash*, Jan. 17, 1940, 3.

141. *Clarion*, Dec. 1938, 5; "M.B.C. News Notes," *EV*, Feb. 28, 1944, 14.

142. "Comments and Items of Interest," *EV*, Feb. 13, 1939, 2; V. L Stump, editorial, "'Hated for His Name's Sake," *EV*, Mar. 10, 1941, 3. A 1939 entry in "News Items and Comments" deplored "Germany's brutal Anti-Semitism" but also noted that "the Jew, as a *Nation*, has failed God." See *EV*, Jan. 2, 1939, 1. Also see responses to "What Are the Conditions for Maintaining Peace in Europe?" *Clarion*, Oct. 1938, 11, and in the same issue, "'Because Hitler Wills It,'" 9; H. G. Brubaker, "National Socialism and Christian-

ity," *EV*, June 3, 1940, 4; "Do Jews Control America?" *EV*, Sept. 9, 1940, 2. "Shall German Refugees Be Admitted to the U.S.?" *Clarion*, Feb. 1941, 7; Theodore E. Miller, "A Few Observations," *EV*, May 19, 1941, 9–10; "Where Can the 'Wandering Jew' Wander?" *SSH*, Jan. 25, 1942, 7; "They Have Lost Their Souls," *EV*, Oct. 26, 1942, 3; "A Word about Atrocities," *EV*, Feb. 28, 1944, 3, 10; "A Struggle For Palestine Which Must End in Defeat," *EV*, Oct. 7, 1946, 2. On biblical prophecy's impact on attitudes about Jewish people, see Boyer, *When Time Shall Be No More*, 181–87.

143. Nelson Hostetter, interview by Joseph Miller, MLA.

144. Mary Olive Lady, interview by author.

145. Responses to "Shall German Refugees Be Admitted?" 7; *Clarion*, Oct. 20, 1944, 2.

146. "We Have Been Challenged!" *SSH*, Sept. 9, 1945, 7. Two BIC students, Ernest Boyer and Harry Paugstat, hitchhiked to Washington, D.C., to see the funeral procession. "In Memoriam," *Clarion*, Apr. 27, 1945, 1, 4

147. *EV*, Nov. 4, 1946, 10; Walter Winger, interview by author.

148. The Christian soldier had to have both an offense and defense, wrote Wilmer Heisey, a student at Messiah Bible College. The Christian faced an enemy with superior numbers, but he worked under a God who never lost a battle. The soldier's equipment included "feet shod . . . with the gospel of peace." "The Christian Soldier," *Clarion*, June 1942, 13, 16.

149. "News of Church Activity," Jan. 5, 1942, 7.

150. "Draftees or Volunteers?" *Echo*, Nov. 1940, 10, 15; Arthur W. Heise, "Question of the Month," *SSH*, Nov. 4, 1951, 5. Also see "Christianity as a Warfare," *EV*, Jan. 16, 1939, 3, 21; James M. Brubaker, "Our Line of Defense," *EV*, Mar. 10, 1941, 5, 16; Joel E. Carlson, "The First Fifth Column," *EV*, June 2, 1941, 5, and "Why Not 'All-Out Aid' for Christ?" *EV*, July 28, 1941, 4; Jesse Lady, "'V' for Victory," *Clarion*, Nov. 1941, 3; Chester Wingert, "Armistice: There Was," *Clarion*, Nov. 1941, 11, 17; "World's Mightiest Warplane Takes Off," selected, *SSH*, Feb. 15, 1942, 7; "Chapel Notes," *Clarion*, Dec. 1942, 15; "A Dangerous Thing," *Clarion*, Jan 1943, 2; Professor Kuhns, "Youth Must Be *Strong*," *Clarion*, Feb. 1943, 1, 10; "A Clear Vision of Peace and Love," *Clarion*, Mar. 1943, 4; *Clarion*, Apr. 1943, 12–15; Anna Wolgemuth, "News from Mission Fields," *SSH*, Apr. 16, 1944, 7; "Why Does God Allow This War?" *SSH*, July 23, 1944, 4; T. C. Bales, "The Muster-Roll of the Church," *SSH*, July 23, 1944, 8; Harriet L. Trautwein, "Wanted," *SSH*, Sept. 9, 1945, 7; J. Edgar Hoover, "Necessity of Discipline," *EV*, Nov. 17, 1947, 3; Eber B. Dourte, "The Foundation of Our Peace Testimony," *EV*, May 26, 1952, 5, 12.

151. "God Answers Prayer: A True Story of the Great War," *EV*, June 19, 1939, 2, 15; "Let Peace Be Our Theme," *Clarion*, Nov. 1940, 14; "A Christian's Attitude in the Present Crisis," *EV*, Mar. 2, 1942, 3; "Liberty in Prison," *EV*, Oct. 12, 1942, 11, 16; Arthur Musser, "A Powerful Hookup," *Clarion*, Nov. 1942, 1; George Kevan, "A Revival in an Army: An Account by a British Soldier," *SSH*, Nov. 29, 1942, 4, 8; "From the Pastor's Mail Bag," *SSH*, May 20, 1945, 4; Joseph H. Smith, "God's Will as to Our Enemies," *EV*, July 2, 1945, 11.

152. Gerald N. Wingert to author, June 17, 1996; Paul Hutchinson, "The President's Religious Faith," *Life*, Mar. 22, 1954, 151–70; Schrag and Sider, "BIC Public Policy," 207.

153. Schrag and Sider, "BIC Public Policy," 207; J. Wilmer Heisey, "R. I. Witter: Fervent in Spirit," *BICHL* 20 (Apr. 1997): 72–73, 76; GC *Minutes*, 1939–54, "Roll Call of Standing Committees." Over 50 percent of Mennonite and much higher percentages of Church of the Brethren and Quaker conscripted men chose military service. Mennonite—Amish and BIC are included in these computations—percentages varied widely between groups.

See Bowman, *Brethren Society,* 389, n. 6; Bush, *Two Kingdoms,* 19, n. 34, 97–99; Keim, *Conscription of Conscience,* Sibley and Jacob, *Conscription of Conscience,* 24, n. 7.

154. Dorothy Sherk, interview by author; Clara Meyer Eberly, Rowena Winger Heise, Esther Tyson Boyer, questionnaires.

155. Rupert Turman, questionnaire; John Fries Jr. interview by author; E. Morris Sider, "Brief Biography of John E. Zercher," in *Lantern in the Dawn: Selections from the Writings of John E. Zercher,* ed. E. Morris Sider and Paul Hostetler (Nappanee, Ind.: Evangel Press, 1980), 17–18.

156. Heisey, "They Also Served," 245–46. Verna W. Heise recalls that while her brother served in the military, his wife and child moved in with Verna's family. Verna's father, John Henry Heise, had been a World War I conscientious objector. See Louis Heise and Verna W. Heise, interview with author. Similarly, Irene Frey Hensel's diary describes her visits with her husband in Civilian Public Service and her brother's visits home when he was on military furlough; June 13, 1941; Sept. 23, Oct. 26, 27, Nov. 25, 1942; May 24, 27, June 1, July 15, Aug. 25, Nov. 9, Dec. 12, 1943; Feb. 5, Mar. 18–19, Apr. 27, June 9, 16, 1944, Irene Frey Hensel, 79–1.1; newspaper clippings, Irene Frey Hensel, Hist. MSS 79–1.2, BICA. Anna Lane Hostetter's diary is filled with details of three sons in Civilian Public Service. But it also notes news about the military service of a brother of Evelyn Poe, a woman living in the Hostetter home. A. Hostetter, Feb. 16, Apr. 16, 1945, Anna Hostetter, Diaries, 79–1.1, BICA

157. John S. Kohler, questionnaire; Harmon, *They Also Serve,* 58.

158. Heisey, "They Also Served," 259.

159. Cumberland, Penn. DC, Feb. 9, 1943, art. 2; Feb. 12, 1946, art. 21; Grantham, Penn., DC, Jan. 28, 1946, art. 10.

160. "Donegal Tidings," n.d., photocopies of two issues in possession of author.

161. *Clarion,* Oct. 11, 1946, 2.

162. GC *Minutes,* 1943, 4.

163. Henry N. Hostetter, "It Is Up to Us," in *They Also Serve,* 53. The question of corporate versus individual aspects of religious faith extended beyond the issue of nonresistance. One response to the mid-1940's indoctrination questionnaire pointed explicitly to the shift from "church salvation" to "individual salvation," which the respondent equated with "individual opinion." Typed responses, Henry N. Hostetter Papers, Correspondence, 13–2.1, "Indoctrination" folder.

164. E. J. Swalm, "A Free *Conscience,*" in *Nonresistance under Test,* comp. Swalm, 268.

165. "Christian Life," First half 1942, BYPW, VIII-2-2.1, BICA.

166. Jesse W. Hoover, "Quill Quirks," *SSH,* Jan. 30, 1944, 4, and "Quill Quirks," *SSH,* Apr. 23, 1944, 4, and "A Question of Liberty," *EV,* Dec. 4, 1944, 3.

167. Adams, *Best War Ever,* chap. 1, esp. 9. On government and media representations of the war, also see Kenneth Paul O'Brien and Lynn Hudson Parsons, eds., *The Home-Front War: World War II and American Society* (Westport, Conn.: Greenwood Press, 1995), chaps. 2–4, 6; George H. Roeder, *The Censored War: American Visual Experience during World War II* (New Haven: Yale Univ. Press, 1993).

168. Clarence Z. Musser, "Christian Youth Facing Militarism," reported on by Alice Grace Zercher, *SS,* Aug. 27, 1944, 7.

169. Jesse W. Hoover, "United—Uncompromising," *EV,* June 21, 1943, 3.

170. *Minutes,* Donegal DC, Feb. 22, 1944, note after art. 4.

171. E. Morris Sider, "The Brethren in Christ Ministry and Peace," BICHL 16 (Apr. 1993): 101. On Mennonite groups, see Redekop, *Leaving Anabaptism*, 111–14. and *Mennonite Society*, 301. On Quakers, see Cecil B. Currey, "The Devolution of Quaker Pacifism: A Kansas Case Study, 1860–1955," *Kansas History* 6 (1983): 120–33; Hamm, *Transformation of Quakerism*, 107–109. On the loss of pacifism among a variety of small religious groups, in Schlabach and Hughes, eds., *Proclaim Peace,* see Casey, Koontz, and Kornweibel. Compromise often accompanies what Hughes describes as the privileging of "a distinctly American virtue: the freedom to choose" (xii).

172. H. G. Brubaker, "Civilized? Guess Again," *EV,* Dec. 4, 1939, 4. Sociologist Leo Driedger argues that Mennonites have been shaped by individualism and diversity at many points in their history. See his *Global Village*, 68, 232.

173. C. N. Hostetter Jr., "War and the Word."

174. Wendell E. Harmon, "Christ and the Machine," *EV,* May 21, 1945, 5.

175. "What Obedience to Conscience Implies," selected, *EV,* July 19, 1943, 2. Another example is Wendell E. Harmon, "Soldiers of Another Kingdom," in *Nonresistance under Test,* comp. Swalm, 13. Also see Ross Nigh, "My Convictions on Peace: Under A.S.W. Contract," *SSH,* Jan. 21, 1945, 4; Eber B. Dourte, "Grounding the Church," *EV,* May 31, 1948, 14.

176. "Dangerous Substitutes," June 21, 1942, BYPW, VIII-2-2.1, BICA.

177. Mary Olive Lady to author, Sept. 22, 1996. MC *Alumni Directory,* 1992, 21.

178. The person commenting on the question, probably Wendell Harmon, acknowledged that in fact it is very hard to neatly separate the two motivations. See "Brethren in Christ C.P.S. Thinks," *SSH,* Jan. 28, 1945, 4.

179. Typed responses, Henry N. Hostetter Papers, Correspondence, 13–2.1, "Indoctrination" folder.

180. Hostetter, "War and the Word."

181. Unsigned questionnaire.

182. Dorothy Sherk, "The Legacy of E. J. Swalm: As an Evangelist," BICHL 16 (Apr. 1993): 65–66.

183. "Brethren in Christ CPS Thinks," *SSH,* Jan. 7, 1945, 4.

184. John A. Climenhaga, "Unity in Diversity," *EV,* Feb. 24, 1947, 3–4.

185. Typed responses, Henry N. Hostetter Papers, Correspondence, 13–2.1, "Indoctrination" folder.

186. Carlton O. Wittlinger, "Are Minority Convictions Out of Date?" *SSH,* Jan. 28, 1945, 7.

187. On evaluations of American religion as a competitive market, see Finke and Stark, *Churching of America;* Marty, *Pilgrims in Their Own Land,* viii–x.

188. Hostetter to Boyer, July 25, 1935, Henry N. Hostetter Papers, Correspondence, 13–2.1, "Young People's Program, 1935–1937" folder Calvin Redekop states that defections of youth are highest among the most evangelically oriented Mennonite churches. See *Mennonite Society,* 28. At the other end of the Anabaptist spectrum, Kraybill and Bowman quote an Amish farmer: "The children are our most important crop." See *Backroad to Heaven,* 236.

189. Wendell E. Harmon, "E Pluribus Unum," *SSH,* May 26, 1946, 4.

190. Typed responses, Henry N. Hostetter Papers, Correspondence, 13–2.1, "Indoctrination" folder.

191. Dorothy Sherk, interview by author.

192. On comparison of Amish groups in Holmes County, Ohio, including a comparison of their accommodations to the larger society and their retention of youth, see Don Kraybill, "Plotting Social Change across Four Affiliations," in *Amish Struggle,* ed. Kraybill and Olshan, 53–74. On defection of "progressive" Mennonite youth, see Redekop, *Mennonite Society,* 26–29.

193. H. G. Brubaker, "Dr. Brubaker Attends Peace Convention," *Echo,* Nov. 1940, 6; and "Non-Resistance Is Not Too Expensive," 2.

194. See the description of this concern in chap. 4, below.

195. Miriam A. Bowers, interview by author.

Chapter 3: Nonresistance and Home Front Life

1. The introductory quotations come from letters, questionnaires, and interviews. Hostetler to author, Apr. 8, 1996; A. Zercher to author, Aug. 26, 1996; R. Zercher, questionnaire; Frances Harmon, telephone interview by author. On popular conceptions of the war, see Adam's overview, *Best War Ever,* 1–19. Also see Blum, *V Was for Victory,* 6; Fussell, *Wartime,* vi, 130, 153; O'Brien and Parsons, *Home-Front War;* Richard Polenberg, "The Good War? A Reappraisal of How World War II Affected American Society," *Virginia Magazine of History and Biography* 100 (July 1992): 295–322; John Tateishi, comp., *And Justice for All: An Oral History of the Japanese American Detention Camps* (New York: Random House, 1984); Terkel, *"The Good War";* Neil A. Wynn, *The Afro-American and the Second World War* (New York: Holmes and Meier Publishing, 1975). Erenberg and Hirsch, on the other hand, describe as "paradoxical," rather than negative, the war's impact on social groups outside the mainstream. See their *War in American Culture,* 2–5; unsigned questionnaire.

2. Many scholars focusing on World War II have drawn on oral history. Roger Horowitz's survey of oral histories notes that the memories of women, racial minorities, and unionized laborers lead to ambivalent evaluations of World War II. Studs Terkel's 1984 collection, still one of the best, challenges the "Good War" of his title. Horowitz's survey, however, faults the narrowness of oral history's emphasis on collecting facts, evaluating accuracy, and drawing increasingly fine-grained portraits of the period. Interviews, he contends, should also be used to consider the construction of "meaning and memory." In this view, the influence of the war lies more in people's memories than in actual events that historians might uncover. The explosion of historical writing on memory responds to larger interdisciplinary discussions about the locus of authority in academic study. In communities such as the Brethren in Christ, who value their heritage, the importance of how the community builds that heritage is obvious. Roger Horowitz, "Oral History and the Story of World War II," *Journal of American History* 82 (Sept. 1995): 617, 620–22. Terkel, *"The Good War."* For a discussion of "History and Memory," see "AHR Forum," *American Historical Review* 102 (Dec. 1997): 1371–412. For a reflection on the importance of this historiographic trend to the BIC, see Sider, "Community, Memory, and the BIC," 396–407.

3. Unsigned questionnaires; Alice Grace Hostetter Zercher to author, Aug. 26, 1996.

4. "C.O. Churches Custodians of Non-Resistance," report on C. F. Derstine sermon, "The Four Horsemen of the Apocalypse and the Attitude of the C.O.'s," *Clarion,* Nov. 1939, 12. On the close scrutiny that writers on biblical prophecy accorded Jews, and their lesser attention to Hitler during the 1930s and 1940s, see Boyer, *When Time Shall Be No More,* 107–12, 187.

5. Harold Kettering, "'Because Hitler Wills It,'" *Clarion,* Oct. 1938, 9.

6. Ulery to Miller, May 15, 1940, Orville B. Ulery Papers, Hist. MSS 38–1.1, "MCC-CPS Correspondence, 1940" folder, BICA.

7. Jesse W. Hoover, "'Be Not Dismayed,'" *EV,* Jan. 5, 1942, 3, 6; Kenneth E. Hess, John C. Reesor, Paul E. Wingerd, Miriam Frey Zook, questionnaires; unsigned questionnaire; Dorothy Sherk, interview by author; Bothwell, Drummond, and English, *Canada,* 316.

8. Engle to Hostetter, Sept. 2, 1942, Hostetter to Climenhaga, Oct. 1, 1942, Henry N. Hostetter Papers, Correspondence, Hist. MSS 13–2.1, "BYPW, 1942–44," folder.

9. From contemporary accounts: Irene Frey Hensel, diary, May 7, 13, 20, July 15, 1942; Jan. 11, 1944, 79–1.1, BICA. Lady to H. Hostetter, Aug. 8, 1942, Henry N. Hostetter Papers, Correspondence, 13–2.1, "BYPW, 1942–44," folder; *EV,* May 25, 1942, 6. From retrospective accounts: Harriet Trautwein Byer, Maurine Rosenberry, questionnaires; Dorothy Sherk, interview by author.

10. Joseph H. Ginder, Anna Heise Reesor, Lucille Mann Wolgemuth, questionnaires; Harold Heise, interview by author.

11. Anna Lane Hostetter, Diary, June 12, 1945, 79–1.1, BICA; *Minutes,* Penn. SC, 1944, art 8; 1946, art. 9; E. Morris Sider, "John J. Engbrecht and the Brethren in Christ in South Dakota," *BICHL* 14 (Apr. 1991): 95.

12. "Do You Expect to Attend General Conference?" *EV,* May 25, 1942, 6; Jesse W. Hoover, "Looking Forward into 1943," and "Less Gas to Go Places," *EV,* Jan. 4, 1943, 3; "The Church and Community," July 18, 1943, BYPW, VIII-2–2.1, BICA; *Minutes,* Pacific Coast SC, 1943, art. 3.

13. "Important Notice," *EV,* Apr. 26, 1943, 2; "Special Notice," *EV,* Apr. 9, 1945, 6–7; Swalm, *Beloved Brethren,* 133.

14. Beulah Arnold, *MSMS,* 5–6; Allen Buckwalter, *MSMS,* 55; Ruth H. Byers, *MSMS,* 79; Anna R. Wolgemuth, *MSMS,* 535; Henry H. Brubaker, "Selections from the Memoirs of a Missionary: The Missionary Years," part 2, *BICHL* 14 (Apr. 1991): 70–72.

15. Climenhaga to Hostetter, Sept. 16, 1942, Henry N. Hostetter Papers, 13–2.1, "BYPW, 1942–44" folder Wilma Wenger Musser, questionnaire. Harriet Trautwein Byer describes becoming business manager of the Beulah College *Echo* as an example of women taking over men's work. See her questionnaire.

16. *Clarion,* Dec. 22, 1944, 1, and Jan. 19, 1945, 1; Miriam Heisey, "Thumb-Way," *Clarion,* Feb. 6, 1945, 2.

17. Harriet Trautwein Byer, Irene Wagaman Engle, questionnaires.

18. "County Boy among First Conscientious Objectors Called," *Intelligencer Journal,* May 8, 1941, clipping in Hostetter Papers, MCC, Misc., Hist. MSS 7–4.3, "C.O." folder.

19. Heisey, "They Also Served," 233, 255; Jeanette Frey Dourte, questionnaire.

20. Ross Nigh, interview by author.

21. Mary Olive Lady, Morris N. Sherk, questionnaires.

22. Harvey R. Sider, E. Morris Sider, Martha L. Lady, Mary Olive Lady, questionnaires.

23. Esther Tyson Boyer, Beulah Heisey, questionnaires.

24. Dorothy Sherk describes the death of her brother James in an interview with author. Rowena Winger Heise notes the death of her cousin and classmate, Joe Nigh, son of community members Joram and Alma Nigh. See her questionnaire. Also see Clara Meyer Eberly, questionnaire.

25. Harriet Trautwein Byer, Clara Meyer Eberly, Dorothy Witter Schrag, questionnaires; "Californian Churches to Protect Loyal Japanese," *EV,* Jan. 19, 1942, 2.

26. Clarence H. Sakimura, interview by author.

27. Beulah Heisey, questionnaire.

28. Judson Hill, questionnaire.

29. Donald Engle, "With God in CPS," SSH, Feb. 27, 1944, 4.

30. Geraldine M. Wenger, questionnaire; *Clarion*, Feb. 1943, 9.

31. On mobilization among the Mennonites, see Melvin Gingerich, *Service for Peace: A History of Mennonite Civilian Public Service* (Akron, Penn.: Mennonite Central Committee, 1949). On mobilization of the larger coalition, see Keim and Stoltzfus, *Politics of Conscience*, chaps. 3–5.

32. "Our Attitude as Nonresistant Christians in the Present Situation," adopted by MCC, Jan. 3, 1942, EV, Feb. 2, 1942, 49–50; *Minutes*, Penn. SC, 1–2 Apr. 1942, art. 13. The most direct condemnation of agricultural profits from war prices came from C. F. Derstine, a Mennonite. See his "C.O. Churches Custodians of Non-Resistance," 12.

33. Jay Gibble remembers being told that the flag decal he put on his bike indicated a willingness to do military service in a telephone conversation with author, Nov. 14, 1996. Gerald N. Wingert remembers a Mennonite classmate who did not salute the flag. See Wingert to author, June 17, 1996. Leone Dearing Sider remembers her parents being threatened when she and her siblings refused to join a pledge in Saskatchewan in an interview by author.

34. PRS News, EV, Nov. 17, 1941, 2, 16; *Minutes*, Dauphin-Lebanon DC, Sept. 1, 1941, art. 6. A book of stamps, each saying "Brethren in Christ 10 cents Relief and Service," can be found in GC, PRS, I-21–1.1, "*Minutes*, 1940–1947" folder, BICA.

35. Ulery to Miller, Feb. 25, 1942; Miller to Ulery, Feb. 27, 1942; Stump to Ulery, May 16, 1942; Ulery to Miller, May 20, 1942; Orville B. Ulery Papers, 38–1.1, "MCC CPS Correspondence" folder Dorothy Meyer Baldwin, questionnaire; PRS News, EV, Feb. 2, 1942, 49–50. For a discussion of patriotism among rank-and-file union members, see Gary Gerstle, "The Working Class Goes to War," in *War in American Culture*, ed. Erenberg and Hirsch, 105–27.

36. Miller to Hoover, June 27, 1942, Orville B. Ulery Papers, 38–1.1, "MCC CPS Correspondence" folder. Also see correspondence on bonds between Hoover and other MCC personnel in MCC Correspondence, IX-6–3, "Jesse W. Hoover, 1943" folder.

37. O. B. Ulery, "Important Notice," EV, July 6, 1942, 2; "The Civilian Bond Purchase Plan," EV, July 20, 1942, 2, 5. Encouraging their purchase, one notice argued that civilian bonds not only provided a peace witness but also were added to county quotas, presumably of war bond purchases. PRS News, EV, May 10, 1943, 2.

38. "Buy Civilian Government Bonds," BC *Bulletin*, Dec. 1942, 2. Also see "Civilian Government Bonds," BC *Bulletin*, Mar. 1943, 2. Other encouragement to buy bonds appeared in *Minutes*, Rapho DC, Jan. 1, 1945, art. 19.

39. "News of Church Activities, Canada," EV, Apr. 27, 1942, 7. E. Morris Sider remembers his parents purchasing such a certificate for him in an interview by author.

40. "Council of Civilian Service Organized," *Clarion*, Feb. 1942, 7. The article gave a list of committee members. Also see "Grantham Joins in Regional Blackout," *Clarion*, June 1942, 6.

41. Mary Olive Lady, questionnaire.

42. Jesse W. Hoover, "Church Service Units Encouraged," EV, May 25, 1942, 2.

43. "Students Do Red Cross Work," *Clarion*, Mar. 1942, 9.

44. Edward Gilmore, "The Alternate Service Work Program," in *Nonresistance under*

Test, comp. Swalm, 81; E. Morris Sider, "Life and Labor in the Alternate Service Work Camps in Canada during World War II," MQR 66 (Oct. 1992): 597.

45. *Minutes,* Dauphin-Lebanon DC, Sept. 1, 1941, art. 6.

46. For an illustration of the close working relationships between the military and pacifist relief efforts, see Grigor, McClelland, *Embers of War: Letters from a Quaker Relief Worker in War-torn Germany* (London: British Academic Press, 1997).

47. GC *Minutes,* 1943, art. 52.

48. "Can We Follow Christ in a Total War?" from *Peace Sentinel, EV,* Feb. 1, 1943, 11.

49. *Minutes,* Wainfleet DC, Dec. 12, 1939, art. 6.

50. Ezra D. Heisey, "In Dairy Farm Work," *Minutes,* OH-KY JC, Mar. 14–16, 1946, 56–57.

51. Irene Wagaman Engle, questionnaire; Martha L. Lady, MSMS, 329, and interview by author.

52. Clara Meyer Eberly, questionnaire.

53. *Minutes,* ON JC, Sept. 13–14, 1939, art. 3.

54. Miriam Statler, "'Think It Over': Women and Non-Resistance," reprinted from *Goshen College Record, EV,* May 5, 1941, [16]. D'Ann Campbell's study of all women during World War II describes women's achievement of fuller military status in various branches of the military. During the war, 350,000 women entered the armed services. A Cadet Nursing Corps program produced 125,000 for work in the war effort between 1943 and 1948. See *Women at War with America: Privates Lives in a Patriotic Era* (Cambridge: Harvard Univ. Press, 1984), 20, 54. Jean Bethke Elshtain might agree with the article's author. Elshtain provides a label for women who not only join war production but also war's fervor—the "aggressive mother" who urges men to "kill them for me." *Women and War,* 191–92.

55. Ulery to Miller, Feb. 25, 1942; Miller to Ulery, Feb. 27, 1942; Orville B. Ulery Papers, 38–1.1, "MCC CPS Correspondence" folder.

56. PRS News, *EV,* June 21, 1943, 9; PRS News, *EV,* May 22, 1944, 2; *Minutes,* OH-KY JC, Mar. 11–13, 1943, art. 5. On the National Service Board for Religious Objectors, see Keim and Stoltzfus, *Politics of Conscience,* 109 and later.

57. Anna Lane Hostetter, diary, Mar. 14, Apr. 24, 1945, 79–1.1, BICA.

58. Goossen, *Women against the Good War,* 77.

59. Jesse W. Hoover, "Quill Quirks," SSH, June 25, 1944, 4. See chap. 1, n. 23.

60. Alderfer to Brubaker, Mar. 23, 1942, GC, PRS, I-21–1.1, BICA; A. James Alderfer, questionnaire. An announcement in the EV asked people to send in names of any medical students who were conscientious objectors. See Apr. 13, 1942, 2.

61. Harold Engle and Mary Elizabeth Engle, interview by author.

62. Alvan Thuma, MSMS, 497. A Canadian writer described conscientious-objector males of draft age who experienced difficulty being admitted to universities; "Peace Churches in Canada," EV, Nov. 8, 1943, 2. E. Morris Sider remembers a story of one conscientious objector who was forced to leave Queen's University during World War II. See Sider to author, July 2, 1998.

63. Sider, *Nine Portraits,* 314–17, 331–32.

64. GC *Minutes,* official directories, 1939–54; Sider, *Leaders,* 193.

65. Heisey, "They Also Served," 252.

66. "Please Read," EV, Mar. 10, 1941, 2.

67. Hostetter to Miller, May 16, 1942, Miller to Hostetter, May 19, 1942, Hostetter Papers, CPS, Hist. MSS 7–5.2, "CPS Letters and Pictures" folder.

68. GC *Minutes,* 1943, art. 52.

69. *Minutes,* Grantham DC, Oct. 4, 1948, art. 13.

70. *Minutes,* Wainfleet DC, Dec. 4, 1945, art. 2.

71. BC *Bulletin,* Sept. 1943, 2.

72. *Clarion,* Feb. 1943, 10, and Nov. 1943, 4.

73. Unsigned questionnaire.

74. E. Morris Sider, interview by author.

75. Paul S. Boyer, questionnaire.

76. Unsigned questionnaire.

77. Grace French, questionnaire.

78. Brother Montgomery, "Testimony," EV, May 22, 1944, 9.

79. George Bundy and Ethel Heisey Bundy, interview by author; George E. Bundy, "Autobiography," typed manuscript in possession of its author.

80. Bundy, "Autobiography." Bundy's wife, Ethel Heisey Bundy, remembers the congregation of God's Love Mission in Detroit praying on George's behalf during his final East Lansing appeal.

81. George Bundy, interview by author. His determination perhaps helped to lead to his election in 1952 as president of the Intercollegiate Peace Fellowship; see chap. 2, note 113; *Minutes,* Intercollegiate Peace Fellowship, Apr. 26, 1952, Dec. 7, 1953, "Results of Planning Conference for Intercollegiate Peace Fellowship, Messiah Bible College, Oct. 17, 1953"; MCC Report Files 2, IX-12–2, "ICPF" folder.

82. GC *Minutes,* 1938, art. 25; *Minutes,* OH-KY JC, 1940, art. 5; 1941, art. 4; Wittlinger, *Quest for Piety,* 401–404.

83. "Statement of George Bundy, Employee of the Hoyt Laundry, May 22, 1951," in possession of George E. Bundy.

84. GC *Minutes,* 1940, art. 13; Hershberger to Boyer, Aug. 21, 1945; Boyer to Hershberger, Aug. 30, 1945, Mennonite General Conference Committee Collection, Committee on Economic and Social Relations, I-3–7, "C. W. Boyer, 1940–1946" folder [hereafter CESR], AMC.

85. C. W. Boyer, secretary of Industrial Relations Committee [hereafter IRC], once wished that nonresistant people working on labor issues could set up a national board similar to the National Service Board for Conscientious Objectors. See Boyer to Hershberger, June 23, 1941, CESR, AMC.

86. The IRC was the name used from 1941 through 1952. Earlier the committee was called the Labor Problems Committee, and later the Committee on Social and Economic Relations. See GC *Minutes* for those years. Guy F. Hershberger, *War, Peace, and Nonresistance,* rev. ed. (Scottdale, Penn.: Herald Press, 1953), chap. 13. For a discussion of Hershberger's work on labor issues, see Toews, *Mennonites,* 102–104.

87. GC *Minutes,* 1939–54, official directories; *Minutes,* OH-KY JC, Mar. 14–16, 1940, art. 5.

88. Ulery to Miller, May 15, 1940, Orville B. Ulery Papers, 38–1.1, "MCC CPS Correspondence" folder; *Minutes,* OH-KY JC, Mar. 14–16, 1940, art. 5; Sider, *Nine Portraits,* 332.

89. Hershberger to Boyer, Aug. 21, 1945; Feb. 26, 1947; Boyer to Hershberger, Dec. 3, 1950, CESR, AMC.

90. GC *Minutes,* 1939, art. 12; 1940, art. 13; 1941, art. 17; 1942, art. 15; 1943, art. 14; 1946, art. 16; 1950, art. 19; 1951, art. 24; 1952, art. 24; 1953, art. 24; *Minutes,* OH-KY JC, Mar. 12–14, 1942, art. 5; Mar. 11–13, 1943, art. 6; Boyer to Hershberger, Feb. 17, 1941; Miller to Boyer

and Stauffer, n.d.; Boyer to Hershberger, Mar. 3, 1941; Hershberger to Boyer, May 6, 1941; Boyer to IRC, n.d.; Boyer to Hershberger, June 23, 30, 1941; Sept. 23, 1941; Nov. 9, 1941; Jan. 25, 1941; Boyer to J. Hostetter, Feb. 18, 1942; Mar. 2, 1942; Boyer to Hershberger, June 1, 1942; Jan. 8, 1943; Hershberger to Boyer, Aug. 21, 1945; Hershberger to Boyer, Jan. 5, 1946; Feb. 9, 1946; Boyer to Hershberger, Feb. 10, 1946; Hershberger to Boyer, Feb. 14, 1946; Apr. 6, 1946; Boyer to Hershberger, July 6, 1946; Hershberger to Boyer, Aug. 1, 1946; Boyer to Hershberger, May 12, 1947; Hershberger to Boyer, May 10, 1949; Boyer to Hershberger, Sept. 5, 1950; Boyer to Green, May 1, 1951; Boyer to Hershberger, May 17, 1951; Hershberger to Boyer, June 26, 1951, CESR, AMC.

91. GC *Minutes,* 1946, art. 16; Boyer to Hershberger, Feb. 26, 1947; May 1, 1951, CESR, AMC.

92. Boyer to Hershberger, Feb. 17, 1941; Mar. 3, 1941; June 23, 30, 1941; Sept. 23, 1941; Jan. 25, 1942; Mar. 1, 1942; June 1, 1942; Dec. 12, 1945. Hershberger to Boyer, May 6, 1941; Feb. 23, 1942; Jan. 5, 1946; Sept. 26, 1946. Boyer to J. Hostetter, Feb. 18, 1942; Mar. 2, 1942. Boyer to Horst, Jan. 11, 1946; Boyer to Byers, Jan. 11, 1946; Musser to Boyer, Feb. 5, 1946; Boyer to Lutz, Sept. 1, 1946; Shearer to Boyer, Dec. 30, 1946; Boyer to Shearer, Jan. 19, 1947; Boyer to Lutz, n.d.; Boyer to Hershberger, May 10, 1953; Mar. 28, 1954, CESR, AMC; OH-KY JC, Mar. 11–13, 1943. The community in Ontario also set up a committee to deal with labor union issues and recorded a number of cases; *Minutes,* ON JC, Aug. 31–Sept. 2, 1946, art. 4; Aug. 30, 1947, art. 3; Sept. 4, 1948, art. 2; Sept. 2–4, 1950, art. 1; Sept. 1, 1951, art. 2. Pennsylvania's Dauphin-Lebanon DC set up a Labor Union Action Committee. See *Minutes,* Feb. 22, 1946, art. 16; Sept. 2, 1946, art. 14.

93. Boyer to Hershberger, Apr. 13, 1946, CESR, AMC. A biographical sketch of O. B. Ulery also describes a cordial relationship with labor leaders. See Sider, *Nine Portraits,* 332.

94. Hershberger to Boyer, Feb. 9, 1946, CESR, AMC.

95. Hershberger was most pleased in negotiations with ILGWU when the charitable organization agreed on the National Mental Health Foundation, which had emerged from CPS work in state mental hospitals. See Hershberger to Boyer, July 2, 1946, CESR, AMC. George Bundy's membership record book with the Teamsters in 1951, however, shows only an initial payment and then a withdrawal in good standing. Official dues book of International Brotherhood of Teamsters, Chauffeurs, Warehousemen and Helpers of A.F.L., and honorable withdrawal card, in Bundy's possession.

96. Ulery to Boyer, Mar. 19, 1941; Boyer to Hershberger, May 10, 1953, CESR, AMC.

97. GC *Minutes,* 1943, art. 14; 1944, art. 15; 1945, art. 13.

98. Paul Carlson, Mae Pyke Knepper, Mary Olive Lady, Benjamin W. Myers, Lloyd S. Myers, Leone Dearing Sider, questionnaires. On children during World War II, see William M. Tuttle Jr., *"Daddy's Gone to War": The Second World War in the Lives of American Children* (New York: Oxford Univ. Press, 1993). Tuttle weaves retrospective accounts of childhood in World War II with theories of child development. He notes the intensity of children's fears for their own lives during the war, since they had not yet developed concepts that would enable them to understand the distance of the war from their homes. See chap. 1.

99. Gerald N. Wingert, questionnaire. Paul S. Boyer also remembers listening to Lowell Thomas's war news reports. One item described American soldiers in the Pacific stringing wire that decapitated Japanese soldiers, "causing them 'to join ancestors rather abruptly.'" It made Boyer laugh, which brought a reprimand from his father. See his questionnaire. Wingert to author, June 17, 1996.

100. Luke L. Keefer Jr., *MSMS*, 301; Paul S. Boyer, questionnaire; Tuttle, *Daddy's Gone to War*, chap. 8. Several oral informants in Terkel's *"The Good War"* describe the excitement of the war to children. See the section "Growing Up: Here and There," 221–50.

101. Lester Fretz, interview by author; E. Morris Sider, questionnaire, and interview by author.

102. Ibid.

103. Esther Tyson Boyer, Paul Carlson, Mildred Charles, questionnaires.

104. Barbara C. Smucker, "Are We Preparing for World War III?" from *The Mennonite, EV*, May 8, 1944, 2, 15; Wendell E. Harmon, "Disarming Our Children," *SSH*, July 21, 1946, 4.

105. Walter Winger, interview by author. Perry Bush includes schoolchildren as targets of hostility toward conscientious objectors. See his *Two Kingdoms*, 92. Mennonites' concerns about the influence of public schools led many to establish new church-run elementary and secondary schools in the 1940s. Donald B. Kraybill, *Passing the Faith: The Story of a Mennonite School* (Intercourse, Penn.: Good Books, 1991), 5–7; 22–92; Toews, 191–94.

106. Tuttle includes a chapter on experiences of minority children during the war, including the experiences of children from conscientious-objector homes. A number of them were singled out in classrooms for having refused to participate in war drives. These children not only dealt with unfriendly teachers and peers but also struggled with internal moral dilemmas about evil and enemies. See *Daddy's Gone to War*, 237, 250–52.

107. Unsigned questionnaire; Myron Mann, J. Norman Hostetter, questionnaires; Tuttle, *Daddy's Gone to War*, 183 (Paul S. Boyer experience); Lester Fretz, interview by author; Benjamin W. Myers, questionnaire. The community provided not only civilian bonds but also small-denomination stamps to be used in Sunday schools and youth programs. *Minutes*, PRS, June 1941, GC, PRS, I-21–1.1, BICA.

108. Gerald N. Wingert to author, June 6, 1996, and June 17, 1996, and Aug. 10, 1996.

109. Paul S. Boyer, questionnaire.

110. James Payne, "In the School," *Minutes*, OH-KY JC, Mar. 11–13, 1943, 47.

111. Wittlinger, *Quest for Piety*, 207–13, chaps. 13, 17.

112. Ibid.

113. Typed responses, Henry N. Hostetter Papers, Correspondence, 13–2.1, "Indoctrination" folder.

114. Hostetter to Dohner, Oct. 27, 1936; Dohner to board members, n.d., Henry N. Hostetter Papers, Correspondence, 13–2.1, "To 1937" and "BYPW, 1942–44" folders.

115. Maurine Speer, "The Kansas Youth Conference," *SSH*, Oct. 18, 1942, 7–8; Leroy Mann, "Sketches from M.B.C. Young People's Conference," *SSH*, Sept. 12, 1943, 7; "Byler Is Speaker at Relief Program," *Clarion*, Dec. 3, 1945, 1; Mildred Kniesly, "Ohio Society Holds Annual Conference," *SSH*, Mar. 7, 1948, 7; Hostetter to committee members, Jan. 19, 1943, Henry N. Hostetter Papers, Correspondence, 13–2.1, "BYPW, 1942–44" folder.

116. Hostetter to Boyer, July 25, 1935, Henry N. Hostetter Papers, Correspondence, 13–2.1, "Young People's Program, 1935–1937" folder.

117. *Flash*, 1940–41, Messiah College, Student Affairs, Misc., IXS-6–14.1, BICA. *Scoop* was announced in the *Clarion*, Mar. 11, 1948, 1.

118. Henry N. Hostetter, "Message for Young People's Societies," *SSH*, Feb. 1, 1942, 7. For similar injunctions, see Hostetter to Harley, Dec. 2, 1936, Henry N. Hostetter Pa-

pers, Correspondence, 13–2.1, "To 1937" folder; Kuhns, "Youth Must Be *Strong,*" *Clarion,* Feb. 1943, 1, 10; Orie O. Miller, "Young People and Tomorrow," *ssh,* Apr. 11, 1943, 7.

119. "Achieving Success" (first half, 1944), BYPW, VIII-2–2.1, BICA.

120. Pawelski, "A Stabilizing Influence," 294; Ray M. Zercher, "It Seems to Me: The Brethren in Christ Experience," *BICHL* 16 (Dec. 1993): 283.

121. Ray M. Zercher, "Keeper of the Charge: M. G. Engle," *BICHL* 9 (Aug. 1986): 101–104.

122. Paul Fussell's cultural study of World War II notes the interrelationship between homogenization in the military, the economy, and mass media. "Uniform and anonymous, undifferentiated in essentials whether Marine replacements or aerial gunners, these boys turned by training into quasi-mechanical interchangeable parts reflect the success of human mass-production between the two world wars . . . assisted by the rapid rise of 'media culture,' with its power to impose national uniformities." See *Wartime,* 66. Also see Blum, *V Was for Victory,* chap. 4; Polenberg, "The Good War?" 297–99.

123. Lela Swalm Hostetler, interview by author.

124. *Minutes,* PRS, June 2, 1943, art. 12; PRS news, *EV,* July 5, 1943, 2; Jesse W. Hoover, "Christian Education," *EV,* July 5, 1943, 3; Hoover to Stoltzfus, Aug. 17, 1943, MCC Correspondence, IX-6–3, "Jesse W. Hoover, 1943" folder: Jesse W. Hoover, "The High School Victory Corps," *EV,* Oct. 11, 1943, 2, 7. The Canadian community raised a similar concern about a home defense course. See "Peace Churches in Canada," *EV,* Nov. 8, 1943, 2.

125. Howard L. Landis, questionnaire.

126. Beulah Heisey, questionnaire.

127. Alice Grace Zercher to author, Aug. 26, 1996. Perry Bush notes the general desire of Mennonites to be seen as good citizens. See *Two Kingdoms,* 13–17.

128. Esther Tyson Boyer, questionnaire.

129. Lois Raser, questionnaire.

130. Beulah Heisey, questionnaire. Others also remember being careful about revealing their nonresistant positions to classmates or coworkers. See Maurine Rosenberry, questionnaire.

131. Earl G. Hensel, questionnaire.

132. Paul Hostetler to author, Dec. 3, 1996.

133. E. Morris Sider, interview by author.

134. Wendell E. Harmon, "Learning by Doing," *ssh,* July 7, 1946, 6.

135. Wendell E. Harmon, "On Christian Vocations," *ssh,* Mar. 24, 1946, 4.

CHAPTER 4: NONRESISTANT MOBILIZATION

1. On the roots of relief work's connections to ideas of citizenship, see Bush, *Two Kingdoms,* chap. 1, esp. 29–31. On Mennonite Central Committee, see John D. Unruh, *In the Name of Christ: A History of Mennonite Central Committee and Its Service, 1920–1951* (Scottdale, Penn.: Herald Press, 1952); Juhnke, *Vision, Doctrine, War,* 243–54; Robert S. Kreider and Rachel Waltner Goossen, *Hungry, Thirsty, a Stranger: The M.C.C. Experience* (Scottdale, Penn.: Herald Press, 1988); Cornelius J. Dyck, ed. *The Mennonite Central Committee Story,* vols. 1–5 (Scottdale, Penn.: Herald Press, 1980–82).

2. Recent works have begun documentation of women's major roles in movements and organizations previously largely described in terms of male leadership. For example, see Julie Roy Jeffry, *The Great Silent Army of Abolitionism: Ordinary Women in the Antislavery Movement* (Chapel Hill: Univ. of North Carolina Press, 1998); Kathryn

Kish Sklar, *Florence Kelley and the Nation's Work: The Rise of Women's Political Culture, 1830–1900* (New Haven: Yale Univ. Press, 1995). On the tensions between the service ethic of Roman Catholic sisters and the hierarchy's desire for low-cost female labor, see Mary J. Oates, "Organizing for Service: Challenges to Community Life and Work Decisions in Catholic Sisterhoods, 1850–1940," in *America's Utopias,* ed. Chmielewski, Kern, and Klee-Hartzell, 150–61. On Mennonite women's sewing circles as auxiliary organizations, see Juhnke, *Vision, Doctrine, War,* 157–58. In the process of detailing women's contributions to peace efforts during World War II, Goossen sometimes compares the invisibility of those efforts to similar problems faced by women in military settings. See her *Women against the Good War,* 2, 45–47.

3. Sibley and Jacob, *Conscription of Conscience,* 326–30; Gingerich, *Service for Peace,* app. 21; Toews, *Mennonites,* 240–41. Canadian districts did raise funds for dependents of men in ASW. *Minutes,* ON JC, Sept. 2–4, 1944, art. 3.

4. Brubaker, "Non-Resistance Is Not Too Expensive," 2.

5. This committee had several different names; to avoid confusion I will use one name throughout. The PRS Committee was also called the Non-Resistance Committee (1939), the Peace Committee (1940), the Relief and Service Committee (1941–46), and the PRS Committee (1947–66).

6. GC *Minutes,* 1940, art. 17; 1941, art. 15.

7. GC *Minutes,* 1944, art. [14]; 1945, art. 12.

8. Pennsylvania districts, presided over by C. N. Hostetter Jr. and Henry N. Hostetter, had set up a system to raise CPS funds earlier that year. See *Minutes,* Manor-Pequea DC, Feb. 4, 1941, art. 16; *Minutes,* Cumberland DC, Feb. 11, 1941, art. 29. Also see *Minutes,* MI DC, Nov. 8, 1941, art. 11.

9. *Minutes,* Rapho DC, Apr. 1, 1943, art. 9

10. *Minutes,* Grantham DC, Feb. 5, 1944, art. 12; Sept. 18, 1944, art. 16; Jan. 28, 1946, art. 11. *Minutes,* Donegal DC, Aug. 3, 1944, art. 5. *Minutes,* MI DC, Oct. 19, 1944.

11. *Minutes,* Dauphin and Lebanon DC, Feb. 22, 1944, art. 2.

12. PRS News, *EV,* Jan. 14, 1946, 2; "Special Notice," *EV,* Mar. 25, 1946, 2; Hostetter to members of Grantham district, Nov. 9, 1945, in *Minutes,* Grantham DC folder; Bush, *Two Kingdoms,* 161; Duis, "No Time for Privacy," 20, 28–34.

13. Rempel to Hostetter, Jan. 21, 1946, Hostetter Papers, CPS, 1944–47, 7–5.1.

14. Swalm, *Beloved Brethren,* 90–91.

15. Anna Lane Hostetter, diary, Jan. 1, 5, 6, 11, 12, 15, 17, 26; Feb. 8, 9, 10, 14; Mar. 12, 13, 21, 22; May 2, 8, 1945, 79–1.1, BICA. Her March 13 entry recorded her helping a man fill out the conscription questionnaire establishing his conscientious objection. Administrative correspondence also documents her work. For example, see Hostetter to Lichti, Jan. 23, 1946, Hostetter Papers, CPS, 1944–47, 7–5.1.

16. PRS News, *EV,* Jan. 19, 1942, 22; "Tour of CPS Camps," *Echo,* Nov. 1943, 7; H. Hostetter to board members, June 26, 1944, Henry N. Hostetter Papers, Correspondence, 13–2.1, "Correspondence, 1942–44" folder; *Minutes,* OH-KY JC, Mar. 8–10, 1945, art. 2; "After C.P.S.—What?" BC *Bulletin,* Dec. 1945, 3–4; Anna Lane Hostetter, diary, Feb. 19, 1945, 79–1.1, BICA; Grace Herr Holland, Naomi Light, Mary Ellen Engle Thuma, questionnaires; Book, "Pursuit of Great Spoil," 125–26; H. Hostetter, "Pastoral Visitation," in *Nonresistance under Test,* comp. Swalm, 159–62.

17. *Clarion,* Apr. 1944, 9; "Quartet Tours C.P.S. Camps," *Clarion,* Oct. 6, 1944, 2; "Quartet Visits C.P.S. Camp," *Echo,* Apr. 1945, 6; Esther G. Book Ulery, questionnaire.

18. Grace Herr Holland, questionnaire; Sider, "Life and Labor ASW," 58.

19. Simon Bohen, "News Notes from Palmyra, Penn." *EV*, Mar. 1, 1943, 8–9; *Minutes*, OH-KY JC, Mar. 8–10, 1945, art. 16.

20. *Minutes*, Grantham DC, Feb. 5, 1944, arts. 9, 11–12, 14; Feb. 5, 1945, arts. 9, 14; Jan. 28, 1946, art. 10; *Minutes*, Manor-Pequea DC, May 13, 1943, art. 4; Feb. 2, 1945, art. 21; *Minutes*, Kans. SC, Apr. 6, 1944, art. 7; *Minutes*, Donegal DC, Jan. 3–4, 1945, art. 10; "'Donegal Tidings' Continues," *SSH*, Jan. 26, 1947, 7. MCC sent out suggestions for items men should bring to CPS camp, starring items that sewing circles might provide. "What to Bring to Camp," Hostetter Papers, CPS, 7–5.2, "CPS Camp Instructions" folder.

21. Vera Clouse Beachy, "To Our Young People," *EV*, Mar. 1, 1943, 12–13.

22. Evelyn Brumbaugh Engle, Esther G. Book Ulery, questionnaires; Lester Fretz, interview by author; Anna Lane Hostetter, diary, Feb. 3, 1945, 79–1.1, BICA.

23. Mildred Charles, audiotaped response to questionnaire.

24. David D. Schrag, "A Camper's View of the Canning and Drying Project," *EV*, Aug. 14, 1944, 2, 8–9.

25. Sider, *Messenger of Grace*, 67–68, and *Messiah College*, 73–74, 171–72. The *Clarion* remarked upon food contributions throughout the 1940s. See *Clarion*, Nov. 1941, 13. A photo of women from Franklin County preparing fruit for school appeared in the *Clarion*, Nov. 1942, 5. For production of food for GC, see *Minutes*, Rapho DC, Mar. 28, 1946, art. 11.

26. *Minutes*, Donegal DC, Feb. 13–14, 1946, art. 16.

27. *Minutes*, Cumberland DC, Aug. 3, 1943, art. 1; *Minutes*, Manor-Pequea DC, Feb. 6, 1945, art. 4. District councils regularly reported amounts and varieties of food contributions.

28. "Home Canning and Drying Project," and William T. Snyder, "Preliminary Report of the Canning and Drying Project," *Women's Activities Letter* [hereafter *WAL*], Dec. 1943, 1–2; William T. Snyder, "Canning and Drying Program Successfully Closing," *WAL*, Dec. 1944, 3, MCC Collection, Periodicals, IX-40–2. By May 1943, Jesse W. Hoover was corresponding with MCC officials about BIC participation in the food production program for CPS. In early 1944, he made certain that community women in Pennsylvania, Indiana, Kansas, and California would receive the *WAL*. See Snyder to Hoover, May 13, 1943; Horst to Hoover, Dec. 11, 1943; Hoover to Horst, Jan. 5, 1944; Hilty to Hoover, Nov. 30, 1944; Hoover to Henard, Feb. 25, 1947; MCC Correspondence, IX-6–3, "Jesse W. Hoover, 1943, 1944, 1947" folders. "PRS News" warned that without food production, CPS men might go hungry the next winter. See *EV*, June 21, 1943, 9.

29. "Food for Relief," *WAL*, May 1945, 2–3, MCC Collection, Periodicals, IX-40–2.

30. "PRS News," *EV*, June 4, 1945, 2; July 16, 1945, 2.

31. "Starvation in Germany," *EV*, June 3, 1946, 2; *Minutes*, Rapho DC, Jan. 1, 1946, arts. 16–17, 21.

32. *Minutes*, Manor-Pequea DC, Feb. 5, 1946, arts. 8–9; *Minutes*, Cumberland DC, Aug. 6, 1946, art. 4.

33. *Minutes*, Cumberland DC, Feb. 12, 1946, art. 22; "Canadian Groups Support Government Meat Coupon Drive," *EV*, Sept. 23, 1946, 12; *Minutes*, Rapho DC, Jan. 1, 1947, art. 22; Jan. 1, 1948, art. 16; *Minutes*, Manor-Pequea DC, Feb. 3, 1948, art. 14.

34. Scrapbook, photo and caption, "'Snitzing' Apples for Europe's Hungry Peoples," clipping, Oct. 1947 (handwritten), Irene Frey Hensel, 79–1.2, BICA.

35. Hoffman to Hoover, Jan. 5, 1946; Hostetter to Hoover, Jan. 5, 1946, Hostetter to "Brother," May 13, 1946, Hoffman to Hostetter, Jan. 18, 1947; "Promoting His Peace through Relief and Service," Jan. 1946, 2, Hostetter Papers, CPS, 1944–47, 7–5.1.

36. Marjorie H. Haines, "'In the Name of Christ,'" *EV*, Feb. 1, 1954, 12. These citations represent only a sampling of the many GC, state or provincial, and district minutes, as well as pieces in the *EV*, that note the emphasis on food production and processing. Also see Verna Mae Winger Heise, interview by author.

37. Community farmers from Kansas also contributed wheat through the Brethren Service Committee Wheat Donation Campaign. See "Is Your Congregation Doing Plus Giving for War Sufferers Relief?" *EV*, Mar. 25, 1946, 2. Jesse W. Hoover corresponded with MCC about a special contribution of dry beans from community farmers in Michigan; Hoover to Snyder, n.d., MCC Correspondence, IX-6–3, "Jesse W. Hoover, 1943" folder.

38. The ON community noted sewing circle production of clothing for the Nonresistance Committee in 1939. See *Minutes*, ON JC, Dec. 12, 1939, art. 6. "PRS News" in the *EV* began noting sewing contributions for relief in financial statements in July 14, 1941, 2. At the beginning of 1942, Jesse W. Hoover reported that the BIC had contributed 1,774 pounds of clothing in "Clothing! More Clothing!" *EV*, Feb. 2, 1942, 10. In 1946, PRS encouraged community members to contribute clothing through MCC rather than through a national "victory clothing collection." See "PRS News," *EV*, Jan. 14, 1946, 2. At the end of the period, calls for relief clothing for war torn Korea appeared. See Harold Yoder, "Korean Relief News," *SSH*, Aug. 8, 1954, 5. Some sewing circles had earlier supplied equipment kits for CPS men. See *Minutes*, Manor-Pequea DC, Feb. 2, 1945, art. 21.

39. Mary Olive Lady, interview.

40. Lela Swalm Hostetler, interview. Also see Rowena Winger Heise, Robert Worman, questionnaires; E. Morris Sider, Verna Mae Winger Heise, interviews by author. Irene Frey Hensel's diary also notes substantial time spent on sewing for relief. See entries for Nov. 14, 20, Dec. 10, 1941; Feb. 13, 4, Mar. 7, 1942, Irene Frey Hensel, 79–1.1, BICA.

41. *Minutes*, South Dickinson DC, Feb. 17, 1954, art. 7; *Minutes*, Ind. SC, Mar. 9, 1951, art. 1.

42. The following are a sampling from across the continent. *Minutes*, Grantham DC, Mar. 3, 1941, art. 10; Feb. 7, 1942, art. 10; *Minutes*, ON JC, Sept. 8–9, 1943, art. 3; Sept. 1–3, 1945, art. 3; Oct. 11, 1952, art. 3; *Minutes*, Chino congregation, Feb. 5, 1947, art. 14; Feb. 4, 1948, art. 10; *Minutes*, Rapho DC, Mar. 30, 1944, art. 5; *Minutes*, IA-SD SC, Mar. 10, 1945, Dallas Center Pastoral Report; Mar. 9, 1946, Dallas Center Pastoral Report; "PRS News," treasurer's report, *EV*, Apr. 9, 1945, 8; "News of Church Activity," Cedar Grove, Penn., *EV*, Feb. 25, 1946, 9; *Minutes*, OH-KY SC, Mar. 19–21, 1947, art. 21; Mar. 17–19, 1948, General Report of Joint Mission Board; *Minutes*, Dauphin-Lebanon DC, Feb. 7, 1948, art. 3; *Minutes*, South Dickinson DC, Mar. 16, 1948, arts. 4–5; Feb. 17, 1949, art. 5; *Minutes*, OK SC, Mar. 4, 1949, art. 23; Mar. 3, 1950, art. 22; *Minutes*, Upland congregation, California, Sept. 14, 1954, art. 8. Jesse W. Hoover's correspondence with MCC noted relief clothing contributed by Michigan sewing circles; Hoover to Snyder, n.d., MCC Correspondence, IX-6–3, "Jesse W. Hoover, 1943" folder. Total contributions by denomination, including the BIC appeared in the *WAL*. For samples, see *WAL*, Jan. 1944, 3; Aug. 1944, 4; Oct. 1944, 4; Dec. 1944, Jan. 2–3, 1946, 2–3, MCC Collection, Periodicals, IX-40–2.

43. *Minutes*, Rapho DC, Mar. 30, 1944, art. 5. The members of the committee are handwritten between the typed lines of the minutes.

44. *Minutes*, Rapho DC, Aug. 3, 1944, art. 3.

45. The program for the 1946 state council meeting listed the sewing issue, but the minutes from that year and following years do not. Handwritten notes in a 1945 program indicate that the report and recommendations were tabled; the section claiming equality for sewing with "any other phase of church work" is lined out. Perhaps del-

egates to the state council, probably all male, took issue with that statement. *Minutes,* Rapho DC, Jan. 1, 1945, art. 5; program, Penn. SC, 1945, "Rapho District to Penn. State Council," 8–9; *Minutes,* Penn. SC, 1945, art. 11; Program, Penn. SC, 1946, "Regarding Sewing Circles and Bible Conferences: Carried Over from Council 1945," 9–10.

46. Anna Lane Hostetter's diary, however, offers a very different explanation. She recorded that the "Sewing Circle question" had been discussed. "The men were sending it right through," until Hostetter spoke. "It was not easy. Very, very nervous before I arose!" She argued that a small group like the Brethren in Christ should focus on the desperate need in war areas. Quoting statistics on people in need of clothing in liberated Europe and comparing the Pennsylvania community's "1,600 sisters" to the Mennonites' 11,000 members in Lancaster County alone, Hostetter apparently made her point. "Many were glad I spoke." One woman's growing awareness of suffering in the larger world and sense of what her small group could realistically accomplish may have defeated the attempts by other members to gain more recognition for women's contributions to community life. See entry for Apr. 5, 1945. Hostetter's diary has many entries related to relief efforts, Jan. 1, 24, 25; Feb. 8, 11, 12; Mar. 14, 21, 27; Aug. 10, 1945, Anna Lane Hostetter, 79–1.1, BICA. Jesse W. Hoover instructed MCC workers to send brochures on relief clothing to Anna Hostetter. See Hoover to Stoltzfus, June 8, 1943, MCC Correspondence, IX-6–3, "Jesse W. Hoover, 1943" folder.

47. Hoover to Wittlinger May 2, 1976, Wittlinger Papers, Quest 1, 35–1.22, "Peace and Service, 1910–50" folder. See Nelson Hostetter's comments on volunteers in chap. 6. Nancy Heisey notes forty BIC people serving on MCC in the 1950s. See "BIC Participation," 201. Also see Ray M. Zercher and Wendell R. Zercher, "Brethren in Christ in MCC Service," *BICHL* 28 (Aug. 1995): 274–75. See app. 6 for participants, many of whom served in years before record keeping was standardized or served in short-term, informal appointments.

48. *GC Minutes,* 1947, art. 16.

49. The text of Dohner's talk appeared in minutes that, as was typical, also reflected this region's strong emphasis on nonresistant activities. The joint council minutes are filled with descriptions of various aspects of mobilization: CPS participants; sewing and canning for that program and for relief; two local men on relief cattle boats; and two members, David and Ruth Hoover, who had just left for three years as relief volunteers in the Philippines. See *Minutes,* OH-KY JC, Mar. 19–21, 1947, arts. 4, 21; Leah Dohner, "Dangers That Threaten the Church," 58–59. Furthermore, Dohner herself had written two articles six years earlier that had encouraged adults and children to contribute to relief efforts in France but had cautioned them not to lower their donations to missions. See Dortha E. Dohner, "Her First Smile: A Story of Relief Work in France," *SSH,* Oct. 19, 1941, 7, and "'Lost, An Orphan': A Story of Relief Work in France," *SSH,* Nov. 2, 1941, 7.

50. In 1970s statistics, BIC ranked first in per capita giving of twenty-one denominations in Canada and fourth in forty-two denominations in the United States. See Kauffman and Harder, *Anabaptists Four,* 234–35. In contrast, in 1989 rankings of stewardship ("the percentage of net household income given to church and charities"), the BIC ranked lowest of the five groups; Kauffman and Driedger, *Mennonite Mosaic,* 219. Yeatts and Burwell question the validity of the 1989 figures in "Tradition and Mission," 93–94.

51. "An Appeal from the Peace Committee: Wanted God's Man for This Need," *EV,* Sept. 9, 1940, 6.

52. *GC Minutes,* 1940, official directory; *Minutes,* PRS, Oct. 5, 1940; Ulery to Brubaker, Dec. 23, 1940, GC, PRS, I-21–1.1, BICA; "PRS News," *EV,* Nov. 18, 1940, 2; "Alumnus Goes to

Europe as Relief Worker," BC *Bulletin,* Dec. 1940, 1; "Rev. Burkholder Asks Release from Relief Post," *Echo,* Jan. 1941, 5; "Appeal from Peace Committee," *EV,* Jan. 13, 1941, 2; "Hoover Sails for France," *EV,* Mar. 10, 1941, 6; "PRS News," *EV,* Dec. 22, 1941, 2. On the 1941 start of Mennonite food programs for children in France, see Bush, *Two Kingdoms,* 288–91.

53. Byer to Brubaker, n.d.; Rosenberger to Swalm, June 16, 1940; Swalm to Brubaker, June 20, 1940; Feather to Brubaker, Nov. 19, 1940; Oldham to Brubaker, Dec. 4, 1940, GC, PRS, I-21–1.1, BICA.

54. Miriam Nolt, "War—Suffering—Why?" *Clarion,* Mar. 1942, 15; Clara E. Stoner, "Copy of a Letter Sent to the Officers of the Peace Committee," *EV,* Oct. 7, 1940, 2.

55. See app. 6.

56. Stoner, "Letter to Peace Committee," 2.

57. Goossen, *Women against the Good War,* chap. 5, esp. 107–11.

58. "1944 Women's Service Units," MCC Report Files 1, IX-12–1, "Voluntary Service Personnel" folder.

59. Heisey, "They Also Served," 233–44.

60. Unsigned to Hostetter, n.d., Hostetter Papers, Correspondence, Family, 7–22.8.

61. Kreider to Heisey, May 2, 1945, unsigned evaluations, "Evaluation of the Women's Summer Service Unit Which Served at Ypsilanti State Hospital," MCC Report Files 1, IX-12–1, Women's Service Unit, "Ypsilanti: Questionnaires" and "Ypsilanti: Applications and Evaluations" folders.

62. Goossen, *Women against the Good War,* 111; Heisey, "They Also Served," 228–63; Jeanette Frey Dourte, diary, 1943, in possession of its author; Gerald N. Wingert, diary, 1947–48, in possession of its author, and questionnaire.

63. "Howard State Hospital: Summer Service Unit: June 4, to Aug. 14, 1946," MCC Report Files 1, IX-12–1, "Voluntary Service Personnel" folder; Clara Meyer Eberly, questionnaire.

64. Harold S. Martin, "Witnessing in the South," in *They Also Serve,* ed. Harmon, 40–41. In 1949, two other BIC men, Irvin Musser and Glenn Hostetter, were also doing voluntary service in Gulfport. See "List of Voluntary Service Workers Serving One Year Terms," Sept. 21, 1949, MCC Report Files 1, IX-12–1, "Voluntary Service Personnel" folder.

65. Harmon, *They Also Serve,* 56.

66. Harold and Ruth Davis, attachment to letter, Ruth Davis to Wittlinger, Mar. 1976, Wittlinger Papers, Quest 1, 35–1.22, "Peace, 1910–50" folder; Harold K. Davis, Ruth Brubaker Davis, questionnaires.

67. Ruth E. Pye, "The Challenge of a Children's Camp" *EV,* Feb. 6, 1950, 14; "Summer Service Personnel," June 14, 1949, MCC Report Files 1, IX-12–1, "Voluntary Service Personnel" folder.

68. Esther G. Book, "In a Migrant Unit," *SSH,* Oct. 14, 1951, 4.

69. "Two Chosen for European Tour," *Clarion,* Mar. 28, 1947, 1; Sider, *Messenger of Grace,* 165–67.

70. "Members of Student Travel Group," "Council of Mennonite and Affiliated Colleges European Summer Tour—1950: Evaluation and Report," MCC Report Files 1, IX-12–1, "Voluntary Service European Short Term, 1950" folder. In that year the pretour conference was held at Messiah Bible College.

71. Esther Tyson Boyer, questionnaire.

72. John Engle, interview by author.

73. Heisey, "BIC Participation," 196–97.

74. Gwinner to author, June 27, 1998. The delays in Gwinner's (Williams in 1945) case and in others are clear in correspondence between BIC leaders. Hoover to PRS members, n.d.; Hostetter to Hoover, Sept. 7, 1945, Hostetter Papers, CPS, 1944–47, 7–5.1. Byler to Hoover, Oct. 2, 1945; Byler to Hoover, Feb. 26, 1946, MCC Correspondence, IX-6–3, "Jesse W. Hoover, 1944, 1945, 1946" folders. Byler to Hoover, May 9, 1946; Byler to Hoover, June 18, 1946; Hoover to Jost, May 9, 1947, MCC Correspondence, IX-6–3, "Jesse W. Hoover, 1946, 1947" folders.

75. Graber to Hoover, Apr. 13, 1944; Hoover to Graber, Apr. 19, 1944, MCC Correspondence, IX-6–3, "Jesse W. Hoover, 1944" folders.

76. Byler to Hoover, May 9, 1946; Byler to Hoover June 18, 1946; Hoover to Jost, May 9, 1947, MCC Correspondence, IX-6–3, "Jesse W. Hoover, 1946, 1947" folders.

77. GC *Minutes,* 1948, art. 25; 1949, art. 25; "Foreign Mission Board: Preamble and Resolutions to Mission Work in the Philippines," n.d., MCC Correspondence, IX-6–3, "PRS Committee, 1948" folder; "Philippine Unit Closes," *EV,* Jan. 8, 1951, 16; Unruh, *In the Name of Christ,* 100. N. Heisey discusses the unit in the Philippines in "BIC Participation," 186–87.

78. Thelma Book, *MSMS,* 24–25.

79. Miriam Stern, *MSMS,* 457, 459.

80. Dorothy Sherk, interview by author. The contemporary record, however, gave health problems as a reason for her not serving as a relief worker. See GC *Minutes,* 1945, art. 27, 1946, art. 30; *Minutes,* PRS, June 18, 1948, art. 8.

81. "PRS News," *EV,* Jan. 17, 1944, 2.

82. Duane Engle, questionnaire.

83. Lester Fretz, interview by author. This family attitude differed from that of some Mennonite church leaders, who feared the isolation of young men volunteering in this program. Fretz's experiences represent those of a number of other BIC Canadian and American young men who traveled on livestock boats. Byler to Waldo, Feb. 5, 1946; Melvin Gingerich, "Recommendations to the Brethren Service Committee and the Mennonite Central Committee Relating to the Sea-Going Cowboys," Sept. 23, 1946; "Information for Livestock Attendants," n.d., MCC Report Files 1, IX-12–1, "Seagoing Cowboys" folder. Royce Saltzman, "To Poland on a Cattle Boat," *SSH,* Sept. 29, 1946, 7–8; *Clarion,* Mar. 28, 1947, 1; Paul Glick, obituary, *EV,* Apr. 7, 1947, 11; Jesse W. Hoover, "Committal," July 28, 1947, 3–5; John C. Reesor, questionnaire. C. N. Hostetter Jr. noted general interest in the program by young men who had graduated from high school and came from farm backgrounds. See Hostetter to MCC, Mar. 18, 1947, MCC Correspondence, IX-6–3, "C. N. Hostetter, Jr., 1947" folder.

84. Lester C. Fretz, interview by author.

85. John H. Engle, interview by author; Engle to editor, "Lamao Bulletin," June 11, 1998, unpaginated, in possession of author.

CHAPTER 5: CONSCIENTIOUS OBJECTION, CIVILIAN PUBLIC SERVICE, AND COMMUNITY LIFE

1. E. J. Swalm described the untitled poem as one "written during the days of the CPS program." Swalm, "A Free Conscience," 273.

2. Excellent sources exist for the wide variety of personal experiences of the 136 BIC men in Civilian Public Service, as well as the sixteen identified women who had connections to the program. See apps. 4, 5. The chapter also considers briefly Canada's

Alternative Service Work program, in which eighty-five community men served, and the U.S. postwar I-W program for conscientious objectors, in which 164 community men served between 1952 and 1958. See Harmon, *They Also Serve,* 47; GC *Minutes,* 1958, art. 16; and see app. 3, 7. This chapter draws on BIC committee correspondence, surveys done during the war, finances of participants and their families, and retrospective questionnaires and interviews.

3. Civilian Public Service has received substantial historical attention. The focus has been institutional or on civic questions, such as religious freedom and church-state relations. Each of the three Historic Peace Churches shortly after the war wrote accounts of its own institutional participation in the program. Mulford Sibley and Philip Jacob's 1952 study evaluates conscription and all forms of conscientious objection in World War II in the context of civil liberties. The authors conclude that governmental handling of both draft-law violators and CPS participants was a denial of liberty, in that both had punitive elements. Mitchell Robinson's more recent dissertation on Civilian Public Service synthesizes other studies of the program and places this World War II experiment in the large context of ongoing tension in American history between the ideals of liberty and of equality. Individual conscience was violated, he concludes, but as a result of a second imperative in a liberal democracy to share equitably the burden of military defense. A Roman Catholic CPS participant, Gordon Zahn, was even more critical of the program's military oversight and the cooperation of the Historic Peace Churches with the state. Zahn's commitment to religious dissent and nonviolent civil disobedience that challenges unjust social structures demonstrates the broad spectrum represented in the CPS coalition. See Keim, *Bender,* 291–94; Gingerich, vi, chap. 23; Keim and Stoltzfus, *Politics of Conscience,* chap. 2; Robinson, "Civilian Pubic Service," 507–20; Sibley and Jacob, *Conscription of Conscience,* chap. 6, esp. 119–24; chap. 20; 483; Gordon C. Zahn, *War, Conscience, and Dissent* (New York: Hawthorn Books, 1967), 12–17, 165–66, 199–200.

4. Perry Bush describes Mennonites as the "good boys" of CPS. See *Two Kingdoms,* 114, also see chap. 3; Toews, *Mennonites,* 155–56; Keim, *Bender,* 284–85.

5. "C.P.S. Questionnaire," Hostetter Papers, CPS, 7–5.2, "CPS Questionnaire—Penn. State Council, 1945" [hereafter QPASC45] folder, BICA. This questionnaire is a key source for determining sentiments of BIC CPS men. All of the questionnaires are signed, but probably their authors were assured of their confidentiality. Therefore, no names are cited here. Statistics from this source are from the author's analysis.

6. Gaeddert to Hoover, Nov. 24, 1944, MCC Correspondence, IX-6–3, "Jesse W. Hoover, 1944" folder. Reports by Titus M. Books, a BIC pastor providing pastoral care in eastern CPS camps in 1943, describe chronic denominational tensions, most between a multiplicity of Mennonite groups. See MCC Correspondence, IX-6–3, "Titus M. Books, 1943" folder. Also see Gingerich, *Service for Peace,* app. 16.

7. QPASC45.

8. "They Also Serve in Camp," 13; Wendell E. Harmon, "The Constant Witness: Around the Clock and in All Parts of the Country the Testimony for Peace Never Lagged," both in *They Also Serve,* 7.

9. QPASC45.

10. Ibid.

11. "Fall Meeting of the MCC," n.d., handwritten report, GC, PRS, I-21–1.1, "*Minutes,* 1940–47" folder, BICA. This report noted, for example, that getting government approval of detached service units was difficult in an election year.

12. Agricultural deferments and those related to the ministry are noted in the sources listed below. Canada's system for conscientious objectors initially placed conscientious objectors in camps. By 1943, however, most were placed on farms or in factory work; Sider. See "Life and Labor ASW," 597. Some informants conflated this Canadian system with agricultural deferments in the United States. Sources below include both Canadian and U.S. references to agricultural work and ministerial deferments. In 1940, PRS approved a form for certifying students of theology. *Minutes,* PRS, Oct. 1940, GC, PRS, I-21–1.1, "*Minutes,* 1940–47" folder; Hostetter to Miller, June 26, 1942, Hostetter Papers, CPS, 7–5.2, "MCC Correspondence" folder; Yoder to Hostetter, Aug. 11, 1944; Hostetter to Stump, Sept. 12, 1944; Stump to Hostetter, Sept. 6, 1944; Hostetter to Montgomery, Sept. 26, 1944; Hostetter to Local Draft Board, Nov. 8, 1945, Hostetter Papers, Home Mission Correspondence, 1944–46, M–Z, 7–2.15, BICA. *Clarion,* Nov. 1943, 4; Ruth Zook Fadenrecht, Eugene H. Feather, Isaiah B. Harley, Millard Herr, Daniel L. Hoover, Erma Lehman Hoover, Maybelle Kanode, Mary Kuhns, Martha M. Long, John A. Musser, Dorothy Sherk, Leone Dearing Sider, Lewis B. Sider, Orpha Geib Wolgemuth, Abe S. Yoder Jr., Alice Grace Hostetter Zercher, unsigned questionnaires; Kenneth Bert Hoover, audiotaped responses to questionnaire; Isaiah B. Harley, interview by author; George Bundy, *MSMS,* 67, and "Autobiography," typed manuscript in possession of its author; David Climenhaga, *MSMS,* 92–93; Erma Lehman Hoover, *MSMS,* 271; Ira Stern, *MSMS,* 458; H. Frank Kipe, "Franklin County Church Leaders," *BICHL* 18 (Dec. 1995): 451.

13. "Please Read," *EV,* Mar. 10, 1941, 2.

14. Jesse W. Hoover, "Quill Quirks," *EV,* May 21, 1944, 4.

15. GC *Minutes,* 1944, art. [14]. A PRS announcement early the next year reported that contributions from deferred draftees would be put into a special fund for postwar benefits for CPS men; PRS News, *EV,* Jan. 29, 1945, 2. Later that year, PRS set up a committee of five, at least some of the members deferred draftees, to promote additional contributions from men receiving deferments. See *Minutes,* PRS, Nov. 2, 1945, Hostetter Papers, CPS, 1944–47, 7–.51. In 1946, the Kansas SC advocated a similar push in its jurisdiction; *Minutes,* Kans. SC, Apr. 4, 1946, art. 9.

16. Hostetler to author, Dec. 3, 1996; Hostetler, questionnaire.

17. Ray M. Zercher, Abe Yoder Jr., questionnaires.

18. Esther Tyson Boyer, Irene Wagaman Engle, Grace Holland Herr, Alice Grace Hostetter Zercher, unsigned questionnaires; Glenn C. Frey, *MSMS,* 151.

19. QPASC45.

20. Many articles in BIC periodicals condemned noncombatant service, although the degree of condemnation differed. However, one piece, written by BIC leader Henry G. Brubaker before the United States entered the war, noted two avenues for conscientious objectors: noncombatant and civilian. Brubaker's statements foreshadowed the confusion and conflicts that would trouble the BIC community throughout the war and into the 1950s; Henry G. Brubaker, "Peace Convention," *EV,* Oct. 21, 1940, 2; Wesley P. Martin, "Non-Resistance in Theory and Practice," *Clarion,* Mar. 1940, 2. Articles in the *EV* and *SSH,* many written or chosen by Wendell E. Harmon or Jesse W. Hoover, saw problems with the noncombatant position. Harmon, who had been participating in the California church, however, often sounded a conciliatory note. See PRS News, *EV,* Apr. 13, 1942, 2; "Can We Follow Christ in a Total War?" from *Peace Sentinel, EV,* Feb. 1, 1943, 2, 11; Wendell E. Harmon, "Our Church—Its Crisis and Its Youth," *EV,* Sept. 13, 1943, 4–5, and "The Post-War Conscience," *EV,* Jan. 3, 1944, 11, 16; "An Open Letter to

C.P.S.: A Former Camper Now in Medical Training," *ssh*, Apr. 16, 1944, 4; Jesse W. Hoover, "Quill Quirks," and "From the Pastor's Mail Bag," *ssh*, June 18, 1944, 4; "What Is Lost," *ssh*, Aug. 13, 1944, 4; R. A. Franklin, "After the War—What Will Our Church Do?" *ev*, Aug. 28, 1944, 16; "A Christian Conscience About War," selected; "Why 1 A-O Is Not for Me," selected, *ssh*, July 1, 1945, 4; "A Testimony from an Ex-C.P.S. Man," from *The Methodist C.O.*, *ssh*, Mar. 31, 1946, 4; "prs News," *ev*, Oct. 16, 1950, 16. A postwar peace conference included the topic, "What about Non-Combatant Service?" addressed by C. N. Hostetter Jr.; "Program of the Brethren in Christ Church Peace Conference," July 3–5, 1953, Hostetter Papers, Lectures, 7–17.5, "Non-Resistance" folder.

21. *Minutes,* Pacific Coast JC, 1943, art. 11; *Minutes,* Chino DC, Feb. 2, 1944, art, 6; "Alvin Burkholder," Feb. 14, 1974, Wittlinger Papers, Quest 1, 35–1.22, "Peace and Service, 1910–50" folder; Arthur M. Climenhaga, questionnaire, and interview by author; Martha Lady and Mary Olive Lady, interview by author; Book, "Pursuit of Great Spoil," 110; Isaac, "P. B. and Edna Friesen," 23–25.

22. *Minutes,* Kans. SC, Apr. 6, 1944, art. 6; A. James Alderfer, Naomi Rettew Hilsher Engle, Mildred M. Hess, J. Norman Hostetter, questionnaires; Curtis O. Byer to author, July 3, 1996; Book, "Pursuit of Great Spoil," 124–25; *Echo,* Mar. 1942, 5; *Clarion,* Dec. 1943, 6; Joe Smith, *msms,* 448; Mary Olive Lady, interview by author; [Hostetter] to Hoover, Apr. 15, 1944, Henry N. Hostetter Papers, Correspondence, 13–2.1, "bypw, 1942–44" folder; Notes from Ira Eyster interview by Carlton Wittlinger, Wittlinger Papers, Quest 1, 35–1.22, "Peace and Service, 1910–50" folder.

23. Arthur M. Climenhaga, questionnaire, and interview by author. Climenhaga's views parallel other community members in California. Frances L. Harmon, *For Christ and the Church: A Biography of Alvin C. Burkholder* (Grantham, Penn.: Brethren in Christ Historical Society, 1995), 49–52; "Alvin Burkholder," Feb. 14, 1974, Wittlinger Papers, Quest 1, 35–1.22, "Peace and Service, 1910–50" folder. In Eldon F. Bert's autobiography, he does not describe the incidents Climenhaga does. Bert indicates that because of their conscientious objection, neither he nor his brother Dwight was required to carry a rifle. Bert also notes, "The Army advanced my rank rapidly" from a private to a technical staff sergeant. See *Walk Memory's Lane* (Harrisburg, Penn.: Triangle Press, 1992), 50–56.

24. Sources include student and alumni news in the *Clarion* and the *Echo;* obituaries in the *ev; dc* minutes; the Hostetter papers, and retrospective accounts. See especially "Addresses of Boys in Service from M.B.C.," May 25, 1944, Hostetter Papers, cps, 7–5.2, "Addresses—Boys in cps & Military Service" folder. This list includes fifty-seven men in military service and thirty-eight in cps. A 2001 obituary records official bic member from Upland, California, Viola Burkholder Jensen Raser's enlistment in the U.S. Army as a nurse in 1942. She served "with distinction until the war's end in 1945, assigned to the 22nd General Hospital in England during most of that time." See *ev*, Nov./Dec. 2001, 27.

25. *Clarion,* May 1941, 13.

26. "Former Student Speaks," *Clarion,* Mar. 16, 1945, 1.

27. Unsigned questionnaire.

28. Lester Fretz, Dorothy Sherk E. Morris Sider, interviews by author; Rowena Winger Heise, questionnaire.

29. Charles Eldon Winger, Verle Winger, obituaries, *ev*, Oct. 22, 1945, 11.

30. Toews, *Mennonites,* 173–74. The statistics used by Toews come from 1944 and 1949 censuses. They differ from numbers in a compilation in C. N. Hostetter Jr.'s papers.

These latter figures give almost identical figures to those listed in Toews of the percentage in CPS. The Hostetter Papers figures, however, place a higher percentage in combatant military service and a smaller fraction in noncombatant military service than do those in Toews but do not materially change the BIC ranking with other Mennonite groups. Tally on untitled ledger sheet, Hostetter Papers, CPS, 1944–47, 7–5.1.

31. Between 1951 and 1957, only 4 percent of drafted BIC men chose noncombatant service, whereas 44 percent chose combatant military service, and 52 percent alternative service. GC *Minutes,* 1958, art. 16.

32. E. Morris Sider, telephone conversation with author, July 7, 1998. Throughout its history, the community disfellowshiped for a variety of offenses. For descriptions of its use, some of which suggest that disfellowshiping meant revocation of membership, see Climenhaga, *History of the* BIC, 279–80; Sider, BIC *in Canada,* 82–85; Wittlinger, *Quest for Piety,* 92–96. GC *Minutes,* 1942, art. 13; 1943, arts. 51–52; 1948, art. 17; 1958, art. 16.

33. Gerald N. Wingert to author, June 17, 1996.

34. Kenneth Bert Hoover, audiotaped response to questionnaire.

35. Sider, *Lantern in the Dawn,* ed. Sider and Hostetler, 17; *Minutes,* Grantham DC, Mar. 6, 1948, art. 18.

36. *Minutes,* Manor-Pequea DC, Jan. 28, 1947, art. 29. For unstated reasons, Hunt then asked for a letter of dismissal from the church and was "freely" given one. For another description of a BIC congregation's system of discipline for those who served in the military in World War II, see Morris Sherk, *A Century on the Hill: The Story of the Mechanicsburg Brethren in Christ Church* (Nappanee, Ind.: Evangel Press, 1990), 134–35.

37. Paul J. Winger, questionnaire. Perhaps not unconnected is his observation that the BIC church provided little support for his parents in their retirement, though they had been missionaries.

38. Gordon H. Schneider, questionnaire.

39. Clara Gibboney Kritzberger, questionnaire.

40. Isaiah B. Harley, interview by author. Also see Ray M. Zercher, questionnaire.

41. Sider, *Lantern in the Dawn,* 17–18.

42. Ray M. Zercher, questionnaire.

43. Brock, *Freedom from Violence,* 215.

44. Frances Harmon, interview by author.

45. Heisey to Hostetter, May 13, 1941, Hostetter Papers, CPS, 7–5.2, "CPS Letters" folder; Hostetter to Harley, Mar. 3, 1956, GC, PRS, Reports and Literature, I-21–1.4, "Testimonials— Peace, 1956" folder, BICA; Unsigned questionnaire; Gerald Wenger, interview by author.

46. See chap. 2 n. 111. Also see Regehr, "Lost Sons," 474–76; Sprunger and Thiesen, "Mennonite Military Service," 485.

47. Toews, *Mennonites,* 164, chaps. 6–7. On BIC interest in relief training and CPS Reserve Force Program, see Hostetter Papers, CPS, 7–5.2, "Civilian P.S. Res. Corps" folder.

48. "County Boy" newspaper clipping, Hostetter Papers, MCC, Misc., 7–4.3, "C.O." folder.

49. For a description of the Grottoes camp, see Gingerich, *Service for Peace,* 95–107. Gingerich's work provides descriptions of many other MCC-administered CPS units.

50. Harmon, *They Also Serve,* 15, 60.

51. J. Wilmer Heisey, interview by author.

52. *The Olive Branch,* Oct. 11, 1941, 2, MCC Collection, CPS Individual MCC CPS Camps [hereafter MCC, CPS], IX-13–1.4, "Camp 4," AMC; John Wolgemuth, "The End of the Dry

River Floods," *ssh*, June 11, 1944, 4. In response to a question about the opening of new work opportunities for small units or individual placements of men, often called "detached service," Wolgemuth balanced his response. He noted the advantages of more adequately utilizing the skills of participants and of providing greater service to the nation. He also pointed to the loss of "group fellowship" that detached service would bring its members. Above all, he urged those leaving camp to live "consistently" and "above the reproach of critics." *The Olive Branch*, Sept. 5, 1942, 4, MCC, CPS, IX-13–1.4, "Camp 4."

53. Harmon, *They Also Serve*, 60.

54. Ray M. Zercher, questionnaire, and "It Seems to Me," 284–88. Zercher found 1930s separatism—especially as expressed in clothing strictures, isolation from other groups, and emphasis on personal religious experiences—oppressive. He dissented by sometimes wearing a tie in public high school and later at Messiah Bible College. Atypically, Zercher connects his nonconformity within the group to his willingness and even zeal for nonconformity in the larger society, especially when military service was at issue. He remembers firing off, while at Howard, a poem he wrote contrasting pacifists playing tennis to planes circling overhead in training for combat. He sent the poem to Henry Hostetter, editor of the youth page in the *Sunday School Herald*. Hostetter did not publish the poem. Perhaps that was just as well, Zercher reflects, noting his unbending standards on war as well as on the ethical standards expected of coworkers in the hospital, a stance that often caused tension. Zercher also remembers his growing respect for his Anabaptist heritage and for Mennonites—"being usually content to be considered a Mennonite"—especially their skill in a cappella singing.

55. Goossen, *Women against the Good War*, chaps. 3–5.

56. Ruth Zercher, "Our Wives," in *Nonresistance under Test*, comp. Swalm, 156–58, and interview by author.

57. President Franklin D. Roosevelt objected to proposed programs for conscientious objectors that included wages. He was undoubtedly influenced by the lobbying of the American Legion against pay for conscientious objectors. Keim and Stoltzfus, *Politics of Conscience*, 111–14; Robinson, "Civilian Public Service," 515–16; Sibley and Jacob, *Conscription of Conscience*, 116–17; Toews, *Mennonites*, 146.

58. Eber Dourte, "The Camp Life," in *Nonresistance under Test*, comp. Swalm, 99; Harmon, *They Also Serve*, 56.

59. C. N. Hostetter Jr., "Relief Work," *ssh*, Nov. 17, 1946, 7.

60. "Fall Meeting of MCC," with PRS *Minutes*, June 2, 1943, art. 9, GC, PRS, I-21–1.1, "*Minutes*, 1940–47" folder, BICA; "Activities during the Past Year," *EV*, June 21, 1943, 9; GC *Minutes*, 1944, art. [14].

61. H. G. Brubaker to CPS Worker in the Home Congregation, Feb. 11, 1946, Hostetter Papers, CPS, 1944–47, 7–5.1.

62. Harmon, *They Also Serve*, 57; J. Wilmer Heisey, account journal, June 10, 1943 to Mar. 19, 1946, in possession of its author, and interview by author.

63. In a number of letters, the PRS treasurer, John H. Hoffman, sounded particularly unhappy with the Rapho district. Its unwillingness to provide dependency payments to a CPS man viewed as an erring member brought two contacts from Hoffman and an urgent plea to C. N. Hostetter Jr. that someone else speak also to "the brethren." Hoffman was distressed that the Selective Service Administration knew that Emmanuel and Mabel Hoffer had had a new baby before the home district did. He was appeased by an apology from

the district for "neglect in taking care of their own dependency cases." Hoffman to Hoover, Jan. 14, 1946; Hoffman to Hostetter, Feb. 7, 1946, Hostetter Papers, CPS, 1944–47, 7–5.1.

64. The MCC statement drew on biblical phrasing of "bearing one another's burdens" to support its contention that such aid was mutual aid rather than charity. That biblical base did not appear in the statement that ran in the *Visitor*. "Statement on Policy in Regard to C.P.S. Dependency Needs," adopted by MCC, Mar. 18, 1944, MCC Report Files 1, IX-12–1, "CPS Dependency" folder; "An Emergency Need," and "Statement on C.P.S. Dependency Adopted," *EV*, Apr. 10, 1944, 2; *GC Minutes*, 1944, art. [14]. Mennonite social thinker J. Winfield Fretz pointed to CPS as an example of mutual aid within the church and as an economic system that stood in contrast to capitalism and industrialism. See J. Winfield Fretz, "Mutual Aid in the Church of Tomorrow," *SSH*, Oct. 29, 1944, 4.

65. Hoover to Byler, May 31, 1944, CPS, Camps, Finances, 1941–46, IX-13–1.2, "Finances, Dependency, BIC Correspondence, 1944–45" [hereafter "BIC Dependency"] folder, AMC.

66. Hoover to Hostetter, Sept. 18, 1945, Hostetter Papers, CPS, 1944–47, 7–5.1. In another case in which MCC did not cover medical costs of a CPS man because he had been in CPS less than six months, Hoover asked if PRS had "an obligation." See Hoover to Hostetter, Mar. 20, 1946, Hostetter Papers, CPS, 1944–47, 7–5.1.

67. *Minutes*, Dauphin-Lebanon DC, Feb. 22, 1945, art. 5.

68. Hostetter to Hoover, Feb. 6, 1946, Hostetter Papers, CPS, 1944–47, 7–5.1; Harmon, *They Also Serve*, 56.

69. [Hostetter] to Wenger, Feb. 26, 1946, Hostetter Papers, CPS, 1944–47, 7–5.1.

70. Hostetter to Hoffman, Mar. 30, 1946; Hoover to PRS committee members, Feb. 21, 1946, Hostetter Papers, CPS, 1944–47, 7–5.1.

71. Betty Grove, interview by J. Wilmer Heisey; Hostetter to camp director, Cantonsville, Maryland, Jan. 3, 1946, Hostetter Papers, CPS, 1944–47, 7–5.1.

72. Harmon, *They Also Serve*, 57; Brubaker to MCC, n.d., stamped July 27, 1944; Bennett to Hoover, July 27, 1944; Hoover to Bennett, Aug. 1, 1944; Bennett to Hoover, Aug. 11, 1944, CPS, Camps, Finances, 1941–46, IX-13–1.2, "BIC Dependency" folder, AMC.

73. PRS committee, financial report, for year ending, May 1, 1945, including "Dependency allowances paid to and including June 1945," Hostetter Papers, CPS, 1944–47, 7–5.1.

74. "MCC-CPS Releases for April, 1945: Brethren in Christ," MCC Report Files 1, IX-12–1, "BIC Men in CPS" folder.

75. PRS committee, financial report, June 1, 1946, including "Total dependency payments made to and including June 1946," Hostetter Papers, CPS, 1944–47, 7–5.1.

76. Correspondence to PRS committee, Nov. 5, 1945; PRS response, Nov. 7, 1945, Hostetter Papers, CPS, 1944–47, 7–5.1.

77. Hoffman to Hostetter, Nov. 9, 1945, Hostetter Papers, CPS, 1944–47, 7–5.1.

78. Anna Mae Rohrer Kohler, John S. Kohler, questionnaires.

79. John S. Kohler, "A Returned Service Man Looks at the Church," *SSH*, Mar. 9, 1947, 7. Not all CPS evaluations of the Amish were positive. See Witmer to Hostetter, Nov. 10, 1941, Hostetter Papers, CPS, 7–5.2, "CO Camp Meetings" folder.

80. "Post-War Needs and Plans of CPS Men: As Revealed in the Findings of a Preliminary [Survey] Made by the Mennonite Central Committee for Brethren in Christ and Total MCC—CPS Men," Mar. 1, 1944, MCC Report Files 1, IX-12–1, "BIC Men in CPS" folder.

Fifty-one of the seventy-six community men in the program at the time responded to the questionnaire.

81. The Hostetter Papers, focused on CPS, show how such confidence might have been built. Hostetter corresponded personally with many of the men. He prepared carefully before visiting CPS camps, requesting statistics from MCC on denominational and educational backgrounds of the men he would be speaking to and visiting with. For Hostetter correspondence with CPS men, see Hostetter Papers, CPS, 7–5.2, "CPS Letters" folder; CPS, 1944–47, 7–5.1. For Hostetter preparation for camp visitation, see correspondence in Hostetter Papers, CPS, 7–5.2, "CO Camp Meetings" folder.

82. QPASC45; six additional responses and "How Shall We Evaluate the Time Our Boys Spend in C.P.S.?" handwritten notes, Hostetter Papers, MCC, Misc., 7–4.3, "C.O." folder.

83. Wendell E. Harmon, "Brethren in Christ C.P.S. Thinks," SSH, Nov. 26, 1944, 4; Dec. 3, 1944, 4, 6; Dec. 10, 1944, 4; Dec. 17, 1944, 4; Jan. 7, 1945, 4; Jan. 14, 1945, 4; Feb. 25, 1945, 4; Mar. 18, 1945, 4.

84. "BIC CPS Thinks: Installment III," SSH, Dec. 10, 1944, 4. Percentages compiled and calculated from QPASC45.

85. Earl G. Hensel, questionnaire.

86. All of the responses come from the QPASC45 and "BIC CPS Thinks"; Gingerich, Service for Peace, 407–409, chap. 18.

87. Jesse Heise, "As I See It," SSH, Oct. 26, 1947, 7.

88. Engle to Hostetter, Mar. 9, 1943, Henry N. Hostetter Papers, Correspondence, 13–2.1, "BYPW, 1942–44" folder; GC Minutes, 1943, art. 44; 1944, art. 38; 1945, art. 28; 1946, art. 30; 1947, art. 28.

89. Henry N. Hostetter, "A Worthwhile Project: C.P.S. Men Express Thanks," SSH, Jan. 7, 1945, 7, and "Excerpts from Letters," in Nonresistance under Test, comp. Swalm, 166.

90. Hostetter Papers.

91. Sibley and Jacob, Conscription of Conscience, 240.

92. Hoover to Hostetter, Jan. 25, 1946, Hostetter Papers, CPS, 1944–47, 7–5.1.

93. Hoover to PRS committee members, Feb. 21, 1946, Hostetter Papers, CPS, 1944–47, 7–5.1.

94. Gerald N. Wingert to author, June 17, 1996.

95. Hostetter to Fast, Dec. 17, 1941, Hostetter Papers, CPS, 7–5.2, "MCC Correspondence—C. N. Hostetter, Jr." folder.

96. Toews, Mennonites, 241; Sider, "Life and Labor ASW," 580–97; Sider, BIC in Canada, 233–37; Swalm, Beloved Brethren, 77–78. Bruce W. Nix, My Life Story and History of the Nix Family (privately printed, 1995), 39–53, includes photographs, copy loaned to author by Mayme Nigh Gingerich. Arthur W. Heise, Harold M. Heise, Rowena Winger Heise, Russell Heise, Grace Holland Herr, Anna Heise Reesor, Erma Jean Heise Sider, Harvey Sider, Gordon Stickley, questionnaires; Lela Swalm Hostetler, Merlin Marr and Naomi Heise Marr, Ross Nigh, Dorothy Sherk, E. Morris Sider and Leone Dearing Sider, Harvey B. Stickley, interviews by author; Lela Swalm Hostetler to author, Apr. 8, 1996. Contemporary accounts of Alternate Service Work (ASW) include: Minutes, ON JC, 1939–54; J. B. Martin, "Canadian Government Contacts," and Edward Gilmore, "The Alternate Service Work Program," in Nonresistance under Test, comp. Swalm, 65–70, 75–81; "They Also Serve in Canada," and E. J. Swalm, "The Canadian Peace Front," in They

Also Serve, 43–44, 51; "The Service of Canadian C.O's," *EV,* Sept. 28, 1942, 15; E. J. Swalm, "Itinerary among the Alternative Service Camps, in the Provinces of British Columbia and Alberta, Canada," *EV,* Jan. 4, 1943, 2; Ross Nigh, "Experiences in Canadian Alternate Service," *SSH,* Jan. 24, 1943, 7; John Andres, "Take Up Thy Cross and Follow Me," *SSH,* June 11, 1944, 4; Wendell E. Harmon, "With God in CPS," *SSH,* July 23, 1944, 4; "PRS News," *EV,* Mar. 25, 1946, 10; and see app. 3.

97. Louis Heise, interview by author.

98. Paul Comly French, quoted in Kreider and Goossen, *Hungry, Thirsty, Stranger,* 62.

99. E. J. Swalm, "The Canadian Peace Front: In Camps and Farms, Canadian CO's Served under a Plan the U.S. Might Well Have Copied," in *They Also Serve,* 44.

100. *Minutes,* ON JC, Sept. 5, 1953, arts. 6, 11.

101. *Minutes,* ON JC, Sept. 4, 1954, art. 18.

102. Keim and Stoltzfus, *Politics of Conscience,* chap. 6. As early as 1944, the community began addressing the issue of postwar conscription. With a new conscription law in 1948 and a new alternative service program established in 1951, conscientious objection remained a focus in the community; Orie O. Miller and Ernest W. Lehman, "Draft Information," *EV,* July 26, 1948, 242; Sherk to ministers of the MCC Constituent Churches, Aug. 11, 1950; Hostetter to Local Board 85, Apr. 14, 1952; Ginder to Hostetter and Thuma, July 14, 1952, Henry N. Hostetter Papers, Manor Church, Hist. MSS 13–8–1.3, "Selective Service-Peace Position" folder, BICA; B. E. Thuma, "Board Member Expression," *SSH,* Feb. 11, 1951, 4; "PRS News," *EV,* Apr. 16, 1951, 16; NSBRO form letter, Sept. 29, 1951; Neufeld to Hostetter, Sept. 4, 1952; "List of Brethren in Christ I-W Men," Aug. 14, 1953; Curry to Hostetter, Aug. 27, 1953, Hostetter Papers, Mennonites Related Papers, 7–6.1 "NSBRO" folder, BICA; "New CO Regulations Still Delayed," *SSH,* Oct. 21, 1951, 4; GC *Minutes,* 1952, art. 25; GC *Minutes,* 1953, art. 22; "Eleven Men Attending Leadership School," *I-W Mirror,* Feb. 11, 1953, 4, and Dec. 2, 1953, 3; Oct. 20, 1954, 1, MCC Periodicals, IX-40–2, AMC. "The Brethren in Christ I-O, His Draft Call, and PAX," *EV,* July 6, 1953, 13; GC *Minutes,* 1954, art. 24; "Indiana C.O.s Jailed," *SSH,* Apr. 11, 1954, 5; "PAX Men to Peru," *EV,* July 19, 1954, 14; Herbert G. Weaver, "I-W Diary: Agricultural Experimentation," *SSH,* Aug. 22, 1954, 2; "PAX Men Tour Britain," *SSH,* Aug. 29, 1954, 5; "Brethren in Christ Serving in I-W," *SSH,* Dec. 5, 1954. Numerous retrospective accounts are also available. See Paul S. Boyer, Paul Carlson, Myron Mann, Lloyd S. Myers, Clarence Sakimura, Benjamin W. Myers, questionnaires; Clarence Sakimura, interview by author; Curtis O. Byer to author, July 3, 1996; Saba, "Carl Ulery," 51; Thelma Book, *MSMS,* 24–25; Joseph G. Ginder, *MSMS,* 161; Marlin Zook, *MSMS,* 567; see also apps. 6–7.

103. On the PAX program, see Keim and Stoltzfus, *Politics of Conscience,* 144–45; Calvin W. Redekop, *The PAX Story: Service in the Name of Christ, 1951–1976* (Telford, Penn.: Pandora Press, 2001); Toews, *Mennonites,* 241–43.

104. Paul S. Boyer, Clarence H. Sakimura, questionnaires. Also see Howard Landis, listed as PAX member, *WAL,* Nov. 1952, 7, MCC Collection, Periodicals, IX-40–2; Howard Landis, questionnaire.

105. Paul B. Carlson, questionnaire; Wilma I. Musser, "Carl and Avas Carlson and the Chicago Mission," *BICHL* 16 (Aug. 1993): 171–74, 180, 192–95.

106. Paul B. Carlson, questionnaire.

107. Ibid.

108. Ibid.

CHAPTER 6: THE PRIVATE LIFE OF NONRESISTANCE

1. Harmon, *They Also Serve,* 41, 58; Unruh, *In the Name of Christ,* 108.

2. The picture of nonresistance established in previous chapters provides a context for these individual experiences. This is important because both family letters and diaries present challenges to the historian. Hostetter's letters to his parents, for example, undoubtedly reflect his desire to please his parents, who were deeply involved in the community's nonresistance to mobilization. However, his letters, as well as a number by his two younger brothers, show that the family did discuss disagreements. Bechtel's diary also includes much more than descriptions of events; it reveals emotions and literary aspirations. Her experiences as a relief worker, however, in many ways parallel those described by others serving in similar settings. Historian David Brion Davis's reflections on his experiences in the same period raise important questions about the relationship between sources from the period being lived and retrospective sources. Davis is certain that his memories of racist incidents in U.S. military forces in occupied Germany are more accurate than his self-censored letters to his parents, whom he did not want to upset. See "World War II and Memory," *Journal of American History* 77 (Sept. 1990): 585.

3. On his father's side, his great-great-grandfather was a minister and bishop in the church; his great-grandfather a deacon; his grandfather a deacon, minister, bishop, leading member of the Foreign Mission Board, a General Conference secretary, and a president of Messiah Bible College; his father a minister, bishop, evangelist, member of several key denominational boards, including the powerful General Executive Board, a moderator of General Conference, president of Messiah Bible College (renamed Messiah College in a 1951 charter), and chair of the Mennonite Central Committee. Two younger brothers of Nelson Hostetter continued other family traditions—S. Lane Hostetter became an ordained minister, and D. Ray Hostetter served as president of Messiah College from 1964 to 1994. C. Nelson Hostetter, questionnaire, and interview by Joseph Miller, MLA; Sider, *Messenger of Grace,*13–16, 35, 43, 49, 56–57, 60, 133, 150, 164, 230; Sider, *Messiah College,* 189, 297.

4. The United Zion Church formed in a mid-nineteenth-century River Brethren schism. Sider, *Messenger of Grace,* 38–39, 63; Wittlinger, *Quest for Piety,* 134–36; *Rio La Plata,* Jan. 1947, 5, MCC Collection, Periodicals, IX-40–2; *Clarion,* Oct. 2, 1947, 3; C. Nelson Hostetter, questionnaire.

5. DCPS, 1996, 179; DCPS, 1947, 67; C. Nelson Hostetter, "Our War against Parasites," *Rio La Plata,* Dec. 1946, 2, MCC Collection, Periodicals, IX-40–2.

6. Sider, *Messenger of Grace,* 58; DCPS, 1996, 179.

7. Because Nelson was in Civilian Public Service for the longest period and because his letters were the most numerous, this study focuses on his letters rather than those of his brothers, and especially those written during his assignments in the United States. However, a number of Lane's and Ray's letters also support this chapter's personal view of nonresistance, as do some of Nelson's writings for BIC and Mennonite periodicals. Nelson Hostetter usually did not date the letters he wrote in Civilian Public Service, indicating only the day of the week and the time of day. If letters have dates or specific dates can be determined, the information is included as an endnote; all information that is not cited comes from the same archival source. Dates from his movements in the alternative service program and details from the letters do provide locations and gen-

eral time periods. All letters of C. Nelson Hostetter, S. Lane Hostetter, and D. Ray Hostetter are located in Hostetter Papers, Correspondence, Family, 7–22.8.

8. Hostetter, "Senior Expresses," 7.

9. N. Hostetter to parents, June 25, 1943, July 5, 1943.

10. *DCPS*, 1996, 285, 443.

11. Gingerich, *Service for Peace*, 254–56; Sibley and Jacob, *Conscription of Conscience*, 140–41.

12. Hostetter, "Senior Expresses," 7.

13. Sibley and Jacob, *Conscription of Conscience*, 228, 230; Toews, *Mennonites*, 162–64.

14. J. N. Hoover had raised this same question about relief efforts reinforcing military objectives in World War I; see chap.1. Grigor McClelland's letters as a Quaker relief worker in occupied Germany detail a close working relationship between his work and the British armed forces. See *Embers of War*, 5. Perry Bush raises similar issues about MCC's relief work during the Vietnam War. See "The Political Education of Vietnam Christian Service, 1945–1975," *Peace and Change* 27 (Apr. 2002): 198–224.

15. Sibley and Jacob, *Conscription of Conscience*, 242.

16. Ibid., 57.

17. Harmon, *They Also Serve*, 58; Sibley and Jacob, *Conscription of Conscience*, 143–49. Lane and Ray Hostetter raised their own questions on the community's expression of nonresistance. Because Lane was inducted only three months before the war ended in Europe and Ray more than three months after Japan surrendered, they experienced CPS life in one of its most difficult periods. Morale sank in camps and units, because demobilization of conscientious objectors proceeded more slowly than that of military personnel and because as CPS men were progressively demobilized, it became harder to maintain programs and a sense of community life among those who remained. See Sibley and Jacob, *Conscription of Conscience*, 462. Letters from his sons must have shaped the empathy of C. N. Hostetter Jr. for men in Civilian Public Service, as well as his leadership on issues concerning their welfare. From Forest Service Camp 28 at Medaryville, Indiana, Lane wrote in late 1945, "Daddy, you ought to hear the fellows around here dis 'cuss' C.P.S. & also Peace-time Conscription. Why don't you have your members write to Congressmen & M.C.C.? Just this morning some of the fellows were saying that everybody is asleep at home; that the churches were asleep when C.P.S. came & that they are now." See L. Hostetter to parents, Dec. 27, 1945. At another point, Lane wrote, "Can you folks tell me why Grantham B.C. Congregation is so pro-military but teach pacifism? Read the bulletin we fellows get at times. Of course I can't exactly blame them, but tell me will Matt Brubaker get as big a home-coming as the soldier boys. No, Matt didn't do anything. O.K. then why teach that way if you want us to be heroes?" Men in the Grantham district, such as Harold and John Zercher, who were disfellowshiped for military service, would undoubtedly have disagreed with Lane's evaluation. Lane perhaps was responding more to the larger society (which championed the military) and to a church community unsure of itself in modern pluralistic America than to actual events at Grantham. See L. Hostetter to parents, Nov. 10, 1945. Matthew G. Brubaker served in CPS from May 28, 1943, to October 28, 1945. See *DCPS*, 1996, 46. Ray Hostetter, a year younger than Lane, expressed a similar ambivalence about the nonresistant position and later noted his frustration in Civilian Public Service. In August 1945, before his induction into the program, he wrote to his parents from Abilene, Kansas. Thinking about filling out the questionnaire necessary to establish his conscientious objection, he wished his father were there to help him.

In the next sentence, he changed course: "It wouldn't surprise me if I end up NonCombatant because right now that [is] where I feel my place is." In another letter from Abilene, he explained that entering the military medical corps as a noncombatant would help him sort out his vocational aspirations. See R. Hostetter to parents, Aug. 31, 1945. Sometime in the next three months, he shifted his position on the draft; by December 1945, his letters to his parents were coming from CPS Camp 45 in Luray, Virginia. See R. Hostetter to parents, July 12, 1946. For the CPS service of three Hostetter brothers, see app. 4.

18. Hostetter, "Senior Expresses," 7. Grantham, Pennsylvania, was the village in which Messiah College was located.

19. Hostetter, interview by Joseph Miller. Hostetter's desire for exciting and even dangerous work parallels that of numerous other men in CPS. The frustrated interest in assignments in war areas reflects that yearning, as did the "glamour" accorded CPS smoke jumpers, members of a Montana unit that parachuted into remote areas to fight fires. See Toews, *Mennonites,* 145.

20. Anna Lane Hostetter did worry about her sons' well being throughout their years in CPS. Nelson told her not to worry about the amount of food he got at the Grottoes base camp. Ray wrote in his first letter from the state hospital in Cleveland, Ohio, "Mother I got into the kind of ward you told me to try not to get into." R. Hostetter to parents, July 12, 1946.

21. On the work of conscientious objectors in state hospitals during World War II, see Alex Sareyan, *The Turning Point: How Persons of Conscience Brought about Change in the Care of America's Mentally Ill* (Washington, D.C.: American Psychiatric Press, 1993); Bush, *Two Kingdoms,* 109–11; Robinson, "Civilian Public Service," 151–54.

22. "Friends Give Farewell," *Clarion,* Feb. 6, 1945, 1.

23. Richard Minter is included as member of the Grantham district on a 1941 listing. In 1950, 1951, 1955 listings, Minter is listed as a member "under discipline for Military Service." "Grantham District Membership Lists," Mar. 3, 1941, Mar. 6, 1950, Feb. 2, 1951, Feb. 15, 1955, with *Minutes,* Grantham DC, IV-11–1.2, BICA.

24. Biographies, family histories, obituaries, and marriage announcements make clear that marriage within the group built up extensive kinship networks. The same sources also show that community members often drew on people outside the community as marriage partners. See Toews, *Mennonites,* 162. In both the nineteenth and twentieth centuries, adherence to nonresistance was sometimes used as a bounding criterion for exogamous marriages. See Schlabach, *Peace, Faith, Nation,* 83–84.

25. Isaiah B. Harley, interview by author.

26. Minter to Hostetter, Feb. 16, 1945, Hostetter Papers, Home Mission Correspondence, 1944–46, M–Z, 7–2.15.

27. Without dates on letters, determining the chronology of the comments is difficult.

28. Wittlinger, *Quest for Piety,* 487.

29. N. Hostetter to parents, May 9, 1944.

30. Gingerich, *Service for Peace,* 254, 466.

31. N. Hostetter to parents, Jan. 2, 1944.

32. Gingerich, *Service for Peace,* app. 16.

33. In his history of the college, E. Morris Sider argues that the music program there both attracted young people to the school and, despite certain tensions over musical innovation, helped build connections between the school and the BIC denomination. Melvin

Gingerich's history of the Mennonite role in CPS notes an important role for music in that setting as well. Sider, *Messiah College*, 101, 216–17; Gingerich, *Service for Peace*, 326–27.

34. R. Hostetter to parents, Dec. 11, 1945.

35. N. Hostetter to parents, Oct. 30, 1944.

36. N. Hostetter to parents, Mar. 9, 1943.

37. Bush, *Two Kingdoms*, 106–14.

38. Ibid., 108–109; Gingerich, *Service for Peace*, 259–60; Sibley and Jacob, *Conscription of Conscience*, 140–41, 157–60.

39. Nelson Hostetter, "A Day with the Jibaro," *Rio La Plata*, Feb. 1947, 2–3, MCC Collection, Periodicals, IX-40–2.

40. N. Hostetter, "Our War," 2–3.

41. Hostetter, "Jibaro," 4–5; Hostetter, "Our War," 5.

42. N. Hostetter, interview by Joseph Miller; Heisey telephone communication with Mennonite Disaster Service office, August 18, 2001.

43. A diary, letters to her family, letters to her administrative superiors, work reports, and public writings for MCC and BIC periodicals are sources during the years of her service. The diary and letters to family are in the possession of their author. Work-related correspondence while in France is located in various folders of the MCC Collection at AMC. Bechtel wrote a letter about her relief work in 1974. See Bechtel to Wittlinger, Aug. 19, 1974, Wittlinger Papers, 35–1.22, "Peace and Service, 1910–1950" file. She also responded on audiotape to a series of questions for this study.

44. If the stories Bechtel heard about her parents' wedding day stressed its austerity, other stories conveyed difficulty and loss. Laura had had dreams of becoming a dress designer, but after her conversion, making "worldly" clothes seemed inappropriate. With Emanuel, she suffered the loss of four children at birth or soon after. Elsie, born after her father had turned fifty, remembers feeling left out at school because of her black stockings, long sleeves, and braids. She envied and pondered the lives of other youth, whose church life included Bible school and picnics. Wittlinger, *Quest for Piety*, 131; Emanuel Bechtel, Obituary, *EV*, Nov. 25, 1929, 4; Elsie C. Bechtel, audiotaped response to questionnaire.

45. "Church Statistics," inside back cover, GC *Minutes*, 1934–39.

46. Alumni News, *Clarion*, Oct. 1939, 12; *Messiah College Alumni Directory, 1992* (Grantham, Penn.: Messiah College, n.d.), 8; Bechtel, audiotaped response to questionnaire. A passionate person, Bechtel describes the examples set by her Messiah teachers as having touched the "fiber of my being." While teaching in Ohio schools during the first half of the 1940s, Bechtel wrote for the BIC *Sunday School Herald*. Her stories promoted the expected BIC virtues of active, dependable participation in church life, endurance in carrying on the church program in difficult times, and peacemaking by women in the home and in the classroom. Her female characters also exhibit talents as speaker, writers, and singers, and they were often ambitious. See "The Torch Burns Low," *SSH*, Oct. 11, 1942, 321–22; "Good Advertising," *SSH*, Nov. 8, 1942, 355, 357; "Peace on Earth," *SSH*, Dec. 20, 1942, 405–406; "William J. Meyers," *SSH*, Jan. 16, 1944, 23.

47. Bechtel, audiotaped response to questionnaire; Personnel Files, MCC Collection, IX-30, "Files, 1976–80 and Summer Service Personnel, 1944–75" folder; Goossen, *Women against the Good War*, 107; Sautters, Denise, "Life Long Giving: Elsie Bechtel Sees Helping Others as a Duty and a Gift," *Repository*, Nov. 15, 1996, copy of clipping in possession of author; "PRS News," *EV*, July 2, 1945, 2.

48. Editorial, *EV*, July 16, 1945, 3; Bechtel, "Why We Should Support Relief Service," *EV*, July 16, 1945, 5.

49. Bechtel, "Why . . . Relief Service," 5.

50. Fussell, *Wartime*, 75.

51. Because many of Bechtel's diary entries have no date or only the day of the week and are recorded in a paginated book, page numbers are always indicated. When specific dates are included, they are also listed. Bechtel, Aug. 29, 1945, 5–11; Relief and Service News, *EV*, Oct. 8, 1945, 2. On experiences of MCC relief work in Europe in the same years, see Atlee Beechy, *Seeking Peace: My Journey* (Goshen, Ind.: Pinchpenny Press, 2001), chap. 5.

52. Bechtel, 12. For Bechtel's memories of these events, see Bechtel to Wittlinger, Aug. 19, 1974, Wittlinger Papers, Quest 1, 35–1.22, "Peace and Service, 1910–1950" folder.

53. The colony was housed in the chateau of Lavercantière. Small Mennonite relief projects began in France in 1940 (Jesse W. Hoover had been involved with them in 1941), but they were quickly hemmed in by events of the war and governmental policies in both occupied France and Vichy France. Opened in 1943 after the Germans requisitioned an earlier colony building, Lavercantière at first housed refugee children from the Spanish Civil War and Jewish children from a Vichy concentration camp at Rivesaltes. Bechtel's article on Lavercantière in *The Sunday School Herald* described these original children as having "rejoined their families or returned to Spain"—a cryptic and rather ominous remark in light of the Vichy's government's collaboration with German officials in the deportation of Jewish people to eastern forced-labor and death camps. Bechtel, 15; "French Workers Assigned," *EV*, Nov. 19, 1945; "Relief in France during the Occupation," *EV*, Apr. 9, 1945, 2, 9; Clipping, "Le Chateau de Lavercantière" (*Patriote du Sud-Ouest*, Toulouse, 5 Mars 1946, handwritten), MCC Collection, IX-19–1, France Relief, 1939–48, "Lavercantière, 1942–48" folder; Unruh, *In the Name of Christ*, 46, 109; Kreider and Goossen, *Hungry, Thirsty, Stranger*, 57; Elsie C. Bechtel, "Lavercantière—Mennonite Children's Home in France," *SSH*, May 5, 1946, 144. On the Rivesaltes concentration camp and the Vichy role in deportation, see Michael R. Marrus and Robert O. Paxton, *Vichy France and the Jews* (New York: Schocken Books, 1981), 165, 173–74, 256, and chaps. 6–7.

54. An organizational chart showing the relationships between the national government, prefecture, and voluntary organizations such as Secours Mennonite, points to a complex setting. The maze of boxes and lines connecting Lavercantière to a variety of other institutions helps to explain the competing pressures in Bechtel's work. See Bechtel, "Mennonite Children's Home in France," 144; attachment to "Report on Children's Homes Now in Operation," n.d., MCC Collection, Basel Relief Unit, 1948, IX-19–3, "France-Lavercantière Background Materials" folder.

55. Bechtel, 19, 27; report, Secours Mennonite aux Enfant, Oct. 7, 1945, MCC Collection, Basel Relief Unit, 1948, IX-19–3, "France-Lavercantière Background Materials" folder.

56. See note 52.

57. Elsie C. Bechtel, report, Nov. 1–21 (1946 handwritten), MCC Collection, Central Correspondence [hereafter MCC Correspondence], 1946, IX-6–3, "France" folder, AMC; Bechtel, 28, 30, 32–33, 35, 37, 41, 46, 54, 58, 79, 84, 87, 102, 106–107, 118; Bechtel, "Lavercantière—Mennonite Children's Home in France."

58. Bechtel, 32, 34, 37–38, 42, 45, 53–55, 63, 83, 93, 98, 114; "Je n'Oublierai Jamais," "Colonie d'Enfants Lavercantière," unpaginated, MCC Collection, France Relief, 1939–

48, IX-19–1, "Lavercantière, Souvenir Book" folder; Elsie C. Bechtel, report, probably to Secours Mennonite aux Enfants, n.d., MCC Collection, IX-19–1, France Relief, 1939–48, "Lavercantière, 1942–48" folder.

59. Bechtel to Cocanower, June 24, 1947, MCC Collection, France Relief, 1939–48, IX-19–1, "Lavercantière, 1942–48" folder.

60. Bechtel, 114.

61. Bechtel, 11, 33, 39, 42, 48–49, 54, 62, 68, 79–80; Bechtel to family, Sept. 30, 1947, loose sheet in diary; Bechtel to Wittlinger, Aug. 19, 1974, BICA; Elsie Bechtel to friends, n.d., loose sheet in diary; Bechtel, 84, 88–89, 103.

62. Bechtel, 13, 14, 37,45, 47, 80; Bechtel to friends, n.d., loose sheet in diary; Bechtel 64–65, 82.

63. Bechtel, 53–55; Bechtel to friends, n.d., loose sheet in diary; Bechtel, 30, 80, 87.

64. Bechtel, 99; Bechtel, audiotaped response to questionnaire; Bechtel, 53, 84, 32, 37, 63; Bechtel to Cocanower, Apr. 14, 1947, MCC Collection, France Relief, 1939–48, IX-19–1, "Lavercantière, 1942–48" file; Bechtel, 31; Bechtel to family, May 4, 1947, loose sheet in diary.

65. Bechtel, Oct. 16, [1946], 81.

66. Elsie C. Bechtel, "France: Lavercantière," *European Relief Notes,* May–June 1948, 8–9, MCC Collection, Periodicals, IX-40–2.

67. Bechtel, untitled loose sheet in diary.

68. Bechtel, 36, 42,59, 82, 106; Bechtel, untitled, "Colonie D'Enfants Lavercantière," unpaginated, MCC Collection, France Relief, 1939–48, IX-19–1, "Lavercantière, Souvenir Book" folder; Bechtel to family, June 7, 1946, loose sheet in diary; Bechtel to Cocanower, June 24, 1947, MCC Collection, France Relief, 1939–48, IX-19–1, "Lavercantière. 1942–48" folder.

69. Bechtel, 61, 113.

70. Bechtel, loose sheet in diary.

71. Miriam Bowers, a BIC relief worker in Germany in approximately the same period, also does not remember distinguishing herself from her Mennonite coworkers; interview by author.

72. Bechtel, 26, 50.

73. Ibid., 84, 103; Bechtel to family, Sept. 22, 1947, loose sheet in diary.

74. Bechtel to family, June 7, 1947, loose sheet in diary.

75. Bechtel to family, Sept. 22, 1947, loose sheet in diary.

76. Bechtel, 41, 49–50, 57, 58, 80, 81.

77. Ibid., 107.

78. Ibid., 60.

79. Ibid., 85.

80. Bechtel, 91. Similarly, French-speaking Waldensians of northern Italy made her think with pleasure of people at home. Mennonites consistently described themselves as kin to Waldensians, descendents of a twelfth-century grouping that stressed biblical authority and ethical daily practice based on the Beatitudes. See Bechtel to family, June 7, 1946; Dyck, *Mennonite History,* 15–16.

81. Bechtel, 16, 40, 50, 60, 91, 99, 103, 109.

82. Bechtel, diary, 91, 61; Bechtel to family, June 7, 1946, and Sept. 22, 1947, loose sheets in diary; Bechtel, 66.

83. Bechtel to Wittlinger, Aug. 19, 1974, Wittlinger Papers, Quest 1, 35–1.22, "Peace and Service, 1910–50" folder.

84. Bechtel to family, Nov. 23, 1946, loose sheet in diary.

85. Bechtel, 91; Bechtel to family, June 7, 1946, loose sheet in diary.

86. Ibid., 33.

87. Ibid., 79.

88. Ibid., 105.

89. Ibid., 31.

90. Bechtel, loose sheet in diary.

91. *Minutes,* ON JC, Sept. 3, 1949, art. 11; Bechtel, audiotaped response to questionnaire.

92. GC *Minutes,* 1948, art 17; Bechtel, audiotaped response to questionnaire; *Minutes,* ON JC, Sept. 3–5, 1949, art. 1; Sautters, "Life Long Giving."

93. Jameson, "Rachel Bella Calof," 146–47.

Chapter 7: Legacy and Conclusion

1. Title quotation, George Bundy, interview by author; Esther Tyson Boyer, questionnaire.

2. Anna Mae Rohrer Kohler to author, Sept. 25, 1996; BIC *Missions,* 76.

3. Donald D. Engle, questionnaire. Stan Engle's classification during the Vietnam War would have been I-O, rather than IV-E, which was Donald Engle's classification in the 1941–47 conscription system. NSBRO form letter, Sept. 29, 1951, Hostetter Papers, Mennonite Related, 7–6.1, "NSBRO" folder; Sibley and Jacob, *Conscription of Conscience,* 56.

4. Curtis O. Byer to author, July 3, 1996; Clarence Byer to Harley, Feb. 2, 1956, GC, PRS, Reports, Literature, I-21–1.4, "Testimonials—Peace, 1956" folder, BICA. For other intergenerational discussions, see Arthur W. Heise, Ray M. Zercher, questionnaires; Merlin Marr, Ruth Niesley Zercher, interviews by author; Nigh, "Shaper of Life," 306.

5. Daniel L. Hoover, questionnaire.

6. Gordon H. Schneider, questionnaire. Also see Millard Herr, questionnaire.

7. Eugene H. Feather, questionnaire.

8. Unsigned questionnaire.

9. Paul S. Boyer, questionnaire. By 1969, "in absolute numbers the Catholic church had more COs than any other religious body." See Patricia McNeal, "Harder than War: Roman Catholic Peacemaking in Twentieth-Century America," in *Proclaim Peace,* ed. Hughes and Schlabach, 241.

10. Grace Herr Holland, questionnaire; MC *Alumni Directory, 1992,* 64; Boyer, *Mission on Taylor Street,* 65.

11. *Constitution: Doctrine, By-Laws, and Rituals,* 1939, art. 7.

12. Zercher has no idea when he heard the story and is not even sure who told it. Ray M. Zercher, questionnaire.

13. GC *Minutes,* 1945, official directory.

14. Clara Meyer Eberly, questionnaire; Ray Hostetter to parents, n.d., Hostetter Papers, Correspondence, Family, 7–22.8.

15. Clarence H. Sakimura, questionnaire. Irene Bishop was a Mennonite who attended Messiah Bible College and worked in various relief assignments between 1946 and 1967. Cornelius J. Dyck, *Something Meaningful for God* (Scottdale, Penn.: Herald Press, 1981), 85–86, 98.

16. Clarence H. Sakimura, questionnaire; Clarence Sakimura and Herta Aschenbrenner Sakimura, interview by author.

17. Wittlinger, *Quest for Piety*, 485–86.

18. Kauffman and Harder, *Anabaptists Four*, 284, 58–63; Kauffman and Driedger, *Mennonite Mosaic*, 38–39, 239; Yeatts and Burwell, "Tradition and Mission," 100–106.

19. "Peacemakers: A Statement on Peace" (Nappanee, Ind.: Evangel Press, 1978), unpaginated, Public Domain, Misc., VIII-10–1.2, BICA.

20. BIC *Missions*, 1998 update, BICA.

21. GC *Minutes*, 1980, art. 17; Arthur M. Climenhaga, interview by author.

22. Driedger and Kraybill, *Mennonite Peacemaking*, 272. On the larger context of Mennonite/BIC attention to justice issues beyond those related to conscientious objection from the 1950s through the 1970s, see Bush, *Two Kingdoms*, chap. 6; Driedger and Kraybill, *Mennonite Peacemaking*, chaps. 4–5.

23. Driedger and Kraybill. These authors perceptively point out that as Anabaptist groups reject coercion to enforce pacifism, they increasingly accept legal force in public life.

24. Yoder, "Unique Role of the Historic Peace Churches," 137–39.

25. Schrag, "BIC Attitude," 54.

26. Ralph S. Lehman announcement, May 21, 1994; Leola Siebert Wiens to Mann, n.d., Leroy K. Mann to Wiens, June 5, 1994, photocopies in possession of author; E. Mann, see app. 6.

Selected Bibliography

✍

PRIMARY SOURCES

Archival Collections

Archives of the Mennonite Church, Goshen, Indiana

  Committee on Economic and Social Relations. Correspondence with Individuals, I.
    Boyer, C. W. 1940–46. I-3-7.

  Mennonite Central Committee Collection

    Central Correspondence. IX-6-3.

      Books, Titus M. Area Pastor. 1943.

      Brethren in Christ Peace, Relief, and Service. 1947–48.

      E. V. Publishing House. 1947.

      France Office. 1946–47.

      Hoover, Jesse W. 1942–44, 1946–48.

      Hostetter, C. N. Jr. 1941, 1947–48.

      Philippine Island Office. 1947.

      Swalm, E. J. 1945.

    Civilian Public Service and Central Correspondence. Personnel Files. 1945–55.
      IX-6-4.

    Civilian Public Service Camps. IX-13-1.

      Camp No. 4, Grottoes, Virginia. *The Olive Branch.*

      Camp No. 5, Colorado Springs. Colorado. *Pike View Peace News.*

      Camp No. 20, Sidling Hill, Wells Tannery, Pennsylvania. *The Turnpike Echo.*

      Camp No. 31, Camino, California. *The Snowliner.*

      Finances. Dependency. Brethren in Christ Correspondence. 1944–45.

      Relief Training Schools. 1941–46.

      Applications for Women's Summer Relief Training Unit. 1944.

      Women's Summer Service Units. 1945.

  Europe and North Africa. European Headquarters, Basel, Switzerland Files. 1945–54.
    IX-19-3.

  Europe and North Africa. Spain and France Relief Files. 1939–48. IX-19-1.

    Lavercantière. 1942–48.

    Lavercantière. Souvenir Book, 1943–48.

France

Cocanower, Charles, Director. 1947.

Buller, Henry, Director. 1946.

Lavercantière Background Materials. 1948.

Le Lien Newsletter.

Miscellaneous. 1946–47.

Periodicals. Assorted Titles. 1942–79. IX-40-2.

I-W Mirror.

European Relief Notes.

Jordan News.

Philippines Relief Notes.

Rio La Plata.

Women's Activities Letter.

Personnel Files. IX-30.

Report Files. Set 1. 1917–65. IX-12-1.

Brethren in Christ Men in Civilian Public Service.

Civilian Public Service Dependency.

Mennonite Relief Work in World War I. Questionnaires—Answered, E–G.

Seagoing Cowboys.

Voluntary Service European Short Term. 1947–48, 1950–52.

Voluntary Service Evaluation Questionnaire. 1947–48.

Voluntary Service Personnel.

Voluntary Service Weekly Logs. 1947–51.

Women's Service Unit. Ypsilanti: Applications and Evaluations; Daily Logs; Questionnaires.

Report Files. Set 2. IX-12-2.

Intercollegiate Peace Fellowship.

Report Files. Personnel Listings. Set 5. IX-12-5.

Mennonite Central Committee Personnel Headquarters. 1946–53.

Mennonite Central Committee Personnel European. 1945–67.

Mennonite Central Committee Personnel Foreign. 1945–49.

Relief Workers. 1937–49.

The Archives of the Brethren in Christ Church and Messiah College, Grantham, Penn.

Bert, Ray D. "Brethren in Christ 'Peacemakers' and World War I." 1970. IX-1-1.17.

Brubaker, H. H. Audiotaped memoirs.

Constitution and By-Laws of the Brethren in Christ Church. rev. 1924.

Constitution, Doctrine, By-Laws, and Rituals of the Brethren in Christ Church. rev. 1941. Nappanee, Ind.: E. V. Publishing House, n.d.

Council, District. California. Chino. 1941–50.

Council, District. California. Upland. 1941–50. 1951–60.

Council, District. Kansas. Brown County. 1941–50.

Council, District. Kansas. South Dickinson. 1941–50, 1951–60.

Council, District. Michigan. Merrill. 1941–50, 1951–60.

Council, District. Oklahoma. Bethany Congregation. 1951–60.

Council, District. Ontario. Wainfleet, 1921–60.

Council, District. Ontario. Waterloo, 1941–50.

Council, District. Pennsylvania. Centre-Clinton-Lycoming. 1941–50.

Council, District. Pennsylvania. Cumberland. 1931–40, 1941–50.

Council, District. Pennsylvania. Dauphin-Lebanon. 1941–50.

Council, District. Pennsylvania. Donegal. 1941–50.

Council, District. Pennsylvania. Grantham. 1911–20, 1941–55.

Council, District. Pennsylvania. Manor-Pequea. 1911–20, 1941–50.

Council, District. Pennsylvania. Rapho. IV-2-1.1.

Council, District. Southern Ohio. Highland. 1951–60.

Council, Joint. Ohio-Kentucky. 1931–40, 1941–50, 1951–60.

Council, Joint. Ontario. 1941–50.

Council, State. California. 1911–40, 1941–50, 1951–60

Council, State. Indiana. 1940–50, 1951–60.

Council, State. Iowa–South Dakota. 1941–50.

Council, State. Kansas. 1910–20, 1941–50, 1951–60.

Council, State. Michigan. 1941–50.

Council, State. Ohio. 1901–10, 1911–20.

Council, State. Oklahoma. 1911–20, 1941–50.

Council, State. Pennsylvania. 1931–40, 1941–50.

Councils, State and Joint. Ontario. III-2-1.1.

Engle, Eli M. Papers. Hist. MSS 3-1.1.

Evangelical Visitor, 1914–19, 1939–54.

Fries, John A., Jr., "The History and Philosophy of the Christian Doctrine of Nonresistance in the Brethren in Christ Church." M.Div. thesis, Western Evangelical Seminary, 1972. IX-1-1.8.

General Conference. Board for Young People's Work. I-4-1.4, 1.5, 1.6.

General Conference. General Executive Board. I-7-1.1, 1.2.

General Conference. Minutes. 1913–54, 1958, 1980.

General Conference. Peace, Relief, and Service Committee. I-21-1.1, 1.4.

Harley, Isaiah. Interview by E. Morris Sider, Aug. 22, 1979.

Heisey, Frances B. Hist. MSS 25-1.1.

Heisey, J. Wilmer. Interview by E. Morris Sider, July 31, 1979.

Hensel, Irene Frey. Hist. MSS 79-1.1, 1.2.

Hess, Abram Z. Hist. MSS 10-1.1

Hoover, Kenneth. Interview by E. Morris Sider, Jan. 17, 1979.

Hostetler, Paul and Lela. Interview by E. Morris Sider, July 29, 1979.

Hostetter, Anna Lane. Hist. MSS 79-1.1.

Hostetter, C. N., Jr. Papers

Civilian Public Service. Hist. MSS 7-5.1, 5.2.

Correspondence, Family. Hist. MSS 7-22.8.

Diaries, Hist. MSS 7-23.1.

Home Mission Correspondence. Hist. MSS 7-2.15.

Lectures, Addresses, Sermons, Seminars. Hist. MSS 7-17.5.

Mennonite Affiliated Colleges. XI-12-8.6.

Mennonite Central Committee. Hist. MSS 7-4.2, 4.3.

Mennonite Related Papers. Hist. MSS 7-6.1.

Peace Conferences. Hist. MSS 7-8.1, 8.2.

Hostetter, Christian N. Papers. Hist. MSS 1-2.1.

Hostetter, Henry N. Papers. Hist. MSS 13-2.1, 13-8-1.3.

Manual of Doctrine and Government of the Brethren in Christ Church. Nappanee, Ind.: Evangel Press, 1961.

Manual of Doctrine and Government of the Brethren in Christ Church. Nappanee, Ind.: Evangel Publishing House, 1998.

Messiah College. Student Affairs. *Clarion,* Monthly, 1935–43. IX-6-11.3.

Messiah College. Student Affairs. Miscellaneous Publications. XI-6-14.1.

Minutes of General Conferences of Brethren in Christ (River Brethren) from 1871–1904. Harrisburg, Penn.: n.p., 1904.

Miscellaneous. Hist. MSS 5-1.6.

Oral History Collection (All on audiotape unless otherwise noted; additional transcriptions as indicated.)

Interviews by author

Bowers, Miriam, Messiah Village, Mechanicsburg, Penn., Nov. 8, 1996, notes only.

Bundy, George, and Ethel Heisey Bundy. Messiah Village, Mechanicsburg, Penn., July 2, 1996, transcript.

Climenhaga, Arthur M. Messiah Village, Mechanicsburg, Penn., Nov. 8, 1996, transcript.

Crouse, Esther Lausch. Akron, Penn., July 14, 1994, transcript.

Dourte, Jeanette Frey. Manheim, Penn., July 7, 1993, transcript.

Engle, Eunice. Victorville, Calif., by telephone, July 16, 1994, transcript.

Engle, Harold, and Mary Elizabeth Engle. Messiah Village, Mechanicsburg, Penn., Nov. 9, 1996, transcript.

Engle, John, and Anna Kreider Engle. Messiah Village, Mechanicsburg, Penn., Nov. 9, 1996, transcript.

Fretz, Lester. Beamsville, Ont., Oct. 30, 1996, transcript.

Fries, John, Jr. Messiah Village, Mechanicsburg, Penn., Nov. 9, 1996.

Harley, Isaiah B., and Doris Brehm Harley. Messiah Village, Mechanicsburg, Penn., Nov. 9, 1996, transcript.

Harmon, Frances. Upland, Calif., by telephone, July 2, 1994, transcript.

Heise, Harold, and Verna Winger Heise; Louis Heise and Verna Heise Heise. Magnetawan, Ont., Oct. 28, 1996, transcript.

Heisey, Bertha Sollenberger Crider. Newville, Penn., July 18, 1994, transcript.

Heisey, J. Wilmer. Richville, N.Y., July 2, 1993.

Heisey, Velma Climenhaga. Richville, N.Y., July 2, 1993.

Hoffman, Laura. Messiah Village, Mechanicsburg, Penn., July 13, 1994, transcript.

Hoffman, Betty Collins. Elizabethtown, Penn., July 12, 1994, transcript.

Hostetler, Lela Swalm. Messiah Village, Mechanicsburg, Penn., July 11, 1996, transcript.

Lady, Martha, and Mary Olive Lady. Messiah Village, Mechanicsburg, Penn., Nov. 9, 1996, transcript.

Light, Faithe M. Messiah Village, Mechanicsburg, Penn., Nov. 9, 1996, notes only.

Marr, Merlin, and Naomi Heise Marr. Townsend, Ont., Oct. 30, 1996.

Nigh, Ross. Stevensville, Ontario, Oct. 31, 1996, transcript.

Rosenberry, Maurine Mitten. Messiah Village, Mechanicsburg, Penn., Nov. 9, 1996.

Sakimura, Clarence, and Herta Aschenbrenner Sakimura. Mechanicsburg, Penn., Nov. 12, 1996, transcript.

Sherk, Dorothy. Waterloo, Ont., Oct. 29, 1996, transcript.

Sider, Dorothy Myers. Ridgeway, Ont., Oct. 30, 1996.

Sider, E. Morris, and Leone Dearing Sider. Grantham, Penn., Nov. 11, 1996, transcript.

Stickley, Harvey, and Gladys Sollenberger Stickley. Waterloo, Ont., Oct. 29, 1996.

Wenger, Anna Mae Lehman. Mechanicsburg, Penn., July 13, 1994, transcript.

Wideman, Harold Bruce. Gormley, Ont., Oct. 29, 1996.

Winger, Walter. Fort Erie, Ont., Oct. 31, 1996.

Zercher, Ruth Niesley. Grantham, Penn., July 7, 1993, transcript.

Other interviews

Grove, Betty Kline. Interview by telephone by J. Wilmer Heisey. McVeytown, Penn., July 21, 1994, transcript.

Hess, Ruth Landis. Interview by J. Wilmer Heisey. Grantham Penn., July 2, 1994, transcript.

Hoover, Ruth Hilsher. Interview by J. Wilmer Heisey. Grantham, Penn., July 4, 1994, transcript.

Orthos. Grantham, Penn.: The Alumni Association of the Messiah Bible School and Missionary Training Home, 1922.

Public Domain. Church Agencies. Board for Young People's Work. VIII-2-2.1.

Public Domain. Miscellaneous. VIII-10-1.2, 1.10.

Sunday School Herald, 1939–48, 1951–52, 1954.

Swalm, E. J. Interview by E. Morris Sider, Mar. 21, 1978.

Swalm, Ernest J. Papers. Hist. MSS 32-1.3.

Ulery, Carl. Interview by E. Morris Sider, Sept. 17, 1977.

Ulery, Orville B. Papers. Hist. MSS 38-1.1.

Upland College. *Monthly Echo,* 1932–40, 1941–49. X-1-1.14, 1.15.

Upland College. Upland College Bulletins, 1927–59. XI-1-1.28.

Witter, R. I. Hist. MSS 28-1.15.

Wittlinger, Carlton O. Papers. Hist. MSS 35-1.22.

Wolgemuth, Mark. Interview by E. Morris Sider, July 30, 1979.

Zercher, John, and Alice Grace. Interview by E. Morris Sider, July 6, 1979.

Mennonite Library and Archives, Bethel College, North Newton, Kans.

Brubaker, Harry. Interview by Allan Teichroew, June 26, 1969. Interview 940.3162 28, transcript.

Hostetter, C. Nelson. Interview by Joseph Miller, Dec. 22, 1977. Interview 940.5316 79.

Personal Holdings

Bechtel, Elsie C. Diary. July 25, 1945, to ca. 1948. In possession of its author.

Brubaker, Harry L., and Theda Brubaker. Interview by author. Mount Joy, Penn., April 21, 1977, notes only. In possession of author.

Bundy, George E. Autobiography. Scrapbook. In possession of its author.

Dourte, Jeanette Frey. Diary. 1943. In possession of its author.

Heisey, J. Wilmer. Diary. Oct. 3 to Nov. 1, 1944, Jan. 1 to Jan. 22, 1946. In possession of its author.

————. Account book. June 10, 1943, to Mar. 19, 1946. In possession of its author.

Questionnaires, in possession of author

Signed, 138.

Unsigned, 13.

Swalm, E. J. Interview by Pauline Cornell, Aug. 17, 1987. Videotape in possession of Lela Swalm Hostetler.

Swalm, E. J. Papers on honorary doctorate. In possession of Lela Swalm Hostetler.

Wingert, Gerald N. Diary. Jan. 1, 1947, to Dec. 31, 1948. In possession of its author.

Published

Beechy, Atlee. *Seeking Peace: My Journey.* Goshen, Ind.: Pinchpenny Press, 2001.

Bert, Eldon F. *Walk Memory's Lane.* Harrisburg, Penn.: Triangle Press, 1992.

Brethren in Christ Missions, 1871–1978. Elizabethtown, Penn.: Brethren in Christ Missions, 1978.

Brubaker, Allen G. *Eighty Years of Learning to Walk with God: An Autobiography.* Shippensburg, Penn.: Beidel Printing House, 1983.

Brubaker, Henry H. "Selections from the Memoirs of a Missionary: Early Years and the Call to Missions." *Brethren in Christ History and Life* 12 (Aug. 1989): 101–14.

Directory of Civilian Public Service, May 1941 to March 1947. Washington, D.C.: National Service Board for Religious Objectors, n.d.

————. rev. and enl. Washington, D.C.: National Interreligious Service Board for Conscientious Objectors, 1994.

————. rev. Washington, D.C.: National Interreligious Service Board for Conscientious Objectors, 1996.

Harmon, Wendell E., ed. *They Also Serve.* Relief and Service Committee and the Board for Young People's Work, n.d.

Hostetter, Henry N. *Seeking First the Kingdom: Reflections on My Heritage, My Ministry, My Beliefs.* Nappanee, Ind.: Evangel Press, 1995.

Hutchinson, Paul. "The President's Religious Faith." *Life,* Mar. 22, 1954.

Long, T. A. *Biblical and Practical Themes: A Dissertation of Themes—Biblical, Practical, and Spiritually Educational.* Harrisburg, Penn.: Evangelical Press, 1922.

Manual for Christian Youth: Doctrines and Practices Based upon the Holy Scriptures as Taught by the Brethren in Christ. Nappanee, Ind.: E. V. Publishing House, 1945.

Messiah College Alumni Directory, 1992. Grantham, Penn.: Messiah College, n.d.

Messiah College Alumni Directory, 1996. Grantham, Penn.: Messiah College, n.d.

Nigh, Ross. "A Shaper of Life: The Brethren in Christ Experience." *Brethren in Christ History and Life* 16 (Dec. 1993): 305–14.

Nix, Bruce W. *My Life Story and History of the Nix Family.* Privately printed, 1995.

Pawelski, Ruth. "A Stabilizing Influence: The Brethren in Christ Experience." *Brethren in Christ History and Life* 16 (Dec. 1993): 293–304.

Peachey, Urbane, ed. *Mennonite Statements on Peace and Social Concerns, 1900–1978.* Akron, Penn.: Mennonite Central Committee U.S. Peace Section, 1980.

Questions and Answers in Bible Instruction. Children's ed. Nappanee, Ind.: E. V. Publishing House, 1931.

Questions and Answers in Bible Instruction: Brethren in Christ Church. Nappanee, Ind.: E. V. Publishing House, 1946.

Rosenberger, A. C. *Universal Peace in the Light of the Prophet Micah.* Souderton, Penn.: n.d.

Sider, E. Morris, ed. *My Story, My Song: Life Stories of Brethren in Christ Missionaries.* Nappanee, Ind.: Brethren in Christ World Missions, 1989.

Sider, Robert D. "Reflections on a Heritage: The Brethren in Christ Experience." *Brethren in Christ History and Life* 16 (Dec. 1993): 326–35.

Swalm, E. J. *"My Beloved Brethren": Personal Memoirs and Recollections of the Canadian Brethren in Christ Church.* Nappanee, Ind.: Evangel Press, 1969.

———. *Nonresistance under Test: The Experiences of a Conscientious Objector, as Encountered in the Late World War by the Author.* Kitchener, Ont.: Cober Printing Service, 1938.

Swalm, E. J., comp. *Nonresistance under Test: A Compilation of Experiences of Conscientious Objectors as Encountered in the Two World Wars.* Nappanee, Ind.: E. V. Publishing House, 1949.

Tidgewell, Lois. "Blooming Where Planted: The Brethren in Christ Experience." *Brethren in Christ History and Life* 16 (Dec. 1993): 315–25.

White, Gwen. "An Unlikely Journey." *Evangelical Visitor,* Jan. 1991, 9–10.

Wingert, Norman A. *A Relief Worker's Notebook.* Nappanee, Ind.: E. V. Publishing House, 1952.

Wolgemuth, Cecelia. "An Autobiographical Account." *Brethren in Christ History and Life* 8 (April 1985): 47–58.

Zercher, Ray M. "It Seems to Me: The Brethren in Christ Experience." *Brethren in Christ History and Life* 16 (Dec. 1993): 281–92.

Zercher, Ray M., and Wendell R. Zercher. "Brethren in Christ in MCC Service." *Brethren in Christ History and Life* 18 (Aug. 1995): 272–309.

Secondary Sources

Adams, Judith Porter, ed. *Peacework: Oral Histories of Women Peace Activists.* Boston: Twayne Publishers, 1991, 184–91.

Adams, Michael C. C. *The Best War Ever: America and World War II.* Baltimore: Johns Hopkins Univ. Press, 1994.

Alderfer, Owen H. "Anabaptism as a 'Burden' for the Brethren in Christ." In *Within the Perfection of Christ: Essays on Peace and the Nature of the Church,* ed. Terry L. Brensinger and E. Morris Sider, 250–64. Nappanee, Ind.: Evangel Press, 1990.

———. "The Mind of the Brethren in Christ: A Synthesis of Revivalism and the Church Conceived as Total Community." Ph.D. diss., Claremont Graduate School, 1963.

Alonso, Harriet. *Peace as a Women's Issue: A History of the U.S. Movement for World Peace and Women's Rights.* Knoxville: Univ. of Tennessee Press, 1989.

Anderson, Karen. *Wartime Women: Sex Roles, Family Relations, and the Status of Women during World War II.* Westport, Conn.: Greenwood Press, 1981.

Anderson, Richard C. *Peace Was in Their Hearts: Conscientious Objectors in World War II.* Watsonville, Calif.: Correlan Publishers, 1994.

Ariès, Philippe, and Georges Duby, eds. *A History of Private Life.* 5 vols. Translated by Arthur Goldhammer. Cambridge: Harvard Univ. Press, 1987–91.

Augsburger, Myron S. "Perspectives on the Brethren in Christ Experience." *Brethren in Christ History and Life* 16 (Dec. 1993): 342–52.

Baecher, Elisabeth, ed. *Mennonite and Brethren in Christ World Directory.* Strasbourg, France, 2000.

Baker, Robert J. "The Calling and Destiny of the Brethren in Christ." *Christian Living,* Dec. 1969, 3–6.

Bicksler, Harriet. *Perspectives on Social Issues.* Nappanee, Ind.: Evangel Press, 1992.

Blum, John Morton. *V Was for Victory: Politics and American Culture during World War II.* New York: Harcourt Brace Jovanovich, 1976.

Book, Thelma Heisey. "In Pursuit of Great Spoil: A Biography of C. R. Heisey." *Brethren in Christ History and Life* 20 (Aug. 1997): 9–288.

Bothwell, Robert, Ian Drummond, and John English. *Canada, 1900–1945.* Toronto: Univ. of Toronto Press, 1987.

Boulding, Elise. *Cultures of Peace: The Hidden Side of History.* Syracuse, N.Y.: Syracuse Univ. Press, 2000.

———. *One Small Plot of Heaven: Reflections on Family Life by a Quaker Sociologist.* Wallingford, Penn.: Pendle Hill Publications, 1989.

———. "Who Are These Women? A Progress Report on a Study of the 'Women Strike for Peace.'" In *Behavioral Science and Human Survival,* ed. Milton Schwebel, 185–200. Palo Alto, Calif.: Science and Behavior Books, 1965.

Bourdieu, Pierre. *Outline of a Theory of Practice.* Translated by Richard Nice. Cambridge, U.K.: Cambridge Univ. Press, 1977.

Bowers, Miriam A. "Henry G. Brubaker: Western Servant of the Church." *Brethren in Christ History and Life* 5 (Dec. 1982): 163–76.

Bowman, Carl F. *Brethren Society: The Cultural Transformation of a "Peculiar People."* Baltimore: Johns Hopkins Univ. Press, 1995.

Boyer, Paul. *By the Bomb's Early Light: American Thought and Culture at the Dawn of the Atomic Age.* New York: Pantheon Books, 1985.

———. "Confronting the Present, Rethinking the Past: Mennonite Life and Thought in Twentieth Century America: A Review Essay." *Brethren in Christ History and Life* 20 (April 1997): 139–47.

———. "The Ironies of Separateness and Assimilation: A New Look at the Mennonite Experience in America: A Review Essay." *Brethren in Christ History and Life* 14 (Dec. 1991): 415–35.

———. *Mission on Taylor Street: The Founding and Early Years of the Dayton Brethren in Christ Mission.* Grantham, Penn.: Brethren in Christ Historical Society, 1987.

———. *When Time Shall Be No More: Prophecy Belief in Modern American Culture.* Cambridge: Harvard Univ. Press, 1992.

Braude, Ann. "Women's History *Is* American Religious History." In *Retelling U.S. Religious History,* ed. Thomas A. Tweed, 87–107. Berkeley: Univ. of California Press, 1997.

Brensinger, Terry L. *Focusing Our Faith: Brethren in Christ Core Values.* Nappanee, Ind.: Evangel Publishing House, 2000.

Brensinger, Terry L., and E. Morris Sider, eds. *Within the Perfection of Christ: Essays on Peace and the Nature of the Church.* Nappanee, Ind.: Evangel Press, 1990.

Brock, Peter. *Freedom from Violence: A History of Sectarian Nonresistance from the Middle Ages to the Great War.* Toronto: Univ. of Toronto Press, 1991.

———. *Pacifism in the United States: From the Colonial Era to the First World War.* Princeton, N.J.: Princeton Univ. Press, 1968.

———. *Twentieth-Century Pacifism.* New York: Van Nostrand Reinhold, 1970.

Brown, Dale W. *Understanding Pietism*. Rev. ed. Nappanee, Ind.: Evangel Publishing House, 1996.

Brubaker, Darrel. "The Pastoral Call in the Brethren in Christ Church." *Brethren in Christ History and Life* 7 (Dec. 1984): 135–48.

Bush, Perry. "Anabaptism Born Again: Mennonites, New Evangelicals, and the Search for a Usable Past, 1950–1980." *Fides et Historia* 25 (winter/spring 1993): 26–47.

———. "The Political Education of Vietnam Christian Service." *Peace and Change* 27 (Apr. 2002): 198–224.

———. *Two Kingdoms, Two Loyalties: Mennonite Pacifism in Modern America*. Baltimore: Johns Hopkins Univ. Press, 1998.

Campbell, D'Ann. *Women at War with America: Private Lives in a Patriotic Era*. Cambridge: Harvard Univ. Press, 1984.

Carden, Maren Lockwood. *Oneida: Utopian Community to Modern Corporation*. Syracuse, N.Y.: Syracuse Univ. Press, 1998.

Carter, Paul A. "The Fundamentalist Defense of Faith." In *Change and Continuity in Twentieth-Century America: The 1920s*, ed. John Braeman, Robert H. Bremner, and David Brody, 179–214. Columbus: Ohio State University, 1968.

Charlton, Lucille. "I Was a Stranger: The Story of Will Charlton." *Brethren in Christ History and Life* 12 (April 1989): 3–49.

———. "Norman A. Wingert: Christian Worker and Writer." *Brethren in Christ History and Life* 5 (June 1982): 3–22.

Charlton, Mark. "Trends in Political Participation among Brethren in Christ Ministers, 1975–1980." *Brethren in Christ History and Life* 4 (Dec. 1981): 142–60.

Chatfield, Charles. *The American Peace Movement: Ideals and Activism*. New York: Twayne Publishers, 1992.

———. *For Peace and Justice: Pacifism in America, 1914–1941*. Knoxville: Univ. of Tennessee Press, 1971.

Chatfield, Charles, and Peter van den Dungen, eds. *Peace Movements and Political Cultures*. Knoxville: Univ. of Tennessee Press, 1988.

Chmielewski, Wendy E., Louis J. Kern, and Marilyn Klee-Hartzell, eds. *Women in Spiritual and Communitarian Societies in the United States*. Syracuse, N.Y.: Syracuse Univ. Press, 1993.

Climenhaga, A. W. *History of the Brethren in Christ Church*. Nappanee, Ind.: E. V. Publishing, 1942.

Confino, Alon. "Collective Memory and Cultural History: Problems of Memory." *American Historical Review* 102 (Dec. 1997): 1386–1403.

Crosby, Alfred W. *America's Forgotten Pandemic: The Influenza of 1918*. Cambridge, U.K.: Cambridge Univ. Press, 1989.

Currey, Cecil B. "The Devolution of Quaker Pacifism: A Kansas Case Study." *Kansas History* 6 (1983): 120–33.

Davis, David Brion. "World War II and Memory." *Journal of American History* 77 (Sept. 1990): 580–87.

Davis, Natalie Zemon. "Who Owns History? History in the Profession." *Perspectives* 34 (Nov. 1996): 1, 4–6.

DeBenedetti, Charles. *The Peace Reform in American History*. Bloomington: Indiana Univ. Press, 1980.

de Certeau, Michel. *The Practice of Everyday Life*. Berkeley: Univ. of California Press, 1984.

Driedger, Leo. *Mennonites in the Global Village.* Toronto: Univ. of Toronto Press, 2000.

Driedger, Leo, and Leland Harder, eds. *Anabaptist-Mennonite Identities in Ferment.* Elkhart, Ind.: Institute of Mennonite Studies, 1990.

Driedger, Leo, and Donald B. Kraybill. *Mennonite Peacemaking: From Quietism to Activism.* Scottdale, Penn.: Herald Press, 1994.

Dyck, Cornelius J. *An Introduction to Mennonite History: A Popular History of the Anabaptists and the Mennonites.* 3d ed. Scottdale, Penn.: Herald Press, 1993.

———, ed. *Responding to Worldwide Need.* Vol. 2. *The Mennonite Central Committee Story.* Scottdale, Penn.: Herald Press, 1980.

———, ed. *Something Meaningful for God.* Vol. 4. *The Mennonite Central Committee Story.* Scottdale, Penn.: Herald Press, 1981.

Early, Frances H. "New Historical Perspectives on Gendered Peace Studies." *Women's Studies Quarterly* 23 (fall/winter 1995): 22–31.

———. *A World without War: How U.S. Feminists and Pacifists Resisted World War I.* Syracuse, N.Y.: Syracuse Univ. Press, 1997.

Ehrenreich, Barbara. *Blood Rites: Origins and History of the Passions of War.* New York: Henry Holt, 1997.

Eller, Cynthia. "Moral and Religious Arguments in Support of Pacifism: Conscientious Objectors and the Second World War." Ph.D. diss., Univ. of Southern California, 1988.

Elshtain, Jean Bethke. *Women and War.* New York: Basic Books, 1987.

Elshtain, Jean Bethke, and Sheila Tobias, eds. *Women, Militarism, and War.* Savage, Md.: Rowman and Littlefield, 1990.

Epp, Frank H. *Mennonites in Canada, 1786–1920: History of a Separate People.* Toronto: Macmillan of Canada, 1974.

———. *Mennonites in Canada, 1920–1940: A People's Struggle for Survival.* Scottdale, Penn.: Herald Press, 1982.

Epp, Marlene. "Purple Clematis and Yellow Pine: On Cemeteries, Irony, and Difference." *Mennonite Quarterly Review* 74 (Jan. 2000): 183–89.

Erenberg, Lewis A., and Susan E. Hirsch, eds. *The War in American Culture: Society and Consciousness during World War II.* Chicago: Univ. of Chicago Press, 1996.

Eshleman, Kenneth L. "Thirty Years of MCC–Washington Office: A Unique or Similar Way?" *Mennonite Quarterly Review* 75 (July 2001): 293–313.

Finke, Roger, and Rodney Stark. *The Churching of America, 1776–1990: Winners and Losers in Our Religious Economy.* New Brunswick, N.J.: Rutgers Univ. Press, 1992.

Fox, Richard Wightman. *Reinhold Niebuhr.* New York: Pantheon Books, 1985.

Frazer, Heather T., and John O'Sullivan. "Forgotten Women of World War II: Wives of Conscientious Objectors in Civilian Public Service." *Peace and Change* 5 (fall 1978): 46–51.

———. *"We Have Just Begun Not to Fight": An Oral History of Conscientious Objectors in Civilian Public Service during World War II.* New York: Twayne Publishers, 1996.

Frazier, Thomas R., ed. *The Private Side of American History: Readings in Everyday Life.* 2 vols. San Diego, Calif.: Harcourt Brace Jovanovich, 1987.

Fussell, Paul. *The Great War and Modern Memory.* New York: Oxford Univ. Press, 1975.

———. *Wartime: Understanding and Behavior in the Second World War.* New York: Oxford Univ. Press, 1989.

Geiser, Ron. "Vietnam Experience Holds Lessons for Today, Prof. Says." *Mennonite Weekly Review,* May 21, 1998, back page.

Gingerich, Melvin. *Service for Peace: A History of Mennonite Civilian Public Service.* Akron, Penn.: Mennonite Central Committee, 1949.

Goossen, Rachel Waltner. *Women against the Good War: Conscientious Objection and Gender on the American Home Front, 1941–1947.* Chapel Hill: Univ. of North Carolina Press, 1997.

Grimsrud, Theodore Glenn. "An Ethical Analysis of Conscientious Objection to World War II." Ph.D. diss., Graduate Theological Union, Berkeley, Calif., 1988.

Hall, David L. "A Critical Analysis of the Hermeneutical Presuppositions in the Brethren in Christ Church on the Peace Position." D.Min. diss., Eastern Baptist Theological Seminary, 1988.

Hamm, Thomas D. *The Transformation of American Quakerism: Orthodox Friends, 1800–1907.* Bloomington: Indiana Univ. Press, 1988.

Handy, Robert T. *A History of the Churches in the United States and Canada.* New York: Oxford Univ. Press, 1976.

Harmon, Frances L. *For Christ and the Church: A Biography of Alvin C. Burkholder.* Grantham, Penn.: Brethren in Christ Historical Society, 199.

Harnden, Philip C. "Those Who Said No." *The Other Side* 21 (July 1985): 28–33.

Hawkley, Louise, and James C. Juhnke, eds. *Nonviolent America: History through the Eyes of Peace.* North Newton, Kans.: Bethel College, 1993.

Hawley, Ellis W. *The Great War and the Search for a Modern Order: A History of the American People and Their Institutions, 1917–1933.* New York: St. Martin's Press, 1979.

Heisey, D. Ray. "The Force of Narrative: Portrait of Bishop B. F. Hoover." *Brethren in Christ History and Life* 11 (Dec. 1988): 229–328.

Heisey, J. Wilmer. "R. I. Witter: Fervent in Spirit." *Brethren in Christ History and Life* 20 (Apr. 1997): 5–108.

Heisey, Mary Jane. "The Also Served: Brethren in Christ Women and Civilian Public Service." *Brethren in Christ History and Life* 18 (Aug. 1995): 228–71.

Heisey, Nancy R. "Brethren in Christ Participation in Mennonite Central Committee: Integral Part or Burden?" *Brethren in Christ History and Life* 18 (Aug. 1995): 177–227.

Hershberger, Guy F. *War, Peace, and Nonresistance.* Rev. ed. Scottdale, Penn.: Herald Press, 1953.

Hewitt, Nancy A. "Beyond the Search for Sisterhood: American Women's History in the 1980s." In *Unequal Sisters: A Multicultural Reader in U.S. Women's History,* ed. Ellen Carol DuBois and Vicki L. Ruiz, 1–14. New York: Routledge, 1990.

"History of Cross Roads Brethren in Christ Church, 1877–1977." Prepared for the One-Hundredth Anniversary Celebration, May 7, 1977.

Homan, Gerlof D. *American Mennonites and the Great War, 1914–1918.* Scottdale, Penn.: Herald Press, 1994.

Horowitz, Roger. "Oral History and the Story of World War II." *Journal of American History* 82 (Sept. 1995): 617–24.

Hostetler, Beulah Stauffer. "Midcentury Change in the Mennonite Church." *Mennonite Quarterly Review* 60 (Jan. 1986): 58–82.

Hostetler, Paul. "The Legacy of E. J. Swalm: A General Conference Leader." *Brethren in Christ History and Life* 16 (Apr. 1993): 49–55.

———. *Preacher on Wheels: Traveling the Road to Sainthood with Happy Abandon.* Elgin, Ill.: Brethren Press, 1980.

Howlett, Charles. *The American Peace Movement: References and Resources.* Boston: G. K. Hall, 1991.

Isaac, Allyne Friesen, "P. B. and Edna Friesen: Reminiscences of a Family." *Brethren in Christ History and Life* 17 (April 1994): 3–49.

Jameson, Elizabeth. "Rachel Bella Calof's Life as Collective History." In *Rachel Calof's Story: Jewish Homesteader on the Northern Plains*, ed. J. Sanford Rikoon, 135–53. Bloomington: Indiana Univ. Press, 1995.

Jeffries, John W. *Wartime America: The World War II Home Front.* Chicago: Ivan R. Dees, 1996.

Johnson-Weiner, Karen. "The Role of Women in Old Order Amish, Beachy Amish and Fellowship Churches." *Mennonite Quarterly Review* 75 (Apr. 2001): 231–56.

Jones, Charles Edwin. *Perfectionist Persuasion: The Holiness Movement and American Methodism, 1967–1936.* Metuchen, N.J.: Scarecrow Press, 1974.

Juhnke, James C. *A People of Two Kingdoms: The Political Acculturation of the Kansas Mennonites.* Newton, Kans.: Faith and Life Press, 1975.

———. *Vision, Doctrine, War: Mennonite Identity and Organization in America, 1890–1930.* Scottdale, Penn.: Herald Press, 1989.

Kauffman, Howard D. "Brethren in Christ Faith and Draft Nonregistrants." *Mennonite Quarterly Review* 58 (Oct. 1984): 520–37.

Kauffman, J. Howard, and Leland Harder. *Anabaptists Four Centuries Later: A Profile of Five Mennonite and Brethren in Christ Denominations.* Scottdale, Penn.: Herald Press, 1975.

Kauffman, J. Howard, and Leo Driedger. *The Mennonite Mosaic: Identity and Modernization.* Scottdale, Penn.: Herald Press, 1991.

Kauffman, J. Howard, and Thomas J. Meyers. "Mennonite Families: Characteristics and Trends." *Mennonite Quarterly Review* 75 (April 2001): 199–209.

Keefer, Luke L., Jr. Review of *Leaving Anabaptism: From Evangelical Mennonite Brethren to Fellowship of Evangelical Bible Churches*, by Calvin W. Redekop. *Brethren in Christ History and Life* 23 (Aug. 2000): 367–71.

Keim, Albert N. *Harold S. Bender, 1897–1962.* Scottdale, Penn.: Herald Press, 1998.

Keim, Albert N., and Grant M. Stoltzfus. *The Politics of Conscience: The Historic Peace Churches and America at War, 1917–1955.* Scottdale, Penn.: Herald Press, 1981.

Kennedy, David. *Over Here: The First World War and American Society.* New York: Oxford Univ. Press, 1980.

Kerber, Linda K. *No Constitutional Right to Be Ladies: Women and the Obligations of Citizenship.* New York: Hill and Wang, 1998.

Kerber, Linda K., and Jane Sherron De Hart. "Gender and the New Women's History." In *Women's America: Refocusing the Past*, ed. Linda K. Kerber and Jane Sherron De Hart, 3–24. New York: Oxford Univ. Press, 2000.

King, Omer E. "From Pennsylvania Dutch to English in the Brethren in Christ Church." *Brethren in Christ History and Life* 8 (Apr. 1985): 37–46.

Kniss, Fred. *Disquiet in the Land: Cultural Conflict in American Mennonite Communities.* New Brunswick, N.J.: Rutgers Univ. Press, 1997.

Kornweibel, Theodore, Jr. "Bishop C. H. Mason and the Church of God in Christ during World War I: The Perils of Conscientious Objection." *Southern Studies* 26 (winter 1987): 261–81.

Kraybill, Donald B. *Passing On the Faith: The Story of a Mennonite School.* Intercourse, Penn.: Good Books, 1991.

Kraybill, Donald B., and Carl F. Bowman. *On the Backroad to Heaven: Old Order Hutterites, Mennonites, Amish, and Brethren.* Baltimore: Johns Hopkins Univ. Press, 2001.

Kraybill, Donald B., and Marc A. Olshan, eds. *The Amish Struggle with Modernity.* Hanover, N.H.: Univ. Press of New England, 1994.

Kreider, Robert S. "The Colonial Experience Which Sticketh Closer than a Brother." *Mennonite Life* 35 (Sept. 1980): 16–20.

———. "CPS: A 'Year of Service with Like-Minded Christian Young Men': CPS Camp No. 5, Colorado Springs." *Mennonite Quarterly Review* 66 (Oct. 1992): 546–79.

Kreider, Robert S., and Rachel Waltner Goossen. *Hungry, Thirsty, a Stranger: The M.C.C. Experience.* Scottdale, Penn.: Herald Press, 1988.

Lapp, John A. "Mennonites in the Year 2000," *Mennonite Quarterly Review* 75 (Jan. 2001): 99–118.

LeFebvre, Henri. *Everyday Life in the Modern World.* Translated by Sacha Rabinovitch. New Brunswick, N.J.: Transaction, 1984.

Leff, Mark H. "The Politics of Sacrifice on the American Home Front in World War II." *Journal of American History* 77 (Mar. 1991): 1296–318.

Lehman, A. Ruth. "Earthen Vessels: Jesse S. Oldham and the Springhope Congregation." *Brethren in Christ History and Life* 15 (Aug. 1992): 191–244.

Litoff, Judy Barrett, and David C. Smith, eds. *Since You Went Away: World War II Letters from American Women on the Home Front.* New York: Oxford Univ. Press, 1991.

Long, Martha M. "Adda Engle Taylor: Pioneer Missionary." *Brethren in Christ History and Life* 7 (June 1984): 65–105.

———. "Miriam A. Bowers: A Self-Giving Woman." *Brethren in Christ History and Life* 17 (Aug. 1994): 204–26.

Luebke, Frederick C. *Bonds of Loyalty: German Americans and World War I.* DeKalb: Northern Illinois Univ. Press, 1974.

Lynd, Staughton, and Alice Lynd. *Nonviolence in America: A Documentary History.* Maryknoll, N.Y.: Orbis Books, 1995.

MacMaster, Richard K. *Land, Piety, Peoplehood: The Establishment of Mennonite Communities in America, 1683–1790.* Scottdale, Penn.: Herald Press, 1985.

Marr, Lucille. "Ontario's Conference of Historic Peace Church Families and the 'Joy of Service.'" *Mennonite Quarterly Review* 75 (2001): 257–72.

———. "Peace Activities of the Canadian Conference of the Brethren in Christ Church." *Brethren in Christ History and Life* 8 (Apr. 1985): 13–36.

Marsden, George, ed. *Evangelicalism and Modern America.* Grand Rapids, Mich.: William B. Eerdmans Publishing, 1984.

Marty, Martin E. *The Noise of Conflict, 1919–1941.* Chicago: Univ. of Chicago Press, 1991.

———. *Pilgrims in Their Own Land: 500 Years of Religion in America.* Boston: Little, Brown, 1984.

Mathies, Ronald J. R. "Leadership and Learning, the Tentativeness and Challenge: The Brethren in Christ in Mennonite Central Committee." *Brethren in Christ History and Life* 18 (Aug. 1995): 340–48.

———. "The Legacy of E. J. Swalm: As a Churchman in the Wider Christian Community in the Witness of Peace." *Brethren in Christ History and Life* 16 (Apr. 1993): 56–62.

Mauss, Armand L. *The Angel and the Beehive: The Mormon Struggle with Assimilation.* Urbana: Univ. of Illinois Press, 1994.

McClelland, Grigor. *Embers of War: Letters from a Quaker Relief Worker in War-Torn Germany.* London: British Academic Press, 1997.

Meigs, Mark. *Optimism at Armageddon: Voices of American Participants in the First World War.* New York: New York Univ. Press, 1997.

Milkman, Ruth. *Gender at Work: The Dynamics of Job Segregation by Sex during World War II.* Champaign: Univ. of Illinois Press, 1987.

Miller, Keith Graber. *Wise as Serpents, Harmless as Doves: American Mennonites Engage Washington.* Knoxville: Univ. of Tennessee Press, 1996.

Morton, Desmond. *When Your Number's Up: The Canadian Soldier in the First World War.* Toronto: Random House of Canada, 1993.

Morton, Desmond, and J. L. Granatstein. *Marching to Armageddon.* Toronto: Lester and Orpen Dennys, 1989.

Morton, W. L. *The Kingdom of Canada.* 2d ed. Toronto: McClelland and Stewart, 1969.

Musser, Wilma I. "Brethren in Christ Churches in Kansas: A Historical Survey." *Brethren in Christ History and Life* 14 (Aug. 1991): 131–314.

———. "Carl and Avas Carlson and the Chicago Mission." *Brethren in Christ History and Life* 16 (Aug. 1993): 171–213.

———. "Rhoda E. Lee." *Brethren in Christ History and Life* 2 (June 1979): 3–52.

Nolt, Steven M. "The Amish 'Mission Movement' and the Reformulation of Amish Identity in the Twentieth Century." *Mennonite Quarterly Review* 75 (Jan. 2001): 7–36.

———. *A History of the Amish.* Intercourse, Penn.: Good Books, 1992.

O'Brien, Kenneth Paul, and Lynn Hudson Parsons, eds. *The Home-Front War: World War II and American Society.* Westport, Conn.: Greenwood Press, 1995.

Offer, Avner. *The First World War: An Agrarian Interpretation.* Oxford, U.K.: Clarendon Press, 1989.

Oyer, John S. Introduction to "Mennonites and Alternative Service in World War II." *Mennonite Quarterly Review* 66 (Oct. 1992): 451–54.

Pawelski, Ruth. "Ohmer U. Herr: Quest for Obedience." *Brethren in Christ History and Life* 11 (Apr. 1988): 52–59.

Pederson, Jane Marie. *Between Memory and Reality: Family and Community in Rural Wisconsin, 1870–1970.* Madison: Univ. of Wisconsin Press, 1992.

Pitzer, Donald E., ed. *America's Communal Utopias.* Chapel Hill: University of North Carolina Press, 1997.

Polenberg, Richard. "The Good War? A Reappraisal of How World War II Affected American Society." *Virginia Magazine of History and Biography* 100 (July 1992): 295–322.

Redekop, Benjamin W., and Calvin W. Redekop, eds. *Power, Authority, and the Anabaptist Tradition.* Baltimore: Johns Hopkins Univ. Press, 2001.

Redekop, Calvin W. *Leaving Anabaptism: From Evangelical Mennonite Brethren to Fellowship of Evangelical Bible Churches.* Telford, Penn.: Pandora Press, 1998.

———. *Mennonite Society.* Baltimore: Johns Hopkins Univ. Press, 1989.

———. *The Pax Story: Service in the Name of Christ, 1951–1976.* Telford, Penn.: Pandora Press, 2001.

Redekop, Gloria Neufeld. *The Work of Their Hands: Mennonite Women's Societies in Canada.* Waterloo, Ont.: Wilfrid Laurier Press, 1996.

Regehr, T. D. "Lost Sons: The Canadian Mennonite Soldiers of World War II." *Mennonite Quarterly Review* 66 (Oct. 1992): 461–80.

———. *Mennonites in Canada, 1939–1970: A People Transformed.* Toronto: Toronto Univ. Press, 1996.

Robinson, Mitchell Lee. "Civilian Public Service and World War II: The Dilemmas of Conscience and Conscription in a Free Society." Ph.D. diss., Cornell Univ. Press, 1990.

Robitaille, Glenn A. "The Sermon on the Mount and the Doctrine of Nonresistance." *Brethren in Christ History and Life* 20 (Dec. 1997): 272–90.

Roeber, A. G. "The Origin of Whatever Is Not English among Us: The Dutch-Speaking and the German-Speaking Peoples of Colonial British America." In *Strangers within the Realm: Cultural Margins of the First British Empire*, ed. Bernard Bailyn, Philip D. Morgan, and A. G. Roeber. Chapel Hill: Univ. of North Carolina Press, 1991.

Roeder, George H. *The Censored War: America Visual Experience during World War Two*. New Haven: Yale Univ. Press, 1993.

Saba, Beth Ulery. "Carl Ulery: Versatile Churchman." *Brethren in Christ History and Life* 11 (Apr. 1988): 44–52.

Sampson, Cynthia, and John Paul Lederach, eds. *From the Ground Up: Mennonite Contributions to International Peacebuilding*. New York: Oxford Univ. Press, 2000.

Sareyan, Alex. *The Turning Point: How Persons of Conscience Brought About Change in the Care of America's Mentally Ill*. Washington, D.C.: American Psychiatric Press, 1993.

Sawatsky, Rodney J. "Translating Brethren in Christ Identity." *Brethren in Christ History and Life* 22 (Aug. 1999): 213–20.

Sawin, Mark Metzler. "Moving Stubbornly toward the Kingdom of God: Mennonite Identity in the Twenty First Century." *Mennonite Quarterly Review* 75 (Jan. 2001): 89–98.

Schlabach, Theron F. *Gospel versus Gospel: Mission and the Mennonite Church, 1863–1944*. Scottdale, Penn.: Herald Press, 1980.

———. *Peace, Faith, Nation: Mennonites and Amish in Nineteenth-Century America*. Scottdale, Penn.: Herald Press, 1988.

Schlabach, Theron F., and Richard T. Hughes, eds. *Proclaim Peace: Christian Pacifism from Unexpected Quarters*. Urbana: Univ. of Illinois Press, 1997.

Schrag, Martin H. "The Brethren in Christ Attitude toward the 'World': A Historical Study of the Movement from Separation to an Increasing Acceptance of American Society." Ph.D. diss., Temple University, 1967.

———. "Henry Lesher, Jr., and the American Revolution." *Brethren in Christ History and Life* 18 (Dec. 1995): 382–407.

———. "A Historical Survey of Brethren in Christ Hermeneutics." *Brethren in Christ History and Life* 9 (Dec. 1986): 203–36.

———. "The Life and Times of Christian Lesher." *Brethren in Christ History and Life* 18 (Apr. 1995): 42–123.

———. "The Military Chaplaincy: An Evaluation from the Brethren in Christ Understanding of the Christian Faith." *Brethren in Christ History and Life* 13 (Dec. 1990): 375–96.

Schrag, Martin H., and E. Morris Sider. "The Heritage of the Brethren in Christ Attitudes toward Involvement in Public Policy." *Brethren in Christ History and Life* 12 (Dec. 1989): 186–220.

Shafer, Donald. "The Pastor and Church Loyalty." In *We Have This Ministry: Pastoral Theory and Practice in the Brethren in Christ Church*, ed. E. Morris Sider, 319–28. Nappanee, Ind.: Evangel Press, 1991.

Sherk, Morris. *A Century on the Hill: The Story of the Mechanicsburg Brethren in Christ Church*. Nappanee, Ind.: Evangel Press, 1990.

Shipps, Jan. "Making Saints: In the Early Days and the Latter Days." In *Contemporary Mormonism: Social Science Perspectives,* ed. Tim B. Heaton and Lawrence A. Young, 64–83. Urbana: Univ. of Illinois Press, 1994.

Shirk, Susan E. M. "The Impetus for Brethren in Christ Foreign Missions." *Brethren in Christ History and Life* 9 (Aug. 1986): 150–64.

Sibley, Mulford Q., and Philip E. Jacob. *Conscription of Conscience: The American State and the Conscientious Objector, 1940–1947.* Ithaca, N.Y.: Cornell Univ. Press, 1952.

Sider, E. Morris. "The Anabaptist Vision and the Brethren in Christ Church." *Brethren in Christ History and Life* 17 (Dec. 1994): 283–96.

———. *The Brethren in Christ in Canada: Two Hundred Years of Tradition and Change.* Nappanee, Ind.: Evangel Press, 1988.

———. *Called to Evangelism: The Life and Ministry of John L. Rosenberry.* Nappanee, Ind.: Evangel Press, 1988.

———. "Community, Memory, and the Brethren in Christ." *Brethren in Christ History and Life* 18 (Dec. 1995): 396–407.

———. "John J. Engbrecht and the Brethren in Christ in South Dakota." *Brethren in Christ History and Life* 14 (Apr. 1991): 74–99.

———. *Leaders among Brethren: Biographies of Henry A. Ginder and Charlie B. Byers.* Nappanee, Ind.: Evangel Press, 1987.

———. "Life and Labor in the Alternate Service Work Camps in Canada during World War II." *Mennonite Quarterly Review* 66 (Oct. 1992): 580–97.

———. *Messenger of Grace: A Biography of C. N. Hostetter, Jr.* Nappanee, Ind.: Evangel Press, 1982.

———. *Messiah College: A History.* Nappanee, Ind.: Evangel Press, 1984.

———. *Nine Portraits: Brethren in Christ Biographical Sketches.* Nappanee, Ind.: Evangel Press, 1978.

———. "A Question of Identity: The Brethren in Christ in the Interwar Years." *Mennonite Quarterly Review* 60 (Jan. 1986): 31–37.

Sider, E. Morris, ed., *Reflections on a Heritage: Defining the Brethren in Christ.* Grantham, Penn.: Brethren in Christ Historical Society, 1999.

Sider, E. Morris, and Paul Hostetler, eds. *Lantern in the Dawn: Selections of the Writings of John E. Zercher.* Nappanee, Ind.: Evangel Press, 1980.

Sider, Harold K. "Willing to Serve: The Story of Christian and Cora Sider." *Brethren in Christ History and Life* 15 (Aug. 1992): 245–303.

Smucker, Donovan E. *The Sociology of Mennonites, Hutterites and Amish: A Bibliography with Annotations, 1977–1990.* Vol. 2. Waterloo, Ont.: Wilfrid Laurier Univ. Press, 1991.

Snyder, Esther Dourte. "The Legacy in Our Hearts: Reflections on the Lives of Monroe and Susie Dourte." *Brethren in Christ History and Life* 13 (Dec. 1990): 324–74.

Sprunger, Keith L., and John D. Thiesen. "Mennonite Military Service in World War II: An Oral History Approach." *Mennonite Quarterly Review* 4 (Oct. 1992): 481–91.

Stayer, James M., Werner O. Packull, and Klaus Deppermann. "From Monogenesis to Polygenesis: The Historical Discussion Anabaptist Origins." *Mennonite Quarterly Review* 40 (1975): 83–121.

Stearns, Peter N. "The New Social History: An Overview." In *Ordinary People and Everyday Life: Perspectives on the New Social History,* ed. James B. Gardner and George Rollie Adams, 4–10. Nashville, Tenn.: American Association for State and Local History, 1983.

Stoner, John K. "Peacemaking and the Church: A Bibliographical Essay." *Brethren in Christ History and Life* 11 (Dec. 1988): 329–45.

Swartley, Willard M., and Cornelius J. Dyck, eds. *Annotated Bibliography of Mennonite Writings on War and Peace, 1930–1980.* Scottdale, Penn.: Herald Press, 1987.

Swerdlow, Amy. *Women Strike for Peace: Traditional Motherhood and Radical Politics in the 1960s.* Chicago: Univ. of Chicago Press, 1993.

Tateishi, John, comp. *And Justice for All: An Oral History of the Japanese American Detention Camps.* New York: Random House, 1984.

Terkel, Studs. *"The Good War": An Oral History of World War II.* New York: Ballantine Books, 1984.

Thelen, David. "Memory and American History." *Journal of American History* 75 (Mar. 1989): 1117–29.

Toews, Paul. *Mennonites in American Society, 1930–1970: Modernity and the Persistence of Religious Community.* Scottdale, Penn.: Herald Press, 1996.

Trautwein, Noreen. "Alma B. Cassel: The A.B.C. of Beulah (Upland) College." *Brethren in Christ History and Life* 16 (Apr. 1993): 3–46.

Tuttle, William M., Jr. *"Daddy's Gone to War": The Second World War in the Lives of American Children.* New York: Oxford Univ. Press, 1993.

Unruh, John D. *In the Name of Christ: A History of the Mennonite Central Committee and Its Service, 1920–1951.* Scottdale, Penn.: Herald Press, 1952.

Vance, Jonathan F. *Death So Noble: Memory, Meaning, and the First World War.* Vancouver: Univ. of British Columbia Press, 1997.

Vaughn, Stephen. *Holding Fast the Inner Lines: Democracy, Nationalism, and the Committee on Public Information.* Chapel Hill: Univ. of North Carolina Press, 1980.

Wittlinger, Carlton O. *Quest for Piety and Obedience: The Story of the Brethren in Christ.* Nappanee, Ind.: Evangel Press, 1978.

Wittner, Lawrence. *Rebels against the War: The American Peace Movement, 1941–1960.* New York: Columbia Univ. Press, 1969.

Wuthnow, Robert. *The Restructuring of American Religion: Society and Faith since World War II.* Princeton, N.J.: Princeton Univ. Press, 1988.

Wynn, Neil A. *The Afro-American and the Second World War.* New York: Holmes and Meier, 1975.

Yeatts, John R., and Ronald J. Burwell. "Tradition and Mission: The Brethren in Christ at the End of the Millennium." *Brethren in Christ History and Life* 19 (Apr. 1996): 67–115.

Yoder, John Howard. "The Unique Role of the Historic Peace Churches." *Brethren Life and Thought* 14 (summer 1969): 132–49.

Yoder, Lawrence M. "Why Changes in Brethren in Christ Hermeneutics? A Sociological and Anthropological Analysis." *Brethren in Christ History and Life* 9 (Dec. 1986): 237–63.

Zahn, Gordon. *War, Conscience, and Dissent.* New York: Hawthorn Books, 1967.

Zercher, David L. "Between Two Kingdoms: Virginia Mennonites and the American Flag." *Mennonite Quarterly Review* 70 (Apr. 1996): 165–90.

———. "Is There a 'Brethren Mindset'? Reflections on the Alderfer Thesis." *Brethren in Christ History and Life* 19 (Apr. 1996): 154–83.

———. "Opting for the Mainstream: The Brethren Join the National Association of Evangelicals." *Brethren in Christ History and Life* 10 (Apr. 1987): 48–70.

Zercher, Ray M. "John N. Hoover: Fervent in Spirit, a Servant of the Lord." *Brethren in Christ History and Life* 8 (Aug. 1985): 124–54.

———. "Keeper of the Charge: M. G. Engle." *Brethren in Christ History and Life* 9 (Aug. 1986): 79–124.

———. *To Have a Home: The Centennial History of Messiah Village.* Mechanicsburg, Penn.: Messiah Village, 1995.

Index

Adam, Michael, 73
Agriculture: and Brethren in Christ (BIC) history, 5, 8, 9, 114, 163, 219 n. 73; and conscription deferments, 85, 115–17, 139; and the peace witness, 47–48, 60–61; and relief contributions, 98, 236 n. 37; and war mobilization, 165, 208 n. 57; and war profits, 27, 35–36, 80, 208–209 n. 58
Alderfer, James, 66, 84, 117–18
Alternative service. *See* Alternative Service Work (ASW); Civilian Public Service (CPS); I-W service
Alternative Service Work (ASW), 59, 82, 90, 101, 110, 130–32, 177–78; compared to CPS, 131–32
American Friends Service Committee (AFSC), 44, 46, 107; relief work in France in WWI and WWII, 13, 38–39. *See also* Religious Society of Friends; Friends Reconstruction Unit
American Relief Board, 44
American War of Independence, 9, 196 n. 29
Amish, 1, 6, 12, 117; in CPS, 17, 127; history, 194 n. 19. *See also* Anabaptism: Old Orders
Anabaptism, xii, 97, 167,194 n.19; American groups and settlements, 6, 19, 165–66; BIC identity, 5, 7, 9; European origins, 6–7; Old Orders, 12, 17–18, 20, 127, 200 n. 71; separation of church and state, 8; student tours, 108
"Anabaptist Vision," 13
Anti-Semitism, 70, 223 n. 142
Arbitration, 28
Baker, Charles, 29
Baker, Lillian, 29, 33
Baker, Newton D., secretary of war, 26
Baldwin, Dorothy Meyer, 80, 125
Baum, Paul B., 42
Bearss, Rose, 131

Bearss, Ross, 131, 177
Bechtel, Elsie C., 17, 75, 150–59, 152; and family, 150, 157–58, 252 n. 44; and historical sources, 252 nn. 43, 46; on peace witness, 58, 64, 151; in relief work in France, 135, 153–59, 186; in Women's Service Unit, 107, 186
Bender, Harold S., 13–14, 210 n. 78
Bert, Dwight, 118
Bert, Eldon F., 243 n. 23
Bert, Orville, 118
Bert, Ray, 41
Beulah College, 53, 55, 59, 82, 85, 101, 129; and student tours, 108
Blum, John M., 77
Board for Young People's Work, 92, 93, 129, 144
Boer War, 29
Book, Doyle, 110, 187
Book, Esther G., 108
Book, Maynard C., 62, 179
Book, Thelma Heisey, 110, 187
Boulding, Elise, 15, 18
Bowers, Miriam, 58, 75, 187
Bowman, Carl, 18, 201 n. 79
Boyer, Clarence W., 36; and BIC on labor unions, 88–89, 231 n. 85
Boyer, Esther Tyson, 50, 94, 109, 160, 187
Boyer, Paul S.: as child, 50, 86, 91–92, 206 n. 27, 211 n. 81, 232 nn. 99, 107; historical scholarship, 194 n. 19, 195 n. 25, 201 nn. 76, 77, 205 n. 19, 217 n. 35, 223 n. 142; on nonresistance/peace witness, 161–62; PAX service, 132, 133, 187
Boyer, Rozella, 32, 36, 206 n. 27, 220 n. 97
Brethren in Christ (BIC): and American identity, 4, 7, 166–67, 96, 151, 155 archives, xiii; financial contributions, 238 n.50; history, 5–12, 193 n. 11; identity formation, 98, 105, 163,

194–95 n. 20, 201 n. 75; membership and size, 5, 11, 64, 167, 193 nn. 8, 13; Mennonite identity, 109, 114; name, 8; periodicals, xiii, 5; scholarship on, xiii, 7, 11, 197 n. 38. *See also* River Brethren

Brethren in Christ History and Life, xiii

Brethren Service Committee, 103

Brock, Peter, 120

Brubaker, Frances, 42

Brubaker, Harry L., 40, 43, 171, 212–13 n. 96

Brubaker, Henry G., 69, 73, 75, 84, 105, on non-resistance/peace witness, 53–54

Bundy, Ethel Heisey, 87, 230 n. 80

Bundy, George, 87–88, 221 n. 113, 231–32 n. 95

Burkholder, Alvin C., 105

Bush, Perry, 13, 14–15, 22

Byer, Clarence, 41, 161, 172

Byer, Curtis, 161

Byer Glen D, 105

Byers, Charlie B., 63, 85

Can a Christian Fight?, 53

Canada: civilian mobilization, 82; entry into World War II, 78; Upper Canada, 196 n. 29; Wartime Elections Act of 1917, 78. *See also* Alternative Service Work; Conference of Historic Peace Churches; Conscientious objection; Conscription; Non-Resistant Relief Organization; Ontario

Canadian Nonresistance Committee, 64, 82

Carlson, Paul, 63, 132–34, 191

Cattle boats. *See* Livestock ships

Centralization: BIC: 8, 67; Historic Peace Churches, 13; U.S., 13, 67

Charles, Mildred Byer, 60, 102

Children: and church life, 2, 3, 5; and civilian bonds, 232 n. 107; and fear, 78, 90, 232 n. 98; and nonconformity, 165; and nonresistance/peace witness, 33, 50, 63, 89–92, 165; in public schools, 79, 90–92, 232 nn. 105–106; and war toys, 90

Christian Peacemaker Teams, 11

Church of the Brethren, 9, 98, 201–202 n. 79, 221 n. 114; and CPS, 146, 147; history, 194 n. 19. *See also* Heifer Project; Livestock ships

Church of Jesus Christ of Latter-Day Saints. *See* Latter-Day Saints, Church of Jesus Christ of

Church service, 5–6, 150, 193 n. 15

Citizenship, 31, 35, 52–53, 69, 94; and Mormons, 22

Civil defense programs, 82

Civil liberties, constriction of: in World War I, 29–30, 34; in World War II, 115–16

Civil rights movement, 14

Civil War, U.S., 30, 195 n. 23; and BIC military

participation, 29, 196 n. 29; and nonresistance, 29, 196 n. 29

Civilian bonds, 80–82; illustration, 81

Civilian Public Service (CPS), xiii, 13, 53, 63, 66, 78–79, 111; assignments, 17, 59, 107, 121, 141–43, 250–51 n. 19; BIC evaluations, 59, 72, 73, 74, 114–15; BIC men, 51, 94, 95, 120, 121–30, 179–83, 242 n. 15; BIC as Mennonites, 10; family support, 80, 100–101; finances of participants, 117, 124–30; funding and administration, 50, 54–55, 97–98, 99–102, 102–103; history, 113–14, 240–41 n. 3; and relief work, 109–10; and volunteer service, 108; women's participation, 19, 123, 129. *See also* Hostetter, Nelson

Climenhaga, Arthur M., 118, 164

Cold War, 2, 40, 56

Coma, Augustin, 152, 154

Committee on Public Information, 29–30

Conference of Historic Peace Churches, 10, 14, 68, 95, 100

Conflict, xi, 1, 3–4; and church discipline, 10; in church districts, 8, 33–34, 65–66; about conscientious objection, 164–65; among Mennonites, 121, 207 n. 43; and historical sources, 207 n. 36, 220 n. 103; and nonconformity, 5, 105; and nonresistance/peace witness, 3, 50, 98, 121, 134; in relief work, 154. *See also* Families: and conflict

Conscientious objection: and BIC definitions, 40–47, 54, 73, 117, 128, 164–65, 196 n. 29; categorized 17, 68, 138, 166–67; and daily life, 59, 79–80, 94–95, 110; in Canada, 10, 26–27, 28–29, 41–42, 43, 46–47, 63, 64, 82, 130–32; and families, 71–72, 160–61; and Cold War era, 132, 149; and gender, 18–19; and medical students, 84; in the U.S., 26–27; in World War I, 38, 47, 113, 171–76, 211 n. 82, 211–12 n. 90, 212 nn. 94–95; in World War II, 34, 113, 122, 245 n. 57, 201 n. 73, 250 n. 17; in the work place, 77, 84–87; and women, 18–19, 63, 104, 140–41, 168

Conscription, military, 9, 69, 99, 111; and BIC men in World War I, 26–27, 40, 115–16, 134, 171–76, 210 n. 78; and BIC men in World War II, 49–50, 113, 115; in Canada, 9, 26, 27, 47, 49, 99, 132, 203 n. 4; in Cold War era, 10, 57, 247–48 n. 102, 255 n. 3; and CPS, 140; and deferments 41, 115–17, 211 n. 82, 241 n. 12; and draft boards, 27; and registration (1980), 164

Church of Jesus Christ of Latter Day Saints, 21–22

Council of Mennonite and Affiliated Colleges, 108

Daily practice, 16, 18, 77–87, 149, 164–66, 198 n. 51; changes by 1950s, 130, 163; and conscientious objection in World War I, 40–41; historical sources, 34–35; and nonresistance/peace witness, 58–66, 141–43; in relief work, 154

Davis, Harold, 108, 180, 187

Davis, Ruth Brubaker, 108, 187

Democracy, 69, 70, 94, 138; and church organization, 67; and CPS, 115

Detweiler, George, 25, 34, 35, 44, 203 n. 1, 207 n. 46

Discipline: Anabaptist roots, 7; church practice, 5, 17, 26; in family, 15, 63; military, 35; for military service, 3, 10, 73, 118–21, 163; for war-related work, 73, 74. See also Disfellowshiping

Disfellowshiping, 66, 243 n. 32; defined, 6; for military service, 6, 64, 118–20, 134, 244 n. 36; and public confession, 6; for violation of nonconformist practice, 6, 64

Districts, church: Bertie (Ont.), 65; California, 117–18; and church structure, 5, 8; Cumberland (Penn.),102; Dauphin-Lebanon (Penn.), 58, 99–100, 125; Donegal (Penn.), 42, 73, 102, 121; Grantham (Penn.), 119, 250 n. 17; Kansas, 129; Manor-Pequea (Penn.), 103, 119–20; Miami (Oh.), 36; and nonresistance/peace witness, 33, 39, 42, 124; Oklahoma, 117; Rapho (Penn.), 39, 69, 99, 103–104, 245 n. 63; South Dickinson (Kans.), 103; Upland (Calif.), 121, 128–29; Wainfleet (Ont.), 51

Doctrine, church: on nonresistance/peace witness, 2, 11, 162, 164

Dohner, Leah, 105

Domestic violence, 200 n. 64. See also Families: and conflict

Dourte, Eber, 124

Dourte, Jeanette Frey, 62, 79

Driedger, Leo, 15, 225 n. 172

Early, Frances, 19

Eavey, C. Benton, 44–46, 45, 172

Eavey, Mabel Wingert, 45

Eberly, Clara Meyer, 79, 83, 107–108, 187

Education: church on nonresistance/peace witness, 10, 51; denominational schools, 8–9; levels of, 163

Ehrenreich, Barbara, 19

Eisenhower, Dwight D., 23, 71, 90

Elliot, Fred, 28–29, 35

Employment: and war-related work, 36, 37, 39–40, 51

Engle, Donald, 79, 160, 180

Engle, Eli M., 28, 30

Engle, Harold, 84, 187

Engle, Irene Wagaman, 83

Engle, John, 109, 111, 187

Espionage Act, 1917, 30

Evangelicalism: and BIC, 5, 15, 166, 198 n. 49. See also National Association of Evangelicals

Evangelical Visitor: Civil War obituaries, 29; editors, 207 n. 46; as historical source, xiii, 6; to promote nonresistance/peace witness, 10, 30, 56; as reading material, 70, 86; women as contributors, 31; in World War I, 25, 34. See also Periodicals

Families: and Anabaptism, 199 n. 61; and conflict, 18, 29; and conscientious objection, 41, 46, 219 n. 88; and marriage, 251 n. 24; with military and alternative service members 71; and nonresistance/peace witness, 3, 29, 59–63, 111, 134–35,160–61, 199 n. 64, 219 n. 88; and religious practice, 18. See also Bechtel, Elsie C.; Domestic violence; Hostetter, Nelson

Feather, Eugene H., 161

Fellowship of Reconciliation, 68, 147

Fishburn, Harry, 43, 173

Flag veneration: and Mennonites, 206 n. 27; in World War I, 27, 32, 36; in World War II, 80, 228 n. 33

France. See American Friends Service Committee; Friends Reconstruction Unit; Mennonite Central Committee; Relief service

Fretz, Lester: and family, 60, 90, 91; as livestock attendant, 110–11, 187, 239–40 n. 83

Friends, Religious Society of. See Religious Society of Friends

Friends Reconstruction Unit, 44, 45

Garman, John, 31

Gender: in Anabaptist groups, 200 n. 66; and conscientious objection, 19, 26; and military service, 220 n. 102; and nonresistance/peace witness, 31–34, 49,61–65, 136; and war, 19

General Conference: committees, 71, 99; and conscientious objection in World War I, 26, 27, 42; and conscription, 117; and funding of CPS, 97, 125; legislation on military service from World War II to 1958, 10, 66, 72, 118–20, 163; legislation on nonconformity, 28, 194 n. 16; legislation on nonresistance, 28, 66; legislation on war-related work, 82, 85

General Executive Board: and conflict, 33, 207 n. 36; as historical sources, 203 n. 3; and nonresistance in World War I, 27, 35, 36, 42; and relief efforts in world War I, 37, 39

German: ethnicity, 208 n. 53; language, 7, 8, 30, 195 nn. 21, 25; surnames, 35, 76

German Baptist Brethren, 6, 7. See also Church of the Brethren

Goossen, Rachel Waltner, 19

Grimsrud, Theodore, 17

Grove, Betty, 79, 125–26
Grove, Lloyd, 126, 181
Haas, Eugene, *141*, 181
Hamm, Thomas D. 24
Harley, Isaiah B., 120
Harmon, Frances, 66, 77, 120–21, 184
Harmon, Wendell E., *57*; as conscientious objector, 66, 121; in CPS, 114, 128, 181; on nonresistance/peace witness, 54–57, 58, 69, 73, 74, 95, 225 n. 178
Heifer Project, 103, 110
Heise, D. W., 42, 47
Heise, Edgar, 41, 43, 173
Heise, Jesse, 129, 181, 188
Heisey, Beulah, 79, 94, 95, 188
Heisey, J. Wilmer, 124, *137*, 181, 188
Hensel, Earl, 95
Hensel, Irene Frey, 69, 225 n. 156
Hensel, John, 63
Herr, Grace, 64–65
Herr, Ohmer, 37
Hershberger, Guy F., 15, 32–33, 88–89
Hess, Enos H. 35
Hess, Raymond, 85, 181
Hess, Ruth Landis, *123*, 184
High School Victory Corps, 93–94
Hiroshima, 56
Historic Peace Churches: and author's identity, xiv; and BIC connections, 67–68, 70, 75, 80, 97; and conscientious objector numbers, 224 n. 153; and CPS, 50, 54, 99, 104, 113, 124, 166–67, 240–41 n. 3; definition of, 9–10, 61, 143; in peace movements, 11; and peace programs in late twentieth century, 11
Hoffman, John H., 245 n. 63
Holiness: and BIC identity, 9; Mennonites, influenced by, 198 n. 49; World War I expressions of, 10, 24, 33; World War II expressions of, 55, 63, 68, 105, 217 n. 35. *See also* National Holiness Association
Holland, Grace Herr, 101, 162
Hoover, B. F., 213–14, n. 117
Hoover, David, 71, 161, 181, 188
Hoover, J. N., 36
Hoover, Jesse W., 78; on democracy, 67; in Historic Peace Church coalition, 67–68, 71; on nonresistance/peace witness, 54–56, 58, 69–70, 72–73, 84, 116; and peace committees of BIC and MCC, 82, 83, 100, 109, 125, 129–30, 235–36 n. 28; in relief work in France, 105–106, *106*, 188
Hoover, Kenneth B., 37, 119
Hoover, Ruth Hilsher, 71
Hostetler, Lela Swalm, 76, 93, *100*, 103

Hostetler, Paul, 95
Hostetter, Abram, 119
Hostetter, Anna Lane: and conscientious objectors, 83–84, 235 n. 15; CPS and volunteer service support, 101, 107; and family, 136, 144, 224 n. 156, 251 n. 20; and relief material aid, 104, 237 n. 45; on war, 69
Hostetter, C. N., Jr. (Christian Neff): and BIC leadership, 14; and conscientious objectors, 84, 133; in CPS and MCC work, *53*, 68, 100, 124, 125, 129–30, 243 n. 30, 246 n. 81; and discipline, church, 119, 120; and family, 70, 101, 136, 249 n. 3, 250 n. 17; in NAE, 14, 198 n. 47; on nonresistance/peace witness, 53–54, 55, 59, 72, 73, 216–17 n. 25; and work camps, 109; in World War I, 25, 212 n. 91; and youth, 74, 92
Hosttetter, C. N., Sr. (Christian N.), 42, 136, 212 n. 91, 249 n. 3
Hostetter, D. Ray, 137, 140, *141*, 181, 249 nn. 3, 7; 250 n. 17; 251 n. 20
Hostetter, Henry N., 72, 101, 144
Hostetter, Lane (S. Lane), 137, 140, *141*, 181, 249 nn. 3, 7, 250 n. 17
Hostetter, Nelson (C. Nelson): in CPS, 135, 136–50, *137*, *142*, 181; and family, 70, 136, 143, 144, 150; and music, 138, 145–46; on nonresistance/peace witness, 17, 138–42, 149; relief training and volunteer service, 135, 138–39, 148, 188
Hunt, Carl, 119–20
Hunter, Richard C., 17
I-W program (Roman numeral *I*), 130, 132–34, 190–91
Individualism, 147, 166–67; and conscientious objection, 120, 134; and corporate church positions, 72–74, 224–25 n. 163
Indoctrination Committee, 214–15 n. 8
Industrial Relations Committee, 88–89; 231 n. 86. *See also* Labor unions
Influenza epidemic, 1918–1919, 35, 208 n. 51
Jameson, Elizabeth, 18
Joint Councils. *See* State Councils
Keim, Albert, 13
Kipe, Keith, 119
Kohler, Anna Mae Rohrer, 126–27, 160
Kohler, John S., 71, 126–27, 182
Korean War, 120
Kraybill, Donald B., 15, 18, 192 n. 7, 200 n. 71, 226 nn. 188, 192, 256 n. 22
Kreider, Ethan, 43
Kreider, H. K., 39
Kritzberger, Clara Gibbonney, 66, 120
Labor unions: nonresistance/nonconformity, 28, 87–89, 204 n. 10, 231 nn. 85, 92, 95. *See also* Industrial Relations Committee

Lady, Martha, *61,* 62, 83

Lady, Mary Olive, *61,* 62, 79, 82, 103, 219 n. 81

Landis, Howard L., 94

Latter-Day Saints, Church of Jesus Christ of. *See* Church of Jesus Christ of Latter Day Saints

Livestock ships (cattle boats), 110, 140, *141,* 239–40 n. 83

Mann, Esther, 107, 168, 188

Martin, Harold S., 55, 144, 185

Marty, Martin E., 1, 61

Martyr's Mirror, 167

Mauss, Armand L., 21–22

Medical doctors: and war mobilization, 40, 84

Memory, and nonresistance/peace witness, 23–24, 98, 167, 197 n. 37, 226–27 n. 2

Mennonite Central Committee: and BIC membership, 10, 50, 75, 97–98, 100, 104–105, 109–10, 184–85; history of, 97–98, 234 n. 1, 249 n. 3; and Hostetter, C. N., Jr., as chair, 14; programs, 13, 80, 85, 102, 103–104, 106, 108–109, 124, 130, 133, 136, 146, 151, 153, 154, 160, 163, 168. *See also* Civilian Public Service; PAX program; Relief service; Volunteer service; Women's Service Units

Mennonite Disaster Service, 136, 148, 252 n. 42

Mennonite Nurses Association, 84

Mennonites: archives, xiii; and BIC affiliation with, xii, 51, 67, 83, 98, 203 n. 3, 215 n. 13; and BIC identity, xii, 10, 75, 105, 127, 129, 136, 148–49, 156–57, 163, 167; history and demographics, 6–7, 73, 109, 193 n. 13, 194 n. 19, 195 n. 27, 197 n. 39, 200 n. 71; in Historic Peace Church coalition, 9; Intercollegiate Peace Fellowship, 221 n. 113, and labor unions, 88–89; women, 107; in military and war–related work, 71, 86, 121; in World War I, 12–13, 48; in World War II, 13, 113, 123, 138

Messiah Bible College. *See* Messiah College

Messiah College: and civil defense, 82; curriculum, 69; faculty and staff, 44, 53, 109, 123, 133–34, 136, 162, 252 n. 46; history, 8, 102, 235 n. 25; and nonresistance/peace witness, 55, 57, 58; and music, 101, 116, 145, 251 n. 33; periodicals, 70, 71, 92; and student tours, 108–109; students, 56, 59, 85, 107, 138, 150, 165

Messiah College Peace Society, 64

Michigan, BIC in, 47–48, 166, 210 n. 77; Adams, Seth, 39–40; Montgomery, "Brother," 86–87. *See also* Bundy, George; Taylor, Melinda; Taylor, Walter

Militarism, 30, 31, 36, 37, 73, 110, 139, 148–49, 161, 164, 165; reflected in language, 35, 70–71

Military camps, World War I, 40–41; Camp Lee, Va., 44, 45; Camp Meade, Md., 42; Fort Levenworth, Kans., 43; Fort Riley, Kans., 41; prisons, 27

Military service: of BIC men in the U.S. Civil War, 29, 196 n. 29; of BIC men in World War I, 38, 171–76, 210–11 n. 81; of BIC men in World War II, 59, 66, 71, 102, 111, 117–21, 126, 128, 142–43, 165, 224 n. 156, 243 nn. 24, 30, 250 n. 17; of BIC women, 243 n. 24; combatant in World War I, 41, 48, 116; and draft boards, 44; prohibitions on, 28, 30, 32, 73, 127. *See also* Conscription; noncombatancy

Miller, Anna Verle, 65

Minter, Richard (Dick), 142–43, 251 n. 23

Missions, BIC, 5, 34, 78, 105, 110, 244 n. 37; and conscientious objection, 128; and relief contributions, 38, 238 n. 49; in urban areas, 8

Mobilization: civilian, 34–37; 77–87; military, 34–37; nonresistant, chap. 4

Mormons. *See* Church of Jesus Christ of Latter-Day Saints

Music: in CPS, *137,* 145, 251 n. 33; at Messiah College, *101, 116, 141. See also* Messiah College; Hostetter, Nelson

Musser, Clarence, 73

Muste, A. J., 23

Myers, Benjamin, 91, 191

Myers, Lyle, *137,* 182;

National Association of Evangelicals: BIC participation in, 11, 14, 198 n. 46

National Holiness Association: BIC participation in, 11. *See also* Holiness

National Service Board for Religious Objectors, 83, 113, 131–32

New Call to Peacemaking, 11

Nigh, Joe, 118

Nigh, Ross, 59, 65, 90, 177

Nolt, Miriam, 106

Noncombatancy: in World War I, 27, 40–42, 161, 171–76; in World War II, 116–19, *116,* 128, 140, 161, 242 n. 20, 243 nn. 23, 30, 250 n. 17. *See also* Conscientious objection; Military service

Nonconformity: 1950s changes in, 10; daily practice of, 20, 62, 105, 111; in dress and appearance, 32, 65; defined, xii, 2, 3, 26, 162–63; and electoral politics, 2, 10, 28, 30, 32, 56–58; and holiness, 9–11; and nonresistance, 4, 28, 32 50, 54, 244–45 n. 54; and women, 63–65

Nonresistance: and church teaching, 41, 50, 57; as daily practice, 17–18, 28–29, 33, 35–36, 49, 54, 58–66, 73, 77–87; definitions of, xi, 2–3, 28, 30–33, 51–54, 57–58, 60, 151, 164–65, 192 n. 7, 218–19 n. 67, 256 n. 22; in families, 30–33, 91–92; and gender, 19, 31–33, 49, 63–65, 98, 104; history of, 7–9, 196 n. 29; and service ethic,

38, 56, 58, 64, 111, 139; and World War I, 25–26, 30, 207 n. 46. *See also* Nonconformity; Pacifism; Peace witness; Persistence

Nonresistance Under Test: 1938 ed., 14, 46; 1949 ed., 58, 123

Non-Resistant Relief Organization, 44

Nonviolence, 11, 23, 31, 52, 54, 58, 68

Noyes, John Humphrey, 21–22

Nurses: and war mobilization, 83–84, 140

Old Orders. *See* Anabaptism: Old Orders. *See also* Amish; River Brethren: Old Order

Oneida Community, N.Y.: compared to BIC, 21–22

Ontario, 5; BIC in World War I, 28–29, 35, 41–42, 43, 46–47; families, 60, 62–63, 90–91, 93, 100, 110–11; men in military service, 118; nonresistance/peace witness, 51, 53; relief efforts, 103; war-related work, 83, 85. *See also* Canada

Ontario Bible School, 76, 93

Pacifism: and force, 54; loss of, 73, 203 n. 89; 225 n. 171; and Nelson Hostetter, 137–40, 146–48; and nonresistance, 1, 2, 4, 12, 23, 52; and tolerance, 162; and World War I, 26

Patriotism: in church education, 69; and CPS, 99, 121, 138, 139; nonresistance as, 44, 53; rituals of, in World War I, 36–37; as zealotry, 70, 73, 161

Pawelski, Ruth Herr, 65, 93

PAX program, 132–33, 186–89

Peace movements, U.S., 23, 25, 28, 31, 56, 161–62

Peace Now, 68

Peace, Relief, and Service Committee (PRS), 71, 75; and conscientious objector support, 83, 84, 115–17; and CPS funding, 99–100, 245 nn. 63, 64, 124–26; 129–30; and disfellowshiping, 120; programs, 80–81, *105*

Peace testimony. *See* Nonresistance; Peace witness

Peace witness: 1960s-1990s, 11; defined, 2–3; and institutionalization, 27, 75, 114; and justice concerns, 256 n. 22; and memory, 4; persistence and loss of, 7, 24, 166; and political participation, 56–58; post-World War II, 10; and service ethic, 17, 164; World War II statements on, 53–58. *See also* Nonresistance; Pacifism

Periodicals, 69; of denomination, xiii, 6, 55, 128; of denominational schools, 55, 59, 92, 138; of districts, church, 71. *See also Evangelical Visitor*

Persistence, cultural, 23, 164; and daily practice, 159; and families, 134–35; and memory, 23–24

Philippine relief unit, 109–10, 238 n. 49

Plainness: and Anabaptist identities, 2, 12, 34, 37; and children, 252 n. 44; in church architecture, 5; in dress and hairstyles, 1, 6, 19, 32, 63, 64, 244–45 n. 54. *See also* Nonconformity

Polity, church: reorganization in 1950s, 11; structure, 5

Premillenialism, influence on BIC, 20–21, 198 n. 49; during World War I, 26, 30, 205 n. 19; during World War II, 52

Prohibition, 28

Prophecy, Biblical: and nonresistance, 205 n. 19, 210–11 n. 81; 227 n. 4

Protestantism, 5, 7, 9

Quakers. *See* Religious Society of Friends

Racism, 70, 108, 147–48

Ransom, I. J., 37

Raser, Evelyn, 59

Raser, Lois, 94

Red Cross, 38, 47, 82, 83; in Canada, 131

Redekop, Calvin, 15, 19, 199 n. 61, 226 n. 188

Relief material aid: in World War I, 27, 37–39, 47; in World War II, 102–104, 238 n. 49. *See also* Heifer Project; Livestock ships; Sewing circles

Relief service: for Armenians in World War I, 37; BIC participation in, 109–11, 145, 186–89, 238 n. 49; in France in World War I, 13, 44–46; in France in World War II, 105–106, *106*, 151–58, 253 nn. 53, 54; and military connections, 36, 139, 249–50 n. 14; training for, 138, 151; and youth, 95. *See also* Bechtel, Elsie C.; Hoover, Jesse W.; Livestock ships; PAX program

Religious Society of Friends: BIC comparison of, 24; CPS administration, 145, 146–47; in Historic Peace Church coalition, 9, 67–68; in World War I, 13, 98; in World War II, 84, 162, 221 n. 115. *See also* American Friends Service Committee

Revivalism, 43, 166, 198 n. 49; and Anabaptism, 14–15; and BIC, 5, 6–7, 43; in holiness tradition

Richer, Menno, 162, 174

River Brethren: to nineteenth-century schisms, 6–8, 194 n. 18, 195 n. 22, 196 n. 29; Old Order, 12. *See also* Brethren in Christ: history

Roman Catholicism: and Anabaptism, 7; and BIC neighbors, 48, 91, 160; and pacifism, 161–62, 255 n. 9; and relief work in France, 156–57

Rosenberger, A. C., 31

Sakimura, Clarence, 79, 132, 162–63, 189

Saltzman, Royce, *141*, 189

Schneider, Gordon, 60, 120, 161

Sedition Amendment, 1918, 30

Selective service. *See* Conscription

Service ethic, 3, 9, 17, 97. *See also* Relief service; Volunteer service

Sewing circles, 103–104, 235 n. 19, 236 n. 38, 237
    n. 45; and nonresistance, 39, 104
Sherk, Dorothy, 64, 65, 74, 75, 110
Sherk, James, 75,118
Showalter, Shirley Hershey, 23
Sider, E. Morris: as child and youth, 62–63, 65,
    79, 86, 90, 95; historical scholarship on BIC,
    endnotes to "Introduction," 205 n. 19, 207 n.
    46, 222 n. 128
Sider, Earl M., 43, 62–63, 175
Sources: church periodicals and records, xiii;
    diaries and letters, 248–49 n. 2, 249 n. 7, 252
    n. 51; oral interviews and questionnaires, xiii
South African War, 29
State Councils: Ohio-Kentucky, 105, 238 n. 49;
    Oklahoma, 68; Pennsylvania, 42, 104, 127
Stoner, Clara E., 106–107
Stump, Vernon L., 38, 44, 51, 203 n. 1
Swalm, Ernest J. (E. J.): as BIC leader, 14; as con-
    scientious objector in World War I, 43, 46–
    47, 175; oratory and writings on nonresis-
    tance/peace witness, 50, 53–54, 58, 60, 68, 70,
    72,74, 132
Taylor, Walter, 44, 47–48, 175, 214 nn. 120, 121
Taylor, Melinda, 47–48
Taxation, for war, 8, 31
Terkel, Studs, 51
They Also Serve, 114, 121, 132
Thomas, Erwin, 58
Thuma, Alvan, 84
Thuma, Dan, 118
Tolerance, 73, 74, 128, 162
Ulery, Orville B. (O. B.), 44, 53–54, 78, 83, 84, 88
United Nations Relief and Rehabilitation Ad-
    ministration (UNNRA), 82, 146
United Zion Church, 136; 249 n. 4
Upland College. *See* Beulah College
Vietnam War, antiwar movement, 14, 22
Visitor. See Evangelical Visitor
Volunteer service, 104–111, 136, 164, 220 n. 94; BIC
    participants, 186–89; MCC programs, 10, 14, 132;
    Puerto Rico, 148. *See also* Mennonite Central
    Committee; PAX Program; Relief service
Waldensians, 254 n. 80
War bonds: and public schools, 91, 94; in World
    War I, 27, 30, 36, 37, 47; in World War II, 80–
    82, 140

Wenger, Geraldine M., 80
Wenger, Rolla Leroy, 43, 175
Wenger, Samuel, 43, 175
Winger, Charles, 118
Winger, Paul, 118, 120
Winger, Walter, 70, 90–91
Wingert, Eunice Lady, 64
Wingert, Gerald N., 50, 90, 91, 119, 130, 219 n. 73
Witter, Ray I., 71, 90, 105, 185
Wittlinger, Carlton O., 74; historical scholarship
    on BIC, endnotes to "Introduction"
Wolgemuth, John M., 79, 121, 122, 183, 244 n. 52
Women: and BIC numbers, 206 n. 28; and con-
    scientious objection, 63, 89, 140–41, 219 n. 88;
    and CPS, 101, 102, 107, 123, 124–27, 129, 184–85;
    in nineteenth century, 8; and nonconformity,
    32, 65; and nonresistance/peace witness, 19,
    31–32, 39, 62, 111, 150, 165; in organizations and
    social movements, 234 n. 2; relief material
    aid, 38–40, 98,103–104, 235–36 nn. 28, 36–38;
    in volunteer service, 64, 106–108; in war, 79,
    80,123–24, 229 n. 54; as writers, 31, 206 n. 23.
    See also Bechtel, Elsie C., Gender; Sewing
    circles; Women's Service Units
Women's Service Units, 107–108, 151, 186–89
World War I: historical scholarship on, 204 nn.
    6, 12; mobilization for, 13, 26–28, 29–30
Young Evangelicals, 15
Young People's Society. *See* Board for Young
    People's Work
Youth: and church education, 2, 74, 90, 204 n.
    10; and church retention, 3, 74–75, 226 nn.
    188, 192; in CPS, 114; education, 5, 232 n. 105,
    233 n. 130; and nonresistance/peace witness,
    55, 62, 64, 92–95; and volunteer service, 97,
    98,104,107–108,129. *See also* Board for Young
    People's Work
Zercher, Alice Grace Hostetter, 76, 94
Zercher, Harold, 119
Zercher, John, 119–20
Zercher, Ray M., 76–77, 93, 162; and conscrip-
    tion, 117; and CPS 121, 123, 183; on nonresis-
    tance/nonconformity, 55, 120, 244–45 n. 54
Zercher, Ruth Niesley, 123, 184
Zook, Mary, 38–39, 44
Zook, Samuel A., 41, 176